# Reality Rules!

# Genreflecting Advisory Series

**Diana Tixier Herald, Series Editor**

Jewish American Literature: A Guide to Reading Interests
*Rosalind Reisner*

African American Literature: A Guide to Reading Interests
*Edited by Alma Dawson and Connie Van Fleet*

Historical Fiction: A Guide to the Genre
*Sarah L. Johnson*

Canadian Fiction: A Guide to Reading Interests
*Sharron Smith and Maureen O'Connor*

Genreflecting: A Guide to Popular Reading Interests, 6th Edition
*Diana Tixier Herald, Edited by Wayne A. Wiegand*

The Real Story: A Guide to Nonfiction Reading Interests
*Sarah Statz Cords, Edited by Robert Burgin*

Read the High Country: A Guide to Western Books and Films
*John Mort*

Graphic Novels: A Genre Guide to Comic Books, Manga, and More
*Michael Pawuk*

Genrefied Classics: A Guide to Reading Interests in Classic Literature
*Tina Frolund*

Encountering Enchantment: A Guide to Speculative Fiction for Teens
*Susan Fichtelberg*

Fluent in Fantasy: The Next Generation
*Diana Tixier Herald and Bonnie Kunzel*

Gay, Lesbian, Bisexual, and Transgendered Literature: A Genre Guide
*Ellen Bosman and John Bradford; Edited by Robert B. Ridinger*

# Reality Rules!

## A Guide to Teen Nonfiction Reading Interests

Elizabeth Fraser

**Genreflecting Advisory Series**
Diana Tixier Herald, Series Editor

**LIBRARIES**
UNLIMITED
A Member of the Greenwood Publishing Group

Westport, Connecticut • London

**Library of Congress Cataloging-in-Publication**

Fraser, Elizabeth, 1970-
    Reality rules! : a guide to teen nonfiction reading interests / Elizabeth Fraser.
        p. cm. — (Genreflecting advisory series)
    Includes bibliographical references and indexes.
    ISBN 978-1-59158-563-3 (alk. paper)
    1. Teenagers—Books and reading—United States—Bibliography. 2. Readers'
advisory services—United States. I. Title.
    Z1037.F843    2008
    016.0285'5—dc22        2007051063

British Library Cataloguing in Publication Data is available.

Library of Congress Catalog Card Number: 2007051063
ISBN: 978-1-59158-563-3

First published in 2008

Libraries Unlimited, 88 Post Road West, Westport, CT 06881
A Member of the Greenwood Publishing Group, Inc.
www.lu.com

Printed in the United States of America

The paper used in this book complies with the
Permanent Paper Standard issued by the National
Information Standards Organization (Z39.48–1984).

10  9  8  7  6  5  4  3  2  1

# Contents

Introduction .................................................................................ix

## Part 1: Nonfiction Genres

**Chapter 1—True Adventure** ..................................................................3
    Definition ............................................................................3
    Appeal ................................................................................3
    Chapter Organization ...........................................................3
    Survival and Disaster Stories ...............................................4
    Sports Adventures ...............................................................7
    War Stories..........................................................................9
    Explorations, Travel, and Historical Adventures ...............10
    Consider Starting with . . . ..................................................13
    Fiction Read-Alikes............................................................13

**Chapter 2—True Crime** ......................................................................15
    Definition ..........................................................................15
    Appeal ...............................................................................15
    Chapter Organization .........................................................15
    Cons and Crimes: Solved and Unsolved ............................15
    Crime Science ...................................................................19
    Intrigue and Espionage.......................................................22
    Consider Starting with . . . ..................................................23
    Fiction Read-Alikes............................................................24

## Part 2: Life Stories

**Chapter 3—Memoirs and Autobiographies** ..........................................27
    Definition ..........................................................................27
    Appeal ...............................................................................27
    Chapter Organization .........................................................27
    Coming-of-Age ..................................................................28
    Overcoming Adversity .......................................................31
    Multicultural Experiences ..................................................36
    Working Life Memoirs.......................................................38
    Humorous Memoirs.............................................................42
    Consider Starting with . . . ..................................................43
    Fiction Read-Alikes............................................................43

**Chapter 4—Biography** .................................................................................45

    Definition ..............................................................................................45

    Appeal ...................................................................................................45

    Chapter Organization ............................................................................46

    American Presidents and Other Political Leaders .................................46

    Problem Solvers and Experimenters: Science Biography .....................48

    Outstanding in Their Fields: Professional Biographies.........................50

    Change-Makers and Activists ...............................................................52

    Historical Biography .............................................................................55

    Partner and Group Biographies ............................................................58

    The Creative Life: Entertainers and Writers ........................................59

    Biography Collections...........................................................................62

    Consider Starting with . . . ...................................................................65

    Fiction Read-Alikes..............................................................................66

    References .............................................................................................66

## Part 3: Nonfiction Subject Interests

**Chapter 5—History** ...................................................................................69

    Definition ..............................................................................................69

    Appeal ...................................................................................................69

    Chapter Organization ............................................................................69

    Defining Times......................................................................................70

    History's Darkest Hours........................................................................74

        Human Cruelties............................................................................75

        Natural Disasters and Disease Epidemics .....................................78

    Micro-histories .....................................................................................81

    Historical Biography: Ordinary People in Extraordinary Times.............85

        Individual Stories ..........................................................................86

        Group Stories.................................................................................86

    Ideas of History ....................................................................................89

    New Perspectives ..................................................................................89

    Consider Starting with . . . ...................................................................90

    Fiction Read-Alikes..............................................................................91

**Chapter 6—Science, Math, and the Environment** ....................................93

    Definition ..............................................................................................93

    Appeal ...................................................................................................93

    Chapter Organization ............................................................................93

    Science Adventures...............................................................................94

    Scientists and Science Enthusiasts .......................................................96

    History of Science ................................................................................97

    Digging into the Past.............................................................................98

        Archaeology ..................................................................................98

        Paleontology................................................................................101

    How Things Work ...............................................................................102

        General ........................................................................................102

        Transportation .............................................................................105

Micro-science ................................................................................................107
Environmental Writing......................................................................................110
    Ecology and Conservation ...............................................................111
    Animals ...............................................................................................112
Consider Starting with . . . ...........................................................................114
Fiction Read-Alikes.........................................................................................115
References ........................................................................................................115

**Chapter 7—Sports** ...........................................................................................117
Definition .........................................................................................................117
Appeal ..............................................................................................................117
Chapter Organization ......................................................................................117
Sports Biographies ..........................................................................................118
Rules and Tips..................................................................................................122
The Greatest Games ........................................................................................126
Sports in Action...............................................................................................128
Consider Starting with . . . ...........................................................................129
Fiction Read-Alikes.........................................................................................129

**Chapter 8—All About You**...............................................................................131
Definition .........................................................................................................131
Appeal ..............................................................................................................131
Chapter Organization ......................................................................................131
Self-Esteem ......................................................................................................132
Health and Nutrition........................................................................................133
Sexuality...........................................................................................................135
Relationships ....................................................................................................137
Tough Stuff .......................................................................................................139
Career Directions.............................................................................................141
Fun Stuff...........................................................................................................144
Consider Starting with . . . ...........................................................................146
Fiction Read-Alikes.........................................................................................146
References ........................................................................................................146

**Chapter 9—How To** ...........................................................................................147
Definition .........................................................................................................147
Appeal ..............................................................................................................147
Chapter Organization ......................................................................................148
General Crafts ..................................................................................................148
Beauty and Style..............................................................................................153
    Beauty..................................................................................................153
    Style.....................................................................................................155
Clothing and Accessories ................................................................................156
Acting ...............................................................................................................159
Drawing ............................................................................................................160
    Techniques ..........................................................................................160
    Anime and Manga ..............................................................................161
Comics and Graphic Novels............................................................................163

**Chapter 9—How To (*Continued*)**

Cooking ...........................................................................................................165

Technology ......................................................................................................166

Games ..............................................................................................................168

Transportation .................................................................................................169

Survival Skills .................................................................................................170

Consider Starting with . . . .............................................................................172

Fiction Read-Alikes.........................................................................................173

References .......................................................................................................173

**Chapter 10—The Arts** ........................................................................................175

Definition ........................................................................................................175

Appeal ..............................................................................................................175

Chapter Organization ......................................................................................175

Visual Arts.......................................................................................................176

    Art ...........................................................................................................176

    Artists .....................................................................................................178

All about Music ...............................................................................................180

    Music .......................................................................................................180

    Musicians ................................................................................................181

Film ..................................................................................................................183

Literature .........................................................................................................185

Poetry ...............................................................................................................186

    About Poetry and Poets...........................................................................187

    Poetry Collections and Anthologies .......................................................188

    Verse Biographies ...................................................................................191

Folklore, Myths, and Legends.........................................................................193

    General ....................................................................................................193

    Urban Legends ........................................................................................194

Consider Starting with . . . .............................................................................195

Fiction Read-Alikes.........................................................................................196

**Chapter 11—Understanding and Changing the World**....................................197

Definition ........................................................................................................197

Appeal ..............................................................................................................197

Chapter Organization ......................................................................................197

Popular Media and Consumer Culture ............................................................197

Social Concerns...............................................................................................199

Religion ...........................................................................................................200

Consider Starting with . . . .............................................................................202

Fiction Read-Alikes.........................................................................................203

Appendix A: Nonfiction Readers' Advisor Resources for YA Librarians.............205

Appendix B: Bibliography ....................................................................................209

Author/Title Index ................................................................................................211

Subject Index.........................................................................................................233

# Introduction

The teenage years are characterized by the tremendous physical, cognitive, and emotional maturations that accompany the transition from childhood to adulthood. Those who work with adolescents and teenagers bear in mind not only these changes but also the wide range of interests and abilities in the racially and ethnically diverse 36.6 million adolescents between the ages of ten and eighteen in the 2000 U.S. Census. One of the places this demographic shift is evident is in nonfiction publishing, which has undergone remarkable changes in a generation of readers.

## Trends in Young Adult Nonfiction

A 1990 *Publishers Weekly* article remarked on the new directions in children's publishing, especially the quality and quantity of recent nonfiction titles. The example cited was Dorling Kindersley's groundbreaking Eyewitness Books series, which delighted readers with its copious illustrations, informative sidebars, and interesting subjects. The publisher is still adding titles to this successful series today. The popularity of biography and history is evident not only in the proliferation of new series but also in new formats. One example that highlights both of these trends is Tokyopop's award-winning manga series Greatest Stars of the NBA. Photobiographies have remained a popular format since Russell Freedman's award-winning *Lincoln: A Photobiography* came out in 1987. Picture book biographies have also become more popular and are being used more in middle school classrooms.

Nonfiction in this century has added new imprints that market directly to "tweens" (nine- to twelve-year-olds) as a result of consumer demand. Consider, for example, Storey Publishing's Storey Kids line. This nonfiction imprint is aimed at middle grade readers and was launched in 2002 after consultations with parents, librarians, teachers, and children.

Today's nonfiction titles often directly address issues of race and identity. For example, Pearl Fuyo Gaskins's *What Are You?: Voices of Mixed-Race Young People* shows teens talking about what race means to their own lives. There is also a growing number of books about civil rights.

In our post-9/11 world teenagers, like adults, are concerned with what is happening around the world. ABDO Publishing launched its successful War on Terrorism series six months after the 9/11 tragedy. Titles explaining current events are available in multiple formats; a graphic novel, *The 9/11 Report: a Graphic Adaptation*, provides one of the best explanations of the 9/11 tragedy and condenses the National Commission's 800-page report.

Another trend is transforming adult books for a younger market. One example of this is Michael Capuzzo's *Close to Shore*, about a terrifying series of shark attacks in 1916. Making books accessible for younger readers often involves adding additional illustrations as well as reformatting the text. The edition Capuzzo adapted for a younger audience features period photographs and newspaper clippings. Al Gore's topical *An Inconvenient Truth: The Crisis of Global Warming* is one of the latest books to be adapted for a younger market.

Today's books are thoughtfully packaged. A book may take the form of a narrative, a diary, or a manual to help support the text and illustrations. As described by Marc Aronson (2006), this is a "marriage of content and appearance." For example, Mavis Jukes's *The Guy Book: An Owner's Manual for Teens,* is presented as a 1950s car manual and gives advice in chapters about interior care, road hazards, and parking to make it more appealing to male readers.

## Purpose, Scope, and Selection Criteria

The number of librarians working with teenagers is climbing alongside the number of teenagers in the United States. In 2007, librarians celebrated the fiftieth anniversary of the Young Adults Library Services Association, the American Library Association's fastest growing division. This guide is intended to help provide young adult librarians with a wide range of choices from which to answer readers' advisory questions.

Although teens asking for something to read are often automatically assumed to be asking for a fictional title, regardless of ability or gender, they frequently choose nonfiction for recreational reading purposes. Les Parsons (2004) encourages teacher-librarians to include "nonfiction in readalouds." Educator David Booth (2002) writes that he chooses to "focus on *literacy* as the goal of developing readers and writers. The term literature refers to one particular and significant art form." It is not what someone reads but reading itself that is important and should be encouraged. Nonfiction should be an automatic and valid choice.

The basic criteria for evaluating nonfiction have not changed, but the formats and audience have broadened considerably. To narrow down their favorite young adult nonfiction titles from the 1970s and 1980s, two *Horn Book* magazine reviewers looked at books' appended material, design, illustrations, and narrative flow. The books were also judged on whether the content was deemed appropriate for the intended age group. The reviewers chose three biographies and two books of poetry. These genres are still very popular, and numbers of titles in them are published annually; at the time of writing, biographies, memoirs, and collections of poetry have been nominated for both YALSA's 2008 Best Books for Young Adults and Quick Picks for Reluctant Readers lists.

Guides currently available to help reviewers, including Kathleen T. Horning's *From Cover to Cover: Evaluating and Reviewing Children's Books,* agree that informational books need to meet standards in five areas: authority, organization, style, design, and illustrations. The books chosen for this guide have been judged in those areas, as well as for popularity among teenagers.

The genres included in this book are those chosen most often by teens for recreational reading. I have taken into account the popularity of "how to" books and poetry books. Dictionaries, almanacs, and reference titles used primarily for homework have not been included. Springboards for the selection were YALSA's Best Books for Young Adults and Quick Picks for Reluctant Young Adult Reader lists, both of which take teen opinions into consideration when the committee casts its final votes. Many of the books included are award winners. Adult books of interest to teens have been included as well.

Although a majority of books in this guide have been published since 2000, acclaimed titles with older publication dates that are still popular with teen readers have also been included. This is a representative sampling rather than a comprehensive list of all nonfiction titles for teens. The book is intended to introduce librarians and readers to the genres and types of nonfiction literature available to teen readers.

Of necessity this book must consider the relative transience of a subject's popularity. Books on ephemeral topics that are available for only a limited amount of time and are of only fleeting interest have not been included here.

## Organization and Features

Readers' advisory guides are generally used to help readers find a book similar to one that they have already enjoyed. Each chapter includes a definition of the genre or literature type, a description of subgenres and themes within it, and annotations for each title. Someone trying to find a new title may start with the author/title index of this book to locate a specific book's listing or with the subject index to find relevant titles or genre areas.

The book is divided into three parts, "Nonfiction Genres," "Life Stories," and "Nonfiction Subject Interests." The first part focuses on two exciting and fast-paced genres, "True Adventure" (chapter 1) and "True Crime" (chapter 2). Part 2, "Life Stories" includes both "Memoirs and Autobiographies" (chapter 3) and "Biographies" (chapter 4). The next part includes the popular subject interests "History" (chapter 5), "Science, Math, and the Environment" (chapter 6) and "Sports" (chapter 7).

Chapter 8, "All About You," contains titles of interest to teens who are developing their own identities, covering a wide variety of subjects such as teen identity, health, nutrition, self-improvement, nutrition, career development, and lighter personal interests. Chapter 9, "How To," contains a wide range of books for both genders, varying from general crafts to cooking, fashion, technology, drawing, and transportation. Chapter 10, "The Arts," examines visual arts, music, film, and literature. The final chapter, "Understanding and Changing the World," lists books about popular media and consumer culture, social issues, and religions.

### The Entries

Entries are filed alphabetically by author within each subgenre or theme. Books in a series that have been written by more than one author are listed under the series title. Each entry includes the book's author, title, publisher, publication date, and ISBN. Dates and ISBNs for reissues have also been given. Each annotated book has been assigned a suggested reading level:

> **M** middle school (ages 6–8)
> **J** junior high school (ages 11–13)
> **H** high school (ages 14–18)

These are suggested guidelines only, based on reviews, publishers' recommendations, and personal experience. Some books published for adult audiences that teens will enjoy have also been included.

The following symbols also appear on the entries:

🎗  title has won award(s)

**A**  books that both teens and adults will enjoy

**BB**  aimed at male readers (books for boys)

**BG**  suitable for use with book groups/clubs

**C**  core titles that have stood the test of time

**RR**  suitable for reluctant readers

The annotations provide enough information about the content and style of the book to help answer a readers' advisory question. Awards won are indicated at the end of annotations for applicable titles, using the following acronyms/short forms:

| | |
|---|---|
| ALA | Association for Library Services to Children Notable books for Children |
| Alex | Alex Award |
| BBYA | Young Adult Library Services Association Best Books for Young Adults |
| BG-HB or BG-HB Honor | Boston Globe-Horn Book Award or Honor |
| CSK or CSK Honor | Coretta Scott King Award or Honor |
| IRA | International Reading Association award |
| JM or JM Honor | James Madison Book Award or Honor |
| Norma Fleck or Norma Fleck Honor | Norma Fleck Award or Honor |
| OP or OP Honor | Orbis Pictus Nonfiction Award or Honor |
| PP | Young Adult Library Services Association Popular Paperbacks |
| Printz or Printz Honor | Michael L. Printz Award or Honor Book |
| Pura Belpre | Pura Belpre Award |
| QP | Young Adult Library Services Association Quick Picks |
| Sibert or Sibert Honor | Robert F. Sibert Informational Book Award or Honor |

Following each annotation are keywords. Some entries also have "Now Try" suggestions, read-alikes that share authors, subjects, themes, or common styles with the main entry.

## "Consider Starting with . . ." and Fiction Read-alike Sections

Two additional sections are provided at the end of each chapter. The first, "Consider Starting with . . ." lists titles from the chapter that are popular and highly accessible books. They represent a great starting point for people who would like more information about a certain genre. The titles listed in the "Fiction Read-Alikes" sections offer additional possibilities for readers interested in particular genres, themes, or subjects.

# References

American Psychological Association. 2002. *Developing Adolescents: A Reference for Professionals.* Available at http://www.apa.org/pi/cyf/develop.pdf.

Aronson, Marc. 2006. "Originality in Nonfiction." *School Library Journal: SLJ* 52 (1): 42–43.

Beneduce, A. 1990. "A Small World [International Children's Book Market]." *Publishers Weekly* 237 (November 2): S8

Booth, David W. 2002. *Even Hockey Players Read: Boys, Literacy, and Learning.* Markham, ON: Pembroke Publishers.

Burns, M. M., et. al. 1999. "Whatever Happened to—? A List of Recovered Favorites and What Makes a Book Memorable after All." *The Horn Book* 75:5 (September/October): 574–86

Carter, Betty, and Richard F. Abrahamson. 1990. *Nonfiction for Young Adults: From Delight to Wisdom.* Phoenix, AZ: Oryx Press.

Kirch, Claire. 2003. "ABDO Current Events Series a Fast Seller." *Publishers Weekly* v. 250 (34) (August 25): 15.

Lodge, S. A. 1996. "DeAgostini Editions Makes U.S. Debut [American Arm of an Italian Publisher Kicks Off a Line of Information Picture Books]." *Publishers Weekly* 243 (May 20): 44.

Lodge, S. A. 2001. "Fresh Takes on the Tried and True [Adaptations of Adult Books for Youth; Bibliographical Essay]." *Publishers Weekly* 248 (48) (November 26): 20–22.

Parsons, Les. 2004. "Challenging the Gender Divide: Improving Literacy for All." *Teacher Librarian* 32 (2): 8–11.

Sullivan, E. 2002. "Race Matters [Issues of Race in Children's Literature; Bibliographical Essay]." *School Library Journal* 48 (6) (June): 40–41.

U.S. Census Bureau. 2001b. Table PC-PS. "Single Years of Age under 30 Years and Sex: 2000." *Census 2000 Summary File 1, Matrix PCT12.* Available at http://factfinder.census.gov (accessed September 5, 2007).

# Part 1

## Nonfiction Genres

# Chapter 1

## True Adventure

## Definition

Adventure is a common genre in fiction. True adventure books have the same characteristics as fictional titles, with the added attraction of being true. The protagonists in these fast-paced stories often face adversity and danger, undergo extreme hardship, and come up against the elements, demonstrating bravery, endurance, and fortitude. Adventure books may cover many subject areas, including survival, intrigue and espionage, war, and sports.

## Appeal

These stories offer readers an escape unlike any other genre. Whether the characters are fighting to survive a tragedy, win a race, or hide from an enemy, readers are given a highly charged, story-driven ride.

The genre is generally skewed toward male readers; sports, exploration, and danger tend to be more popular topics with boys. This gives librarians an opportunity to provide books to readers who might not think about nonfiction. *Within Reach: My Everest Story* and *Shadow Divers: The True Adventure of Two Americans Who Risked Everything to Solve One of the Last Mysteries of World War II* are both page-turners that feature heroes who refuse to give up their goals.

## Chapter Organization

The subgenre survival and disaster stories is first. The story of Sir Ernest Shackleton and his crew, one of the most famous true adventures, is listed in this section. These harrowing tales are followed by sports adventures, a subgenre that demonstrates endurance and determination. The next section covers war stories. More leisurely adventures may be found in the last section, "Explorations, Travel, and Historical Adventures." Readers interested in learning "survival skills" of their own should consult chapter 9.

## Survival and Disaster Stories

The popularity of survival and disaster stories crosses both age and gender. Reading about difficult and harrowing experiences allows readers to vicariously share the experience of natural disasters and death-defying trips that are more exciting than armchair travel, with the added benefit of their being true. With their fast pace and atmosphere of imminent danger, these tales keep readers on the edges of their seats. Readers may relive the San Francisco earthquake here. Those who prefer to know what to do in the event of a disaster should check the "Survival Skills" section of chapter 9.

### Armstrong, Jennifer.

🏃 *Shipwreck at the Bottom of the World: The Extraordinary True Story of Shackleton and the* **Endurance.** New York: Crown Publishers, 1999. ISBN 0517800144. **M** **J** **H** **BB**

When Ernest Shackleton set off in 1914 with a crew of twenty-seven to cross the Antarctic continent, he had no idea what dangers awaited. This riveting depiction of the crew's amazing journey finds their ship stuck in the ice for seven months, followed by a treacherous expedition to try to get help. The text is supplemented by photographs from the expedition's photographer. This remains one of the most amazing survival stories of the twentieth century. **BBYA**

**Keywords:** 1914–1917 • Adventurers • Antarctic • Imperial Trans-Antarctic Expedition • Shackleton, Sir Ernest • Shipwreck

**Now Try:** A longer, more poetic retelling of the horrific journey undertaken by Sir Ernest Shackleton and his crew may be found in Caroline Alexander's BBYA and Alex award-winning title *The* Endurance: *Shackleton's Legendary Antarctic Expedition.* Readers interested in the Antarctic may find out about conditions there in Sophie Webb's *My Season with Penguins.*

### Calabro, Marian.

🏃 *The Perilous Journey of the Donner Party.* New York: Clarion Books, 1999. ISBN 9780395866108. **M** **J** **H**

The thirty-two people who made up the Donner Party left Illinois in the spring of 1846. They were ill-equipped for the journey, having neither a guide nor any experience with the wilderness they would cover in the 2,500 miles they had to cross to get to California. The story of their trip, created from the letters and diaries of the survivors of this tragic expedition, is one of the most horrific in the oeuvre of pioneer tales. Eventually there were eighty-one people in the wagon train; they ended up trapped for the winter in the Sierra Nevada Mountains facing snow drifts twenty-two feet deep and purportedly resorted to cannibalizing the dead to survive until rescue arrived. Additional materials include a chronology and a list of further resources that covers books, videos, and Web sites. **BBYA**

**Keywords:** Cannibalism • Donner Party • Pioneers • Survival

### Banyard, Antonia.

*Dangerous Crossings!* **True Stories from the Edge.** Toronto: Annick Press, 2007. ISBN 9781554510863. **M** **J**

People undertake trips for different reasons: adventure, escape, love, or to accomplish something that has never been done before—often no matter the danger. The ten tales described here include all of these aspects, from pilot Beryl Markham's first Atlantic crossing to the remarkable fourteenth-century journey of Ibn Battutah that lasted twenty-nine years. Sources are included for students interested in these fascinating travels.

**Keywords:** Adventure • Nonfiction collections • Travel • Voyages

## Butts, Ed.

*SOS: Stories of Survival: True Tales of Disaster, Tragedy, and Courage.* Toronto: Tundra Books, 2007. ISBN 0887767869. **M**

In the age of television and the Internet, disasters have become recognized as a universal experience, expanding beyond borders to touch the lives of us all. Butts presents thirteen emotionally devastating tales of disaster and the people who survived them. Black-and-white photographs show the extent of the devastation. The disasters run the gamut from the man-made, such as the Chernobyl nuclear accident and the Triangle Fire, to the horrible weather disasters at the Frank Slide and Mont Pelee volcano. All had lasting consequences and became international news. A list of further reading is included.

**Keywords:** Disasters • Nonfiction collections • Survival

## Karwoski, Gail, and John MacDonald.

*Tsunami: The True Story of an April Fools' Day Disaster.* Plain City, OH: Darby Creek Publishing, 2006. ISBN 9781581960440. **M**

The massive waves that hammered Laupâhoehoe, Hawaii, in 1946 killed more than 150 people. It was a horrific and frightening disaster that illustrates the destruction these terrible storms can wreak. Readers will find out about how tsunamis happen and how scientists work to detect them. Supplementary information includes photographs, diagrams and maps, as well as lists of books and Web sites.

**Keywords:** Disasters • Hawaii • Tsunamis • Weather

## Kyi, Tanya Lloyd.

*Fires!: Ten Stories That Chronicle Some of the Most Destructive Fires in Human History.* True Stories from the Edge. Toronto: Annick Press, 2004. ISBN 9781550378771. **M** **J**

The devastation wrought by a rampaging fire is considerable, as may be seen in the ten tales in this volume from the True Stories from the Edge series. Readers will be thrust into settings as disparate as Chernobyl, Kuwait, London, and Halifax harbor. The individual tales detail the reasons for each fire, as well as the events and people involved, ensuring page-turning stories of both heroes and cowards. Background information includes the evolution of firefighting methods and changes in preventative measures.

**Keywords:** Disasters • History of fires • Nonfiction collections

*Rescues!: Ten Dramatic Stories of Life-saving Heroics.* <u>True Stories from the Edge</u>. Toronto: Annick Press, 2006. ISBN 9781554510344. **M** **J**

No matter the precipitating cause of the situation, the ten rescues described in this volume have in common true heroism and gripping accounts of people coming together in times of trouble and tragedy, in attempts that occasionally prove deadly for the rescuers. For example, UN observer Mbaye Diagne disobeyed orders in Rwanda to save Tutsi refugees. An international crew set out without permission to rescue climbers from one of the world's most dangerous mountains. These are just two of the amazing tales of the brave things people have done.

**Keywords:** Rescues • Rwanda

## Markle, Sandra.

*Rescues!* Minneapolis, MN: Millbrook Press, 2006. ISBN 9780822534136. **M** **J**

Disasters can happen anywhere, putting people in grave danger. It takes very special individuals, usually with a great deal of training and technical support, to rescue those caught unprepared. Readers will go behind the scenes to find out how ten different rescue operations were carried out, as rescuers take on situations including a fire, an earthquake, a burning house, a tsunami, and more.

**Keywords:** Nonfiction collections • Rescue work • Survival

## Philbrick, Nathaniel.

🐾 *Revenge of the Whale: The True Story of the Whaleship* **Essex**. Penguin Putnam/G. P. Putnam's Sons, 2002. ISBN 039923795X. **M** **J**

Whaling was a common practice in the early nineteenth century; it is described accurately here, with the addition of an astounding true story. In 1820 the whaleship *Essex* was attacked and sunk by a sperm whale. This remarkable and unusual event caught the attention of Herman Melville and became the inspiration for the novel *Moby Dick*. **BBYA**

**Keywords:** Sperm whales • Whaling

## Scandiffio, Laura, and Stephen MacEachern.

*Escapes!* <u>True Stories from the Edge</u>. Toronto: Annick Press, 2003. ISBN 9781550378238. **M** **J**

Throughout the ages, people have faced incredible odds to free themselves from untenable situations, such as slavery, war, and political imprisonment. Ten amazing tales of such escapes are presented in this book, showing how people fought for their freedom using ingenuity, either alone or with the help of other courageous people.

**Keywords:** Adventure • Escapes • Nonfiction collections

## Swanson, Diane.

*Tunnels!* <u>True Stories from the Edge</u>. Toronto: Annick Press, 2003. ISBN 9781550377811. **M** **J**

Tunnels provide the setting for tales of daring, drama, and terror. People who built tunnels, dug for coal in them, or worked in them in any capacity have faced different and ongoing dangers, such as the baffling and inexplicable 1999 truck fire in the Mont Blanc tunnel. Of course, tunnels have also been favorite routes for outlaws, escaping convicts, drug runners, and prisoners of war. From Howard Carter discovering King Tut's tomb in 1922 to the 1996 takeover of the Japanese embassy in Peru, the reader will find fast-paced and fascinating tales here.

**Keywords:** Adventure • Nonfiction collections • Tunnels

## Tanaka, Shelley, and David Craig.

*Earthquake!: On a Peaceful Spring Morning Disaster Strikes San Francisco.* A Day That Changed America. New York: Hyperion Books for Children, 2004. ISBN 9780786818822. **M** **J**

There is a reason that the earthquake that shook San Francisco in 1906 is referred to as the "Great Earthquake and Fire." Readers will find out what happened in the city through the stories of four people who were there. Photographs, maps, diagrams, paintings, and artifacts help readers learn exactly what happened during this awful event, with additional sidebars explaining how earthquakes occur and what the Richter scale is, and providing other supplemental information. Readers will witness the horror and gravity of a terrible event in a fast-paced and accessible format.

**Keywords:** Disasters • Earthquakes • San Francisco earthquake • San Francisco fire

# Sports Adventures

The characters in these books exhibit admirable qualities, such as mental and physical endurance, the underdog fighting to the end, and a competitor determined to finish. Readers vicariously experience adventure, often in a sport that interests them, as well as developing empathy for the protagonists' battles.

## Breashears, David.

🎗 *High Exposure: An Enduring Passion for Everest and Unforgiving Places.* New York: Simon & Schuster, 1999. Reprinted 2000. ISBN 0684865459. **H**

Breashears is a world-renowned climber and cinematographer. He is best known for the Emmy award-winning IMAX movie *Everest,* which he made after climbing the mountain for the fourth time in 1996. In this book readers find out how he became interested and involved in both pursuits, as they follow him through ever more difficult climbs, from Yosemite to Europe, Nepal, and Tibet. In relating the story of his triumphs and tragedies, Breashears also gives the reader a sense of what drives him back to the top of the mountain repeatedly, if only to recover the bodies of those who were unable to finish the ascent. **Alex**

**Keywords:** Cinematography • Mount Everest • Mountaineering • Sports

## Colton, Larry.

🏅 *Counting Coup: A True Story of Basketball and Honor on the Little Big Horn.* New York: Warner Books, c2000. ISBN 9780446526838. **H**

Colton visited a Crow Indian Reservation in Hardin, Montana, intending to write about the boys' basketball team. Instead he spent fifteen months there, following Sharon LaForge and the girls' team from their preseason workouts to the state championship. Here the reader will find a picture of the players' lives in a mixed community, along with a view of the difficulties faced by the star player, who had an alcoholic mother, a difficult home life, and several of the uglier problems associated with her community. Also included is a front-row seat to the basketball games and the community, with an update several years after the season ended. **Alex, BBYA**

**Keywords:** Basketball for women • Hardin High School • Indian athletes

**Now Try:** Readers who empathize with Sharon's belief that basketball was everything will find another group of heroes in Michael D'Orso's *Eagle Blue: A Team, a Tribe, and a High School Basketball Team in Arctic Alaska.* This Alex award winner follows a basketball team from Fort Yukon, just inside the Arctic Circle, to the 2005 state championships. This is an especially remarkable achievement in a place where the school usually has an enrollment of thirty-two.

## Hillenbrand, Laura.

*Seabiscuit: An American Legend.* New York: Random House, 2001. ISBN 9780375502910. **H** **A**

The Great Depression is more than a label for the economic situation of the country during the 1930s, it is an apt description of the country's morale as a whole. Into this era stumbled a descendant of the great Man o' War, a runt with no characteristics of a champion, who was nurtured and brought on as a great talent by three men. In a story that captured the nation, Seabiscuit became a media darling whose career was eagerly followed by the American people, including the president, as his owner, trainer, and jockey helped him become one of the greatest racehorses of all time.

**Keywords:** Economic depression • Gambling • Horse racing • Horses • Seabiscuit (race horse) • Underdogs

## Pfetzer, Mark, and Jack Galvin.

🏅 *Within Reach: My Everest Story.* New York: Dutton Books, 1998. Reprint: Puffin Books, 2000. ISBN 9780141304977. **J** **H** **BB**

We've all heard it before: If we decide we want something enough, we can make it happen. If a thirteen-year-old decides to climb Mount Everest, it might surprise people when that person reaches the summit two years later. This story of how one determined climber raised money, learned to climb, and found himself on Everest's "Death Zone" during a very dangerous storm is just as amazing. **QP**

**Keywords:** Mount Everest • Mountaineering • Mountaineers • Pfetzer, Mark

### Scdoris, Rachael, and Rick Steber.

*No End in Sight: My Life as a Blind Iditarod Racer.* Prineville, OR: Two Star/Bonanza Publishing, 2005. Reprint: St. Martin's Press, 2006. ISBN 0312352735. **H**

> Rachael Scdoris was introduced to sled dogs by her father, a musher, and developed a love for the sport of sled dog racing at an early age. Legally blind since birth, she faced not only merciless teasing at school, but also the prejudices of people in the sledding community, who thought a girl with a disability should not compete, even if she could pass the qualifying races. Readers have a front-row seat as Rick Steber and Scodoris tell how she overcame childhood obstacles and ultimately earned the right to compete in the 2005 Iditarod, a grueling, 1,200-mile sled dog race.
>
> **Keywords:** Blindness • Iditarod • Scodoris, Rachael • Sled dog racing

### Venables, Stephen.

*To the Top: The Story of Everest.* Cambridge, MA: Candlewick Press, 2003. ISBN 9780763621155. **M J H**

> Venables's experience climbing Mount Everest frames a history of various attempts made to climb the world's tallest mountain. From George Mallory's failed expedition in 1924 to Sir Edmund Hillary's successful one in 1953, the necessary equipment, stamina, and life-threatening difficulties make for an exciting read. The continuing dangers presented by the mountain are aptly demonstrated.
>
> **Keywords:** Adventure • Everest • Hillary, Edmund • Mountaineering • Venables, Stephen

# War Stories

The books in this section offer gripping narratives that take place during times of war. These stories often show the lengths to which people will go to survive, with an emphasis on endurance, courage, and strength. Those characteristics separate these stories from the books in the "Human Cruelties" subsection of chapter 5.

### DeSaix, Deborah Durland, and Karen Gray Ruelle.

*Hidden on the Mountain: Stories of Children Sheltered from the Nazis in Le Chambon.* New York: Holiday House, 2007. ISBN 9780823419289. **M J**

> Based on extensive research, the authors share a remarkable story. During World War II a town in Nazi-occupied south-central France, a Protestant community whose people had once been persecuted for their religious beliefs, banded together and rescued several thousand Jewish children. The book includes a background, time lines, information about the rescuers, and the diaries of the children, with extensive photographs and source notes.
>
> **Keywords:** Jewish children in World War II • Le Chambon • World War II

1

2

3

4

5

6

7

8

9

10

11

## Levine, Ellen.

🌻 *Darkness over Denmark: The Danish Resistance and the Rescue of the Jews.* New York: Holiday House, 2000. ISBN 9780823414475. **M** **J** **H** **C**

Hitler's plan to purify the Aryan race is familiar, but its failure in one country in Europe is not as well known. This complex and thrilling story covers Nazi occupation, ongoing resistance, and tales from both survivors and victims who were deported to Theresienstadt. Although there is acknowledgment of Danish Nazi sympathizers, betrayals for money, and political conflict, the continuing determination of the Danes to protect Jewish citizenship and property, before and after the war, differentiated them from every other Nazi-occupied nation. **BBYA**

**Keywords:** Danish history • Ethnic relations • German occupation of Denmark • Holocaust • World War II

## Shapiro, Stephen, and Tina Forrester.

*Hoodwinked: Deception and Resistance.* Outwitting the Enemy: Stories from the Second World War. Toronto: Annick Press, 2004. ISBN 1550378325. **M** **J** **RR** **BB**

Shapiro introduces readers to diversions, deceit, and tricks used to turn the tide of the war. Readers may know about a false town that was constructed in England, but not necessarily false radio broadcasts and impersonating superior officers or Operation Mincemeat, which misled Axis forces into expecting an attack from a different direction. These tactics are discussed and supplemented with additional materials to draw readers into the study of history and its effects.

**Keywords:** Espionage • Resistance • World War II

*Ultra Hush-Hush: Espionage and Special Missions.* Outwitting the Enemy: Stories from the Second World War. Toronto: Annick Press, 2003. ISBN 1550377787. **M** **J** **RR** **BB**

This introduction to espionage and its importance is presented strictly through examples that illustrate some of its most important uses in World War II. The reader will learn about covert operations, daredevils, and double agents. Sidebars add more and intriguing information.

**Keywords:** Code talkers • Covert operations • Enigma machine • Espionage • World War II

# Explorations, Travel, and Historical Adventures

These titles provide readers with a wealth of exciting possibilities—from experiencing travel to searching for new frontiers. They give readers a chance to gain an understanding of new places, cultures, and historical periods. Readers will visit the Solomon Islands with Maria Coffey, find out why historians debate the truth about Marco Polo's trips, or dive to the depths of the Pacific Ocean.

## Aronson, Marc.

🌻 *Sir Walter Ralegh and the Quest for El Dorado.* New York: Clarion Books, 2000. ISBN 9780395848272. **J** **H**

The Elizabethan age was the perfect time for an intelligent, ambitious, and determined man to improve his position. Ralegh, now commonly spelled "Raleigh," gained enough favor from Queen Elizabeth I to become a courtier and go off adventuring to the New World in search of gold. Of course, the same arrogance that readers witness in this close view of Elizabeth's court also caused his eventual imprisonment and death. This book was awarded both the 2000 Boston Globe-Horn Book Award and the 2001 Robert F. Sibert Informational Book Award. **BG-HB, Sibert**

Keywords: Courtiers in Great Britain • Discovery of Guiana • Raleigh, Sir Walter

## Benanav, Michael.

*Men of Salt: Crossing the Sahara on the Caravan of White Gold.* Guilford, CT: Lyons Press, 2006. ISBN 9781592287727. **H**

Wanting to experience a means of travel and a way of life before modern technology rendered them obsolete, Michael Benanev crossed more than 1,000 miles of desert with a camel caravan to the salt mining outpost of Taoudenni. Salt mining, a difficult way of life, has been practiced for over a millennium without benefit of medical help or electricity. Benanav's travels provide a glimpse into a culture that provides a sharp contrast to our own.

Keywords: Caravans • Sahara • Salt industry • Salt trade • Travel in Africa

## Blumberg, Rhoda.

*Shipwrecked!: The True Adventures of a Japanese Boy.* New York: HarperCollins, 2001. ISBN 9780688174842. **M** **J**

Novelists would have a hard time dreaming up Manjiro's life story. Shipwrecked in 1841 at the age of fourteen when he was working to support his family, he was rescued by a passing whaler, on which he managed to learn English and navigation skills. The whaler's captain took him along to the United States, where Manjiro not only became Japan's first visitor to the country but also earned a death sentence should he ever try to return to Japan. But this was only the start of his adventures; he became a prospector, a samurai, and a politician, among other things. Blumberg provides a very interesting picture of Japanese culture and viewpoints, along with this fascinating life story.

Keywords: Japanese history • Manjiro • Mung, John

## Coffey, Maria, Dag Goering, and Debora Pearson.

*Jungle Islands: My South Sea Adventure.* Adventure Travel Books. Toronto: Annick Press, 2000. ISBN 9781550375961. **M**

When she was young, Maria almost drowned. She had to overcome an overwhelming fear of water to make some incredible trips, one of which she recounts in this book, taking readers with her on the trip of a lifetime through the Solomon Islands. Using shell money, swimming with sharks, visiting Skull Island, and encountering a whole new culture are just a few of the things readers can experience in this colorful and enticing real-life adventure. A list of Web sites is included.

Keywords: Coffey, Maria • Goering, Dag • Sea kayaking • Solomon Islands

**Now try:** Armchair travelers have many opportunities to learn about the world. They may prefer to learn about cultures, geography, or politics. Readers interested in a hot, dry climate may try Laurie Raskin and Debora Pearson's *My Sahara Adventure: 52 Days by Camel,* in which the modes of transport include jeep, bus, boat, train, and camel. Readers who have wondered what it is like to live in colder climates can go along on an often dangerous, 5,000-mile round-trip drive from Vancouver to Tuktoyaktuk to deliver food, in *By Truck to the North: My Arctic Adventure,* the other book in the <u>Adventure Travel</u> series. Authors Andy Turnbull and Debora Pearson were awarded the 1999 Norma Fleck Award for Canadian children's nonfiction.

## Freedman, Russell, and Bagram Ibatoulline.

*The Adventures of Marco Polo.* New York: Arthur A. Levine Books, 2006. ISBN 043952394X. **M** **J**

Marco Polo was either the greatest explorer of all time or the greatest storyteller in history. Even his family did not believe he could have accomplished all he said he did; in the thirteenth century, as he lay dying, they asked him to tell the truth. Freedman shares Polo's remarkable adventures with readers as he travels from Venice to the court of Kublai Khan, becoming the first person to see the marvels of the orient, including the use of coal and paper money. Ibatoulline adds beautiful illustrations and period artwork to help transport the reader to the cultures that Polo visits. As Freedman points out in his author's note, the debate among historians about the truth of the journey is still going strong, due in no small part to the 150 versions of the tale that exist. The evidence on both sides of the debate is presented and draws readers' attention to the difficulty of confirming historical events.

**Keywords:** Adventurers • Asia • Exploration • Polo, Marco

**Now Try:** Although the dispute about Marco Polo continues to catch the attention of historians, the importance of his claims is not in doubt. Diana Childress addresses both points in *Marco Polo's Journey to China.* A volume in the <u>Pivotal Moments in History</u> series, this text not only explains the difference between primary and secondary sources but also includes a primary source with a direct translation.

## Gunderson, Jessica.

*The Lewis and Clark Expedition.* <u>Graphic Library</u>. Mankato, MN: Capstone Press, 2007. **M** **RR**

This is a fast-moving, graphic summary of the basic events of the expedition on which Meriwether Lewis and William Clark traveled overland to find a passage west to the Pacific Ocean. Interested readers will find a list of some of the pertinent facts from the expedition, a source list to guide them to additional books and Web sites, and a glossary.

**Keywords:** Clark, William • Exploration and discovery of the Western U.S. • Explorers • Graphic nonfiction • Lewis, Meriwether • Lewis and Clark expedition

## Kurson, Robert.

🐾 *Shadow Divers: The True Adventure of Two Americans Who Risked Everything to Solve One of the Last Mysteries of World War II.* New York: Random House, 2004. ISBN 9780375508585. **H** **A**

Deep-water diving is very dangerous; while trying to recover shipwrecks, divers often lose their lives. This gripping adventure follows Richie Kohler's and John

Chatterton's seven-year attempt to identify the wreck they found in 1991 off the coast of New Jersey, which turned out to be the World War II German submarine U-869. The men and their team were driven to succeed and to give some peace to the families of the fallen. They faced sharks, suffered from decompression sickness, and even lost some team members. **Alex**

**Keywords:** U-869 • Archaeological excavations • Chatterton, John • Deep-water diving • Kohler, Rich • Shipwrecks—New Jersey • Underwater archaeology

## Consider Starting with . . .

Armstrong, Jennifer. *Shipwreck at the Bottom of the World: The Extraordinary True Story of Shackleton and the* Endurance.

Breashears, David. *High Exposure: An Enduring Passion for Everest and Unforgiving Places.*

Hillenbrand, Laura. *Seabiscuit: An American Legend.*

Kurson, Robert. *Shadow Divers: The True Adventure of Two Americans Who Risked Everything to Solve One of the Last Mysteries of World War II.*

Pfetzer, Mark, and Jack Galvin. *Within Reach: My Everest Story.*

Tanaka, Shelley, and David Craig. *Earthquake!: On a Peaceful Spring Morning Disaster Strikes San Francisco.*

## Fiction Read-Alikes

- **Fama, Elizabeth.** Fama based *Overboard* on the true tale of an accident that occurred in 1996. In this book a young American girl fights for her life after the ferry she is on sinks off the coast of Sumatra.

- **Hobbs, Will.** Will Hobbs is one of the most consistent writers of survival and adventure fiction. Readers may find danger, wild weather, and daring, such as in *Wild Man Island,* as well as female protagonists (*Jackie's Wild Seattle*.)

- **McKernan, Victoria.** Take another look at the adventures of Shackleton and his crew, from the point of view of the youngest member of the voyage, in *Shackleton's Stowaway*. Readers can experience this remarkable journey through eighteen-year-old Perce Blackborow's eyes.

- **Mikaelson, Ben.** Readers looking for adventure and survival will find both in Mikaelson's *Red Midnight*. The only hope for a twelve-year-old Guatemalan boy and his sister escaping from the soldiers who killed his family is a kayak and the open water that separates his country from the United States.

- **Smith, Roland**. Mountaineering may be in Peak Marcello's blood, but the judge isn't amused when Peak is caught climbing skyscrapers. Peak's parents come up with a plan to help keep him out of trouble, but is it really to his benefit to be the youngest person ever to climb Mount Everest? Readers can find out in *Peak.*

- **Sweeney, Joyce.** Four friends decide to go spelunking to get away from their various problems. In *Free Fall*, their survival skills are seriously tested when they get lost in the Ocala National Forest; none of them has left word at home of their destination.

- **Tullson, Diane.** In *Red Sea*, when Libby is purposely late for her family's group sailing trip, her family misses the launch and sets off alone. When Mediterranean pirates and a fierce storm kill her stepfather, seriously injure her mother, and leave her sailboat in a mess, Libby's mother's fate rests in her hands.

# Chapter 2

## True Crime

## Definition

True crime is neither a very large nor a very old genre in young adult nonfiction. It is, however, becoming more popular. One indication of this increase in popularity is the number of detective and forensic titles on television (*CSI, Veronica Mars, Cold Case Files*). The traditional true crime book focuses on an actual crime, either real or unsolved, with an examination of the events, the investigations, and the real people involved in it. True crime books have now evolved beyond chronological presentations of a crime, although these are still found. It is possible to find debates about a crime's ramifications; criminal profiling; explanations of forensic procedures and methods; and stories about famous criminals, spies, and espionage.

## Appeal

These stories offer readers an escape unlike any other genre. Whether characters are hiding from an enemy or trying to discover a killer, readers are given an adrenaline-fueled, story-driven ride. Many of these stories also give readers a glimpse into the criminal mind, as well as a taste of crime-solving techniques.

## Chapter Organization

The first section, "Cons and Crimes," includes books that cover crimes, scams, and the people who have tried to get away with them. This is followed by works that investigate the methods used by criminal investigators, in "Crime Science." Readers may learn how to use these methods and find out how they have been used by agents and double agents in the books listed in "Intrigue and Espionage."

## Cons and Crimes: Solved and Unsolved

This subgenre includes stories of criminals trying to escape justice as well as tales about law enforcement agents trying to catch them, throughout history and into the present. Two series describe notable crimes, including some that remain mysteries more than a hundred years after they happened (<u>A Treasury of Victorian Murder</u>) and others that acknowledge the inventiveness of the crooks (<u>True Stories from the Edge</u>.)

## Boese, Alex.

🎋 *Hippo Eats Dwarf: A Field Guide to Hoaxes and Other B.S.* Orlando, FL: Harcourt, 2006. ISBN 9780156030830. **H** **A**

What happens when someone says something that sounds absurd, yet he or she seems to be sure of and believe that information? Readers will learn about all of the amazing, amusing, and outright criminal kinds of fakery possible in today's world. Real-life examples follow "reality rules" to provide the reader with commonsense guidelines in areas including birth, entertainment, the Internet, politics, food, news, business, and war. As Reality Rule 11.4 says, "technology can hide even the most glaring lack of talent." This title was listed in the Addictive Nonfiction section of the 2007 Popular Paperbacks list. **PP**

**Keywords:** Fraud • Humor • Imposters and imposture • Law • Popular culture • Social science

**Now Try:** Writing about fakery is not new to Boese, who maintains the Web site museumofhoaxes.com and whose first book will let readers know that hoaxes are not just common to the dot-com era. His *The Museum of Hoaxes: A Collection of Pranks, Stunts, Deceptions, and Other Wonderful Stories Contrived for the Public from the Middle Ages to the New Millennium* is a chronological history of some outrageous and astounding pranks. It is a good thing that Boese also explains why things were believed possible at the time.

## Geary, Rick.

## A Treasury of Victorian Murder. **J** **H**

This collection of Victorian true crimes presents some of the most horrendous and most puzzling crimes of the age, from the first serial killer in the United States to a crime that inspired Edgar Allan Poe. The artwork takes readers behind the scenes and lets them decide what actually happened, while providing realistic period details.

**Keywords:** Graphic nonfiction • Murder mysteries • True crime

*A Treasury of Victorian Murder.* **Volume 1.** New York: NBM Publishing, 1987. Reprinted 2002. ISBN 9781561633098. **J** **H** **RR**

A short introduction to the Victorian age, including some of the important names in literature, the arts, and murder, precedes three cases from the times. Readers follow along with the investigations of three sensational cases that combine true crime and history in graphic format. The Ryan Mystery presents a mysterious and unsolved murder, Glasgow physician E. W. Pritchard's crimes brought him both accusers and defenders, and the "abominable Mrs. Pearcey" committed both scandalous and vicious crimes.

**Keywords:** Criminal investigations • Graphic nonfiction • Great Britain • Nineteenth-century murders

*The Mystery of Mary Rogers.* New York: NBM/ComicsLit, 2001. 9781561632749. **H**

The unsolved murder of a Manhattan tobacconist's assistant in 1841 caused a sensation in the news when her beaten body was recovered from the Hudson River days after her disappearance. There were many possible suspects and causes of death; and the case was never solved. This fifth volume in the series includes the usual attention to setting and also lets the reader decide which of the posited solutions is the most likely. This astounding case inspired Edgar Allan Poe's short story "The Mystery of Mary Roget."

**Keywords:** Graphic nonfiction • Murder—New York State • Rogers, Mary

**Now Try:** Another unsolved and lingering murder in popular culture is the famous case of Lizzie Borden. Did she or didn't she commit one of the most heinous crimes of the nineteenth century? Rick Geary gives readers a chance to make up their own minds, presenting all of the facts in *The Borden Tragedy* (volume 3 of the series).

*The Beast of Chicago.* New York: NBM/ComicsLit, 2003. ISBN 9781561633623. **H**

The first serial killer in the United States, H. H. Holmes, remains one of the most frightening, with a legacy of between 100 and 200 victims. His trail of swindles and scams followed his three families across several states on his way to Chicago, where he built "The Castle," the sight of his most horrendous crimes. Illustrations show the mazes, trapdoors, and panels in his house of horrors, which Holmes used during the 1893 World's Fair to perpetrate and hide his grisly crimes. Readers follow the complicated schemes and travels of this industrious bigamist and murderer. This is volume 6 of the series.

**Keywords:** Graphic nonfiction • Mudgett, Herman • Murderers • Serial killer • World's Fair

**Now Try:** Erik Larson takes on the stories of both the architect behind the 1893 World's Fair and America's first serial killer, who used the Exposition as the base for his most horrific crimes. More mature readers will find this fast-moving story in Larson's *The Devil in the White City: Murder, Magic, and Madness at the Fair That Changed America.*

*The Murder of Abraham Lincoln: A Chronicle of 62 Days in the Life of the American Republic, March 4–May 4, 1865.* New York: NBM ComicsLit. 2005. ISBN 151634255. **J** **H**

The most famous American murder of the Victorian period is undoubtedly the assassination of President Abraham Lincoln by John Wilkes Booth. This story, told in graphic format, breaks it down into its key parts: introductions of the president and the conspirators, followed by the day of the conspirators' attacks, Booth's escape, and the president's final journey. Artwork highlights the plots, conspiracies, and period details. This is volume 7 of the series.

**Keywords:** Assassinations—pictorial works • Booth, John Wilkes • Graphic nonfiction • Lincoln, Abraham • Presidents—assassinations

🎗 *The Case of Madeleine Smith.* New York: NBM ComicsLit, 2006. 9781561634675. **H**

Emile L'Anglier's death in Glasgow in 1857 left few clues: correspondence from a young lady named "Mimi," a journal, keys, and evidence of the poison that was used to kill him. The trail led to a respectable young lady named Madeleine Smith, who had been involved in a clandestine and forbidden romance with L'Anglier, until she became involved with a more suitable gentleman. Her subsequent trial was followed closely in Victorian Scotland. This is volume

8 of the series. This title was chosen for YALSA's 2007 Great Graphic Novels for Teens list.

**Keywords:** Graphic nonfiction • Poisonings • Scottish murders • Smith, Madeleine Hamilton

## Jacobs, Thomas A.

🌺 *They Broke the Law—You Be The Judge: True Cases of Teen Crime.* Minneapolis, MN: Free Spirit, 2003. ISBN 1575421348. **J H**

A former juvenile court judge presents a variety of real-life cases of teen crime. Readers are presented with twenty-one cases, ranging from truancy to drug trafficking, along with related information to take into consideration, such as the teen's background, the particulars of the crime, sentencing options, and additional questions that could affect sentencing. Readers may then compare what they would do with the sentence the teen received, and read about what actually happened to the teens in question. The variety of crimes considered, along with the questions and role-playing possibilities posed, offer an interesting and relevant introduction to the law, ethics, and how teens feel about both. **QP, PP**

**Keywords:** Crime • Law • Nonfiction collections • Teenage crime

**Now Try:** Teens interested in more information about their rights under the law have many choices. For information about the legal system and personal rights, start with Thomas Jacobs's *What Are My Rights?: 95 Questions and Answers about Teens and the Law.* Readers who enjoyed the chance to give their opinions about true cases of crime may take a look at some cases in which teens fought in the courts to change the status quo, in Jacobs's *Teens Take It to Court: Young People Who Challenged the Law—and Changed Your Life.* Readers who are interested in becoming a lawyer will find the *Young Person's Occupational Outlook Handbook* in the "Career Directions" section of chapter 8.

## Larson, Erik.

*Thunderstruck.* New York: Crown, 2006. ISBN 1400080665. **H A**

Larson pairs the story of Guglielmo Marconi's race to develop and be acknowledged as the wizard behind wireless communication with a murder mystery that ultimately depends on those communications to catch a murderer. Larson presents the backgrounds of both Marconi and the mild-mannered Hawley Harvey Crippen, on the run with his mistress after murdering his overbearing wife, before showing how these plots intertwine in a gripping final chase.

**Keywords:** Crippen, Hawley Harvey • Marconi, Guglielmo • Murder

## Schroeder, Andreas.

*Scams!: Ten Stories That Explore Some of the Most Outrageous Swindlers and Tricksters of All Time.* True Stories from the Edge. Toronto: Annick Press, 2004. ISBN 9781550378538. **M J**

Why are people so often willing to believe things that are too good to be true? Who are the people with the ability to fool millions? This volume answers these questions before presenting ten of the most amazing and inventive swindles in history. They range from very successful Nazi counterfeiters to the invention of an entire culture in the 1970s.

**Keywords:** Counterfeiters • Fraud • Nonfiction collections • Swindlers

*Thieves!* <u>True Stories from the Edge</u>. Toronto: Annick Press, 2005. ISBN 9781550379334. **M** **J** **BB**

> Over the course of 150 years, some amazing thefts have been committed. The thefts, robberies, and burglaries that are related here are some of the most mind-boggling, either for their execution or for the horrific ways in which the plans went awry. A careful theft of the *Mona Lisa* went according to plan; so why were the robbers unable to get paid for their crime? A disastrous escape attempt by bank robbers left without a pilot for their plane adds humor.
>
> **Keywords:** Nonfiction collections • Robbery • Theft • Thieves

## Schroeder, Lucinda Delaney.

*A Hunt for Justice: The True Story of a Woman Undercover Wildlife Agent.* Guilford, CT: Lyons Press, 2006. ISBN 1592288820. **H** **A**

> Lucinda Schroeder presents the true tale of a takedown that she could not reveal until after her retirement from thirty years with the U.S. Fish and Wildlife Service, much of that time spent as one of a handful of undercover special agents. In 1991 Schroeder went undercover as "Jayne," looking for evidence against a known poacher, who was also running an illegal hunting ring in Alaska that guaranteed a kill of a wolf, sheep, caribou, or bear. Would the poachers ever suspect a woman? "Jayne" and her partner were in grave danger and under terrible pressure to gather evidence. With information about crime, justice, hunting, and nature, this is a gripping read.
>
> **Keywords:** Criminology • Environmental protection • Schroeder, Lucinda • True crime

# Crime Science

The popularity of forensics is readily seen in both fiction and popular culture. *CSI*'s explosion onto television was followed by two spin-offs. Kathy Reichs's novels, based on her own experience, have also been adapted for television. This subgenre does not include true crime stories per se; rather, it shows readers how forensic science is used to solve crimes. Readers will also find read-alike titles in which criminologists depend on forensic science to solve their cases.

## 24/7: Science Behind the Scenes: Forensic Files. **RR**

> This series takes a closer look at the scientists who work behind the scenes to solve crimes. Each of the twelve books in this series examines an aspect of crime science, providing the reader with an overview of the science and how it is used to solve crimes. Each book highlights three real-life cases that depended on the science in question. "Help Wanted" sections provide information about careers in forensics as well as where to go for further information.
>
> **Keywords:** Criminal investigations • Forensics

## Beres, D. B.

*Dusted and Busted!: The Science of Fingerprinting.* New York: Franklin Watts, 2007. ISBN 9781417785070; 9780531154571pb. **M** **J**

What makes fingerprints unique? How are they gathered? Readers will learn how to tell them apart and find out how a fingerprint analyst helped solve a robbery, identify a victim and killer, or find out if a burglar could be identified by footprints.

**Keywords:** Fingerprint analysis • Fingerprints

*Killer at Large: Criminal Profilers and the Cases They Solve!* New York: Franklin Watts, 2007. ISBN 9780531120651; 9780531175262pb. **M** **J**

Criminal profiling involves the use of psychological analysis and observation to catch criminals. Readers may find out how law enforcement made use of criminal profilers to help catch criminals such as a computer hacker and a murderer, as well as whether or not they might be interested in profiling as a career.

**Keywords:** Criminal investigations • Criminal profiling,

## Denega, Danielle.

*Gut-Eating Bugs: Maggots Reveal the Time of Death!* New York: Franklin Watts, 2007. ISBN 9780531118245; 9781428724761pb. **M** **J**

Viewers of *CSI* know that bugs follow a time line on decomposing tissue, and that entomologists can track the development of these bugs to determine someone's time of death. The cases here show how these very specialized scientists work and help solve crimes.

**Keywords:** Criminal investigations • Forensic entomology

*Have You Seen This Face?: The Work of Forensic Artists.* New York: Franklin Watts, 2007. ISBN 9780531154588; 9781428728431pb. **M** **J**

Readers may learn how artists use forensics to create replicas of murder victims that help investigators in the process of identification. The real-life examples include the use of an age-progression photo to help a father find his daughter years after her disappearance.

**Keywords:** Composite drawing • Criminals • Facial reconstruction • Forensic artists

## Joyce, Jaime.

*Bullet Proof!: The Evidence That Guns Leave Behind.* New York: Franklin Watts, 2007. ISBN 9780531154557; 9781428724259pb. **M** **J**

What kind of evidence do forensic firearms examiners look for when they search a scene or a witness? When guns are fired, they leave evidence both on the person who fired the gun and at the scene. Readers may follow the 1929 St. Valentine's Day Massacre as well as two newer mysteries that are solved by ballistics evidence.

**Keywords:** Ballistics • Criminal investigations

## Prokos, Anna.

*Guilty by a Hair!: Real-Life DNA Matches!* New York: Franklin Watts, 2007. ISBN 9780531118214; 9780531187333pb. **M J**

What is DNA, and how do forensic scientists use it to solve crimes? Readers will find out exactly what this chemical unique to each person, found in every cell of the body, can tell an investigator. How did a cat hair help convict a man of murder, and what is a typical day like for a forensic scientist?

**Keywords:** Criminal investigations • DNA profiling • Forensic scientists

*Killer Wallpaper: True Cases of Deadly Poisonings.* New York: Franklin Watts, 2007. ISBN 9780531154595; 9781428725102pb. **M J**

What happens in the case of a suspected poisoning? Readers will learn the specific steps a forensic toxicologist takes in analyzing blood and tissue samples. The sample cases include the Washington State Excedrin case.

**Keywords:** Criminal investigations • Forensics • Toxicology

## Webber, Diane.

*Do You Read Me?: Famous Cases Solved by Handwriting Analysis!* New York: Franklin Watts, 2007. ISBN 9780531154564; 9781428728011pb. **M J**

This book shows how handwriting is used as evidence, with cases that are both famous and notorious. The Lindbergh kidnapping, Hitler's supposed diaries, and a forged will are examined and used to show how the experts can use handwriting to help solve crimes.

**Keywords:** Criminal investigations • Forged documents • Handwriting analysis

*Shot and Framed: Photographers at the Crime Scene.* New York: Franklin Watts, 2007. ISBN 9780531154601; 9781428729292pb. **M J**

One of the key investigators in a criminal investigation is a crime scene photographer. The cases that help show how this exacting and detailed work is done include photographs from a fifty-year-old murder and video evidence that helps to exonerate an innocent man after several years in jail.

**Keywords:** Crime scene photography • Criminal investigations

## Winchester, Elizabeth Siris.

*The Right Bite: Dentists as Detectives.* New York: Franklin Watts, 2007. ISBN 9780531187340; 9780531187340pb. **M J**

Forensic dentistry is not a very old science, but is has made its mark in legal evidence. A case in point is the trial of Ted Bundy, whose bite mark was used to tie him to a victim. In another case a single tooth was also used to identify a victim. The reader will find out about a forensic dentist's background and what he does with his time.

**Keywords:** Criminal investigations • Forensic dentistry • Murder victims

## Bowers, Vivien.

*Crime Scene: How Investigators Use Science to Track Down the Bad Guys.* Illustrated by Martha Newbigging. Toronto: Maple Tree Press, 2005. ISBN 9781897066553. **M**

> The police rely on scientists to help them solve all sorts of crimes: counterfeiting, theft, computer hacking, even murder. This book discusses what kind of evidence a criminal leaves behind and how forensics is used to help solve cases, showcasing a variety of forensic specialists.
>
> **Keywords:** Criminal investigations • Forensic sciences

## Owen, David.

**❦** *Hidden Evidence: Forty True Crimes and How Forensic Science Helped Solve Them.* Willowdale, ON: Firefly Books, 2000. ISBN 9781552094839. **BB**

> The reader will travel hundreds of years through the evolution of science and crime investigation with David Owen as he examines how forensic science was used in forty cases, including Jack the Ripper's killings, presidential assassinations, and recent serial killings. **BBYA, PP, QP**
>
> **Keywords:** Forensic science • Law • True crime

## Platt, Richard.

**❦** *Crime Scene: The Ultimate Guide to Forensic Science.* New York: Dorling Kindersley, 2003. ISBN 0789488914; 0756618967pb. (2006). **J H**

> In this thorough look at forensics and the processes involved in investigating crimes, Platt breaks down the procedures and techniques used by the team into seven chapters, highlighting each with a real-life case study in which a specific technique led to a solution. Each step has ample additional material, including illustrations, charts, time lines, and photographs. **QP**
>
> **Keywords:** Crime sciences • Forensics • Investigative sciences

# Intrigue and Espionage

Author David Owen refers to espionage as the world's "second oldest profession." It has been a popular subject in film and fiction since Sean Connery became the first James Bond. This genre gives readers a chance to apply the knowledge they gain from the "Crime Science" titles and learn how it has been used in real-life situations.

## Bursztynski, Sue.

*This Book Is Being Bugged.* **It's True! Series**. Toronto: Annick Press, 2007. ISBN 9781554510795. **M RR**

> Here is a fun and straightforward book about spies and spying. In this introductory guide, readers will find some of the amazing, and notorious incidents of espionage in history and across different cultures, from the Trojan horse to women spies to the truth about ninjas. Also included are a glossary and a guide on where to find more information.
>
> **Keywords:** Espionage • Ninjas • Spies

## Coleman, Janet Wyman.

*Secrets, Lies, Gizmos, and Spies: A History of Spies and Espionage.* New York: Abrams Books for Young Readers, 2006. ISBN 0810957566. 🇯 🇭

> Written in partnership with the International Spy Museum, this book presents a survey of the world of espionage, from the people involved in it to the evolving techniques and methods. Using actual stories to illustrate the good and the bad of espionage Coleman helps readers better understand the implications of the actions, whether of a spy, double agent or traitor. Fascinating wartime stories have the possibility of supplementing curriculum. Almost all stories have accompanying photographs.
>
> **Keywords:** Espionage • Intelligence service • Traitors

## Janeczko, Paul B.

*Top Secret: A Handbook of Codes, Ciphers, and Secret Writing.* **Illustrated by Jenna LaReau.** Cambridge, MA: Candlewick Press, 2004. ISBN 9780763609719. 🇲 🇯

> Paul Janeczko's knowledge of codes is impressive. Here he discusses ciphers and other forms of cryptography used historically to exchange secret information. It is his ability to clearly explain the difference between codes and ciphers, and let readers know just how they can be used that makes this a captivating book. The chapters are divided into three sections: codemaking, codebreaking and concealment. Readers are given instructions for making codes, as well as devices from invisible inks, St. Cyr slides, and cipher squares, along with background on how they were originally used and practice questions to help them get started. Readers are encouraged to make their own codes and ciphers, having been shown how they work.
>
> **Keywords:** Codes • Ciphers • Cryptography

## Owen, David.

*Hidden Secrets: A Complete History of Espionage and the Technology Used to Support It.* Toronto; Buffalo, NY: Firefly, 2002. ISBN 1552975649. 🇭 🇦

> A careful examination of the world's "second oldest profession," looked at through case studies primarily from the twentieth century, allows for examination of various technologies. The numerous photographs and illustrations help show the development and importance of the techniques and equipment used in espionage and how they affected the outcomes of historical events.
>
> **Keywords:** Espionage • History • Spies

# Consider Starting with . . .

Boese, Alex. *Hippo Eats Dwarf: A Field Guide to Hoaxes and Other B.S.*
Geary, Rick. *The Beast of Chicago.*

Jacobs, Thomas A. *They Broke the Law—You Be the Judge: True Cases of Teen Crime.*

Owen, David. *Hidden Evidence: Forty True Crimes and How Forensic Science Helped Solve Them.*

Schroeder, Andreas. *Thieves!*

## Fiction Read-Alikes

- **Ferguson, Alane**. Fans of *CSI* are a natural fit for Ferguson's mysteries. Starting with *The Christopher Killer*, readers will be introduced to Cameryn Mahoney, a very determined young detective. Cammie makes full use of her forensic knowledge, so readers will find some gory scenes in *Angel of Death* and *The Circle of Blood*.

- **Horowitz, Anthony**. When Alex Rider is informed of his uncle's death, he has no idea of the dangerous escapades that are in store for him. Starting with *Stormbreaker*, which has just been released as a graphic novel, this junior MI6 agent has a number of exciting adventures in *Point Blank*, *Skeleton Key*, and *Eagle Strike*.

# Part 2

## Life Stories

# Chapter 3

## Memoirs and Autobiographies

## Definition

A memoir is essentially a snapshot: a person's recording of a series of events from his or her own life. Memoirs differ from biographies in that in most cases they are reconstructed directly from an author's memory, without the source material that would be used in biographies. They rely heavily on an author's feelings, impressions, and emotions, rather than incorporating the varying viewpoints and impartiality that are expected from biographers and historians.

Autobiographies tell the complete life story of the author, usually in chronological order, rather than focusing on one part of it. They often have coauthors, who are able to make use of primary and secondary sources. Readers will then have the added benefit of a number of formats and reading levels and a wide variety of supplementary materials.

## Appeal

Like biographies, memoirs and autobiographies allow readers to explore other lives, usually concentrating on one character. The difference is that with memoirs and autobiographies, readers experience events from the character's perspective. Memoirs and autobiographies may be tragic, funny, or eye-opening. They provide an intimate experience through which a reader may relate on a personal level to the actions, tragedies, and foibles of the author. The wide variety of subgenres and themes in this type of literature allows readers to choose from a broad range of experiences. These books are not necessarily written by famous or notable people; it is the stories that are shared with readers that make them worthwhile.

## Chapter Organization

There are many different types of memoirs. In the "Coming-of-Age" section, authors reminisce about the experiences that helped them become adults. In "Overcoming Adversity," stories of tragedy and triumph dominate, including Lori Gottlieb's fight with anorexia and Lance Armstrong's battle with cancer. Experiences with other countries and cultures are found in "Multicultural Experiences," giving readers a chance to see what it is like to grow up in another country or with a multicultural background.

Musings about work are found in the section "Working Life." Readers may share the travels of cartoonist Guy Delisle to China and North Korea or learn with first-year teacher Esmé Raji Codell. The wry humor often found in these books leads into the "Humorous Memoirs" section. Here authors' contemplations often provide a new way of looking at things. Examples of this include David Almond's assertions about the world's worst candies and Gary Paulsen's tales of invented extreme sports. Autobiographies have been integrated into the appropriate categories and are identified by keyword.

# Coming-of-Age

Anyone familiar with young adult literature knows the term *coming-of-age*. In these books the authors contemplate the times and events that marked their transition from childhood into maturity. These experiences had a direct influence on the paths of their lives. The books deal with issues relevant to teens, from the point of view of a person who has actually had these experiences.

## Conroy, Pat.

🌹 *My Losing Season*. New York: Nan A. Talese, 2002. Reprint: Bantam, 2003. ISBN 0553381903; 9780553381900. **H** **A**

Author Pat Conroy remembers his senior season at the Citadel military college, where he was a point guard, although admittedly not the world's greatest. He follows his team through their games, ascribing much of what he has done as a writer to what he learned on the court. Readers may be surprised to flearn that the greatest suffering he endured was not as a plebe at the military college, but at the hands of his coach, which made him a stronger man in the end. He developed a strong camaraderie with his team and achieved victories in friendships, writing, and a love of the game. **Alex**

Keywords: Basketball • The Citadel • Conroy, Pat • Writing

## Dowd, Olympia.

*A Young Dancer's Apprenticeship: On Tour with the Moscow City Ballet.* Brookfield, CT: Twenty-First Century, 2003. ISBN 076132917X. **M** **J**

Olympia Dowd recalls the time she spent studying and touring with the Moscow City Ballet at the age of fourteen. She is able to write about the highs and lows of going from being a Canadian student to being a guest principal performing in *Carmen, Cinderella,* and *The Nutcracker*. Descriptions include the difficulties of constant performing and the differences between the tours in Asia, Europe, and America. Photographs of her life as a young dancer complement the text, which ends with her starting the next phase of her career.

**Keywords:** Ballet • Dance • Performing arts

## Frank, Anne, Otto Frank, Mirjam Pressler, and Susan Massotty.

🌹 *Anne Frank: The Diary of a Young Girl.* **Definitive ed.** New York: Doubleday, 1995. ISBN 0891902236. **M** **J** **H** **C**

One of the most evocative pictures of the Holocaust can be found in the diary of Anne Frank, who spent two years hiding from the Nazis with her family in an annex in Amsterdam, only to be discovered and sent to Bergen-Belsen concentration camp. Her father, the only survivor from her family, edited and published her diary after the war. After his death in 1990, Susan Massotty translated this version, adding approximately 30 percent more material and giving a much clearer picture of Anne and the life she lived in the attic. Readers will experience her rages, tensions, and vulnerabilities, along with her poignant observations. **BBYA**

**Keywords:** Frank, Anne • Holocaust • World War II

## Mace, Nancy.

*In the Company of Men: A Woman at the Citadel.* New York: Simon & Schuster/Simon Pulse, 2001. ISBN 0689840039. **H**

In 1995 South Carolina's famed military college, The Citadel, was ordered to accept women as students. The first female student, Shannon Faulkner, lasted only a week. Four more women entered El Cid's hallowed halls in 1996. Among them was Nancy Mace, who became the first female graduate. The reader is shown not only the trials of being a freshman "knob" but also the abuse that Nancy endured because of her gender and her position as the daughter of The Citadel's commandant and most decorated living graduate.

**Keywords:** Mace, Nancy • The Citadel military academy of South Carolina • Military cadets

**Now Try:** Readers interested in the military might want to read Eric Haney's behind-the-scenes memoir *Inside Delta Force,* or books in the Inside Special Forces series, which covers military branches in the United States and Great Britain (see the "Career Directions" section of chapter 8). A fiction title that complements Nancy Mace's book is Amy Efaw's *Battle Dress.* Efaw used her own military background to add realism to the tale of a female freshman dealing with the "Beast" training at West Point.

## Myers, Walter Dean.

🎗 *Bad Boy: A Memoir.* New York: HarperCollins, 2001. ISBN 0060295236. **J H**

This is an honest and forthright account of Meyers's adolescence in Harlem. The writing ably balances the quick temper and an indifferent attitude toward school with the voracious appetite for words that would eventually turn Myers into the 1994 winner of the Margaret A. Edwards Award for lifetime achievement in young adult literature. **BBYA**

**Keywords:** Autobiography • Harlem • Writer

## Parks, Rosa, and James Haskins.

*Rosa Parks: My Story.* New York: Dial Books, 1992. Reprint: Puffin Books, 1999. ISBN 0141301201. **M J H**

Rosa Parks will forever be remembered as the mother of the civil rights movement. This rendition of her life gives the reader a better understanding of the context in which this dignified woman lived. Tired of her lowly status and aware of her own rights, Parks was not the first person to refuse to give up a seat on the bus. Nevertheless, because of her background with the NAACP, once she had been arrested she was perfectly placed to be the plaintiff in a test case. The description of the year-long bus boycott and its participants, including Dr Martin Luther King Jr., provides a vivid picture of the times.

**Keywords:** Autobiography • Civil rights • Civil rights workers • Montgomery bus boycott • Parks, Rosa

## Rosen, Christine.

*My Fundamentalist Education: A Memoir of a Divine Girlhood.* New York: Public Affairs, 2005. 9781586482589. **H**

The devout Keswick Christian School wasn't in line with Rosen's parents' philosophy; they simply chose it because it was in a better neighborhood. The early religious education Rosen received, attending the school through eighth grade, is recounted with humor and warmth. Early on she applied Bible stories to her everyday life eagerly, such as when she saw parallels between the ten plagues and her Florida home's insect problems. As she matured, the author increasingly questioned doctrines, leading to an eventual break with fundamentalism. Nevertheless, she is appreciative of her background, speaking of the rewards of childhood education in general and hers in particular.

**Keywords:** Christian lives • Florida childhoods • Florida fundamentalists • Religious biographies • Rosen, Christine

## Siegel, Siena.

🔖 *To Dance: A Ballerina's Graphic Novel.* New York: Atheneum Books for Young Readers, 2006. ISBN 0689867476; 9780689867477. **M** **J**

For Siena Cherson Siegel, dance was more than a way to correct her flat feet. It was a driving force and a part of her. This lovely memoir, told in graphic novel format with watercolor images, follows her from her youth in Puerto Rico to her teen years at her mentor George Balanchine's School of American Ballet and her performances with the New York City Ballet. Readers will learn about both the hardships and the rewards of Siegel's time with the ballet. This was an honor book for the 2007 Robert F. **Sibert** Informational Book Medal.

**Keywords:** Ballerinas • Ballet • Dance • Graphic nonfiction • Siegel, Siena Cherson

## Waldman, Neil.

*Out of the Shadows: An Artist's Journey.* Honesdale, PA: Boyds Mills Press, 2007. ISBN 1590784111. **M** **J**

How does someone become an artist? Waldman reflects on the childhood that led him to his career. His comforting relationship with his grandparents and their instruction in traditions, family history, and art helped to demonstrate his growing interest in the world around him. Art became a refuge for Waldman and several members of his family from the incessant fighting in his home. The varied artworks they produced illustrate this story of family, home, and finding one's own way.

**Keywords:** Artists • Illustrators • Waldman, Neil

## Walker, Rebecca.

🌶 *Black, White and Jewish: Autobiography of a Shifting Self.* New York: Riverhead Books, 2001. Reprinted 2002. ISBN 1573229075. **H** **A**

Walker looks at her life as the biracial daughter of a liberal Jewish lawyer and well-known author Alice Walker. She was an emblem of her parents' civil rights activities, a "Movement child" until her life was torn apart by her parents' divorce. Her life then became a series of changes, reflected in the shifts she made between her parents' families. She was unable to fit in either with her mother's bohemian lifestyle in San Francisco or with her father's suburban New York family. With perfect candor Walker describes how she tested the boundaries of sex, drugs, and school, as well as enduring the prejudices of friends along the way and determining where she belonged. **Alex**

**Keywords:** African Americans • Biracial • Jewish • Memoir

## Zenatti, Valerie.

🌶 *When I Was a Soldier: A Memoir.* New York: Bloomsbury Children's Books, 2005. Reprinted 2007. ISBN 1599900599. **H**

Valerie Zenatti's life changed after her family emigrated from France to Israel. This book recounts the months up to her eighteenth birthday and the following two years, during which time she served her compulsory military service. The transition she experienced while in uniform makes for an enlightening read and presents a view of modern life in Israel not often seen. **BBYA**

**Keywords:** Israel • Israeli army • Military • Zenatti, Valerie

# Overcoming Adversity

Stories of remembered problems, pain, unfortunate events, and turbulent personal pasts can be very wrenching to read. The subject matter, which can include disease, death, depression, attempted suicide, drug addiction, and different forms of abuse, often makes these stories more appropriate for older teens. At the same time, these stories can deeply move and inspire readers, as they learn how teens have coped with situations beyond their control.

There is a popular crossover with fiction covering the same material, especially as the authors come to terms with or find ways to overcome their situations.

## Angelou, Maya.

*I Know Why the Caged Bird Sings.* New York, Random House, 1970. Reprinted 2002. ISBN 9780375507892. **H** **A** **C**

Regarded as Angelou's masterwork, this is the first volume of six that make up her complete autobiography. She tells of the lessons she learned when she was sent to live with her grandmother in Arkansas, which helped her through some of the extraordinary hardships she endured later in life. Originally published in 1970, this dignified portrayal of racism, sexism, and abuse suffered and overcome is a remarkable achievement.

**Keywords:** Abuse • American authors • Angelou, Maya • Autobiography • Poetry • Racism • Sexism

**Now Try:** Readers interested in accessible, strong poetry may be drawn to Maya Angelou's work. A sense of growth and development, as well as a number of relatable themes, may be found in *The Complete Collected Poems of Maya Angelou*. Readers may follow her work from her earliest productions to the 1993 collection she delivered at President William Clinton's inauguration.

## Armstrong, Lance.

🏆 *It's Not About the Bike: My Journey Back to Life.* New York: Putnam, 2000. Reprint: Berkley Books, 2001. ISBN 0425179613. **H**

Best known for winning the Tour de France seven consecutive times, Lance Armstrong's hardest race was fraught with pain and aimed at an entirely different finish line. Having secured a place in the history books as one of the greatest cyclists in the world by his mid-twenties, he received the devastating diagnosis of his cancer. His battle with the disease that had spread to his lungs and brain is handled openly and serves as a great inspiration. **BBYA, PP**

**Keywords:** Armstrong, Lance • Cancer • Cycling • Sports

## Corrigan, Eireann.

*You Remind Me of You: A Poetry Memoir.* New York: PUSH, 2002. ISBN 0439297710. **H**

Corrigan's difficult journey with anorexia is told in verse, detailing her struggle, her difficulty in finding something meaningful in life as she entered several treatment facilities, and finally her recovery alongside a previous boyfriend after his own attempted suicide.

**Keywords:** Anorexia • Attempted suicide • Bulimia • Eating disorders • Poetry • Verse novel

## Deng, Alephonsion, Benson Deng, Benjamin Ajak, and Judy Bernstein.

*They Poured Fire on Us from the Sky: The True Story of Three Lost Boys from Sudan.* New York: Public Affairs, 2006. ISBN 9781586483883. **H** **A**

The Sudanese civil war forced thousands of boys from their homes. This is the story of three of the "lost boys" and their journey of nearly a thousand miles to Ethiopia and then back to Kenya. All of them were under the age seven when they started this walk; they endured unrelenting hunger, "hissing bullets," and the many deprivations that accompany war. The contrast between the boys' lives in the war and their relocation to San Diego, where they started to write the journals that become this book, underscores the hardships of day-to-day survival and separation from their families during the war.

**Keywords:** Ajak, Benjamin • Deng, Alephonsion • Deng, Benson • Lost boys • Sudan • War

## Gantos, Jack.

★ *Hole in My Life.* New York: Farrar, Straus & Giroux, 2002. ISBN 0374399883. **J** **H**

Author Jack Gantos shares his remarkable journey and the changes he made in his life—from helping smuggle hash as a youth to his subsequent arrest, conviction, and time in prison; to his decision to attend college to learn to write. This was a 2003 honor book for both the Michael L. Printz Award and the Robert F. Sibert Informational Book Award. **BBYA**

**Keywords:** Biography • Gantos, Jack • Jail • Writing

## Gottlieb, Lori.

★ *Stick Figure: A Diary of My Former Self.* New York: Simon & Schuster, 2000. ISBN 0684863588. **J** **H**

Gottlieb polished a diary dating from the 1970s to retell the story of her struggle with anorexia. In a family and society in which a girl in Beverly Hills "can never be too rich or too thin" her story shows how Gottlieb, a film executive turned medical doctor, can be a positive example in a world obsessed with physical appearance. **BBYA, QP**

**Keywords:** Anorexia • Diary • Memoir

## Irwin, Cait.

★ *Conquering the Beast Within: How I Fought Depression and Won . . . and You Can, Too.* New York: Random House/Three Rivers Press, 1998. Reprint: Times Books, 1999. ISBN 9780812932478. **J** **H**

Irwin wrote this book, complete with illustrations that depict depression as a scary storybook wolf, to show that depression is a serious, threatening, but ultimately curable illness. Her own battle with depression started at the age of thirteen; and the book speaks directly to teens, describing the route to recovery and its likely steps, including medication and possible hospitalization, but above all the necessity to get help. **QP**

**Keywords:** Depression • Irwin, Cait • Journal • Writing

## Mah, Adeline Yen.

★ *Chinese Cinderella: The True Story of an Unwanted Daughter.* New York: Delacorte Press, 1999. Reprint: Dell Laurel-Leaf, 2001. ISBN 9780440228653. **M** **J** **H**

Wu Mei (Fifth Younger Sister) was told that because her mother died giving birth to her, she was unlucky. Her father's subsequent remarriage left her with a horrid stepmother determined to provide the best for the marriage's new children and a life for Wu Mei that is taken right out of Grimm, including separation from the few family members who cared for her, as well as ongoing emotional and physical abuse. This real-life Cinderella's academic success and determination to please her father during the confusing times of the Communist revolution in China make for a gripping and engrossing story. **BBYA**

**Keywords:** China • Chinese Americans • Chinese social life and customs • Mah, Adeline Yen

## Musgrave, Susan.

🎗 *Nerves Out Loud: Critical Moments in the Lives of Seven Teen Girls.* Toronto: Annick Press, 2001. ISBN 9781550376937. **J** **H**

The pivotal moment for one of the seven girls occurred when she was abused in a foster home by her foster father. A second maintained a façade of health for six years while suffering with anorexia before seeking help; and a third fell in love with her female best friend. These events changed these girls' lives forever and helped them to become the women that they are today. Seven authors contribute deeply personal and honest essays about their lives and some of the painful moments they have dealt with. **Norma Fleck**

Keywords: Abuse • Bulimia • Life-changing events • Rape • Teenage girls • Women authors

## Runyon, Brent.

🎗 *The Burn Journals.* New York: Alfred A. Knopf, 2004. ISBN 0375826211. H.

At the age of fourteen, eighth grader Brent Runyon poured gasoline on himself and set himself alight. The burns covered 85 percent of his body and required six months of treatment, both mental and physical. The trauma he endured during his recovery was so traumatic that it is often difficult to comprehend that this is nonfiction, making for an engrossing, if at times difficult, read. **IRA, PP**

Keywords: Attempted suicide • Burns • Family relationships • Memoir • Runyon, Brent

## Sebold, Alice.

🎗 *Lucky.* Boston: Back Bay Books, 1999. Reprinted 2002 . ISBN 9780316096195. **H**

Being raped at age eighteen was enough pain for any lifetime; yet Sebold's hardships did not end there. Sebold endured a trial and fallout that followed her for years. **PP**

Keywords: Law • Rape • Sebold, Alice • Trial

## Shivack, Nadia.

*Inside Out: Portrait of an Eating Disorder.* New York: Atheneum Books for Young Readers, 2007. ISBN 9780689852169. **J** **H**

Shivack grew up in a family that required her to finish everything on her plate, while being the daughter of a Holocaust survivor who ate one meal a day. Shivack's "E.D." (eating disorder) became her companion, her monster, and her lifelong battle after the age of fourteen. Her struggle is accompanied by the drawings and paintings that illustrate her struggles, and the ongoing battles faced by the millions who, the reader is informed, deal with this difficult disorder. A list of eating disorder resources is included.

Keywords: Bulimia • Eating disorders • Shivack, Nadia

Now Try: Joan Ryan gives readers an inside look at a world in which eating disorders are a normal thing in *Little Girls in Pretty Boxes: The Making and Breaking of Elite Gymnasts and Figure Skaters.* When a smaller body can increase an athlete's jumps and leaps, bulimia and anorexia are often seen as a necessary evil.

## Stone, Miriam.

*At the End of Words: A Daughter's Memoirs.* Cambridge, MA: Candlewick Press, 2003. ISBN 9780763618544. **H**

Miriam Stone's memoir, written in powerful, beautiful poetry and short prose, describes her life and feelings during her senior year of high school and first year of college, when her mother lost her battle with cancer. Stages of grief and healing are expressed in poetry, which stands as a tribute to and expression of the author's love for her mother.

**Keywords:** Breast cancer • Cancer • Death and dying • Family relationships • Mothers and daughters • Poetry • Stone, Miriam

## Traig, Jennifer.

*Devil in the Details: Scenes from an Obsessive Girlhood.* New York: Little, Brown, 2004. ISBN 9780316158770. **H** **A**

Jennifer Traig was eventually able to find help for her obsessive-compulsive disorder. She recounts the forms it took during her teen years in this surprisingly funny memoir. She was a square peg in her mixed-faith family, which dealt with her anorexia but was unable to deal with her scrupulosity, a form of OCD she turned toward her body and her religious studies in turn.

**Keywords:** Anorexia • Obsessive-compulsive disorder (OCD) • Scrupulosity • Traig, Jennifer

## Vincent, Erin.

*Grief Girl: My True Story.* New York: Delacorte Press, 2007. ISBN 9780385903684. **J** **H**

Erin Vincent recalls the difficult and anguishing time following the car crash that took the lives of her parents at age fourteen. This is a smooth first-person presentation that could easily be mistaken for fiction. Among the other issues discussed that make for an engrossing read are the continuing problems she and her sister encountered—insufficient funds, arguments over parenting responsibilities, grasping and greedy adults, and the normal feelings associated with such a horrible loss.

**Keywords:** Bereavement • Family relationships • Grief • Vincent, Erin

## Zubli, Rita la Fontaine de Clercq.

*Disguised: A Wartime Memoir.* Cambridge, MA: Candlewick, 2007. ISBN 9781428763661. **J** **H**

Faced with becoming Japanese prisoners of war, an innocent twelve-year-old girl's family decided to protect her from the indignities older women were subjected to by pretending she was their son "Rick." Little did she know that she would end up learning Japanese and working for war camp commandants in Sumatra and Java, making her a unique witness to the devastation suffered by prisoners all over the Dutch East Indies.

**Keywords:** Children in World War II • Clercq Zubli, Rita la Fontaine de • Prisoners of war • World War II • World War II personal narratives

# Multicultural Experiences

Books written to help people understand other cultures have enjoyed an increase in popularity in the last several years. In a country where a majority of people can trace their lineage to another country, it makes sense that books containing themes about getting to know a new culture are particularly meaningful. Readers who enjoy these titles may also be interested in titles listed in Pearl Gaskins's *What Are You?: Voices of Mixed-race Young People* (see chapter 8).

### Abu-Jaber, Diana.

*The Language of Baklava: A Memoir.* New York: Pantheon Books, 2005. ISBN 9780375423048. **H** **A**

Growing up in a multiracial family can be difficult and confusing; for Diana it meant straddling New York and Jordan. Her recollections are evoked strongly and centered around the foods of her families, which helped form, preserve, and pass on both love and identities. The dishes vary widely and evoke the settings and cultures, from her American grandmother's pot roast to the goat dish she shared in a Bedouin camp. Recipes may encourage would-be chefs to share in her enjoyment.

**Keywords:** Abu-Jaber, Diana • Jordan • Middle Eastern cookery • Recipes

### Ahmedi, Farah, and Mir Tamim Ansary.

🌺 *The Story of My Life: An Afghan Girl on The Other Side of the Sky.* New York: Simon Spotlight Entertainment, 2005. ISBN 1416906703. **H**

This complicated and moving life story depicts a childhood in Afghanistan starting at the time when the mujahideen were fighting the Soviets, and goes on to describe life under the Taliban. Ahmedi, who lost her leg to a land mine and her father and brothers to the war, transmits hope and her belief in the kindness of strangers as she adapts to life in a new land with her mother. **PP**

**Keywords:** Afghanistan • Ahmedi, Farah • Emigrant • Perseverance

### Akbar, Said Hyder, and Susan Burton.

🌺 *Come Back to Afghanistan: A California Teenager's Story.* New York: Bloomsbury, 2005. ISBN 9781582345208. **H** **A**

Hyder went to Afghanistan for his summer vacation. After the fall of the Taliban, his father returned to Afghanistan and became the governor of the province of Kunar. Hyder spent three summers with him, acquiring a view of the country that offers some rather unusual and intriguing sights, including a wedding ceremony, an accusation of smuggling, and a tour of Osama bin Laden's house. This is one American teenager whose amazing summer vacations offer social and political insights into an important part of the world. **BBYA**

**Keywords:** Afghanistan • Akbar, Said Hyder • Political science • Travel

## Barakat, Ibtisam.

🎗 *Tasting the Sky: A Palestinian Childhood.* New York: Farrar, Straus & Giroux, 2007. ISBN 0374357331. **M J H BG**

This searing and powerful memoir starts with the teenage author's removal from a bus traveling to Ramallah by Israeli soldiers in 1981. Her subsequent move to a detainment center brought back memories of her life during the Six-Day War, which involved fleeing with her family to Jordan, living in a refugee camp, bombings, living alongside the Israeli army, and constant political upheavals. Against the background of the war is her wonder at being allowed to attend a United Nations school and stay with her family. A bibliography leads readers to further information. **ALA**

**Keywords:** Arab–Israeli conflict • Barakat, Ibtisam • Israel • Middle East • Palestine • Six-Day War

## Ebadi, Shirin.

*Iran Awakening: A Memoir of Revolution and Hope.* New York: Random House, 2006. ISBN 1400064708. **H A**

In the 1970s, when Islamic fundamentalists took over in Iran, Shirin Ebadi's life changed radically. Although she was stripped of her judgeship by Ayatollah Ruhollah Khomeini's theocracy in 1980, she fought back, becoming a human rights lawyer in Iranian courts. A devout Muslim, she stayed in Tehran during dangerous times, determined to speak out, facing an assassination attempt and an arrest; and ending up in prison while trying to protect her home and family. She was awarded the Nobel Peace Prize in 2003 and continues to practice law and lecture today.

**Keywords:** Ebadi, Shirin • Human rights advocates • Iran • Nobel Peace Prize winners

## Moaveni, Azadeh.

*Lipstick Jihad: A Memoir of Growing up Iranian in America and American in Iran.* New York: Public Affairs, 2005. ISBN 9781586481933 **H A**

As a teenager in California, being "Persian" seemed the politically correct way to describe oneself after the 1979 Iranian hostage crisis. Moaveni had never been able to fully acclimate herself to the United States, but when she was assigned as a journalist to Tehran, she had to come to terms once again with a country completely outside her own experience. Neither family memories nor her California home were comparable to the loud, restricted city where the Morality Police could beat people for breaking rules, and the political and social climates were only slowly changing.

**Keywords:** Iran • Journalism • Moaveni, Azadeh • Oppression • Political science • Women's studies

## Satrapi, Marjane.

🎗 *Persepolis: The Story of a Childhood.* New York: Random House/Pantheon, 2003. ISBN 0375422307. Reprinted 2004; ISBN 1415575037. **J H A**

Marjane, the daughter of radical Marxists and a descendant of the last Emperor of Iran, grew up in Iran during the time of its revolution and subsequent war with Iraq. Her description of life in Tehran in the 1970s and 1980s is by turns outrageous, funny, and sad. The use of a graphic format helps present a child's point of view, while depicting the horrors of war and living under a totalitarian regime. **Alex, BBYA**

**Keywords:** Alex • Biography • Graphic nonfiction • Iran • Totalitarianism

✿ *Persepolis 2: The Story of a Return.* New York: Pantheon, 2004. ISBN 0375422889. **H** **A**

Part two of Satrapi's autobiography recounts her life after her parents sent her to Vienna at the age of fourteen to receive an education and she escaped from the religious police. Satrapi's journey was a long one; she learned about the dangers of secular freedom, finally moving back to Iran, where she had to learn to fit into a culture that was alien to her. The artwork is deceptively simple, lending deeper meaning to the text. **BBYA**

**Keywords:** Austria • Graphic nonfiction • Satrapi, Marjane • Tehran

## Working Life Memoirs

Authors who use their work as a vehicle to present information offer a view into new worlds. Readers may gain insight on professions, cultures, and places. This genre offers the possibility to cross not only borders, but also formats, as demonstrated in the graphic novel remembrances of Guy Delisle's time in China and Korea.

### Child, Julia, and Paul Prud'homme.

*My Life in France.* New York: Alfred A. Knopf, 2006. ISBN 9781400043460. **H** **A**

Julia Child remains one of the best known chefs and promoters of French cooking in the world; it is almost impossible to picture her as someone arriving in France never having tasted the cuisine as well as a being a complete novice in the kitchen. The reader will join her as she experienced her introduction to the Cordon Bleu, recording her experiences with the enthusiasm and dedication that led her to create her revolutionary cookbook. Readers might be inspired to create some of their own masterpieces.

**Keywords:** Child, Julia • Cooking • French cooking

### Codell, Esmé Raji.

✿ *Educating Esmé: Diary of a Teacher's First Year.* Chapel Hill, NC: Algonquin Books of Chapel Hill, 1999. Reprinted 2001. ISBN 1565122798. **H** **A**

Esmé remembers her first year of teaching as one in which she was determined to give her students the education they deserved. Her unconventional approach, whether using dance lessons to teach math, or having a student show another student what teaching required, was not always appreciated by the students or her principal. Her love of teaching and determination to keep working in the cause of learning make this a book worth reading. **Alex**

**Keywords:** Codell, Esmé Raji • Teaching

**Now Try:** Erin Gruwell began her teaching career with much the same idealistic spirit that Esmé did, except that she started off with a roomful of "unteachable, at-risk" students. In Erin Gruwell's *The Freedom Writers Diary: How a Teacher and 150 Teens Used Writing to*

*Change Themselves and the World around Them,* she and her students learned from each other and took a step to making the world a better place. Unlike in Esmé's classroom, the themes here are the Holocaust, civil rights, and a stunning visit by Miep Gies.

## Delisle, Guy.

🏵 *Pyongyang: A Journey in North Korea.* Montreal: Drawn & Quarterly Publications, 2005. ISBN 1896597890. **H**

When Guy Delisle spent two months in North Korea to oversee some animators working for his French film company, he was kept under close watch by a government "guide" and not given free rein to see the real country. His journal of his visit depicts both the government's ruses and the oppression of the average citizen, in a graphic format that allows a sense of humor to come through. **BBYA**

Keywords: Graphic nonfiction • Memoir • North Korea

*Shenzhen: A Travelogue from China.* Montreal: Drawn & Quarterly Books, 2006. ISBN 1894937791. **H**

Guy Delisle was again sent to supervise animators in a communist country. This travelogue covers his three months in the city of Shenzhen in the south of China, which he compares to the West, as well as to other cities he visited while there. Readers are shown the day-to-day lives of the people he met and the loneliness and rigidity he endured as part of his day, highlighted in the graphic novel format.

Keywords: China • Graphic nonfiction • Memoir

## Greenlaw, Linda.

🏵 *The Hungry Ocean: A Sswordboat Captain's Journey.* New York: Hyperion, 1999. ISBN 0786864516 **H** **A**

Greenlaw was a woman doing a man's job—the only woman in the world to have been the captain of a swordfish boat. As one of the most successful captains in the Grand Banks fleet, she didn't take kindly to being called a fisherwoman. Here she describes a month's journey in her boat, the *Hannah Boden,* with her five-man crew. They spent a month in a 100-foot space, working twenty hours a day to catch 40,000 pounds of fish. It was a difficult, demanding job, and Greenlaw describes the hardships of managing the crew, the boat, and the weather in language that effectively conveys her experience to the reader. **Alex**

Keywords: Fishing • Grand Banks • Greenlaw, Linda

## Haney, Eric L.

*Inside Delta Force: The Story of America's Elite Counterterrorist Unit.* New York: Delacorte Press, 2002. Reprinted 2006. ISBN 1428715851; 9780385336031. **H** **A**

Retired Army Command Sergeant-Major Haney didn't have any understanding of what the army was trying to do in 1977 when he agreed to become part of its new Delta Force. The physical and psychological tests that winnowed the first 163 candidates down to a dozen finalists are grueling enough to fatigue the reader. Delta Force, dedicated to special operations warfare and counterterrorism, became the inspiration for the television program *The Unit*.

**Keywords:** Delta Force • International security • Terrorism prevention • United States Army

## Krüger, Kobie.

🌷 *The Wilderness Family: At Home with Africa's Wildlife.* New York: Ballantine Books, 2001. ISBN 0345444264. **H** **A**

Kobie Kruger's memoir recounts the seventeen years she and her family spent in the remote Mahlangeni section of South Africa's Kruger National Park, where her husband Kobis worked as a game warden. She was warned about the difficulties to expect, including disease, lack of schooling, medical attention and the plentiful and dangerous animals. However, her happiness during those years, despite the problems they encountered, shines through in this exciting story. The wonders and dangers of their home are illustrated through tales of the family's adventures (including a lion attack on Kobis) and a menagerie of animals, which included badgers, hyenas, and an orphaned lion cub the family adopted. **Alex**

**Keywords:** Kruger, Kobie • Kruger National Park • Lions • South Africa • Zoology

## Pepin, Jacques.

*The Apprentice: My Life in the Kitchen.* Boston: Houghton Mifflin, 2003. ISBN 0618444114. **H**

Pepin quit school at age thirteen to begin the long process of working his way up to becoming a chef. He succeeded, eventually working in top restaurants and as the chef to France's prime minister before leaving for America in 1959. The story of his succession of jobs in the United States, including choosing to work for Howard Deering Johnson instead of the Kennedys, is one of luck, determination, and skill. Always underlying his words is a love of family and food. The reader will even be treated to some of his favorite recipes while reading about his transformation from chef to teacher and TV personality.

**Keywords:** Chef • Cooking • Pepin, Jacques • Recipes • Television personality

## Rall, Ted.

🌷 *To Afghanistan and Back: A Graphic Travelogue.* New York: Nantier Beall Minoustchine, 2002. ISBN 1561633259. **H** **A**

In this graphic travelogue, syndicated cartoonist and columnist Ted Rall shares the details of his fascinating and dangerous fall 2001 trip to Afghanistan, along with his liberal political views. Rall, a frequent traveler to Central Asia, includes a memoir as well as several short essays that explain exactly why that small piece of landscape so far, far away is so very, very important to so many countries, and also so very, very dangerous. **BBYA**

**Keywords:** Afghanistan • Essays • Graphic nonfiction • Politics • Travelogue

## Salzman, Mark.

🎗 *True Notebooks: A Writer's Year at Juvenile Hall.* New York: Knopf, 2003. Reprint: Vintage, 2004. ISBN 0375727612. 🇯 🇭 🇦

When author Salzman suffered writer's block while writing about a delinquent, he accompanied a friend to a juvenile center for some firsthand experience with young criminals. The friend, a volunteer creative writing instructor working with serious criminals, set Salzman on a new path with his own class. Salzman's time at L.A.'s Central Juvenile Hall, where he discovered boys with remarkable talents, described in essays covering everything but their crimes, was a life-changing experience for him. Questioned repeatedly about what good could come of spending time with these kids when it wouldn't change their futures, Salzman was able to say and demonstrate that he remained a part of their lives, as they did of his. **Alex, PP**

**Keywords:** Creative writing • Juvenile delinquents • Salzman, Mark • Teaching

## Steinberg, Jacques.

🎗 *The Gatekeepers: Inside the Admissions Process of a Premier College.* New York: Penguin Putnam/Viking, 2001. ISBN 0670031356. 🇭

Steinberg, the national education correspondent for the *New York Times,* offers a behind-the-scenes look at the college admissions process. By shadowing a Wesleyan admissions officer for a year, he was able to gain detailed knowledge. At a time when increasing numbers of students are competing for college places, this is both a how-to and a consolation. **BBYA**

**Keywords:** Careers • College • Immersion journalism

## Webb, Sophie.

🎗 *My Season with Penguins: An Antarctic Journal.* Boston: Houghton Mifflin, 2000. Reprint: Sandpiper, 2004. ISBN 1415532907. 🇲

Ornithologist Sophie Webb recounts her two-month stay in 1996 on Cape Royds Island off the coast of Antarctica studying a colony of Adélie penguins. The reader will find a full account of her trip, from her initial survival school training to the rigors of polar life and the varying scientific methods used, including induced vomiting and banding 400 chicks in a day. Beautiful watercolor illustrations, painted by Webb, highlight an interesting and difficult journey and allow readers to experience her fascination with this interesting bird. This title was an honor book for the 2001 Robert F. Sibert Informational Book Medal. **Sibert Honor**

**Keywords:** Adélie penguins • Antarctica • Ornithology • Penguins • Polar regions

**Now Try:** Readers may find books about both penguins and the Antarctic in chapter 6. Elaine Scott's *Poles Apart: Why Penguins and Polar Bears Will Never Be Neighbors* discusses the two regions; Evelyn Daigle's *The World of Penguins* contains a plethora of information about an astonishing variety of penguins.

## Humorous Memoirs

Memoirs are occasionally simply stories to be enjoyed. Some authors are able to reminisce in such a way that their stories make one smile while reading, whether or e lessons are imparted.

### Almond, Steve.

🏆 *Candyfreak: A Journey Through the Chocolate Underbelly of America.* Chapel Hill, NC: Algonquin Books of Chapel Hill, 2004. Reprint: Harcourt, 2005. ISBN 9780156032933. **H** **A**

What does it take to be a true candyfreak? According to Almond, whose name justifies his complex, one must have a complete, utter dependence on candy, proven by the daily ingestion of chocolate and the maintenance of copious stores just in case. His devotion to the candy cause leads him not only to explain what the "mistakes" in the candy world were, but also to take readers with him on a delicious journey to find the makers of the best candy bars and chocolates, bemoaning the loss of some artists and celebrating the quality he found. **Alex**

Keywords: Candy • Candy industry • Chocolate

### Crutcher, Chris.

🏆 *King of the Mild Frontier: An Ill-Advised Autobiography.* New York: Greenwillow Press, 2003. ISBN 0060502495; 0060502517pb. **J** **H**

Margaret Edwards Award-winning author Chris Crutcher presents a funny, bittersweet, and brutally honest journey, from a boyhood misspent in remote Cascade, Idaho, to his present life as a writer. Readers will find the same impeccable comedic timing that characterizes his young adult novels. Among the many laugh-out-loud episodes he recalls are his older brother's knack for always gaining the upper hand and many misadventures in small-town sports, including his days as a terrified, 123-pound freshman "with all the muscle definition of a chalk outline." **BBYA**

Keywords: Crutcher, Chris • Humor • Writing

### Paulsen, Gary

*Caught by the Sea: My Life on Boats.* New York: Delacorte Press, 2001. ISBN 0385900252. **M** **J**

A lifelong love of water is shared through some of the noted author's adventures at sea with his boats. Included are stories that demonstrate dangers that may be encountered by either a novice or an experienced sailor, as well as meetings with sharks and lovely lagoons.

Keywords: Boats • Paulsen, Gary • Sailing

Now Try: Paulsen has been incorporating events from his own life into his survival stories for many years. His best-selling and award-winning series about Brian Robeson was inspired by events that actually occurred. Readers will learn about these in *Guts: The True Stories Behind Hatchet and the Brian Books*, a gripping tale that describes real-life hunting, fishing, and weather adventures. It is evident that the outdoors is a major part of Paulsen's life. Another example of how it was an important part of his growing up, chosen for the

1995 Quick Picks for Reluctant Readers, is Paulsen's *Father Water, Mother Woods: Essays on Fishing and Hunting in the North Woods.*

🎗 *How Angel Peterson Got His Name: And Other Outrageous Tales about Extreme Sports.* New York: Random House Children's Books/Wendy Lamb Books, 2003. ISBN 0385729499. Reissued by Yearling, 2004; ISBN 0440229359. **M J BB RR**

Paulsen's collection of autobiographical anecdotes celebrates that innate impulse to try *really stupid stunts*, just to see what happens. What sort of ideas can a group of young teens in a small Minnesota town come up with for fun? Speed is usually a required element; safety is definitely not required. **BBYA**

**Keywords:** Humor • Paulsen, Gary

## Sedaris, David.

*Dress Your Family in Corduroy and Denim.* New York: Little, Brown, 2004. Reprint: Back Bay Books, 2004. ISBN 031601790. **H A**

Sedaris's collection of essays covers assorted topics from family life in this smooth and quick read. The situations brought vividly to life manage to balance humor, pain, and compassion, such as when his neighbors go trick-or-treating on November first.

**Keywords:** Essays • Family relationships • Humor • Pop culture

# Consider Starting with . . .

Barakat, Ibtisam. *Tasting the Sky: A Palestinian Childhood.*

Codell, Esmé Raji. *Educating Esmé: Diary of a Teacher's First Year.*

Gantos, Jack. *Hole in My Life.*

Haney, Eric L. *Inside Delta Force: The Story of America's Elite Counterterrorist Unit.*

Mah, Adeline Yen. *Chinese Cinderella: The True story of an Unwanted Daughter.*

Myers, Walter Dean. *Bad Boy: A Memoir.*

Satrapi, Marjane. *Persepolis: The Story of a Childhood.*

Sedaris, David. *Dress Your Family in Corduroy and Denim.*

Zenatti, Valerie. *When I Was a Soldier: A Memoir.*

# Fiction Read-Alikes

- **Alexie, Sherman**. Alexie has many things in common with his protagonist Junior, in *The Absolutely True Diary of a Part-Time Indian.* Junior knows how much trouble he will face in both places when he transfers from the school on his Spokane reservation to a better academic one in a white town twenty-two miles away, but he is going to do it anyway to secure a better future.

- **Chambers, Aidan**. Readers who enjoy a lyrical, rich examination of a life have an opportunity to transfer that experience to prose with Chamber's *This Is All: The Pillow Book of Cordelia Kenn*. Nineteen-year-old Cordelia writes the unfiltered, complete story of her life for the daughter she is expecting, intending to give the book as a present to her child on her sixteenth birthday.

- **Paulsen, Gary**. In *The Beet Fields*, Paulsen used the events from his sixteenth summer to create a gritty, realistic coming-of-age novel. During one summer after running away, he finds work in beet fields before working with a traveling carnival and having his first sexual encounter. *The Beet Fields* was chosen as a top ten Best Book for Young Adults in 2001.

- **Thomas, Rob.** In *Rats Saw God*, readers will find a believable teenager telling his life story to fulfill a high school requirement. The realities of Steve York's life in this funny, frank novel include his first experience with sex and his past and present relationship with his astronaut father.

# Chapter 4

## Biography

## Definition

A biography is the history of an individual's life. The term comes from the Greek *bios* (meaning life) and *graph* (meaning writing), and its first English usage was in Dryden's *Life of Plutarch* in 1663. People's lives are recorded in biographies, and this is one of the largest and oldest genres. Historians and biographers make use of primary and secondary sources when compiling a life story, making sure that the events recorded are factual, verifiable, and as complete as possible. Unlike memoirs, biographies and autobiographies share someone's whole life, rather than part of it.

## Appeal

Humans are fascinated with other human beings. There is an inherent appeal in looking at how other people live. Biographies are the clearest window into another time, place, and perspective. Readers who do not enjoy any other type of nonfiction are often drawn to biographies because of an interest in the person or the subject. An interest in music may lead someone to open *The Book of Rock Stars* or *Tupac Shakur*; the apparent impossibility of the accident may tempt a reader to delve into *Phineas Gage: A Gruesome But True Story about Brain Science.*

Today's young adult reader of nonfiction will find many options in biography. As Marc Aronson so compellingly remarks, "[E]very biography should have a freshness, a creativity, an interesting tension that makes it different from every other one" (2003, 69–72). Authors may start at any point in a person's life, or indeed look at a moment in time and present all of the other people involved in it, as in Catherine Thimmesh's remarkable *Team Moon: How 400,000 People Landed* Apollo 11 *on the Moon*, which presents the remarkable achievements of the veritable army working behind the scenes. Biographies are also readily available in diverse formats. Russell Freedman's 1988 *Lincoln: A Photobiography* was the first nonfiction title to be granted the Newbery Award in thirty years. Freedman used so many illustrations that the term "photobiography" was coined to call attention to their use; it has been a popular format ever since. Reluctant readers will be very happy with graphic nonfiction, photobiographies, and picture book biographies. Readers will also find alternatives listed under "Sports Biographies" in chapter 7. Another recent trend involves writing in verse format. Biographies written in verse are listed in the "Poetry" section of chapter 10.

Biographies are a popular source of information. They contain accurate content, usually with supplementary material such as source notes, Web sites, photographs, and an index. This makes them good resources for schoolwork as well. Readers are often surprised at the quality of the narrative.

## Chapter Organization

The first section covers some of the most influential people in our history: "American Presidents and Other Political Leaders." The following sections group the biographies into subject categories for which the biographees are best remembered. Science biographies and professional biographies are the life stories of people associated with science and various careers. Change-makers and activists are remembered for a lifetime of trying to make a difference socially and politically. The historical biographies provide unique pictures of individuals and the times in which they lived.

The section on partner and group biographies includes stories told by or about more than one individual, such as Shannon Lanier's and Jane Feldman's *Jefferson's Children: The Story of One American Family*. There is no doubt that there is an innate fascination with famous people, as reflected in the next category, which is concerned with people in the public eye, including entertainers and writers.: The final section, "Biography Collections," covers titles that tell the stories of a number of people.

## American Presidents and Other Political Leaders

Readers are fascinated by the lives of the people who run their country. Teachers like students to know about decisions that shape our lives and our history. These interests make a good match with authors who focus on national or world leaders. This subgenre provides not only the details of the time and someone's part in it, but also a sense of how people in power got there and how they affected the countries they led. Readers may also look under "Biography Collections" for titles about more than one person in this category and in the "Change-Makers and Social Activists" section for more political heavyweights.

### Bober, Natalie.

*Thomas Jefferson: Draftsman of a Nation.* Charlottesville: University of Virginia Press, 2007. ISBN 9780813926322. **H** **A**

The author of the Declaration of Independence was a man of many contradictions, including his owning of slaves and his "shadow family" with Sally Hemings. It isn't often that a historian has a chance to revisit one of his or her works. Bober has done just that in this book, offering a well-rounded look at the education, opinions, and life of the third president of the United States that incorporates research done with the heirs to the Jefferson and Hemings families.

**Keywords:** Jefferson, Thomas • Monticello (VA) • Plantation life • Presidents • Slavery

## Marrin, Albert.

🌳 *George Washington & the Founding of a Nation.* New York: Dutton Children's Books, 2001. ISBN 9780525464815. **H**

Biographies about George Washington often deal with his youthful eagerness, talents as a general, and leadership abilities, and occasionally add in the colonies' fight for independence; but rarely do they look at his feelings about slavery. This is a rare book that covers all of these topics. Marrin also alerts readers to what is actually known and what we will always wonder about the first president. **BBYA**

**Keywords:** U.S. generals • U.S. presidents • Washington, George

## Shecter, Vicky Alvear.

*Alexander the Great Rocks the World.* **Illustrated by Terry Naughton.** Plain City, OH: Darby Creek Publishing, 2006. ISBN 9781581960457. **M**

Shecter presents this biography of Alexander the Great with an irreverent tone and cartoon drawings to match. The youthful language is appropriate to discuss someone who became a conqueror long before he was thirty. Alexander's story is told chronologically, with a number of supplemental facts that are sure to attract interest, including information about the Greeks, Alexander's incredibly vindictive family, and ancient warfare. The information is all the more compelling because of headings, such as "How Bad a Whooping Do You Need?" and "Olympias, the Queen of Mean"; yet the book still presents a thorough and balanced picture of Alexander and of Greece at the time. Source notes and a bibliography are included.

**Keywords:** Alexander the Great • Greek generals • Kings and rulers of Greece

**Now Try:** Alexander's triumphs in war were the stuff of legend, and they certainly merit a more complete examination. The events of his thirty-three years are explored in Alison Behnke's *The Conquests of Alexander the Great*, part of the Pivotal Moments in History series.

## St. George, Judith.

🌳 *In the Line of Fire: Presidents' Lives at Stake.* New York: Holiday House, 1999. ISBN 9780823414284. **M** **J**

The presidency of the United States is one of the most powerful, as well as the most dangerous, jobs on the planet. A chapter is presented about each of the four presidential assassinations: Lincoln, Garfield, McKinley, and Kennedy. Covered are the life and times of each president, his accomplishments, the attack, and its outcome, including the transfer of power and the political changes that resulted. Seven unsuccessful attempts are also examined and lead into an explanation of the increasing security around the presidents and today's Secret Service. **BBYA**

**Keywords:** Assassination attempts • Presidents • Presidents—Assassinations • Secret Service

## Winget, Mary.

*Gerald R. Ford.* Presidential Leaders. Minneapolis, MN: Twenty-First Century Books, 2007. ISBN 9780822515098. **M J**

The thirty-eighth president of the United States occupies a unique position in history: He was the first person to hold the office who had not been officially elected. In fact, Gerald Ford's goal was never to be president at all, but to be speaker of the House. Among the difficulties he faced were the fallout from the Watergate scandal and the economic troubles of the Vietnam War, as well as two assassination attempts.

**Keywords:** Ford, Gerald R. • Presidents • Vice presidents

# Problem Solvers and Experimenters: Science Biography

This subgenre focuses on people whose lives were memorable because of one thing—a scientific discovery or breakthrough. In at least one case the subject may not have set out to make a discovery, but in all cases the people included in this section are notable because they furthered knowledge about a scientific area and ultimately changed our lives.

## Delano, Marfé Ferguson.

🎋 *Genius: A Photobiography of Albert Einstein.* Washington, DC: National Geographic, 2005. ISBN 9780792295440. **M J**

Not only did Albert Einstein win the Nobel Prize for Physics, he was named "Person of the Century" by *Time Magazine* more than forty years after his death. This quick biography provides a well-rounded picture of Einstein, following his life and causes, with numerous photographs and quotes enhancing the text. A chronology and list of resources are also included in this accessible volume. **OP Honor**

**Keywords:** Einstein, Albert • Nobel Prize • Physicists

**Now Try:** Another solid effort, which combines photographs with reproductions of lab sketches and letters, is Delano's *Inventing the Future: A Photobiography of Thomas Alva Edison.* Edison's many inventions are shown and explained in a resource that will help readers understand his contributions and influence on the scientists and technologies that followed.

## Fleischman, John.

🎋 *Phineas Gage: A Gruesome But True Story about Brain Science.* Boston: Houghton Mifflin, 2002. Reprinted 2004. ISBN 0618052526. **J H**

In 1848 a tamping iron accidentally blasted through the head of Phineas Gage, a foreman on a railroad construction gang. He recovered physically, but the mental and emotional changes he exhibited set science and medicine on a new course. Even today, his case continues to provide new insights into the workings of the human brain, all of which are clearly discussed in this book. Photographs and other media are used to illustrate this fascinating case in the history and development of neurosciences. **BBYA, JM Honor**

**Keywords:** Brain damage • Medicine • Neurology

## Fleming, Candace.

🏵 *Ben Franklin's Almanac: Being a True Account of the Good Gentleman's Life.* New York: Atheneum Books for Young Readers, 2003. ISBN 0689835493. **M J**

The life of the printer, writer, scientist, statesman, and inventor, and the only Founding Father who signed all four of the documents that are the basis of the United States today, is presented in this unique biography. In a facsimile of Franklin's own *Poor Richard's Almanack,* information is given about his childhood, family, scientific accomplishments, community achievements, and political contributions. Here is the man who invented and organized not only his famous electrical experiments but also modern garbage collection as we know it, the fire department, the library . . . . **BBYA**

**Keywords:** Franklin, Benjamin • Political biography • Science and technology

**Now Try:** David Adler's *B. Franklin, Printer* presents the different aspects of Franklin's life as a statesman, printer, politician, inventor, writer, and scientist. Student researchers will find many different information tools, including chronologies, maps, period illustrations, facsimiles of documents, quotations, and excerpts from Franklin's *Pennsylvania Gazette,* as well as a list of suggested books and Web sites for further research.

## Krull, Kathleen.

*Isaac Newton.* **Illustrated by Boris Kulikov.** Giants of Science. New York: Viking, 2006. ISBN 9780670059218. **M J**

Einstein considered Newton to be a genius. He invented calculus, developed the modern scientific method, postulated the Laws of Motion, and made landmark discoveries in light and optics, yet he was secretive and prone to feuding with other scientists. This balanced portrayal of a fascinating figure explains both the man and his discoveries.

**Keywords:** Newton, Isaac • Physicists • Scientists

## Levine, Ellen.

*Rachel Carson: Environmentalist.* Up Close. New York: Viking, 2007. ISBN 0670062200. **J H**

Rachel Carson changed the way people looked at the environment. She was lauded and laughed at, usually depending on whether her critics worked for chemical companies. *Time Magazine* named her one of the hundred most influential people of the twentieth century. Ellen Levine recounts how a woman's love of science and the outdoors led her to fight for an education and make the discovery that eventually changed scientific practices in regard to pesticides. The books that Rachel Carson wrote affected science across the world, not only regarding pesticide use but also arguably opening the door for women in scientific research.

**Keywords:** Carson, Rachel • DDT • Environmentalists • Pesticides • Science

## Marrin, Albert.

*Dr. Jenner and the Speckled Monster: The Search for the Smallpox Vaccine.* New York: Dutton Children's Books, 2002. ISBN 9780525469223. **M** **J**

Smallpox has had a phenomenal impact on world history, not only decimating the Aztec empire, but also infecting other North American Indian tribes. Its importance as a disease that crossed to humans from animals is mirrored by Dr. Edward Jenner's discovery of milkmaids' immunity to it if they had already been infected by cowpox. This discovery led him to experiment with and develop a vaccine. Many period photographs and illustrations are included. Although the vaccine eliminated smallpox in many parts of the world, a warning against the possible rise of smallpox today concludes the book.

**Keywords:** Diseases • Jenner, Edward • Smallpox • Smallpox vaccine

## McClafferty, Carla Killough.

🌸 *Something Out of Nothing: Marie Curie and Radium.* New York: Farrar, Straus & Giroux, 2006. ISBN 0374380368. **M** **J**

Anyone who says that girls don't have the same aptitude for science as boys has never heard of Marie Curie. Her determination to complete her education and her discoveries of both radium and polonium, which led to her becoming the first woman to win the Nobel Prize, are phenomenal accomplishments. This is a well-balanced biography, giving a picture of Curie's life with her family and her husband and showing some of her other work. Readers will be very impressed with her humanitarian contributions in World War I. Photographs and reproductions of Curie's own documents supplement the text. **BBYA, OP Honor**

**Keywords:** Curie, Marie • Nobel Prize • Radiation • Radium

**Now Try:** Marie Curie is a very popular role model and the subject of numerous biographies. Barbara Goldsmith's *Obsessive Genius: The Inner World of Marie Curie* concentrates on her scientific accomplishments and presents a particularly interesting view of the Nobel laureate, because it allows readers to consider the gender bias she overcame.

## Sis, Peter.

🌸 *The Tree of Life: A Book Depicting the Life of Charles Darwin, Naturalist, Geologist & Thinker.* New York: Farrar, Straus & Giroux/Frances Foster, 2003. ISBN 0374456283. **M**

This is an introduction to Charles Darwin, the nineteenth-century scientist who sailed around the world and wrote a book that changed it, with material from Darwin's diaries and detailed illustrations by the author. Incorporating details of Darwin's life, journeys, and achievements into visuals that draw readers into the story, this is a great book for the nonlinear thinker to pore over. **BBYA**

**Keywords:** Biography • Natural selection • Science

# Outstanding in Their Fields: Professional Biographies

This section includes biographies of people (other than presidents, scientists, and social activists) who are thought of in conjunction with their chosen professions. In either single or group biographies, the subjects of these books are leaders, exemplars, and innovators in their fields. The books usually offer information pertinent to the subjects' work that will give interested teens a glimpse of possibilities for their own futures.

## Collins, Mary.

*Airborne: A Photobiography of Wilbur and Orville Wright.* Washington, DC: National Geographic Society, 2003. ISBN 9780792269571. **M J**

The reader will follow the Wright brothers as they conceive, develop, test, and undertake the first successful powered flight at Kitty Hawk, North Carolina. Clear and compelling narrative expresses the different personalities of the two brothers. Diagrams and illustrations help to explain aeronautics and the challenges the brothers managed to overcome. In addition to the many photographs, there are a chronology and a list of further resources.

**Keywords:** Aeronautics • Wright, Orville • Wright, Wilbur

## Johnson, Dolores.

*Onward: A Photobiography of African-American Polar Explorer Matthew Henson.* Washington, DC: National Geographic, 2006. ISBN 079227914X. **M J**

Although Robert E. Peary's ninth expedition was the first to reach the North Pole in 1909, his "manservant," Matthew Henson, was actually the first man there. Because Henson was African American, he did not, receive recognition until 2001 for his remarkable achievements, which are retold here. Readers can relive the dangers, repeated failures, and Henson's role in assuring the team's final success, including his positive relationship with the Inuit, ongoing equipment maintenance, and unflagging loyalty. The comparison of his achievements to his reception outside the Arctic is shocking and makes his posthumous award and quotes from his family members all the more affecting.

**Keywords:** Explorer • Henson, Matthew • North Pole

**Now Try:** Katherine Kirkpatrick tells the story of Robert Peary's daughter, who was born in 1893 in Greenland and spent much of her childhood traveling with her father, in *The Snow Baby: The Arctic Childhood of Admiral Robert E. Peary's Daring Daughter.* Marie Ahnighito Peary's unusual childhood, exploring in the Arctic circle, presents a very young perspective on the discovery of the North Pole. The book does not omit Marie's half-Inuit step-siblings or Matthew Henson.

## Partridge, Elizabeth.

*Restless Spirit: The Life and Work of Dorothea Lange.* New York: Viking, 1998. Reprint: Puffin, 2001. ISBN 0142300241. **M J H**

Elizabeth Partridge has a personal connection with this photobiography of the world-famous photographer: Her father was one of Dorothea Lange's assistants in the 1930s. In fact, she herself had a personal acquaintance with Lange and knew the photographer's exacting standards. Lange was the country's primary conduit to the plight of the migrant sharecroppers in the 1930s and the Japanese Americans interned in World War II. Partridge presents an even-handed biography, rich in both Lange's work and her words, giving readers the story of this remarkable woman and the times in which she lived. **BBYA, PP**

**Keywords:** Great Depression • Japanese internment • Lange, Dorothea • Photographer • Photographs

**Now Try:** This is not the only book that provides a close-up picture of the world through the work of someone who devoted her life to using a lens. In *Witness to Our Times: My Life as a Photojournalist,* Flip Schulke shares the story of his life and career, covering friendships with the Kennedy family and Martin Luther King Jr., as well as pioneering underwater photography and photos of Elvis Presley, Fidel Castro, and Muhammad Ali. Photography is a career in which determined and dedicated women have excelled and been recognized. Readers looking for inspiration as well as a fascinating story will find an excellent example in photojournalist Margaret Bourke-White. Susan Goldman-Rubin's *Margaret Bourke-White: Her Pictures Were Her Life* is illustrated with samples of Bourke-White's works. This title was chosen for the 2000 BBYA list.

# Change-Makers and Activists

The people featured in these books are worthy of respect. It is not only the end result of their battles, but the endurance they showed in pursuing causes in which they believed, that makes them memorable. Of course this makes for engrossing reading, giving food for thought far beyond the turn of the last page and demonstrating the difference between right and wrong.

## Aronson, Marc.

*Robert F. Kennedy: Crusader.* Up Close. New York: Viking, 2007. ISBN 0670060666.
**M J H**

This biography does not focus only on Robert F. Kennedy as a man—it examines his position as the "runt" in the Kennedy family, covering the major events in his life to evaluate his actions and determine why and how he became so important to America. Historical events in which he took part, including John F. Kennedy's political career, the civil rights movement, the Vietnam War, and the Cuban Missile Crisis are given context and meaning. Quotes are attributed to their sources, and a list of further reading is included.

**Keywords:** Assassination • Kennedy, Robert F. • Politicians • Politics

**Now Try:** Arthur Schlesinger Jr. won the National Book Award for his scholarly look at the forces that shaped RFK, *Robert F. Kennedy and His Times.* Although it is considerably longer than Marc Aronson's book, both books were written by historians and give a sense of time, place, and the reasons for Robert Kennedy's importance. As a friend of Kennedy's, Schlesinger was also given access to private letters and papers.

## Bausum, Ann.

*Freedom Riders: John Lewis and Jim Zwerg on the Front lines of the Civil Rights Movement.* Washington, DC: National Geographic, c2006. ISBN 0792241738. **M J**

The May 1961 freedom rides are described through a presentation of two strikingly disparate individuals: Jim Zwerg, a white, middle-class student from Wisconsin, and John Lewis, a black student and seminarian who later became a congressman in Georgia. They met in Nashville, where students were protesting segregation, and joined the freedom bus rides. They were both beaten badly, Swerg more so for being seen as a "nigger lover." Ironically, the violence actually acted to enhance the success of the rides. Both riders have contributed forewords to the volume. This was an honor book for the 2007 Robert F. Sibert Informational Book Medal. **BBYA**, **Sibert Honor**

Keywords: Bus integration • Civil rights workers • Freedom rides • Lewis, John • Zwerg, Jim

## Bolden, Tonya.

🏵 *M.L.K.: Journey of a King.* New York: Harry N. Abrams, 2007. ISBN 9780810954762. **M** **J** **H**

This biography of the Nobel Peace Prize winner starts off with a personal touch, introducing him by a nickname given to him by his father, "M.L." Each page is amply illustrated, with well-captioned photographs. Bolden concentrates on the details and events that help readers understand "the dream." King's gift for oratory is explained, as are his difficulties when his own view of nonviolence conflicted with current events. A time line and source notes help interested researchers gather more information. **OP**

Keywords: Civil rights workers • King, Martin Luther, Jr. • Nobel Peace Prize winners

## Fleming, Candace.

🏵 *Our Eleanor: A Scrapbook Look at Eleanor Roosevelt's Remarkable Llife.* New York: Atheneum Books for Young Readers, 2005. ISBN 0689865449. **M** **J**

What makes Eleanor Roosevelt stand out in history? In a time when women did not have much power or education, she did everything she could to change that. Helping her husband's presidential campaign and standing beside him, instead of behind him, was just the start for this truly remarkable and fascinating woman. The children, women, and underprivileged people she represented owe this first-rate crusader a lot. Readers can learn about her through anecdotes supplemented by photographs and copious information about her times, for a well-rounded sense of a complicated woman living through a difficult era. **BBYA**

Keywords: Presidents' spouses • Roosevelt, Eleanor

## Fradin, Dennis Brindell, and Judith Bloom Fradin.

🏵 *Fight On! Mary Church Terrell's Battle for Integration.* New York: Clarion Books, 2003. ISBN 0618133496. **M** **J**

This is a carefully researched tale of a girl born to former slaves in 1865, who went on to become an early civil rights leader, with a career spanning sixty years. Mary Eliza Church, or "Mollie," who graduated from Oberlin College in 1884, was "the first black woman appointed to the Washington, D.C., Board of Education" as well as a cofounder of the NAACP. In her late eighties she conducted a successful campaign to integrate D.C. restaurants and movie theaters. This title was chosen for both the 2004 Teachers' Choices list of the International Reading Association and the Best Books for Young Adults list. **BBYA, IRA**

Keywords: Biography • Civil rights • Integration • Terrell, Mary Church

## Fradin, Judith Bloom, and Dennis Brindell Fradin.

🐾 *Jane Addams: Champion of Democracy.* New York: Clarion Books, 2006. ISBN 0618504362. **M** **J** **H**

Jane Addams was one of America's most prominent women in the twentieth century, lauded for her charitable works and despised for her unwavering stance against war. The narrative demonstrates her resolve with an anecdote detailing her post as Chicago's first female garbage collector, a job taken to help the denizens of Hull House, the settlement house she founded in 1889. Her work at Hull House actually decreased the death rate in Chicago's 19th Ward. The reader will find a surprising woman in this cofounder of the NAACP, determined pacifist, and winner of the Nobel Peace Prize. **ALA**

**Keywords:** Addams, Jane • Nobel Peace Prize winners

*The Power of One: Daisy Bates and the Little Rock Nine.* New York: Clarion, 2004. ISBN 061831556X; 9780618315567. **J**

This biography combines the Fradins' careful research with numerous period photographs, providing powerful proof of the difference one determined person can make. Daisy Bates's early history with segregation is explored, but it was the integration of nine African American students into Little Rock's Central High School in 1957 that brought her into prominence, bringing her death threats while she worked to help the teens stand together.

**Keywords:** Civil rights workers • Little Rock (AR) • Racism • School Integration

## Freedman, Russell.

🐾 *The Voice That Challenged a Nation: Marian Anderson and the Struggle for Equal Rights.* New York: Clarion Books, 2004. ISBN 0618159762; 9780618159765. **M** **J** **H** **BG**

Marian Anderson's contralto voice was applauded by European royalty, championed by Eleanor Roosevelt, and described by Arturo Toscanini as a voice "heard once in a hundred years." Without intending to, she became a symbol of the different treatment accorded to performers in America because of their color, epitomized by the 75,000 people who attended the outdoor concert she gave after being denied permission to perform at Constitution Hall in 1939. Freedman shows that this was by no means the end of her journey or her influence. This title was awarded the 2005 Robert F. Sibert Informational Book Medal and chosen for the 2005 Teachers' Choices list of the International Reading Association. **BBYA, IRA, OP Honor, Sibert**

**Keywords:** Anderson, Marian • Civil rights • Musicians • Singers

## Lawlor, Laurie.

🐾 *Helen Keller: Rebellious Spirit.* New York: Holiday House, 2001. ISBN 9780823415885. **M** **J**

Helen Keller is known as the deaf and blind child who learned how to communicate with the help of her teacher, Annie Sullivan. This biography gives readers a chance to find out much more about this extraordinary woman and her mercurial relationship with her lifelong companion. Her achievements in education, activism, lecturing, and writing are just some of the things that she accomplished against impossible odds in circumstances that would have made them impossible for almost any woman. **BBYA**

Keywords: Blind • Deaf • Keller, Helen • People with disabilities

## Winick, Judd.

🐾 *Pedro and Me: Friendship, Loss, and What I Learned.* New York: Henry Holt, 2000. ISBN 0805064036. **J** **H** **RR**

Winick introduces readers to Pedro Zamora, his roommate during MTV's *Real World San Francisco* series. The would-be cartoonist, who presents this biography in graphic novel format, introduces readers to sensitive topics carefully and thoroughly. Zamora, a gay man diagnosed at an early age with the AIDS virus, responded by becoming an HIV educator to various audiences, including schools. The friendship between these roommates can enlighten and inform, continuing Zamora's work. The many recognitions this title received include being named an honor book for the 2001 Robert F. Sibert Informational Book Medal, as well as being chosen for several lists by YALSA. **BBYA, PP, QP, Sibert Honor**

Keywords: AIDS • Biography • Diseases • Graphic nonfiction

## Woelfle, Gretchen.

*Jeannette Rankin: A Political Pioneer.* Honesdale, PA: Calkins Creek, 2006. ISBN 9781590784372. **M** **J**

Rankin remains the poster child for standing up for what she believed in, which in her case was women's rights and peace. As a result, she wasn't very popular in the U.S. Congress, where she was its first female representative, elected four years before women in the United States had the right to vote. She also voted against both the World War I and II declarations of war, the only representative to do so in 1941. She never changed her mind about the necessity to stand for peace and remained an activist for the rest of her very fascinating life.

Keywords: Feminism • Feminists • Rankin, Jeannette • U.S. Congress • Women legislators

Now Try: Readers looking for stories about pioneering women have a great example in Jeannette Rankin. They might like to try other books about women who stuck to their beliefs or blazed a trail for others. Sue Davidson writes about two political role models in *A Heart in Politics: Jeannette Rankin and Patsy T. Mink*. Readers interested in finding out about more great women who are less familiar should check the "Biography Collections" section for Elizabeth Cody Kimmel's *Ladies First: 40 Daring American Women Who Were Second to None*.

# Historical Biography

These books are about people who have become noteworthy or notorious because of their achievements and have remained a part of history. The presentation of their stories uses the setting, the history itself, as another character. It is the person, not the place and time, that is the main focus of these books. Historical biographies are found in chapter 5 as well.

## Bolden, Tonya.

🦋 *Maritcha: A Nineteenth-century American Girl.* New York: Harry N. Abrams, 2005. ISBN 9780810950450. **M** **J**

Maritcha Remond Lyons was born in 1848 to a family of free blacks in Manhattan, where she learned the importance of education and her right to it. Her remarkable story includes her family's efforts to shelter runaway slaves and her struggles to attend the local, all-white school. Educating others was an important and lifelong goal for Maritcha, as shown by her years as a vice principal. *Maritcha* was awarded the James Madison Book Award as well as being named a Coretta Scott King honor book in 2006. **BBYA, CSK Honor, JM**

**Keywords:** Lyons, Maritcha Remond • New York history • Slavery

## Brown, Chester.

*Louis Riel: A Comic-Strip Biography.* Montréal: Drawn and Quarterly, 2003. Reprinted 2006. ISBN 9781894937894. **H**

Louis Riel is the founder of the Province of Manitoba, a traitor who incited Canada's only civil war, a defender of aboriginal and Métis rights, and a madman convinced he was a prophet, who was found guilty of high treason. His role in history has been argued for over a century. Here, in graphic novel format, is a retelling of Riel's story and the Red River Rebellion that may allow readers to make up their own minds.

**Keywords:** Graphic nonfiction • Métis • Riel, Louis

## Cooper, Michael L.

*Hero of the High Seas: John Paul Jones and the American Revolution.* Washington, DC: National Geographic, 2006. ISBN 9780792255475. **J** **H**

Stories say that Captain Jones yelled, "I have not yet begun to fight!" Historians don't believe it, but no one would argue that it is both a great tale and true to his character. An ambitious sailor and dedicated fighter for the American Revolution, he is considered the father of the U.S. Marines. This is a well-rounded presentation that doesn't overlook Jones's many personal difficulties, desire for fame, and turbulent nature, while giving the reader a front seat at his shipboard adventures.

**Keywords:** American Revolution • Jones, John Paul • U.S. admirals • U.S. Navy

## Freedman, Russell. Illustrated by Frederic Clement.

*Confucius: The Golden Rule.* New York: Arthur A. Levine, 2002. ISBN 0439139570. **M**

Freedman faces two difficulties in writing about Confucius: There is a common misconception about him today, and almost no information is available about someone who died 2,500 years ago. Both challenges offer a talented historian opportunities, and this well-known writer takes full advantage of them. Readers can discover what Confucius thought about his times; read many examples of what he actually did say through quotations from the Analects; and learn about the influence he has had on politics and governments in Asia, Europe, and North America since his death.

**Keywords:** Confucianism • Confucius • Philosophers • Religion

## Giblin, James Cross.

🎗 *The Life and Death of Adolf Hitler.* New York: Clarion Books, 2002. ISBN 0395903718. **J** **H** **BG**

Rather than discussing World War II, Giblin's introduction states that his book is an examination of Hitler himself, and seeks to answer three questions: What kind of person could make the plans that he did? How could he win support for them? And why did nobody stop him until it was too late for so many? The result is a gripping and evenhanded presentation of a notorious and disturbed figure from birth to death. This book was awarded the 2003 Robert F. Sibert Informational Book Medal. **Sibert**

**Keywords:** Germany • Hitler, Adolf • National Socialism • World War II

## Murphy, Jim.

*The Real Benedict Arnold.* New York: Clarion Books, 2007. ISBN 9781428763845. **J** **H**

Benedict Arnold is recognized as one of the country's worst and most dishonorable traitors. This book examines his life, taking into consideration the few of his writings that were not destroyed to find out how close he came to actually being one of the American Revolution's great figures. Without disputing his treasonous acts, the author shows how historical revisionism may rewrite history almost as it happens, in this meticulously sourced biography and great research resource.

**Keywords:** American Revolution • Arnold, Benedict • Traitors

## Robertson, James I.

🎗 *Robert E. Lee: Virginian Soldier, American Citizen.* New York: Atheneum Books for Young Readers, 2005. ISBN 9780689857317. **J** **H**

Why is General Lee so important, almost 150 years after the Civil War? There is no doubt that he was an outstanding soldier; he turned down the command of the federal forces in order to defend his home state. This examination of the Civil War also explores some of the social questions of the time, including slavery, through the choices that Lee made. His importance is underscored by the respect that he was shown by the whole country. **BBYA**

**Keywords:** Civil War • Confederate generals • Confederate States of America • Lee, Robert E.

## Zhang, Ange.

🎗 *Red Land, Yellow River: A Story from the Cultural Revolution.* Toronto: Groundwood Books, 2004. ISBN 9780888994899. **M** **J**

In 1966 Zhang's life was turned upside down when his father's fame as a writer resulted in him being automatically branded a "counterrevolutonary" in China. After his father's arrest by the Red Guards, Chairman Mao's Youth Group, the boy was left without a home, eventually moving to the country to be re-educated as a farmer with millions of other urban youth. Ironically, it was during the period when the country's art was being systematically destroyed that Zhang discovered books and his love of art. This is an engrossing, beautifully illustrated introduction to a difficult time. This title was awarded the 2005 Bologna Ragazzi Award.

**Keywords:** China • Cultural Revolution • Zhang, Ange

## Partner and Group Biographies

Occasionally it is impossible to relate a life story without talking about that person's relationships with other people. The interactions of these subjects make for involving reading. The challenge a biographer faces when describing the accomplishments of multiple lives has resulted in creative, often award-winning books, such as Catherine Thimmesh's splendid *Team Moon: How 400,000 People Landed Apollo 11 on the Moon*.

### Bausum, Ann.

*Muckrakers: How Ida Tarbell, Upton Sinclair, and Lincoln Steffens Helped Expose Scandal, Inspire Reform, and Invent Investigative Journalism.* Washington, DC: National Geographic Society, 2007. ISBN 9781426301377. **M** **J**

Nowadays people are used to the media covering government, corporations, and people in the public eye. This book covers the first reporters to investigate and publish stories on what Theodore Roosevelt called "muck": the unseemly matters of corruption, scandal, and wrongdoing. Ida Tarbell, Upton Sinclair, and Lincoln Steffen's work in the field affected governments and largest corporations, as well as the course of journalism. **ALA Notable, OP Honor**

**Keywords:** Investigative reporting—History • Sinclair, Upton • Steffens, Lincoln • Tarbell, Ida

### Lanier, Shannon, and Jane Feldman.

**🏆** *Jefferson's Children: The Story of One American Family.* New York: Random House Children's Books, 2000. Reprinted 2002. ISBN 0375821686. **J** **H**

Lanier, a fifth great-grandson of Thomas Jefferson through Sally Hemings's son Madison, presents interviews with more than twenty-five Jefferson descendants, including their reminiscences and feelings about the family tree. Many articulate their feelings about family, heritage, and pride in their race. Also included is an explanation of the 1998 DNA study and a discussion of the Monticello Association's reluctance to acknowledge Jefferson's relationship with Hemings. **BBYA**

**Keywords:** Discrimination • Genealogy • Hemings, Sally • Race

### Thimmesh, Catherine.

**🏆** *Team Moon: How 400,000 People Landed Apollo 11 on the Moon.* Boston: Houghton Mifflin, 2006. ISBN 0618507574. **M** **J**

One of the best known moments in astronautics is Neil Armstrong's famous first walk on the moon. How the men on the Apollo 11 mission actually got to the moon is the subject of this engrossing story, starting with the press release written in case of disaster and filling in all the blanks in this incredible journey. *Team Moon* won the 2007 Robert F. Sibert Informational Book Medal. **BBYA, OP Honor, Sibert**

**Keywords:** Aeronautics • Astronautics • Space flight • Space science

# The Creative Life: Entertainers and Writers

A life devoted to one's creative passion is not an easy thing. The phrase "suffering for one's art" is familiar to most people and is demonstrated in the pages of each of these volumes. The books here are not reverential or unbiased pictures. The subjects of the biographies are examined under a clear and often unflattering light, along with all of their foibles and problems. The end result is not only a picture of a subject's life and an examination of the times in which he or she lived, but an understanding of some truly remarkable achievements. Books about artists may be found in chapter 11. Readers will also find books about the dancers Siena Siegal and Olympia Dowd in the "Coming-of-Age" section of chapter 3.

## Cooper, Ilene.

*Oprah Winfrey: Media Queen.* <u>Up Close</u>. New York: Viking, 2007. ISBN 067006162X. **J H**

Anyone familiar with Oprah Winfrey's larger-than-life persona likely knows about her television series, acting career, and magazine. But readers may be surprised by her background, which included overcoming sexual abuse and a teenage pregnancy. Cooper's recounting of Oprah's tale makes for an engrossing read: a poor child who capitalized on every opportunity, overcame mistakes to find a perfect niche, and started a thirty-year career in broadcast television, among other media. In an even-handed and well-documented biography, Cooper covers both Oprah's philanthropic pursuits and criticisms of her wealth.

**Keywords:** Actress • Philanthropists • Television • Winfrey, Oprah

## Fleischman, Sid.

🎗 *Escape!: The Story of the Great Houdini.* New York: Greenwillow Books, 2006. $18.99. ISBN 0060850949. **M J**

Fleischman, who started out as a magician himself, understands that he could not reveal any of a fellow magician's secrets, yet he still manages to bring forth an involving picture of the "monarch of manacles." Houdini was a master not only of illusion but also of reinvention. In this book he is shown from his beginnings as Ehrich Weiss in Budapest through his miraculous career, including his developing show business career. Fleischman's own connection to the Houdini family is also explained. **BBYA**

**Keywords:** Escape artists • Houdini, Harry • Magicians

**Now Try:** Readers interested in Houdini will find another view of him in Jason Lutes's and Nick Bertozzi's graphic novel *Houdini: The Handcuff King.* They include an introduction to give readers some background about Houdini, but it is through the story of his escape from the frigid waters after jumping off the Harvard Bridge that readers see the man, Bess, the crowds waiting above, and the men determined to prove him a fraud. Endnotes offer readers further insight into the pictures.

## Freedman, Russell.

*Martha Graham: A Dancer's Life.* New York: Clarion, 1998. ISBN 0395746558; 9780395746554. **J** **H**

Martha Graham defines living for one's art against all odds. She didn't start to study dance until age nineteen, was told she had the wrong body type, continually fought critics and a public who didn't understand her work, but ultimately left a legacy of 181 dances that revolutionized modern dance. The many photographs illustrate the development of her style.

**Keywords:** Choreographers • Dancers • Graham, Martha • Modern dance

## Golus, Carrie.

*Tupac Shakur.* Just the Facts Biographies. Minneapolis, MN: Lerner Publications, 2007. ISBN 9780822566090. **J** **H**

Tupac Shakur led a complicated life. He was a talented actor who is named on the list of the Recording Industry Association of America's top-selling artists, but he is equally well known for his "gangster image," prison sentence, and murder. Tupac's turbulent, influential, and eventful twenty-five years are supplemented with a glossary, bibliography, and list of further sources.

**Keywords:** Rap musicians • Shakur, Tupac

**Now Try:** Several years after his death, Tupac's mother Afeni Shakur helped to produce a movie about him to let people know the complete truth about her son. The accompanying book also bears her name and shares so many of the actor/musician's own ideas and writings that he is listed as one of the coauthors. Fans and interested readers can find out more from and about Tupac in *Tupac: Resurrection, 1971–1996.* Serious fans of rap might be interested in another Quick Pick title, Cheo Hodari Coker's *Unbelievable: The Life, Death, and Afterlife of the Notorious B.I.G.,* which presents a complete picture of another complicated and talented artist and incorporates pictures from friends and family.

## Hampton, Wilborn.

*Elvis Presley, a Twentieth Century Life.* Up Close. New York: Viking, 2007. ISBN 9780670061662. **J** **H**

Thirty years after his death, Elvis still remains the King of Rock and Roll. He came from a background of poverty, but his love of music enabled him, with the help of Sam Phillips, to take his love of gospel and singing and turn it into a new kind of music. Readers will follow his journey from the early days when only the girls in the audience knew "what the fuss was all about" to his rising career to the musical heights, his less than memorable movie career, and the personal difficulties and excesses that led to his early demise.

**Keywords:** Presley, Elvis • Rock musicians • Singers

## Lee, Bruce, and John R. Little.

🎗 *Bruce Lee: The Celebrated Life of the Golden Dragon.* Boston: Tuttle, 2000. ISBN 9781413140583. **H**

It is easy to see why Bruce Lee remains a star in the world of martial arts. This book shows that there was much more to him. Highly illustrated and with ample quotations, a complete picture of the devoted family man emerges that traces his journey from a Hong Kong childhood through his television and movie careers, to his unexpected and early death. **BBYA**

Keywords: Film stars • Lee, Bruce • Martial arts • Movie stars

## Neimark, Anne E.

*Johnny Cash: A Twentieth-century Life.* Up Close. New York: Viking, 2007. ISBN 0670062154. **J** **H**

Anne Neimark ably demonstrates both the difficulties in Johnny Cash's life as well as the genius he brought to his songwriting. The self-destructive behaviors that warred with his spiritual side and fights for justice are illustrated not only by quotes, but also with Cash's own lyrics. Readers are given a strong sense of the times in which Cash lived and may be drawn to the list of further resources.

Keywords: Cash, Johnny • Country music • Musician

## Partridge, Elizabeth.

🎗 *John Lennon: All I Want Is the Truth: A Biography.* New York: Viking, 2005. ISBN 0670059544. **H**

Readers will meet the genius behind some of the twentieth century's greatest songwriting and witness the self-destructive acts and debaucheries that formed a part of his life. Partridge's biography presents an unbiased picture of the man who was told not to waste time on a guitar hobby because he "could never make a living at it," while demonstrating how the events of the times affected his life and music, both as a Beatle and after. There are helpful supplementary materials, including numerous photographs, source notes, and a bibliography, for interested readers. This title was a Michael L. Printz honor book in 2006. **BBYA, Printz Honor**

Keywords: Composers • Lennon, John • Music

🎗 *This Land Was Made for You and Me: The Life & Songs of Woody Guthrie.* New York: Viking, 2002. ISBN 0670035351. **J** **H**

Many argue that Woody Guthrie was America's greatest folk singer. Partridge's portrait of Guthrie includes all his complexities, from his talent and drive to the difficulties in his personal life and his legacy of over 1,000 songs. Appended information includes information about Huntington's disease and the Woody Guthrie Foundation. **BBYA**

Keywords: Biography • Folk music • Guthrie, Woody

## Reich, Susanna.

🦋 *Clara Schumann: Piano Virtuoso.* New York: Clarion, 1999. Reprinted 2005. ISBN 1415603367. **M J**

> Clara Schumann's personal triumphs as a performer are only equaled by the hardships she faced and overcame in her personal life. She gave herself to her music from her first piano recital at age nine through a lifetime of concert tours in front of devoted audiences. Reich manages to convey how amazing this was in the face of a lifetime of family difficulties, from an autocratic father to her husband's mental illness and the death of several of her children. **BBYA**
>
> **Keywords:** Biography • Pianists • Schumann, Clara

# Biography Collections

Biography collections serve several purposes. By thematically linking biographies, they provide a great starting point for students looking for a research project, as well as a great way to introduce readers to important people in a particular area or to biography as a genre. Readers interested in Kathleen Krull's *Book of Rock Stars* may also want to consult the "Music" section of chapter 10. Elizabeth Cody Kimmel's book may lead readers to the "Change-Makers and Activists" section of this chapter. Readers interested in the brave experimenters covered in *Guinea Pig Scientists* will find more fascinating subjects in the "Problem Solvers and Experimenters" section of this chapter. There are far too many biographical dictionaries and collections to be adequately covered in a guide such as this one. The selection here is simply a sampling of some of the most popular and notable collections for teen readers.

## Bausum, Ann.

*Our Country's First Ladies.* Washington, DC: National Geographic Society, 2007. ISBN 9781426300066. **M J**

> Forty-four women have stood beside a president, acting without a job description or a paycheck, in a position that has consistently influenced the nation. Each biography includes a sidebar with dates, children's names, and a morsel of trivia; a full-page portrait; and a profile that sets out information about the first lady's background, marriage, and role in the administration. The roles are an interesting reflection of both the ladies and the changing times. A list of references and Web sites is included.
>
> **Keywords:** First ladies • Presidents' spouses

*Our Country's Presidents.* Washington, DC: National Geographic, 2007. ISBN 9780792293309. **M J**

> This volume tells the reader many things about the first forty-three presidents of the United States, including their family backgrounds, education, election highlights, important events that happened during their presidencies, and the significance of each leader, as well as a "fact box" listing their nicknames, birth and death dates, and other information about them. What makes this more than a simple chronological biographical presentation are the fifteen thematic essays that help explain the presidency and how it has changed over the years. These topics include the electoral college, former presidents, and presidential landmarks.

**Keywords:** Presidents • U.S. presidents

**Now Try:** Readers interested in a lighter, more irreverent look at the presidents should see Barbara Holland's *Hail to the Chiefs: Presidential Mischief, Morals, & Malarky from George W. to George W.* Picture this funny introduction to the presidents and their foibles as a high school history text reimagined by Dave Barry or Jon Stewart.

## Dendy, Leslie, and Mel Boring.

🎀 *Guinea Pig Scientists: Bold Self-experimenters in Science and Medicine.* **Illustrated by C. B. Mordan.** New York: Henry Holt, 2005. ISBN 0805073167. **M J H**

In this fascinating biography readers will learn about the scientific exploits of ten largely unknown scientists whose determination to succeed in their research was so strong that they participated in their own experiments. These experiments ranged from a doctor inserting a heart catheter into his own arm to a medical student injecting himself with a deadly disease. Not all of these scientists survived, but their contributions to their scientific fields are listed at the end of each chapter. **BBYA**

**Keywords:** Doctors • Medicine • Science • Scientists

## Hoose, Philip.

🎀 *We Were There Too!: Young People in U.S. History.* New York: Farrar, Straus & Giroux, 2001. ISBN 0374382522. **M J**

This volume includes stories about sixty-seven young people who made their mark in different areas of U.S. history, presented chronologically, from a twelve-year-old who sailed with Columbus to nine-year-old Kory Johnson, who started Children for a Safe Environment. Many supplementary documents and illustrations are included, and each story includes a "What Happened to" paragraph. **BBYA**

Children in history • Group biography • U.S. history

## Kimmel, Elizabeth Cody.

*Ladies First: 40 Daring American Women Who Were Second to None.* Washington, DC: National Geographic, 2006. ISBN 0792253949. **M J**

From politics to arts to sports, the forty women represented in this volume stepped to the front of their chosen fields and opened the door for others to follow. In three pages each, with a portrait on a fourth page, the subjects are presented in a short biography featuring important dates and a quote. The volume includes well known and historical figures such as Sacagawea and Helen Keller, but readers might not yet be familiar with Captain Kathleen McGrath, the first woman to command a U.S. Navy warship.

**Keywords:** American women • Pioneers • Women

## Krull, Kathleen.

*The Book of Rock Stars: 24 Musical Icons That Shine Through History.* **Illustrated by Stephen Alcorn.** New York: Hyperion Books for Children, c2003. ISBN 9780786819508. **M J**

> Any introduction to rock music that only contains twenty-four biographies will no doubt start a discussion about who was omitted. Nevertheless, the stars here are all recognized as being major influences on the music and musicians who came after them, a testament to their talent and place in music history. The portraits, readings, and discographies that go along with the short, witty, and often irreverent biographies make this a pleasure to read, even if the stars being introduced, as stated in the introduction, "aren't always the greatest of role models." After all, hasn't that in itself been part of rock's fascination since Elvis appeared on TV from the waist up?
>
> **Keywords:** Musicians • Rock music • Rock stars

🏵 *Lives of Extraordinary Women: Rulers, Rebels (and What the Neighbors Thought).* **Illustrated by Kathryn Hewitt.** San Diego: Harcourt, 2000. ISBN 9780152008079. **M J**

> It may be a truism that behind every man there is a good woman, but these powerhouse women show that history has had its share of strong female rulers and politicians and that they have rarely led easy lives or been appreciated. From historical figures such as Cleopatra and Elizabeth I to Burma's Nobel Peace Prize winner Aung San Suu Kyi, who remains in danger today, readers will learn a little about some of the most interesting women who have helped shape our world. A list of further readings for each of the women is included. This was chosen for the United States Teachers' Choices list for the International Reading Association in 2001. **IRA**
>
> **Keywords:** Nobel Peace Prize • Rulers • Women heads of state • Women in politics

## Meltzer, Milton.

*Ten Kings: And the Worlds They Ruled.* **Illustrated by Bethanne Andersen.** New York: Orchard Books, 2002. ISBN 1428736085. **M J**

> Meltzer describes some of the most powerful rulers in history, those men who, according to the introduction, were "the supreme ruler over a nation or a territory." Each biography looks at the life of a ruler in terms of the particular time, place, and culture in which the king's power was used. Meltzer also examines their effectiveness and the effects the kings had on their own kingdoms. Andersen's illustrations include maps, portraits, and additional pictures to add depth to the biographies, such as an image of the gardens of Versaille for Louis XIV and a Greek temple for Alexander the Great. Readers will find enough basic information for a report and smoothly integrated sidebars about problems for historical study and additional information in other subject areas.
>
> **Keywords:** Kings • Queens • Rulers • World history
>
> **Now Try:** Meltzer introduces readers to life as the second choice for ruler: Historically, women only succeeded to a throne if there was no male heir. Any queen must prove herself worthy of being in power, and Meltzer highlights some powerful women in *Ten Queens: Portraits of Women in Power.* Whether the rulers were warrior queens, living through times of crisis, or dealing with politicians and plotters, readers will see their different styles of

leadership and the ways that these women needed to adapt in ruling their realms because of their gender.

**Sills, Leslie.**

*In Real Life: Six Women Photographers.* New York: Holiday House, 2000. ISBN 9780823414987. **J H**

> What does it take to be a great photographer? Is photography an art? Analyses of the photographs, lives, and careers of six photographers will certainly go a long way to help provide readers with answers to these questions. The six women profiled here, from early pioneers Dorothea Lange and Imogen Cunningham to the more contemporary artist Cindy Sherman, have made different choices in their photography. In this illuminating volume readers will find out how to look at photography and about the mechanics of photography and the significance of each photographer's work.
>
> **Keywords:** Art • Photography • Women photographers

**Taylor, Yuval.**

*Growing Up in Slavery: Stories of Young Slaves as Told by Themselves.* Chicago: Lawrence Hill Books, 2005. ISBN 9781556525483. **J**

> What was life like under slavery? Readers can find out from African Americans who grew up in slavery and published their life stories. They do not omit the violence, cruelty, and misery that was inherent to their situations, yet the rebellions and triumphs that went along with education and a continuing desire for freedom are never overlooked. Subjects include Frederick Douglass and Harriet Jacobs.
>
> **Keywords:** Child slaves • Nonfiction collections • Slavery • Slaves' writings

# Consider Starting with . . .

These are some recommended titles that are both accessible and captivating for readers new to the genre.

> Dendy, Leslie; Mel Boring. *Guinea Pig Scientists: Bold Self-experimenters in Science and Medicine.*
>
> Fleischman, John. *Phineas Gage: A Gruesome But True Story about Brain Science.*
>
> Fleming, Candace. *Our Eleanor: A Scrapbook Look at Eleanor Roosevelt's Remarkable Life.*
>
> Freedman, Russell. *The Voice That Challenged a Nation: Marian Anderson and the Struggle for Equal Rights.*
>
> Murphy, Jim. *The Real Benedict Arnold.*
>
> Partridge, Elizabeth. *John Lennon: All I Want is the Truth: A Biography.*
>
> Shecter, Vicky Alvear and Terry Naughton. *Alexander the Great Rocks the World.*

1
2
3
4
5
6
7
8
9
10
11

Thimmesh, Catherine. *Team Moon: How 400,000 People Landed* Apollo 11 *on the Moon.*

Winick, Judd. *Pedro and Me: Friendship, Loss, and What I Learned.*

## Fiction Read-Alikes

- **Jansen, Hanna.** In the novel *Over a Thousand Hills I Walk with You,* Jansen adapted the true story of her adoptive daughter Jeanne, who was the only member of her family to survive the 1994 Rwandan massacre. Translated from German by Elizabeth Crawford, this is an emotional and powerful story that helps bring to light an important and recent part of history about which too little is known. Readers may look for more options in the "Overcoming Adversity" section of chapter 3.

- **Miller, Sarah.** Helen Keller is a well-known and beloved figure. Her companion, Anne Sullivan, is often overlooked. In *Miss Spitfire,* Miller examines the relationship between the two in terms of the young Annie Sullivan and the obstacles she faced when starting to teach the tenacious and obstinate blind-deaf girl.

- **Moses, Sheila P.** It is a daunting task to write a historical narrative based on a real person, although that can make the story all the more attractive. In *I, Dred Scott: A Fictional Slave Narrative Based on the Life and Legal Precedent of* Dred Scott, Moses uses facts from the Supreme Court case to present one of the little-known causes of the Civil War.

- **Taylor, Mildred D**. Taylor has composed a warm and beautiful family story in nine volumes, basing it on her own family's history. Readers will meet Cassie Logan in the Newbery Award–winning title *Roll of Thunder, Hear My Cry* and will find out how Paul was able to obtain the family's home in *The Land*, the 2002 winner of the Coretta Scott King Award.

- **Walters, Eric.** Terry Fox started a "Marathon of Hope" across Canada, running to raise money for cancer research despite his amputated leg. He did not finish his run, but he inspired the nation, and runs continue annually in his name more than twenty years later. Eric Walters was chosen by the Fox family to write Terry's story, which is fictionalized in *Run.* A young, troubled, and troublesome boy ends up joining the marathon and learning much from Terry, giving readers a chance to learn about him.

## References

Aronson, Marc. 2003. "Biography and Its Perils." In *Beyond the Pale: New Essays for a New Era*. Lanham, MD: Scarecrow Press.

# Part 3

## Nonfiction Subject Interests

# Chapter 5

## History

## Definition

Nonfiction history books recount events in the past relating to a thing, person, time, or country. Selecting titles for this genre is akin to choosing the winners for an awards list; there is no way to do so without leaving out someone's favorite. The entries here are meant as an introduction to the various subgenres and were chosen using established criteria for nonfiction, including accuracy, documentation, style, and design. Readers are generally drawn to a particular time period or subject matter and may find a wealth of formats and styles from which to choose. Historical books describe a wide variety of people and places, inspiring contemplation about how others lived and live.

## Appeal

History is so much more than its obvious connections to school curricula. There are the additional benefits of offering new points of view, introducing new evidence, and showing readers what actually happened during desperate times. Recent trends include authors showing how historians work. Jim Murphy's *The Real Benedict Arnold* shows readers how Arnold's reputation was tainted before and after his death, letting readers know that it is possible that he was both a hero and a traitor. It is only through history that a reader may experience another time from the point of view of someone who was there, as in Jim O'Donnell's *Japan 1945* or Wilborn Hampton's books.

There are several options for appealing to readers who believe history is boring. In the section "New Perspectives" are titles that introduce history from an unexpected angle, such as Terry Deary's *The Wicked History of the World: History with the Nasty Bits Left In*. Choices for reluctant readers include graphic formats and the Eyewitness Books series, which contain numerous illustrations and a format that breaks up the text so it doesn't overwhelm the reader.

## Chapter Organization

Most readers are used to thinking about history in terms of dates. They will not be surprised to find "Defining Times" leading off the subgenres. "History's Darkest

Hours" follows, containing tales of disaster that is both man-made and natural. Next the very large subgenre "Micro-histories" provides readers with examinations of specific historical events and topics, such as *The Library of Alexandria* or *Six Days in October: The Stock Market Crash of 1929*.

The entries in the next section, "Historical Biography," differ from those in the parallel section in chapter 4 in that they emphasize the time and place rather than the people; for example, the participants in the Hitler Youth movement are a part of history because of their participation, or lack thereof, in the group, rather than being famous in their own right.

"Ideas of History" follows the development of one thing through time. The subjects explored in "New Perspectives" deal with changing times. They demonstrate how historical viewpoints change in response to new information, revisions in law, and changing attitudes.

# Defining Times

Dates are needed to understand history. Of all of the ways of looking at history, the chronological is the most common approach. People interested in history look for materials relating to particular time periods and apply questions specifically to that time. Students are taught to start with a particular time period and then look at the dates and settings, asking what happened and how the events of that time changed the course of history.

Each book in this section is a thorough examination of a period in history, covering the settings, people, and culture of that time. Readers will find that Wilborn Hampton used his experiences in the Middle East to bring an immediacy to his presentation in *War in the Middle East: A Reporter's Story: Black September and the Yom Kippur War*. Historian David Hackett Fisher gives readers a very readable and thorough portrait of *Washington's Crossing* to show how the tide of war was turned.

## Caputo, Philip.

🖈 *10,000 Days of Thunder: A History of the Vietnam War.* New York: Atheneum Books for Young Readers, 2005. ISBN 9780689862311. **J** **H**

Why should readers learn about the Vietnam War? This account sets out three reasons: It was the "[1] longest, [2] most controversial war in U.S. history and the [3] only war the United States ever lost." Readers will learn about the background of, people involved in, battles of, and impact of the war. Supplementary photographs, sidebars, and quick fact boxes are included. Readers will find out about life in both Vietnam and the United States during the war. A time line from 1945 to 1993 appears on the endpapers. IRA named this title to the 2006 Teachers' Choices list.

**Keywords:** Vietnam War (1961–1975)

**Now Try:** Readers looking for a more concise account of the Vietnam War will find an option in Stuart Murray's *Vietnam War*, a volume in the Eyewitness Books series. The photographs and short paragraphs normally found in this series' volumes cover the major players, both military and civilian, as well as equipment, the progress of the war, and personal stories.

## Fischer, David Hackett.

*Washington's Crossing.* <u>Pivotal Moments in American History</u>. Oxford; New York: Oxford University Press, 2004. ISBN 0195170342. **H** **A**

1

Fischer is a historian who ably draws readers into his book. He starts by examining the famous painting *Washington Crossing the Delaware,* wondering if that is really how the famous event happened. Readers are given an in-depth examination of the times, including the American, British, and Hessian troops; and are shown how the Americans, with Washington leading the way, were able to turn the tide of the war. Copious illustrations, including maps, portraits, and drawings, enhance the volume. Appendixes include a historiography and lists of primary sources.

2

**Keywords:** Delaware crossing • Presidents • Revolutionary War • U.S. history • Washington, George

3

**Now Try:** Readers who only know about Paul Revere from his famous ride might be interested to find out that his role in pre-revolutionary Boston was not limited to that one moment. David Hackett Fischer's *Paul Revere's Ride* is another example of this historian's ability to start with a particular incident and examine it in the context of other, similar actions.

4

## Galloway, Priscilla. Illustrated by Martha Newbigging.

5

*Archers, Alchemists, and 98 Other Medieval Jobs You Might Have Loved Or Loathed.* Richmond Hill, ON; Buffalo, NY: Annick Press, 2003. ISBN 1550378112. **M** **J**

In this fun and unusual introduction to medieval Europe, readers learn about living in medieval times from a unique viewpoint: a short, amusing crash course in the occupations available at all levels of society, from equal-opportunity serf positions to noble or artistic positions. The authors explain how society was organized and how it differed from modern-day life. Historical and cultural information is added in sidebars.

6

**Keywords:** Medieval history • Medieval life • Medieval occupations

**Now Try:** Getting a picture of a society through its occupational choices is a novel presentation. Laurie Coulter tackles this challenge for the nineteenth century, taking into consideration the vast changes wrought by the Industrial Revolution and presenting a time line of what was happening in America. Readers are given a novel look at the country in her *Cowboys and Coffin Makers: One Hundred 19th-Century Jobs You Might Have Feared or Fancied.*

7

8

## Gourley, Catherine.

9

*War, Women, and the News: How Female Journalists Won the Battle to Cover World War II.* New York: Atheneum Books for Young Readers, 2007. ISBN 9780689877520. **M** **J**

Before World War II, the styles of journalism, as well as opportunities for women writers, were radically different than they are today. A few women changed the face of both, becoming field investigators, war correspondents, and influences on photographers and journalists to come. Suggestions for further reading are included.

10

**Keywords:** Journalists • War correspondents • World War II

11

**Now Try:** In *Where the Action Was: Women War Correspondents in World War II*, Penny Colman introduces eighteen brave female reporters and photographers who spent World War II in the thick of things. Through these women's words and pictures, readers get a different perspective on the war than most textbooks impart. Colman is also able to convey some of the difficulties these women faced in doing their jobs, including harassment, disobeying direct orders, and lying when necessary to obtain needed paperwork.

## Greene, Meg.

*Into the Land of Freedom: African Americans in Reconstruction.* People's History. Minneapolis, MN: Lerner Publications, 2004. ISBN 9780822546900. **J**

The signing of the Emancipation Proclamation in 1860 did not signal the immediate victory over slavery that readers might think. After the war the South was in ruins, families had been torn apart, and freed slaves were left with no guarantees of jobs, education, rights, or homes. The dangers and freedoms that were a part of their lives during Reconstruction are introduced through the forty years of adjustments that included the Fourteenth and Fifteenth Amendments to the Constitution, both of which are appended.

**Keywords:** African Americans • Emancipation Proclamation • Freedmen • Reconstruction

## Hampton, Wilborn.

*War in the Middle East: A Reporter's Story: Black September and the Yom Kippur War.* Cambridge, MA: Candlewick, 2007. ISBN 9780763624934. **J H**

The Middle East is a complicated place, with a longer history of disputes than any other region on the planet. Although it would be impossible to explain centuries of disagreements in one volume, Hampton's explanation of the twentieth-century events that led up to the two wars covered in this book help give readers an understanding of the area as a powder keg. The journals of a UPI reporter covering a war bring to life the dangers of covering the 1970 Black September conflict in Jordan and the 1973 Yom Kippur War. Events following the war are also mentioned, from the assassinations of Anwar Sadat and Yitzhak Rabin to the fighting that broke out along Israel's border in 2006. This is an important chapter in the ongoing cycle of violence in this area.

**Keywords:** Middle East • Middle East in the twentieth century • Yom Kippur War (1973)

## Jennings, Peter, and Todd Brewster.

🎗 *The Century for Young People.* New York: Doubleday, 1999. ISBN 0385327080. **M J H**

Two news veterans divide the century into twelve chapters, examining the events of those years with a view to illustrating the major events and changes through the eyes of the people who were there. The result is a fast-moving and accessible work that, instead of strictly relying on dates and times, conveys the impressions of the teens who lived through those events, adding to an overall picture of the times. **BBYA**

**Keywords:** Twentieth century • U.S. history • World history

## Josephson, Judith Pinkerton.

*Growing Up in Pioneer America, 1800 to 1890.* Our America. Minneapolis, MN: Lerner Publications, 2003. ISBN 9780822506591. **M**

For readers who have wondered what life was like for children of the pioneers, this book is their chance to find out. Six chapters look at aspects of pioneer life, including moving west, dangers on the trail, life and school on the prairie, and what young people's options were as they grew up. Readers will find primary source material such as diaries, stories, letters, and interviews, as well as archival photographs and drawings that help portray the real West.

**Keywords:** Frontier life in the West • Overland journeys to the West • Pioneer children

**Now Try:** Readers interested in finding out what life was like for kids in the past have other options in the Our America series. Judith Pinkerton Josephson used the same format in the other volumes, integrating the first-person stories of young people and using archival photographs to let readers see how youths played, learned, and lived in different times. One of the more appealing time periods is addressed in Pinkerton's *Growing Up in World War II, 1941–1945*. Readers wanting to find out how much things have changed can find a benchmark in *Growing Up in a New Century, 1890 to 1914*.

## McPherson, James M.

🏶 *Fields of Fury: The American Civil War.* New York: Atheneum, 2002. ISBN 0689848331 **M** **J**

This overview of the war, with its short, readable chapters, provides an introduction to the major events and participants as well as broader subjects. These are supplemented by period photographs, paintings, prints, maps, a time line, and additional historical documents, as well as sources for further exploration and study. **BBYA**

**Keywords:** American history • Civil War • Emancipation Proclamation

*Into the West: From Reconstruction to the Final Days of the American Frontier.* New York: Atheneum Books for Young Readers, 2006. ISBN 9780689865435. **J**

The Civil War left a lot of work to be done in Washington. The steps involved in Reconstruction are presented in short chapters that start with the signing of the Homestead Act and add more subjects for the expanding American West. These include a variety of interesting topics, from immigrants to cowboys, to outlaws and lawmen, to frontier arts and letters.

**Keywords:** Cowboys • Frontier and pioneer life • Indians of North America • Reconstruction

## McWhorter, Diane.

🏶 *A Dream of Freedom: The Civil Rights Movement from 1954 to 1968.* New York: Scholastic, 2004. ISBN 141556471X. **M** **J**

This Pulitzer prize–winning author presents a chronological account of the landmark events in civil rights, from *Brown v. Board of Education* to Dr. Martin Luther King's assassination. She adds to these powerful events her own feelings as a white child in the South, illuminating the triumphs and trage-dies of the era. **BBYA**

Keywords: Civil rights • Civil rights movement

## Murphy, Jim.

🕯 *Inside the Alamo.* New York: Delacorte Press, 2003. ISBN 0385900929. **J**

In this smoothly written description of the 1836 battle, readers are put in the thick of things when General Santa Anna and the Mexican Army fought and massacred almost all of the men holed up inside the complex of the Alamo Mission, which was defending the newly formed territory of Texas. This account is unique and useful, particularly when Murphy explains historical research and how it changes as new evidence or interpretations emerge. **BBYA**

Keywords: Alamo • History • Research • Texas

**Now Try:** Readers interested in a comprehensive account of the events at the Alamo can find it in Shelley Tanaka's *The Alamo: Surrounded and Outnumbered, They Chose to Make a Defiant Last Stand.* In this book, a volume in the A Day That Changed America series, readers are given the causes and the aftermath of the rebellion, along with a careful ac-count of the final day of the siege. Enough supplemental information is given that read-ers will have an understanding of why this day fits into the series. Sources for further research are included.

## Van der Vat, Dan, and John S. D. Eisenhower.

🕯 *D-Day: The Greatest Invasion—A People's History.* New York: Bloomsbury, 2003. ISBN 9781582343143. **H A**

The importance of the liberation of his town in Nazi-occupied Holland shines through in the explanation of Operation Neptune, the initial assault on Nor-mandy's five beaches, which determined the outcome of Operation Overlord. The Normandy invasion, complete with the immense amount of planning and result-ing carnage, is covered in a balanced, well-illustrated presentation that explains the difficulties encountered and pays tribute to the many contributions of the vari-ous Allied forces. The text includes maps, photographs, and firsthand accounts. **BBYA**

Keywords: D-Day • Normandy • Operation Neptune • Operation Overlord • World War II • World War II campaigns

# History's Darkest Hours

It is often a particular time or event that captures a reader's attention. This subgenre represents the unfortunate, catastrophic stories that are a part of our past, whether naturally occurring or visited upon humans by humans. Stories of humanity's past intentional inhumanity carry important lessons for us today. Readers have the op-portunity to learn from the past through suspenseful, detailed books with high subject access and numerous fiction read-alikes. Readers will also find books about the victims of tragedies and desperate times. The stories here are not only about suffering but also about endurance, struggles, and triumph. Those drawn to these titles will find per-sonal accounts in the "Overcoming Adversity" section of chapter 3.

## Human Cruelties

These are stories of dark times, tragedies, and unfortunate events, visited upon people by other people.

### Cooper, Michael L.

*Remembering Manzanar: Life in a Japanese Relocation Camp.* New York: Clarion Books, c2002. ISBN 0618067787. **M** **J**

Michael Cooper tells the story of Japanese internment during World War II, focusing on Manzanar, the largest of the relocation centers. Photographs by Dorothea Lange and Ansel Adams show the facilities and the people there, while Cooper integrates oral histories, records from Manzanar's newspaper, and accounts from detainees to give readers a picture of the history and day-to-day life of the prisoners. Cooper adds his own photographs from the 2001 Manzanar Pilgrimage, taken at the dismantled camp, where a memorial now stands. Resources for further study are included.

**Keywords:** Evacuation and relocation • Japanese Americans • Manzanar War Relocation Center • World War II

**Now Try:** A timely reprinting of Jeanne Wakatsuki Houston's 1973 book offers further information about Manzanar and the dangers of misjudgment that internment represented. In *Farewell to Manzanar: A True Story of Japanese American Experience During and after the World War II Internment*, readers share not only her childhood experience of being interned at Manzanar but also the devastation that the internment wrought on her family. It is hoped that the overwhelming fears and prejudices of the time that led to the forcible relocation of over 100,000 people will not be repeated.

### Crowe, Chris.

🖈 *Getting Away with Murder: The True Story of the Emmett Till Case.* New York: Phyllis Fogelman, 2003. ISBN 0803728042. **H**

The Emmett Till case was not the sole cause of the civil rights movement, but it may well have been the final indignity that caused the flood of outrage to overflow the dam of racial injustice. This is a sobering and insightful account of the 1955 Mississippi murder trial of two white men for the killing of a fourteen-year-old black boy from Chicago. Readers are told early on that half-brothers Roy Bryant and J. W. Milam, later described as smoking cigars and reading the newspaper during their trial, were found not guilty, despite strong evidence to the contrary. Four months after Till was killed, Rosa Parks refused to give up her seat on the bus, and the wheels of the civil rights movement were set in motion. **BBYA**

**Keywords:** Civil rights • History • Murder

### Fradin, Dennis Brindell.

🖈 *Bound for the North Star: True Stories of Fugitive Slaves.* New York: Clarion, 2000. ISBN 0395970172. **J** **H**

Twelve tales of dangerous escapes, illustrated using photographs and archival prints, demonstrate not only why the slaves were attempting to escape but also why freedom was so highly sought. All stories, including that of Henry "Box" Brown, who mailed himself to freedom, demonstrate the suffering endured before, during, and after becoming fugitives and explain why people would endure anything rather than be owned. **BBYA**

**Keywords:** Abolitionists • Antislavery movements • Fugitive slaves • Underground railroad

## Fradin, Judith Bloom, and Dennis Brindell Fradin.

*5,000 Miles to Freedom: Ellen and William Craft's Flight from Slavery.* Washington, DC: National Geographic, 2006. ISBN 0792278852. **J H**

A retelling of the remarkable journey of Ellen Craft and William Craft, who escaped from Georgia in 1848. Ellen was dressed as a white man, and William acted as her slave, in a desperate bid for freedom. Reproductions of contemporary newspaper clippings, artwork, and archival photographs help bring to life the story of two of the best-known heroes of the abolitionist movement.

**Keywords:** Abolitionists • Antislavery movements • Fugitive slaves

## Hampton, Wilborn.

🏵 *September 11, 2001: Attack on New York City.* Cambridge, MA: Candlewick Press, 2003. ISBN 0763619493. **J H**

The story of 9/11 is traced through the experiences of several people: a married couple who worked in the World Trade Towers, one of whom was lost; a blind man and his dog, both of whom escaped; as well as several firefighters who stopped their own evacuation to help a woman who couldn't go any farther. The book also touches on the motives of hijacker Mohammad Atta. Hampton re-creates the terrible events of that day clearly, giving readers a sense of what may happen to ordinary people during extraordinary times. **BBYA**

**Keywords:** September 11, 2001 • Terrorism

## Jacobson, Sid.

🏵 *The 9/11 Report: A Graphic Adaptation.* New York: Hill and Wang, 2006. ISBN 0809057387; 9780809057399. **H**

This graphic novel adaptation reduces the almost 800 pages of the original report, *National Commission on Terrorist Attacks upon the United States,* to 15 percent of its original size, in a format that is clear and understandable. Events, people, and the background are all explained. The graphic format allows for the presentation of the multiple events of 9/11 to be laid out and seen, allowing readers to grasp the significance of the time line and its eventual evaluation by the commission. **BBYA**

**Keywords:** Al-Qaeda • Graphic nonfiction • September 11, 2001 • Terrorism • Terrorism prevention

## Jurmain, Suzanne.

🏵 *The Forbidden Schoolhouse: The True and Dramatic Story of Prudence Crandall and Her Students.* Boston: Houghton Mifflin, 2005. ISBN 0618473025. **M J H**

Readers are treated to a little-known and fascinating chapter in the history of school integration and people who fight for the rights of the oppressed. In 1831, when the parents of her students would not allow their children to attend her school with the African American teenager she had given permission to attend,

Prudence Crandall shook up all of Connecticut by founding a school devoted entirely to educating African American girls. What followed was a vicious persecution that included harassment, lawsuits, arrests, and the creation of a state law expressly to keep African American students from entering the state to attend her school. **BBYA, OP Honor, JM Honor**

**Keywords:** African Americans • Civil rights • Crandall, Prudence • Discrimination in education • Educators

## Levine, Karen.

🏆 *Hana's Suitcase.* Morton Grove, IL: Albert Whitman, 2003. ISBN 0807531480. **M J**

In 2000, Fumiko Ishioka obtained several artifacts from the Auschwitz Museum to help her teach Japanese children about the Holocaust at the Tokyo Holocaust Education Resource Center Museum. One of the items was an empty suitcase, marked with a name, Hana Brady, and the German word for orphan. Fumiko and the children set out to learn everything they could about Hana. In alternating chapters, readers learn Hana's story and how Fumiko and the children of the "Small Wings" group of the museum tracked Hana through Thieresienstadt and Auschwitz before finding the last surviving member of her family, in a very touching story of children who determine that their knowledge of the past can affect the future. This title was chosen for the 2004 Teachers' Choices list of the International Reading Association. **IRA**

**Keywords:** Holocaust • Holocaust history • Jewish children in the Holocaust

## O'Donnell, Joe.

🏆 *Japan 1945: A U.S. Marine's Photographs from Ground Zero.* Nashville, TN: Vanderbilt University Press, 2005. ISBN 9780826514677. **H A**

Covering the aftermath of the U.S. bombing raids on western Japan in September 1945 affected this twenty-three-year old Marine photographer so deeply that he kept his photographs locked away for forty-five years. They show the suffering and wreckage in Japan, especially in Nagasaki, as well as the initial reconstruction efforts, and remain a permanent and important reminder of the devastation that accompanies war. **BBYA**

**Keywords:** Military • photojournalism • Nagasaki • Pictorial record of World War II • War photography

## Opdyke, Irene Gut, and Jennifer Armstrong.

🏆 *In My Hands: Memories of a Holocaust Rescuer.* New York: Laurel-Leaf Books, 2004. ISBN 9780553494112. **J H A**

Sorrow, loss, and atrocities are not uncommon in a Holocaust story, but they are unexpected in this tale of a blonde, Catholic teenage student nurse. When the Nazis invaded Poland, Irene Gut was separated from her family, abused by Russian soldiers, and eventually assigned to work for a Nazi major. She took slow steps toward helping the residents of a Jewish ghetto, from leaving them food to passing messages, finally hiding several of them in the major's house. Her continuing journey from schoolgirl to partisan is the story of one woman's decision to fight for what she believes is morally right, no matter the possible consequences. **BBYA**

**Keywords:** Holocaust • Opdyke, Irene Gut • Personal narratives • Poland • World War II

**Now Try:** One of the classic biographies concerning the Holocaust is now available as a single volume in *The Complete Maus*. Art Spiegelman presents both his own troubled relationship with his father and the horrors his father experienced during the Holocaust in a masterful, graphic novel presentation. His approach—presenting the Nazis as cats, Jews as mice, Poles as pigs, and French as frogs—allows readers to concentrate on the themes and emotions in the book, not just the violence inherent to the times. The volumes are available individually, as well, and begin with *Maus I: A Survivor's Tale: My Father Bleeds History*. The second volume, *Maus II: A Survivor's Tale: And Here My Troubles Began*, was awarded a Pulitzer prize. A complement to the tale of this World War II rescuer is available in the World War I tragedy recounted by Jack Batten in *Silent in an Evil Time: The Brave War of Edith Cavell*. Cavell's determination to use her Brussels hospital to help Allied soldiers escape from behind enemy lines, as well as her heroic and tragic end, brought her to world attention.

## Natural Disasters and Disease Epidemics

These are the records of naturally occurring incidents and traumas, either due to plagues, weather, or some other unforeseen and uncontrollable event. Readers interested in the effects of these events may also be drawn to the stories about the scientists and doctors who studied them: some of their stories may be found in the "Problem Solvers and Experimenters: Science Biography" section of the Biography chapter.

### Barnard, Bryn.

🐾 *Outbreak: Plagues That Changed History.* New York : Crown Publishers, 2005. ISBN 9780375829864; 9780375929861lib. bndg. **J H**

In a surprisingly readable book, Barnard looks at six plagues that occurred over the course of history, starting with the bubonic plague in the Middle Ages and moving through smallpox, yellow fever, cholera, tuberculosis, and influenza. Taking a unique approach, he starts with an explanation of each disease, including a map of its spread, while keeping perspective on how it affected history—for example, in changes to the social structure and the erosion of the Church's monopoly in Europe after the plague. Readers will also learn about microbes' abilities to mutate and resist eradication, as well as new diseases. This title was chosen for the Teachers' Choices list of the International Reading Association. **IRA**

**Keywords:** Communicable diseases • Epidemics • Microbes

**Now Try:** A more in-depth look at three plagues may be found in James Cross Giblin's *When Plague Strikes: The Black Death, Smallpox, AIDS*. Giblin examines each outbreak in detail, from both a scientific and a sociological point of view. The causes, symptoms, treatments, and effects of the diseases are described in detail. A comparison of smallpox to AIDS leads to a discussion of the disturbing lack of progress toward a cure for the latter and of how in both cases the diseased were blamed for being ill. In *Invisible Enemies: Stories of Infectious Disease*, Jeanette Farrell provides readers with two distinct and opposite points of view of microscopic invaders, examining seven different diseases and human reactions to them. Reader may be surprised at how much we need microbes. In addition to those found in the body, microbes are used for everything from food production to waste treatment, as readers find out in the fascinating *Invisible Allies: Microbes That Shape Our Lives*.

## Bartoletti, Susan Campbell.

🏺 *Black Potatoes: The Story of the Great Irish Famine, 1845–1850.* Boston: Houghton Mifflin, 2001. ISBN 1413109861. Reprint: Sandpiper, 2005. ISBN 1415592128. **M J H**

The Great Irish Famine of 1845–1850 crossed class lines, killing one million people and causing another two million to emigrate. Readers are shown the devastating effects of years of blighted crops in a country where an entire economy was based on one product. Relief efforts were inadequate, leaving a country without shelter, food, or medical attention. The text is supplemented by illustrations, maps, first-person narratives, and a time line. This is the winner of the 2002 Robert F. Sibert Informational Book Medal. **BBYA, Sibert**

**Keywords:** Famine • History • Ireland

**Now Try:** A good companion book to this is *Feed the Children First: Irish Memories of the Great Hunger,* in which Mary E. Lyons shows the horrors of the Irish potato famine from the Irish point of view. She uses a combination of excerpts from Irish oral histories, historical paintings, and photographs from a nineteenth-century recurrence of the fungus. This gives the reader a firsthand picture of the tragedy from both people who managed to survive the famine and those whose lives were altered drastically. A reminder of continuing problems with hunger worldwide and Web sites for further information are provided.

## Capuzzo, Michael.

🏺 *Close to Shore: The Terrifying Shark Attacks of 1916.* New York: Crown, 2003. ISBN 0375922318. **J**

Hysteria gripped the New Jersey shore in the summer of 1916 when there was a series of vicious attacks in the water. During a one-month period, three men and one boy were killed. What was the source of these attacks. A killer whale? A swordfish? A sea turtle? Newspaper articles, photographs, and presentation of the shark's viewpoint build a phenomenal atmosphere of suspense about the creature, its wanderings, and its means of attack, from a time when nothing was known about the great white. **BBYA**

**Keywords:** Investigation • Science • Sharks

## Hampton, Wilborn.

🏺 *Meltdown: A Race Against Nuclear Disaster at Three Mile Island: A Reporter's Story.* Cambridge, MA: Candlewick Press, 2001. ISBN 0763607150. **J H**

A *New York Times* editor, then a UPI reporter, Wilborn Hampton offers an eyewitness account of the escalating danger of the Three Mile Island nuclear power plant accident of 1979. Through this firsthand account that both explains the events and sets them in the context of the Hiroshima atomic bombing and Chernobyl power plant explosion, readers are clearly shown the scientific underpinnings and the terror of the events. **BBYA**

**Keywords:** Chernobyl • Hiroshima • Nuclear power • Radioactivity

**Now Try:** Wilborn Hampton gives readers a sense of immediacy in his books. By 1979 he was a seasoned reporter. In his first book, *Kennedy Assassinated!: The World Mourns: A Reporter's Story*, he not only conveys a sense of the importance of the story, but also transmits how it felt when he was a novice reporter covering the UPI news desk and the call came in with the news about shots fired at the president's motorcade.

## Lemke, Donald B., Richard Dominguez, and Charles Barnett. Illustrated by Dave Hoover.

*The Schoolchildren's Blizzard.* Graphic Library. Mankato, MN: Capstone Press, 2008. ISBN 9781429601573. **M RR**

On January 12, 1888, an unexpected blizzard ripped through the Great Plains The storm lasted between twelve and eighteen hours, stranded students in their schoolhouses for several days, separated family members, and caused the deaths of up to 235 people. The basic facts of the storm and how some people dealt with its hardships are recounted in this easy-to-read graphic novel. Additional materials include a glossary and reading list; readers may also use the book's identification number at facthound.com to find further information.

**Keywords:** Blizzards • Frontier and pioneer life • Graphic nonfiction • Hypothermia • Immigrants • Nineteenth century • Pioneers • Prairies

**Now Try:** This particular storm easily captures the attention of readers with its ferocity and dire consequences. Readers interested in looking at the storm and its consequences from another perspective may want to try David Laskin's *The Children's Blizzard.* Not only does Laskin devote several chapters to storms and how they work, he also examines why and how some people were able to withstand such brutal cold. Readers will also find out exactly how this storm affected pioneers, in some cases drastically enough to make them leave the prairie.

## Lieurance, Suzanne.

*The Triangle Shirtwaist Fire and Sweatshop Reform in American History.* In American History. Berkeley Heights, NJ: Enslow Publishing, 2003. ISBN 0766018393. **M J**

In one of the worst industrial disasters in American history, 146 people died in a fire at New York City's Triangle Shirtwaist Company. The tragedy alerted the American people to the horrendous conditions endured by factory workers on a daily basis and spurred cities and states to pass new fire codes and laws to protect the workers and their rights. Lieurance examines the fire and the reforms that attempted to address the appalling conditions that made it inevitable, and traces ongoing issues of exploitation in the garment business.

**Keywords:** Labor reform • Triangle Shirtwaist Company fire

**Now Try:** For a broader look at problems in the labor force, Catherine Gourley investigates the history of female children working under horrendous conditions for starvation wages in *Good Girl Work: Factories, Sweatshops, and How Women Changed Their Role in the American Workforce.* It was not in fact "good work for girls," as the author found out, but rather backbreaking work for little money that often led these turn-of-the-century workers, as they attest, to lead the reform efforts as they became older. This title was named to the 2000 BBYA list.

## Murphy, Jim.

🪶 *An American Plague: The True and Terrifying Story of the Yellow Fever Epidemic of 1793.* Boston: Houghton Mifflin, 2003. ISBN 9780395776087. **M** **J** **H**

1

History, science, politics, and public health come together in this dramatic account of the disastrous yellow fever epidemic that hit many cities around the world in 1793. Drawing on firsthand accounts, medical and nonmedical, Murphy re-creates the fear and panic in Philadelphia, the social conditions that caused the disease to spread, and the arguments about causes and cures. Readers also learn about those who fled and those who stayed, among them the heroic group of free blacks who nursed the ill and were later vilified for their work. Archival prints, photos, and contemporary newspaper facsimiles, including lists of the dead, enhance the story. This book was a 2004 Newbery Honor book as well as the winner of the Robert F. Sibert Informational Book Medal. **BBYA, BG-HB, JM, Newbery Honor, OP, Sibert**

2

3

**Keywords:** Disease • Medicine • Science

4

# Micro-histories

*Wikipedia* defines *micro-history* as "the study of the past on a very small scale." Comprising a large subgenre for young adults, these books allow authors to narrow their focus to a single person, action, or object that fascinates them, starting when and where they like and adding as much detail as they choose. A study of one thing may then draw attention to its context and consequences—such as when author Barbara Freese first discusses coal as a pretty jet decoration and ultimately brings attention to the environmental implications of its overuse.

5

6

## Blumenthal, Karen.

7

🪶 *Six Days in October: The Stock Market Crash of 1929.* New York: Atheneum Books for Young Readers, 2002. ISBN 0689842767. **M** **J** **H**

Blumenthal traces the crash that occurred between October 24 and 29, 1929, ushering in the Great Depression. Explaining who the major players were and what led to the crash, she also gives a fascinating glimpse into the "Roaring '20s." Readers do not need a previous understanding of the market to understand this story; they will learn how investing works. **Sibert Honor**

8

**Keywords:** Great Depression • New York Stock Exchange • Stock market

9

## Conniff, Richard.

🪶 *Rats!: The Good, the Bad, and the Ugly.* New York: Crown, 2002. ISBN 037591207X. **M** **J**

Conniff's chatty book introduces readers to one of the most successful animals on the planet. The author, a natural history writer, starts out with basic biology, before debunking rat myths and sharing other trivia with readers. Readers discover the different uses for rats, from laboratory animals to

10

11

pets. All are bound to find out something they didn't know before, whether it's rats' phenomenal breeding rate, their intelligence, their ability to turn up in places as unusual as the White House, or their ability to withstand nuclear radiation. **QP**

**Keywords:** Animals • Rats

**Now Try:** Albert Marrin's *Oh Rats! The Story of Rats and People* covers the next best survivor in the animal kingdom and its relationship to man. Rats are introduced in stories intended to show their various interactions with people, from pet to pest to potential cuisine. Through statistics and stories showing their many roles, rats emerge as "champions of survival." The tenacity and habits of these amazing and prolific creatures are explored much more thoroughly and throughout history in Robert Sullivan's *Rats: Observations on the History and Habitat of the City's Most Unwanted Inhabitants*. Sullivan spent a year observing rats in New York alleys with night vision before writing his Alex award–winning book.

## Freedman, Russell.

🐾 *Give Me Liberty: The Story of the Declaration of Independence.* New York: Holiday House, 2000. ISBN 0823414485. **M** **J**

Freedman begins with the Boston Tea Party, explaining that it was the culmination of a series of events that finally erupted in 1773. He explains those events with a sense of immediacy that brings them to life, along with all of the different people who were affected by the revolution and its major events, which are presented in a sequence leading up to the formation of the Continental Congress and the writing of the Declaration of Independence. The importance of the declaration is also emphasized, not only by the efforts that have been made to preserve the physical document, but also in the effect that the words themselves and their meaning have continued to have in American culture, from gender rights to civil rights. **BBYA**

**Keywords:** Boston Tea Party • Continental Congress • Declaration of Independence

🐾 *In Defense of Liberty: The Story of America's Bill of Rights.* New York: Holiday House, 2003. ISBN 0832415856. **J** **H**

The first ten amendments to the U.S. Constitution, ratified in 1791, listed the individual freedoms guaranteed to Americans. Over the years they were adapted by court cases and societal changes in widely varying areas, including birth control, drug searches, civil rights, book censorship, gun control, war protests, and terrorism. Beginning with their roots in English law and the development of the U.S. Constitution, Freedman provides an exceptionally clear exposition of the history and the nature of each amendment, including examples of applicable situations and the court cases that have led to current laws. This title was chosen for the 2004 Teachers' Choices list of the International Reading Association. **BBYA, OP Honor**

**Keywords:** Civil rights • Law • U.S. Constitution

## Freese, Barbara.

🐾 *Coal: A Human History.* New York: Perseus, 2003. ISBN 1413176550. **H** **A**

Initially coal was seen as a prized ornament, a pretty, shiny substance. Its value for providing heat was soon discovered, making it invaluable, first as it spurred the Industrial Revolution in Great Britain and Europe, then across the Atlantic in the United States, and finally in China. A complete history follows, covering all aspects and ramifications of coal's use. Coal is an interesting and important topic in today's world. **BBYA**

**Keywords:** Coal • Energy • Global warming

## Hoose, Philip M.

🌷 *The Race to Save the Lord God Bird.* New York: Farrar, Straus & Giroux/Melanie Kroupa Books, 2004. ISBN 0374361738. **M** **J**

Readers will explore the ivory-billed woodpecker's history as it faced extinction from loggers and settlers reducing its habitat and those seeking it for its beautiful plumage because its very rarity made it more valuable to collectors. They will learn about the dwindling numbers of this fantastic bird and their importance to naturalists and environmentalists, including the National Audubon Society and the Endangered Species Act. This book was the 2005 winner of the Boston Globe-Horn Book Awards for nonfiction. **BBYA, BG-HB, OP Honor**

Keywords: Audubon Society • Extinction • Habitat • Ivory-billed woodpecker

## Kendall, Martha E.

🌷 *Failure Is Impossible: The History of American Women's Rights.* Minneapolis, MN: Lerner, c2001. ISBN 0822517442. **M** **J**

It is difficult to believe now that at one time an American woman could be tried for the "crime of voting." The guilty party, Susan B. Anthony, was one in a long line of brave women who fought to own their own property, get an education, hold jobs, vote, and do a number of other things that would make them "equal" to men. These women and their struggles are explored in this fascinating and eye-opening history. **BBYA**

Keywords: Equal Rights Amendment (ERA) • Suffrage • Women's rights

## Kyi, Tanya Lloyd.

🌷 *The Blue Jean Book: The Story Behind the Seams.* Toronto: Annick Press, 2005. ISBN 155037916X. **M** **J**

Kyi looks at the blue jean, one of the most common fashion items and a pop culture phenomenon around the world. She provides a historical examination of this most popular pant, from Levi Strauss and his original patent in 1873 to the rise of his competitors, marketing strategies, differing fashions, and changing consumer concerns. Readers may be surprised at how much is behind that little red tab. **PP**

Keywords: Blue jeans • Inventions • Manufacturing • Marketing • Strauss, Levi

*Burn: The Life Story of Fire.* Toronto: Annick Press, 2007. ISBN 9781554510818. **M** **J**

Greek mythology tells us that fire was a gift from Prometheus; charcoal remnants one million years old have been found by archaeologists. Readers will learn how humans' relationship with fire, from its possession, to its adaptation, and to mastering it, has allowed cultures to develop from merely surviving to dominating their surroundings. Discussions also include the problems with this mighty force of nature, whether accidental or man-made.

Keywords: Fire • Science and nature

## Love, Ann, and Jane Drake. Illustrated by Claudia Davila.

*Sweet!: The Delicious Story of Candy.* Toronto; Plattsburgh, NY: Tundra Books, 2007. ISBN 9780887767524. **M**

In this broad look at the history of candy, the authors examine sweet flavors and where they actually come from, including transformed "bee barf, mammal secretions, aphid poop and . . . squished roots." It is noted that kids generally prefer candy from their own part of the world. Candy is then looked at from a historical and international perspective, starting with ancient Egypt's marshmallows and going on to milk, maple sugar, jelly beans, and a number of different processes for making chocolate. A running time line of candy moments from around the world highlights the text.

**Keywords:** Candy • History of candy

## Murphy, Jim.

🏵 *Blizzard!: The Storm That Changed America.* New York: Scholastic Press, 2000. ISBN 9780590673099. **M** **J**

There weren't any long-range forecasting devices in 1888. Three days of hurricane force winds and snow crippled the Northeast, without warning or relief. A train outside of Albany crashed into a snowdrift; people living in tenements resorted to burning their furniture to stay warm. Monumental changes in communications, transportation, and weather monitoring occurred as a direct result of this blizzard and are enumerated here. **BBYA, Sibert Honor**

**Keywords:** Blizzards • New York State blizzards • New York State history

## Ross, Val.

🏵 *The Road to There: Mapmakers and Their Stories.* Toronto; Plattsburgh, NY: Tundra Books, 2003. ISBN 0887766218. **J** **H**

The story of cartography is not just pictures on a page, as readers will learn in this wide-reaching book. The thirteen chapters reflect different eras that possessed different knowledge, using explorations and mapmaking for different purposes, from monetary to political. Readers will meet unusual teams, such as the unlikely collaboration of Roger II and the Muslim scholar Al-Idrisi during the Crusades, and the more familiar Lewis and Clark. Also covered is the evolution of mapmaking techniques from pen and ink to aerial photography, including historically interesting facts such as the quilts used by slaves to help guide them on their escape routes. **Norma Fleck**

**Keywords:** Cartographers • Cartography • Geography • Mapmakers • Maps

## Springer, Jane.

*Genocide.* Groundwork Guides. Toronto: Groundwood Books, 2006. ISBN 9780888996817. **J** **H**

It is a sad statement in today's world that genocide (mass ethnic killing), exist in some twenty countries around the globe. The evolution and history of these particular crimes against humanity is traced in this slim volume in a fascinating and eye-opening journey. Recent atrocities in Rwanda and Darfur are just the latest in a string of crimes that include the slave trade, the Holocaust, and the actions of the Khmer Rouge in Cambodia. Looking at these events is a fine starting point to encourage debate about human rights and the responses to and prevention of genocide.

**Keywords:** Ethnic killings • Genocide • Social science • Violence in society

## Trumble, Kelly.

*The Library of Alexandria.* **Illustrated by Robina MacIntyre Marshall.** New York: Clarion Books, c2003. ISBN 9780395758328. M J

Both the city and the library of Alexandria were very important in the ancient world. Ptolemy I conceived of the library as a way to attract important minds. He and his successors then exponentially increased its collections. Scholarship conducted in the library was stunning and controversial at the time; it included works by Copernicus, Archimedes, and Euclid, whose mathematical text was used until the twentieth century. The library's destruction makes for a sad ending to this amazing tale.

**Keywords:** Alexandrian library

## Walker, Sally M.

🌹 *Secrets of a Civil War Submarine: Solving the Mysteries of the* H.L. *Hunley.* New York: Carolrhoda Books, 2005. ISBN 1575058308. M J

Sally Walker presents a history of the ongoing mystery of the *H.L. Hunley*, the first Confederate submarine to sink a ship. She covers its fascinating history, from the several design attempts through its disappearance during the Civil War, discovery 130 years later, and the many scientists from various fields who have worked together to uncover its secrets. In addition to this book being chosen for the BBYA and IRA's Teacher's Choices lists, Sally Walker was awarded both the 2006 Coretta Scott King/John Steptoe Award for New Talent and the Robert F. Sibert Informational Book Medal. **BBYA, IRA, Sibert**

**Keywords:** Archaeology • Civil War • Forensics • *H.L. Hunley* submarine • Naval history

# Historical Biography: Ordinary People in Extraordinary Times

This subgenre provides a place for books about people caught up in extraordinary times. Their names may be immediately recognizable for their own works and lives, or they might become known only through their presence at a place or event. In either case, it is the history itself that is at the forefront, rendered through the research and details in the writing, rather than the person or people in the story. This differentiates these books from those in the "Historical Biography" section in chapter 4. This section is divided into books about individuals and groups.

## Individual Stories

### Hillman, Laura.

*I Will Plant You a Lilac Tree: A Memoir of a Schindler's List Survivor.* New York : Atheneum Books for Young Readers, c2005. ISBN 0689869800. **J** **H**

> Hannelore Wolff was born in Germany in 1924. Here she recalls what happened to her from 1940 to 1945. Desolate after hearing of her father's death in Buchenwald and the impending deportation of the rest of her family, Hannelore asked the Gestapo for permission to join her family. She spent the rest of the war being shuttled from the Polish ghetto through eight different concentration camps before miraculously ending up on Oscar Schindler's list. The horrors and loss endured in the camps are in stark contrast to the future she was able to find there when she met her husband.
>
> **Keywords:** Auschwitz (Poland) • Hillman, Laura • Holocaust • Schindler, Oscar

### Maurer, Richard.

*The Wright Sister: Katharine Wright and Her Famous Brothers.* Brookfield, CT: Roaring Brook, 2003. ISBN 0761315462. **M** **J**

> Katherine Wright was a model for women of her time. The only college graduate in her family, she gave up her career to run the home and business of her more famous brothers, only to be disowned by her brother when she did marry later in life. The sacrifices she made for her family while maintaining her sense of humor and fighting for equity at her alma mater are highlighted here for the first time.
>
> **Keywords:** Aviation • Wright, Katharine • Wright, Orville

### Poole, Josephine. Illustrated by Angela Barrett.

*Anne Frank.* New York: Alfred A. Knopf, 2005. ISBN 0375932429. **M**

> Two picture book collaborators take on a somber subject: the life of Anne Frank, from her birth to the discovery of her family in their hiding place during World War II. Poole concentrates on Anne's vibrant personality and the changes in the "grown-up world," to set the context for the difficulties her family, as Jewish people living in Amsterdam, would encounter. The increasingly dark tones used in Josephine Poole's illustrations reflect the hardships encountered by the Frank family. Readers will also meet Otto Frank's secretary Miep Gies, who saved Anne's diary and passed it on to him. A detailed chronology of events is included.
>
> **Keywords:** Frank, Anne • Jewish children in the Holocaust • Nonfiction picture book

## Group Stories

### Bartoletti, Susan Campbell.

🔖 *Hitler Youth: Growing Up in Hitler's Shadow.* New York: Scholastic Nonfiction, 2005. ISBN 0439353793. **M** **J** **H** **BG**

> In 1926 the Hitler Jugend was founded to turn the youth of Germany into followers of the führer. Bartoletti follows twelve German youths connected with the group in some way, from those who were ardent followers to those who became staunch resisters. Readers will learn why youth joined, what it was like, how they

were used, and what became of them. The accolades for this title include being made an honor book for both the 2006 Newbery Award and the Robert F. Sibert Informational Book Medal. **BBYA, Newbery Honor, OP Honor, Sibert Honor**

**Keywords:** Germany • Hitler Jugend • Hitler youth • World War II

*Kids on Strike!* Boston: Houghton Mifflin, 1999. ISBN 0395888921. **M J**

Bartoletti takes a broad look at the history of child labor to give readers a chance to ponder the complex issue of whether children were always simply helpless victims in inhumane situations. She shows them joining in the fight for unionization and better working conditions. The conditions they were striving to improve are shown clearly through the author's trademark use of several different research formats, which include memoirs, oral histories, newspaper reports, and over a hundred archival photographs. **BBYA**

**Keywords:** Child labor • Lockouts • Strikes

**Now Try:** Readers who enjoy Bartoletti's trademark combination of writing forms may find an additional resource in *Growing Up in Coal Country,* in which she explores what life was like for children in Pennsylvania's mines. This top-ten BBYA title also gives readers an idea about what life was like for children in coal towns 100 years ago. Readers will learn about the different levels of mine work for children as well as their home lives and the ultimate necessity for unionization. For a more up-to-date look at the dangerous work children are still doing around the world, in both industrialized and developing nations, readers may consult Jane Springer's *Listen to Us!: The World's Working Children*, an illuminating and provocative discussion of different types of exploitation at the end of the twentieth century.

## Freedman, Russell.

*Children of the Great Depression.* New York: Clarion Books, 2005. ISBN 9780618446308. **M J**

Russell Freedman pairs his clear, compelling narrative with photographs taken by the best photographers of the day, including Dorothea Lange and Walker Evans, to give a picture of what life was like for children and teens after "Black Tuesday." Although it explains the factors that triggered the collapse of the stock market and its effects on the nation's economy, the story is told from the children's perspective. History comes alive as they remember the soup kitchens, migrant work, and diversions of the times. Readers will be amazed by tables that show the differences in costs, salaries, and available entertainment between today and the 1930s. **OP**

**Keywords:** Children and social conditions • Great Depression

*Freedom Walkers: The Story of the Montgomery Bus Boycott.* New York: Holiday House, 2006. ISBN 0823420310. **M J**

Freedman sets the stage for his clear, compelling explanation of the 381-day boycott and its importance in the civil rights movement by explaining racial segregation and the damage it inflicted. An engrossing account of the boycott follows: how it came about, the leaders, the organization necessary to maintain it, and the damage inflicted upon those brave enough to maintain their beliefs. This title was chosen for the

2007 Teachers' Choices list of the International Reading Association. **BBYA, IRA, JM Honor, OP**

Keywords: Civil rights movement • King, Martin Luther, Jr. • Montgomery (AL) • Montgomery bus boycott • Parks, Rosa • Segregation

## Galloway, Priscilla, ed.

🏹 *Too Young to Fight: Memories from Our Youth During World War II.* Toronto; New York: Stoddart Kids, 1999; Markham, ON: Fitzhenry and Whiteside, 2004. ISBN 9781550050905. **M J H**

Canadian author Priscilla Galloway was shocked when during a school visit a young student said that World War II didn't have anything to do with the people at home in Canada, so she promptly gathered eleven different and equally insightful accounts by other authors and illustrators who had been affected by a war fought thousands of miles away. Ranging from Joy Kagawa's time in an internment camp, to Janet Lunn hiding her family's German surnames, to Monica Hughes's participation in the war, these stories are just as relevant today given the current political strife in the world. This title was awarded the 2000 Bologna Ragazzi Award.

Keywords: Children in war • History • World War II

## Giblin, James.

🏹 *Good Brother, Bad Brother: The Story of Edwin Booth & John Wilkes Booth.* New York: Clarion, 2005. ISBN 0618096426. **M J**

Both Edwin and John Wilkes Booth were trained actors, following in the footsteps of their father, Junius. Edwin spent his life in the theater world, and his contributions to it are largely forgotten. Better known is his brother, John Wilkes Booth, who assassinated Abraham Lincoln and led a plot to bring down the U.S. government. Giblin presents a lively and engaging picture of these contrasting personalities in a time of war. **BBYA, BG-HB Honor**

Keywords: Actors • Assassination • Biography • Booth, Edwin • Booth, John Wilkes • Civil War • Lincoln, Abraham

## Oppenheim, Joanne.

🏹 *Dear Miss Breed: True Stories of the Japanese American Incarceration During World War II and a Librarian Who Made a Difference.* New York: Scholastic, 2006. ISBN 0439569923. **H**

Joanne Oppenheim's search for a former classmate led her to the story of Clara Breed, former Children's Librarian at San Diego Public Library, and the letters that a group of incarcerated Japanese American children wrote to "Dear Miss Breed." Miss Breed, who was passionate in her opposition to imprisoning Japanese Americans in the wake of the attack against Pearl Harbor, remained in contact with her young friends for the duration of the war, sending them care packages of books and sundries. The children's letters supplement the text and help provide a picture of what life was really like for them in hostile times. Readers will also learn what happened to the correspondents after the war, as the imprisoned attempted to face the climate of fear and mistrust and start their lives over again. This title was chosen for the 2007 Teachers' Choices list of the International Reading Association. **IRA**

Keywords: Breed, Clara • Epistolary nonfiction • Japanese Americans • World War II

# Ideas of History

This section encompasses stories in which the main subject is an idea important to history that at the same time cannot be defined as belonging to one specific point in history. Tonya Bolden gives readers some intriguing examples that enlighten them about the changing views on women's rights.

## Bolden, Tonya.

*33 Things Every Girl Should Know About Women's History: From Suffragettes to Skirt Lengths to the ERA.* New York: Crown, 2002. ISBN 0375911227. **J** **H**

With the help of a number of authors, both contemporary and historical, Tonya Bolden offers a chronological look at thirty-three turning points in the development of women's rights. Bolden starts with a 1776 letter from Abigail Adams to her husband, asking him to "Remember the Ladies," then discusses women's achievements and participation in areas that vary from suffrage, to civil rights, to women's involvement in the war, to information on fashion, music, and beauty. Readers will also find bibliographies, profiles, photographs, quotes, and an index.

**Keywords:** Fashion history • Feminism • Suffrage • Women's rights

**Now Try:** Readers might also enjoy Tonya Bolden's *33 Things Every Girl Should Know: Stories, Songs, Poems, and Smart Talk by 33 Extraordinary Women.* Writers, artists, actors, entrepreneurs, athletes, and scholars give their advice to girls on some of the trials encountered during adolescence.

## Gottfried, Ted.

*The Fight for Peace: A History of Antiwar Movements in America.* People's History. Minneapolis, MN: Twenty-First Century Books, 2006. ISBN 9780761329329. **J** **H**

There is a long history of people willing to stand against wars, stretching back to the U. S. Civil War. During each war since then, some have protested the fighting, whether singly or in groups. An individual's attitudes toward war frequently differ from the government's, and international politics changed significantly in the years leading up to the war in Iraq. Discussion here includes politicians, struggles, and potential repercussions of standing up for one's beliefs.

**Keywords:** Activists • Peace movements • Politics

# New Perspectives

History is not set in stone. Over time, new discoveries make it necessary to change how we interpret the past. This can happen for any number of reasons, including changes in law, cultural mores, new evidence, and scientific advancement. These books provide new and often enlightening takes on historical subjects.

1

2

3

4

5

6

7

8

9

10

11

## Deary, Terry, and Martin Brown.

*The Wicked History of the World: History with the Nasty Bits Left In.* New York: Scholastic, 2006. ISBN 0439877865. **M**

> Deary and Brown present 8,000 years of evils, horrible acts, and gruesome practices culled from history. Relishing in the gory subject manner, the authors throw in puns and treat the whole book with a lighthearted air that is well-matched with the cartoon illustrations. Although there isn't enough detailed information on any particular topic for a report, readers will likely derive a lot of enjoyment from and be led to new topics by this book, which the authors state is written to "teach you nothing."
>
> **Keywords:** History • World history

## Freedman, Russell.

🏮 *Who Was First?: Discovering the Americas.* New York: Clarion, 2007. ISBN 9780618663910. **M J**

> A schoolyard rhyme tells us when Columbus "discovered" America. However, archaeologists, historians, and scientists know about other people living in the Americas way before 1492. So, by whom and when was it actually discovered? Readers will learn of mysterious runes and towers that have led scientists and historians to put forth theories about different peoples having traveled to North America. The Vikings were in Newfoundland as early as AD 1000, but how and when did Stone Age peoples migrate here? Reevaluating that which has been considered "fact" is part of both history and science and makes for an engrossing and enlightening read. **ALA Notable**
>
> **Keywords:** American explorers • Discovery and exploration of America • Exploration and discovery • Pre-Columbian discovery and exploration

## Nelson, Peter.

🏮 *Left for Dead: A Young Man's Search for Justice for the USS* **Indianapolis.** New York: Delacorte Press, 2002. Reissued by Laurel Leaf, 2005. ISBN 0440229456. **J**
**H BB BG**

> The USS *Indianapolis* was torpedoed by a Japanese submarine in the last days of World War II. More than fifty years later, a teen worked with the survivors of the disaster to clear the name of the *Indianapolis*'s captain, who was wrongly court-martialed for the tragedy. **BBYA**
>
> **Keywords:** History • Tragedy • War

# Consider Starting with . . .

These are some of the more captivating and accessible titles in the history genre.

Bartoletti, Susan Campbell. *Hitler Youth: Growing up in Hitler's Shadow.*

Bolden, Tonya. *33 Things Every Girl Should Know About Women's History: From Suffragettes to Skirt Lengths to the ERA.*

Crowe, Chris. *Getting Away with Murder: The True Story of the Emmett Till Case.*

Fradin, Judith Bloom, and Dennis Brindell Fradin. *5,000 Miles to Freedom: Ellen and William Craft's Flight from Slavery.*

Freedman, Russell *Freedom Walkers: The Story of the Montgomery Bus Boycott.*

Giblin, James. *Good Brother, Bad Brother: The Story of Edwin Booth & John Wilkes Booth.*

Jennings, Peter; Todd Brewster. *The Century for Young People.*

McWhorter, Diane. *A Dream of Freedom: The Civil Rights Movement from 1954 to 1968.*

Nelson, Peter. *Left for Dead: A Young Man's Search for Justice for the USS Indianapolis.*

Walker, Sally M. *Secrets of a Civil War Submarine: Solving the Mysteries of the H.L. Hunley.*

## Fiction Read-Alikes

- **Alvarez, Julia.** A young girl finds out the truth about the dangers of living in General Trujillo's Dominican Republic dictatorship in *Before We Were Free.* Alvarez was awarded the Pura Belpre Award for this title, which is based on her own experiences growing up.

- **Anderson, Laurie Halse**. Readers interested in epidemics and the devastation they wreak will find a gripping story in Anderson's exploration of the yellow fever outbreak in Philadelphia, *Fever, 1793.*

- **Blackwood, Gary**. Blackwood has penned an intriguing alternative history title for young adults, *The Year of the Hangman.* A young wastrel named Creighton is press-ganged and sent off to help his uncle, a colonial colonel, but when he arrives in America in 1777 he finds that George Washington has just been defeated.

- **Gray, Dianne E.** Gray's novels, set in late nineteenth-century Nebraska, combine realistic settings and period details with strong characters. *Together Apart* takes place a few months after the schoolchildren's blizzard. *Tomorrow the River* takes place a number of years later.

- **Hobbs, Will.** History need not always be depressing. Will Hobbs provides several stories (*Jason's Gold, Down the Yukon, Far North*) about the Gold Rush that offer readers a chance to be swept to another time by his trademark action.

- **Matas, Carol.** Several of this Canadian author's novels take place in wartime settings and feature Jewish families facing discrimination. *The War Within: A Novel of the Civil War* features a main character discovering divided loyalties and realizing that the Jewish families in her town are facing the same prejudices as the African Americans. A fifteen-year-old Jewish girl passes for Polish and works for the Nazis to save herself in *In My Enemy's House.*

- **Naidoo, Beverly.** Experiences of individuals of different genders and races in South Africa between 1948 and 2000, during the five decades of apartheid, are presented in *Out of Bounds: Seven Stories of Conflict and Hope*. A time line is appended.

- **Skrypuch, Martha Forchuk.** The Armenian massacres are not a part of history common to informational literature, but they add realism and a compelling backstory to several of Martha Skrypuch's books. The main character in *The Hunger* combats her own anorexia and hears about her grandmother escaping from Armenia; *Nobody's Child* is about a survivor of the massacre and how she copes.

- **Toksvig, Sandi.** Denmark's position in World War II is explored in a novel by Sandi Toksvig, *Hitler's Canary*. The story revolves around a theatrical family whose members decide not to sing Hitler's tune. Urged on by ten-year-old Bamse, the entire family eventually become resisters.

- **Walters, Eric.** Adventure, history, realistic dialogue, and engaging stories are all common attributes of Eric Walters's stories. Two of his books examine Japanese internment in World War II. *War of the Eagles* deals with a boy who has lost both his best friend to an internment camp and his father to the Royal Air Force, and *Caged Eagles* follows Tadashi Fukushima and his family in the camps.

# Chapter 6

## Science, Math, and the Environment

## Definition

One definition of *science* has remained relatively constant since 1775, as found in the *Oxford English Dictionary*: a branch of study concerned with demonstrated truths, backed up by classified observations, with the possibility for the gathering of new truths. Although the original definition does allow this to be applied to any body of study, a classification was added in 1860 to specify particular fields. Modern usage separates pure mathematics from the natural sciences, while maintaining several large subdivisions: physical sciences, earth sciences, medicine, engineering, biology, and social science. Science nonfiction, then, focuses on literature with scientific themes. It provides a wide range of materials: reflective explanations of the natural world, fast-paced chronicles of scientific endeavors, and fascinating biographies of the scientists and researchers who struggle to gain new knowledge.

## Appeal

Science and math writing provides answers about Earth's many mysteries. It appeals to the reader's curiosity, or "need to know." Readers interested in these unknowns, or who have questions about how we got here and what might be happening in the world around us, are in the right place to find books to satisfy their curiosity. Some of the greatest achievements in science are explained in Bill Brysons's fascinating *A Short History of Nearly Everything.* Books on archaeology give readers a chance to learn from the past; environmental books help prepare us for the future. Readers interested in how things work can find out about everything from bicycles to rockets.

## Chapter Organization

The chapter starts off with "Science Adventures," fast-paced stories about the people, discoveries, and research that bring about advances in scientific knowledge. This is followed by true tales in "Scientists and Science Enthusiasts" and longer, more detailed works in "History of Science." Scientists learn an immense amount about the planet and its denizens from studying remains. Paleontology and archaeology are included in "Digging into the Past." Titles in "How Things Work" investigate a variety of subjects, in a "General" subsection that covers astronomy and manufacturing, as well as in a "Transportation" subsection that provides information for car lovers and future engineers.

Subject-specific sections follow. "Micro-science" focuses on specific topics, such as tattooing and X-rays. "Environmental Writing" contains subsections on both "Ecology and Conservation" and "Animals."

Readers may find more information about scientists and field research in the "Problem Solvers and Experimenters" section of chapter 4. Information about health and nutrition is covered in chapter 8.

## Science Adventures

These books focus on the people, discoveries, research, and technological achievements that herald advances in our scientific knowledge. They are descriptive and fast-paced, providing information about efforts undertaken around the world to gain knowledge as well as following the work of scientists endeavoring to ensure the survival of the planet and its denizens, several examples of which may be found in the Scientists in the Field series. Readers who enjoy titles in this section may also be interested in the action stories and fast reads found in chapter 1.

### Miles, Victoria.

*Wild Science: Amazing Encounters Between Animals and the People Who Study Them.* Vancouver, BC: Raincoast Books, 2004. ISBN 1551926180. **M**

Miles presents the stories behind ten different scientists at work in the wild. Each profile is divided into four parts. The first takes the reader into the scientist's daily world, whether rescuing a beached blue whale in Newfoundland or teaching bat-handling in Arizona. This is followed by a profile of the scientist, the science, and the animal in question. The habitats, technology, and daily lives of both the animals and scientists are vividly and clearly transmitted.

**Keywords:** Animal habitats • Biologists • Endangered species • Environmentalists • Nonfiction collections • Scientific research • Zoologists

**Now Try:** Readers interested in zoology and scientific research will be drawn to the various titles in Houghton Mifflin's Scientists in the Field series. Titles allow readers to explore areas of interest to them, such as Pamela Turner's *Gorilla Doctors: Saving Endangered Great Apes* or Stephen Swinburne's *The Woods Scientist.*

### Montgomery, Sy.

*Quest for the Tree Kangaroo: An Expedition to the Cloud Forest of New Guinea.* **Photographs by Nic Bishop.** Scientists in the Field. Boston: Houghton Mifflin, 2006. ISBN 0618496416. **M** **J**

Montgomery and her photographer, Nic Bishop, trekked with researchers deep into New Guinea for a sight of an animal that looks like a small bear, climbs like a monkey, and is rarely seen. Readers will gain a strong sense of the difficulties and rewards of this work. Included in the appendixes are Web resources, conservation notes, and a glossary of Tok Pisin, the local Papuan language. This was an honor book for the 2007 Robert F. Sibert Informational Book Medal. **Sibert Honor**

Keywords: Matschie's tree kangaroo • Papua New Guinea • Scientific research

🦟 *The Tarantula Scientist.* **Photographs by Nic Bishop.** Scientists in the Field. Boston: Houghton Mifflin, 2004. ISBN 9780618147991. **M** **J**

In trying to track down the world's largest spider, the Goliath bird-eating tarantula, arachnologist Sam Marshall ventured into rain forests in Guiana, found some incredible specimens, formed a team of dedicated scientists, and was never bitten once—by a spider. What can they learn about this spider and its habitat, and where will it take them next? This book is an honor book for the 2005 Robert F. Sibert Informational Medal. **Sibert Honor**

Keywords: Arachnologists • Field biology • French Guiana • Scientific research • Tarantulas

## Morgan, Jody.

*Elephant Rescue: Changing the Future for Endangered Wildlife.* Firefly Animal Rescue. Toronto: Firefly Books, 2004. ISBN 1552975940. **M**

This volume in the Firefly Animal Rescue series examines the physiology, behavior, and habitats of the world's largest land mammal in both Africa and Asia. Several of the individual ecologists working to create an environment in which this endangered species, whose numbers have shrunk from 1.6 million to 44,000, are profiled. The reasons for this are explored, but the main problem is generally agreed to be humans, including loss of habitat, poaching, sport hunting, and the ivory trade. Readers will also find out about the latest technology ecologists are using in trying to save the elephants and will be directed to contact information for conservation clubs and organizations.

Keywords: Conservation • Elephants • Endangered species

**Now Try:** Readers interested in pairing knowledge about a species with an understanding of the dangers faced by that species and the people who are fighting for its survival may also be interested in Erich Hoyt's *Whale Rescue: Changing the Future for Endangered Wildlife*. This, another title in the Firefly Animal Rescue series, discusses the impact commercial whaling has had on the mammoth creatures of the sea and then shows readers the efforts being made by scientists and environmentalists to protect whales. Cetacean projects are profiled, as are several researchers.

## Walker, Sally M.

*Fossil Fish Found Alive: Discovering the Coelacanth.* New York: Carolrhoda Books, 2002. ISBN 1575055368. **M** **J**

The scientific process is shown to great advantage in Walker's description of a decades-long search for answers about the coelacanth, a fish long thought to be extinct. Beginning with its appearance in the fossil record, Walker shares the surprise, continuing questions, and difficulties of the scientists discovering the remains of the specimen, from preservation to international rights. Web sites are offered for interested readers to find more information.

**Keywords:** Coelacanth • Endangered animals • Fish • Marine research • Scientific research

**Now Try:** Readers interested in the search for a mysterious creature can read about scientist Clyde Roper's quest to find a living giant squid in Bradford Matsen's *The Incredible Hunt for the Giant Squid*. Readers are told what is known and what has been speculated about these elusive and mysterious beasts of the deep, including the remains found on beaches, in fishing nets, and in whales' stomachs. The photos in this title from the <u>Incredible Deep-Sea Adventure</u> series show why Roper has made this a lifelong hunt. In Laurie Lindop's *Venturing the Deep Sea,* readers will find out about the submersibles that have been developed by underwater biologists and geologists to explore the sea's depths and what mysteries still wait there.

## Scientists and Science Enthusiasts

Although scientific information plays an important part in these accounts, it is the individual researcher or person behind a study who is the focus. In *The Radioactive Boy Scout,* readers will be amazed at the extent of David Hahn's experiments. Those interested in more information about scientists and their discoveries will find titles dedicated to them in the "Problem Solvers and Experimenters" section of chapter 4.

### Fradin, Dennis Brindell.

*With a Little Luck: Surprising Stories of Amazing Discoveries.* New York: Dutton, 2006. ISBN 0525471960. **M** **J**

The book starts off with an explanation of serendipity to explain that the discoveries in this book took both luck and timing, in addition to the research already being done. Fradin presents eleven exceptional stories in which people were at a point in their study or efforts to be able to take advantage of something unexpected and use that as a revelation. Whether writing about Charles Goodyear's accidental burning of rubber or Isaac Newton's theories of gravity and motion, Fradin makes history interesting and the concepts behind the stories understandable.

**Keywords:** Explorations • Inventions • Nonfiction collections • Scientific research

### McCutcheon, Marc. Illustrated by Jon Cannell.

*The Kid Who Named Pluto: And the Stories of Other Extraordinary Young People in Science.* San Francisco: Chronicle Books, 2004. ISBN 081183770X. **M**

Inventions, discoveries, and scientific contributions have changed the course of people's lives. Some were even made by children and young adults. In this book Marc McCutcheon tells nine such remarkable stories. They include a few people who are fairly well known, including Louis Braille, who created a way for the blind to read and write, becoming a teacher at the age of nineteen. Not as well known is Philo Farnsworth who, at the age of fourteen, made the first design for a television, and was eventually awarded the first patent for it. Others were mathematicians, paleontologists, and writers—and all demonstrate the rewards of curiosity and persistence.

**Keywords:** Inventors • Nonfiction collections • Science and technology

## Silverstein, Ken.

🏆 *The Radioactive Boy Scout: The Frightening True Story of a Whiz Kid and His Homemade Nuclear Reactor.* New York: Random House, 2004. ISBN 03755031X. Reissued by Villard, 2005. ISBN 0812966600. **J** **H**

David Hahn was not an average Boy Scout. While working for his atomic energy merit badge, he turned his obsession with chemistry into over-drive and set in motion a chain of events that endangered 40,000 residents in his Detroit suburb and necessitated the intervention of the EPA. How this could happen makes for an amazing and true story about family, ambition, and science. **BBYA**

**Keywords:** Atomic energy • Biography • Nuclear energy • Science

# History of Science

These books provide a combination of narrative and detail that makes them appealing to fans of both history and pure science. Readers are offered a leisurely reading experience incorporating a wealth of information.

## Bryson, Bill.

*A Short History of Nearly Everything.* New York: Broadway, 2003. ISBN 9780805059687. **J** **H** **A**

The mysteries of the universe remain unsolved because they are so complex that they took dedicated scientists, including geniuses, years of study and work to discover, much less comprehend. This magnificent volume does not try to explain all of them, yet with Bryson's trademark humor and willingness to look beyond the obvious, readers will learn the real story behind some of science's great discoveries, such as the age and weight of the earth, the Big Bang, and plate tectonics. These insights not only include how often the original people responsible have been left out of the historical record, but also the changes in scientific thought as new discoveries were made and acknowledgment of how much is left to learn.

**Keywords:** Essays • Science • Science history

## Hakim, Joy.

*The Story of Science: Aristotle Leads the Way.* Washington, DC: Smithsonian Books, 2004. ISBN 9781588341600. **M** **J** **H**

This book starts with ancient Sumer and follows the development, refinement, and advancements in science as it made room for physics, mathematics, and geometry up to the Renaissance. This highly illustrated, involving book demonstrates that science is "about uncertainty" by demonstrating the ideas, including that the earth was flat and has no history, that were "proved," accepted, and disproved as more knowledge was gained around the world.

**Keywords:** History of science • Scientific discoveries

## Thimmesh, Catherine, and Melissa Sweet.

*Girls Think of Everything: Stories of Ingenious Inventions by Women.* Boston: Houghton Mifflin, 2000. Reprint: Sandpiper, 2002. ISBN 141315297X. **M**

From the everyday practicalities that led women to invent liquid paper and the windshield wiper to the hard work and genius behind the inventions of Kevlar™ and the first computer compilers, women have been behind some of the most important inventions. Thimmesh covers twelve inventions that changed the way things were being done in a significant way, whether by saving time, making lives easier, or even saving lives. Two were the ideas of young girls; for example, Becky Schroder invented her glo-sheet at the age of ten. All of the women are presented in a few pages, with pertinent information about the inventions and quotations from the inventors themselves. A time line of women's inventions and further information for young inventors are included.

**Keywords:** Inventions • Inventors • Nonfiction collections • Women inventors

# Digging into the Past

In these books, readers have the opportunity to explore the past through everything from remains to monuments. Readers interested in history and forensics may find books they'll enjoy in these categories. The section is divided into two subsections, "Archaeology" and "Paleontology."

## Archaeology

These titles address the recovery and study of human remains and artifacts.

## Bahn, Paul G.

*Written in Bones: How Human Remains Unlock the Secrets of the Dead.* Toronto; Buffalo, NY: Firefly Books, 2003. ISBN 9781552976852. **J H**

Is it really possible to learn anything about someone's life when all one has to study is a skeleton? The forensic anthropologists who uncover the remains explored here in case studies show readers how science is used to inform and enlighten about many things: cause of death, burial rites, battle histories, religions, customs, and details about daily lives and cultures.

**Keywords:** Burial rites • Forensics • History of burials • Human remains (archaeology) • Tombs

## Deem, James M.

🐾 *Bodies from the Ash: Life and Death in Ancient Pompeii.* Boston: Houghton Mifflin, 2005. ISBN 0618473084. **M J**

The 20,000 citizens of Pompeii, one of Rome's largest cities, were killed when the long-dormant Mount Vesuvius erupted over two days in August AD 79, burying the entire city with lava. It wasn't until 1863 that an excavator found a method of using plaster casts to study the excavated human remains. James Deem explains the earthquakes and eruptions as well as the centuries of excavations, giving readers a glimpse into Pompeian society that includes depictions of several houses and stories about the lives of individual residents. His own photographs of Pompeii are added to photographs of the historic excavations, giving readers an insight into the discoveries that have been made about the city and the science used. **BBYA**

**Keywords:** Ancient history • Archaeology • Human remains (archaeology) • Mount Vesuvius • Pompeii

**Now Try:** This book does an exemplary job of explaining and illustrating the archaeology of excavating human remains. Deem's earlier book about the use of human remains as a window to the past in Iron Age northern Europe is *Bodies in the Bog,* in which readers are introduced to these finds as well as the ecology of the bogs that helped to preserve bodies since the 1600s and what archeologists have learned from them.

## Goldenberg, Linda.

*Little People and a Lost World: An Anthropological Mystery.* Discovery! Minneapolis, MN: Twenty-First Century Books, 2007. ISBN 9780822559832. **M** **J**

When a team of Australian archaeologists discovered a skeleton on the Indonesian Island of Flores in 2003 they assumed it was a child because of its diminutive size. They were astounded when it became evident that it was actually the remains of a three-foot-tall, thirty-year-old woman. Their discovery set off a storm of controversy and scientific argument when they announced that the skeleton was actually a new species. Find out about the roles of the geologists, palynologists, paleobotanists, paleoecologists, and paleobotanists on the team and their journey to try to identify the ancient fossil.

**Keywords:** Archaeology • Fossil hominids • Indonesia • Paleontology • Pygmies

## Lauber, Patricia.

*Who Came First: New Clues to Prehistoric Americans.* Washington, DC: National Geographic, 2003. ISBN 9780792282280. **M** **J**

Archaeological discoveries, coupled with scientific contributions from several fields including genetics, have contributed to the development of new theories about how people came to the American continents, bringing into question the belief that the first Native Americans were from the "Clovis" culture. To this day, this debate remains unresolved. Readers will learn about the different theories and how they have been adapted, modified, and outright disproved as new evidence has been discovered in this ongoing and fascinating mystery.

**Keywords:** American antiquities • Archaeology • Indian origins

## Sloan, Christopher

*Bury the Dead: Tombs, Corpses, Mummies, Skeletons & Rituals.* Washington, DC: National Geographic, 2002. ISBN 0792271920. **M** **J**

For thousands of years, cultures around the world have followed different practices for burying their dead. The study of those practices and of the dead, through both anthropological and archaeological means, reveals much about the cultures. Using photographs from *National Geographic*, Christopher Sloan shows remains and tells readers what can be inferred from different customs and rites, some of which are quite disturbing. Sloan goes beyond the standard Egyptian mummies and covers historical peoples around the world, including the Qin dynasty's terra-cotta soldiers, Scythians, and pre-Incans. Time lines and maps will also be useful in research projects.

**Keywords:** Ancient Egypt • Anthropology • Archaeology • Burial customs • Funeral rites • Mummies • Qin dynasty • Scythians • Tombs

**Now Try:** Readers interested in anthropology are often confronted with the grisly facts of death. In *Corpses, Coffins, and Crypts: A History of Burial,* Penny Colman examines the history of death and burial rites in cultures around the world. She balances the facts with anecdotes to make this a surprisingly readable book. Readers are given answers to many questions about death and burial, as well as a look at some of the most famous burial sites around the world.

## Tanaka, Shelley.

*Mummies: The Newest, Coolest & Creepiest from Around the World.* Toronto: Madison Press; New York: Harry N. Abrams, 2005. ISBN 0810957973. **M**

Although most people link the Egyptians to the process of mummification, Tanaka points out that they were not the only culture that practiced this procedure; it also happened naturally after death in several parts of the world because of the climate. Through grisly photographs, readers are shown mummies from different continents and different ages, from the oldest known mummy to newly preserved and maintained modern mummies. Tanaka introduces the technological advances that allow scientists to find out what life was like for the people who became the mummies, introducing readers to the scientific importance that accompanies research.

**Keywords:** Archaeology • Mummies • Social science

**Now Try:** Egyptian archaeologist Zahi Hawass uses the fascinating superstitions surrounding King Tut's tomb as the starting point of *The Curse of the Pharaohs: My Adventures with Mummies.* What will keep readers interested are his descriptions of excavations involving hundreds of mummies at Bahariya Oasis, complete with pictures of both mummies and artifacts, as well as the stories of archaeology's dangers and excitements, told in a storytelling style with panache and enthusiasm.

## Wilcox, Charlotte.

🐾 *Mummies, Bones & Body Parts.* Minneapolis, MN: Carolrhoda Books, 2000. ISBN 9781575054285. **M** **J**

The author starts with the death of a noble woman 2,400 years ago and considers what her tribe would do with her remains. Through case studies, she explains what scientists can learn from mummies and skeletons. Anthropologists and archaeologists can tell us a lot about a culture from human remains, and science has progressed to the point where we now can learn about people's lives and deaths from their remains and the ceremonies with which they were laid to rest. The photographs certainly don't make this one for the squeamish, but if interested in the subject, readers will be quickly drawn in and offered many additional resources. **QP**

**Keywords:** Anthropology • Archaeology • Funeral rites • Mummies • Human remains (archaeology)

**Now Try:** Readers fascinated with this subject are not alone. A title that looks at specific cases is Johan Reinhard's *The Ice Maiden: Inca Mummies, Mountain Gods, and Sacred Sites in the Andes*. Donna M. Jackson explores the job done by forensic anthropologists in *The Bone Detectives*.

## Paleontology

Books in this subgenre examine the recovery and identification of fossil evidence.

### Halls, Kelly Milner, and Rick Spears.

*Dinosaur Mummies: Beyond Bare-Bone Fossils.* Plain City, OH: Darby Creek, 2003. Reprinted 2007. ISBN 1428717811. **M J**

Halls's passion for her subject shines through in this book, which starts with an explanation of her interest in reptiles and paleontology. Readers will learn about fossilization and the various forms of dinosaur fossils that have been found, including dinosaur mummies. Unlike most dinosaur books, this one concentrates on specific finds, from the 1908 Sternberg discovery of an Edmontosaurus to Leonardo, an almost complete Brachylophosaurus discovered in 2000. Stories are packed with information about the scientists, the dinosaurs, photographs, and drawings of what the dinosaurs might have looked like. Further research is easy with the lists of resources, Web sites, dvds, and dig sites.

**Keywords:** Dinosaurs • Fossils • Paleontology

**Now Try:** Dinosaurs continue to engage readers' interests because of the new and exciting discoveries and evolutions in science and paleontology. The third edition of *Dougal Dixon's Dinosaurs* includes twelve new finds in its dinosaur profiles, as well as updated information about fossil formations. The table of contents and index will help interested readers find specific information in the wealth of facts offered in this one book. Readers will find some predictions for possible evolutionary developments after the next ice age in Dixon's *The Future Is Wild*, which is listed in the "How Things Work" section.

### Dingus, Lowell, Luis M. Chiappe, and Rodolfo A. Coria.

*Dinosaur Eggs Discovered!: Unscrambling the Clues.* Minneapolis, MN: Twenty-First Century Books, 2008. ISBN 9780882567912. **M J**

In 1997 three scientists set off to Argentina on a mission to find fossils of birds in Patagonia. On only their second day, they were stunned to find themselves in a basin of sandstone that contained an absolute treasure for paleontologists: fossilized dinosaur eggs, in what would prove to be a dinosaur nesting ground. Readers will join this scientific team as they unravel the mysteries of the eggs and the rock layers in which they were found.

**Keywords:** Dinosaur eggs • Fossils • Paleontology • Patagonia

## Sabuda, Robert.

*Mega-beasts.* Encyclopedia Prehistorica. Cambridge, MA: Candlewick Press, 2007. ISBN 9780763622305. **M RR**

The final volume of the Encyclopedia Prehistorica will undoubtedly change readers' minds about pop-up books being only for kids. Starting with the Mesozoic era on the first of the six double-page spreads of this book, a mighty quetzalcoatlus cleverly unfolds from the pages and towers over them. Each page has at least one additional three-dimensional pop-up, integrating information with colorful engineering more appropriate for older children. The combination of interesting facts and the multiple leaves of many of the pop-ups will ensure that readers will go through this repeatedly in order not to miss anything.

**Keywords:** Extinct animals • Fossil animals • Pop-up books

# How Things Work

The books in this section center on technology and the experimentation and work required to advance scientific knowledge. They serve as a reminder that the hard work required to attain knowledge is time-consuming and a part of a lengthy, rigorous process. This category is divided into two subsections, "General" and "Transportation."

## General

The books here cover scientific investigations, inner workings, and various technologies. They provide a narrower scope for looking at research, inventions, and how the scientific method is being put to use than those works found in the "History of Science" section.

## Dixon, Dougal, and John Adams.

*The Future Is Wild.* Toronto; Buffalo, NY: Firefly Books, 2003. ISBN 9781552977248. **J**

Taking into consideration the changes that have affected our planet over the millennia, scientists posit what the future could bring 5, 100, and 200 million years from now, after an ice age or in a global "hot house." The creatures that will populate the planet after the "human" era are described and illustrated, making for an intriguing discussion of continental drift, evolution, and ecology. Scientists in many different fields were consulted for this fun look at what could lie ahead for the planet's denizens.

**Keywords:** Ecological succession • Evolution • Natural history

## Ferris, Timothy.

♟ *Seeing in the Dark: How Backyard Stargazers Are Probing Deep Space and Guarding Earth from Interplanetary Peril.* New York : Simon & Schuster, 2002. ISBN 0684865793. **H A**

Timothy Ferris is a science writer and lifelong stargazer. Here he recounts how he became entranced by the night sky, and tells tales of other amateur astronomers and their amazing discoveries. Advancements in technology, to which he introduces readers along with the astronomers, have allowed these dedicated nonprofessionals to make such astounding discoveries as James O'Meara's measurement of the length of Uranus's day. The inclusion of star charts may entice new stargazers into their backyards. **Alex**

Keywords: Astronomers • Astronomy

## Macaulay, David.

*The New Way Things Work.* Boston: Houghton Mifflin, 1998. ISBN 0395938473. **M J**

This update of Macaulay's original version of this work expands a section on computers and removes obsolete mechanisms such as record players. The book itself remains a combination of text, illustrated cutaways, and mammoth guide, providing a reliable and fun explanation of technology and science.

Keywords: Science and technology • Technology

## Roach, Mary.

♟ *Stiff: The Curious Lives of Human Cadavers.* New York: W.W. Norton, 2003. ISBN 0393050939. **H A**

What happens to their bodies after people die? Readers are offered a thorough examination of all possible uses of cadavers. What could have been very grotesque subject matter is infused with humor, empathy, and care. The practical uses that scientists make of every part of the human body are interspersed with several amazing and even absurd stories. Overall the book sends a profound message dealing with the respect with which these bodies are treated and lets readers know that death is definitely *not* a boring subject. **Alex, BBYA**

Keywords: Cadavers • Death and dying • Forensics • Medical ethics • Medical research

Now Try: After discussing what happens to the body after death, Roach next tackled the subject of the soul. In *Spook: Science Tackles the Afterlife,* she employs scientific and occult methods to try to find evidence of the soul and what happens to it. Her travels around the world as a dubious believer on a trail to find evidence make for an enjoyable journey. Readers with a much stronger stomach and an inclination toward crime can find out about Annie Cheney's investigation into the extremely grisly, macabre, and profitable selling of body parts. Her award-winning article became the basis for her book *Body Brokers: Inside America's Underground Trade in Human Remains.*

## Slavin, Bill.

🌷 *Transformed: How Everyday Things Are Made.* Toronto: Kids Can Press, 2005. ISBN 1553371798. **M**

Slavin shows the process, including the raw materials and manufacturing steps, in the production of sixty-nine items from baseballs to ice cream and books. Historical information is included, along with artwork to aid understanding and add interest. This title was awarded the 2006 Norma Fleck Award for best Canadian children's nonfiction. **Norma Fleck**

**Keywords:** Manufacturing • Science and technology

## Szpirglas, Jeff.

*They Did What?!: Your Guide to Weird & Wacky Things People Do.* **Illustrated by Dave Whamond.** Toronto: Maple Tree Press, 2005. ISBN 1897066228. **M** **RR** **BB**

The author looks at strange things that people have done, whether they were fads that are best forgotten, hoaxes that people like to think happened, or errors that led to actual inventions or scientific advances, such as the discoveries of penicillin and shatterproof safety glass. Tales are told in short, amusing vignettes with accompanying brightly colored illustrations. This is a book that may be read a bit at a time, and the oddity of the trivia is likely to appeal to reluctant readers.

**Keywords:** Fads • Hoaxes • Inventions

## Swanson, Diane.

*Nibbling on Einstein's Brain: The Good, the Bad and the Bogus in Science.* **Illustrated by Warren Clark.** Toronto: Annick Press, 2001. ISBN 1550376861. **M** **J**

Swanson offers a clear way to assess scientific claims and research and to understand how to differentiate between good and bad science. She explains the "stepping stones" of science and how critical thinking may be applied to science, the media, and any other source of information. Advice is given about where and when to apply a healthy skepticism about scientific claims. Readers will find this information useful in many ways, particularly in research.

**Keywords:** Advertising • Experimentation • Research • Science • Scientific method

## Tambini, Michael.

*Future.* Eyewitness Books. New York: DK Publishing, 2004. ISBN 9780756606848. **M** **J**

Looking through a historical time line of the major innovations and changes of the twentieth century, one can see that much has changed. Just one example is Internet use; the first transatlantic radio broadcast was in 1901. Readers are invited to consider what might happen in biology, technology, habitats, the environment, and so much more as people continue to learn, expand their horizons, multiply, and develop new technologies to deal with a changing world and environmental concerns.

**Keywords:** Forecasting • Technological forecasting

## Wilson, Daniel H.

🎗 *How to Survive a Robot Uprising: Tips on Defending Yourself Against the Coming Rebellion.* New York: Bloomsbury, 2005. ISBN 1582345929. **H**

A roboticist from Carnegie Mellon University felt the best way to protect humanity from an impending and inevitable robot mutiny was to inform people about all of the advances in robotics that have put humans in danger. Once readers have an awareness of these remarkable advances, they will understand his proposed defenses and thus be able to save humanity from the machines. **PP, QP**

**Keywords:** Humor • Robots • Technology

**Now Try:** Information on the development and uses of robotics, without the humorous overtones, is readily available in Rodger Bridman's *Robot*. Readers will find the short, clear text and photographs they expect from an <u>Eyewitness</u> book, along with examples of many automated devices and systems used in a number of different fields. They will go beyond the history and uses of robots to a discussion of artificial intelligence and philosophical implications in David Jones's *Mighty Robots: Mechanical Marvels That Fascinate and Frighten*.

## Transportation

A child's early interest in pictures of cars and trains evolves into a teen's desire to own a vehicle or to travel: These are the enthralling books that help explain the different modes of transportation and how they work. How does a plane stay in the air? Readers will find out in the *Book of Flight: The Smithsonian National Air and Space Museum*. Repair manuals may be found in chapter 9.

## Rinard, Judith E.

*Book of Flight: The Smithsonian National Air and Space Museum.* Richmond Hill, ON: Firefly Books, 2007. ISBN 9781554072927. **J H**

Following a path through the discoveries that enabled humans to create flying machines, this book covers every step in the journey—from the first model gliders to the building of the International Space Station and the potential for a mission to Mars. Readers will discover how aviation was used and adapted in the twentieth century; meet the great pilots; and see awesome photos of the different planes, jets, and space vehicles.

**Keywords:** Aeronautics • Astronautics • Aviation • Space flight

## Smedman, Lisa.

*From Boneshakers to Choppers: The Rip-roaring History of Motorcycles.* Toronto: Annick Press, 2007. ISBN 9781554510160. **M J H**

Motorcycles have come a long way from the 1800s, when a steam engine was mounted to a "penny-farthing" bicycle. This chronological history looks at the evolution of motorcycles and the people who ride them, as they were given safety features, developed wider use, and entered popular culture. One of the interesting and ongoing features of this book is an examination of the changing demographics for motorcyclists, demonstrated in the changing marketing and media use, and in the different ridership, including women, clubs, and ongoing competition with scooter riders.

**Keywords**: Motorbikes • Motorcycles

## Sutton, Richard.

*Car*. <u>DK Eyewitness Books</u>. New York: DK Publishing, 2005. ISBN 9780756613938. **M** **J**

How did we get from the horseless carriage to the high performance vehicles that tear around racetracks? Who are the major figures behind the developments in engineering, and how does an engine work, anyway? Readers can count on this volume in the <u>DK Eyewitness Books</u> series to take them on a well-illustrated journey through the history of cars, guaranteed to make them appreciate all the comfort and technology that go into a modern car.

**Keywords**: Automobiles • History of transportation • Machinery

## Willson, Quentin.

*The Ultimate Classic Car Book*. New York: Dorling Kindersley, 1995. ISBN 0756618851. **J** **H**

Quentin Willson starts out by defining what makes a car a "classic" in order to set out the parameters for the choices that make this a book for all car buffs. Ninety of his favorite models are laid out in double-page spreads, with color pictures, specifications, brief histories, and features noted.

**Keywords**: Antique cars • Automobiles • Classic cars

## Wilson, Hugo.

*Ultimate Harley-Davidson*. New York: Dorling Kindersley, 2003. ISBN 0789499746. **J** **H** **A**

A century of Harley-Davidsons are presented in this glossy book, designed to show how Harley-Davidson evolved into one of the great names in motorcycles. Organized chronologically, Wilson offers a history of the company and the developments that accompanied the fifty bikes he chose to present in his gallery of the best Harley-Davidson models. Readers will see not only the 1999 models but also the Twin Cam engine and how it works. A complete Harley-Davidson catalog is included.

**Keywords**: Harley-Davidson • Motorcycles

## Zimmermann, Karl.

*All Aboard!: Passenger Trains Around the World*. Honesdale, PA: Boyds Mills Press, 2004. ISBN 9781590783252. **M**

A true devotee of trains and train travel has produced a colorful introduction to the history and current status of passenger trains. The main chapters cover the development of passenger cars, followed by trains in the United States, Canada, and Europe. The trains and routes they travel are highlighted by a number of photographs. A final chapter covers excursions, a popular form of train travel today.

**Keywords**: Passenger trains • Railroads • Trains

**Now Try:** With a passion for travel and exploring the history of forms of transportation, Karl Zimmerman next turned his attention to the water in *Steamboats: The Story of Lakers, Ferries, and Majestic Paddle-Wheelers.* Readers looking for information on trains might not be as enthusiastic as Zimmerman about the passenger aspect of train travel. For those readers, John Coiley's *Train* may provide an acceptable alternative. With the trademark combination of photographs and information expected in the Eyewitness Books series, this title covers developments in trains and takes readers behind the scenes.

# Micro-science

As mentioned by Sarah Statz Cords, (2006), *micro-science* is not yet an accepted term. However, it is adapted for use here based on the popularity of the "micro-history" category. The authors in this category focus on a narrowly defined subject. Authors on these subjects—which include diseases, technology, and food—have a wide range of styles and themes.

## Beck, Gregor Gilpin.

*Watersheds: A Practical Handbook for Healthy Water.* **Illustrated by Clive Dobson.** Willowdale, ON: Firefly Books, 1999. Reprinted 2001, ISBN 1552093301; 9781552093306. **J** **H**

This book introduces readers to the paths taken as water passes in and out of the various watersheds in North America. The author and illustrator provide a readable and logical discussion of the biomes water may enter and the various ecosystems found there, as well as the issues faced by scientists, environmentalists, and ecologists.

**Keywords:** Air pollution • Biomes • Ecology • Water pollution • Watersheds

## Buckingham, Alan.

*Photography.* Eyewitness Books. New York: Dorling Kindersley, 2004. ISBN 9780756605438. **M** **J**

This book follows the development of the camera from the camera obscura to the digital camera in this volume in the DK Eyewitness Books series. As cameras become more sophisticated, so does photography, allowing for advances in movement, color, and special effects. A time line, index, glossary, and list of facts will help readers find specific information. Browsers will find interesting facts on any page.

**Keywords:** Cameras • Photography

## Buller, Laura.

*Food.* Eyewitness Books. London; New York: DK Publishing, 2005. ISBN 9780756611729. **M** **J**

This guide shows many different aspects of food, from how and where it is produced to what food means to different cultures. Readers will also find out how opinions have changed about nutrition, allergies, and food preparation as well as information about eating a balanced diet. Numerous enticing illustrations enhance the text.

**Keywords:** Digestion • Food • Nutrition

**Now Try:** *Hungry Planet: What the World Eats* presents a truly unique introduction to food and how it is seen around the world, showing how thirty families in twenty-four countries eat over the course of a week. Photojournalist Peter Menzel and Faith D'Aluisio share the pictures that show a German family's $500 weekly budget as well as a Darfur family's $1.44 weekly allotment. A completely different look at food is Eric Schlosser's and Charles Wilson's *Chew on This: Everything You Don't Want to Know About Fast Food*. With obesity on the rise and a corporate mentality that has been copied not only among the various fast food companies but in the nation's schools, perhaps it is a good thing to find out what is going on behind the counters of one's favorite franchise and how it got that way.

## Diclaudio, Dennis.

🦋 *The Hypochondriac's Pocket Guide to Horrible Diseases You Probably Already Have.* New York: Bloomsbury Publishing, 2005. ISBN 1596910615. **H**

Diclaudio has gathered the forty-five most repugnant, unpleasant, absolutely real maladies into one journal. Each is presented with a list of symptoms, diagnosis, prognosis, and tips for prevention. A perfect way to make sure all hands are washed, if not boiled, is to read about Bejel, otherwise known as endemic syphilis, which is transmitted by touch alone. Never fear, prevention is very simple: "Don't touch anyone. Don't let anyone touch you." This is a very handy guide from a member of Elsevier's Infectious Disease Department, with an index in case the reader hasn't had time to make it through enough medical journals to track down symptoms from the friend-of-a-friend. **PP**

**Keywords:** Disease • Humor

## Gay, Kathlyn, and Christine Whittington.

*Body Marks: Tattooing, Piercing, and Scarification.* Brookfield, CT: Millbrook Press, 2002. ISBN 9780761323525. **J H**

Ears certainly aren't the only things that are pierced anymore. Celebrities have multiple tattoos. We have come a long way from the days when a tattoo or brand was a symbol of ownership. Readers will find out about the history of these practices, from ancient civilization to modern times. The potential drawbacks of a permanent body decoration are also explained. This is a must read for anyone considering undergoing a piercing or getting a tattoo.

**Keywords:** Body marking • Body piercing • Scarification • Tattooing

**Now Try:** Readers seriously interested in body art will definitely want to do some research with books such as Jean-Chris Miller's *The Body Art Book: A Complete, Illustrated Guide to Tattoos, Piercings, and Other Body Modification*. This book, which was chosen for the 1999 Popular Paperbacks list, looks at different kinds of body art. Readers more interested in a superficial look at tattoos may prefer *Tattoo Nation: Portraits of Celebrity Body Art*. This title was chosen in 2004 as a Quick Pick for Reluctant Readers.

## Koppes, Steven N.

*Killer Rocks from Outer Space: Asteroids, Comets, and Meteorites.* Discovery! Minneapolis, MN: Lerner Publications, 2004. ISBN 9780822528616. **M** **J** **H**

In 1994 comet SL9 collided with Jupiter. Although such impacts have happened many times, this was the first time that scientists had witnessed an actual impact. Readers will see what a crater looks like, what craters tell scientists about Earth's history, and what scientists are doing with their increasing knowledge.

**Keywords:** Asteroids • Comets • Meteorites

**Now Try:** Astronomy is a captivating science, with new discoveries and developments to fire the imagination happening all the time. Readers will find both scientific history and particulars of the individual subjects in the Worlds Beyond series. Ron Miller gives readers a chance to get a close look in *Asteroids, Comets, and Meteors* or *Stars and Galaxies,* which starts with the birth of the solar system and follows scientific developments up to the present day. Numerous photographs, a glossary, and further resources are some of the additional material offered in these thorough series books.

## Langley, Andrew.

*Hurricanes, Tsunamis, and Other Natural Disasters.* Boston: Kingfisher, 2006. ISBN 9780753459751. **M** **RR**

This fast-paced, highly illustrated book divides natural disasters into four major types. First, the restless earth covers both earthquakes and tsunamis. Then chapter 2 looks at volcanoes. This is followed by storms, floods, and snow in chapter 3, and the final chapter covers at droughts, fires, and diseases. Each chapter considers the major causes and effects of the disasters on human populations and brims with photographic material, maps, and suggested Web sites. Readers will also learn about the science behind predicting events and be given a look at relief efforts.

**Keywords:** Floods • Hurricanes • Natural disasters • Storms • Tsunamis

## McClafferty, Carla Killough.

*The Head Bone's Connected to the Neck Bone: The Weird, Wacky, and Wonderful X-ray.* New York: Farrar, Straus & Giroux, 2001. ISBN 0374329087. **M** **J**

William Roentgen's discovery of X-rays in 1895 amazed the world, becoming as popular as a sideshow treat as it was for medical purposes. McClafferty's time line points out how long it took for science to become aware of the dangers of radiation and discusses the numerous fields that make use of this invention, supplementing all with photographs.

**Keywords:** Inventions • Radiography • Science • X-rays

### Symes, R. F., and R. R. Harding.

*Crystal & Gem.* <u>Eyewitness Books</u>. New York: DK Publishing, 2007. ISBN 9780756630010. **M** **J**

> Crystals, solid materials in which the basic materials are arranged in a regular pattern, are explained, examined, and illustrated in a captivating discussion of these sparkling and useful substances. The book takes a close look at some of the best known gems and crystals, and readers will also find out about the natural and man-made production of crystals and some of the other uses of these often hidden wonders, from liquid crystal displays to vitamin C.
>
> **Keywords:** Crystallography • Crystals • Precious stones

### Szpirglas, Jeff. Illustrated by Ramon Perez.

*Fear This Book: Your Guide to Fright, Horror, & Things That Go Bump in the Night.* Toronto: Maple Tree Press, 2006. ISBN 189706666X. **M**

> Jeff Szpirglas looks at different types of fear, from involuntary reactions to emotional responses. The body's reactions are described and ways of dealing with fears are suggested. Many different and amusing frightful things are examined, from ghosts and superstitions to reptiles and phobias. Cartoon artwork livens up what could otherwise be a spooky subject.
>
> **Keywords:** Emotions • Fear • Feelings • Ghosts • Monsters

### Szpirglas, Jeff.

🏃 *Gross Universe: Your Guide to All Disgusting Things under the Sun.* Toronto: Maple Tree Press, 2004. Reprinted 2005. ISBN 1894379640. **M** **J** **RR**

> Szpirglas discusses the bodily emissions of humans, animals, and insects, acknowledging that they are entirely gross, meaning that they are presented in a way that is interesting and fun. Some thirty-eight researchers and experts are thanked for their help in gathering the information presented. **PP**
>
> **Keywords:** Bacteria • Health education • Human anatomy • Human behavior • Human biology • Science
>
> **Now Try:** Szpirglas shows science in a way that engages readers by bringing in fun adjectives and nouns, such as *fear, gross,* and *bodily emissions.* His titles catch a reader's eye. Sylvia Branzei's *Grossology: The Science of Really Gross Things* works in the same way. It is particularly appropriate for readers who can pair an interest in the subject of how their bodies work with a strong stomach.

## Environmental Writing

Readers looking for an acknowledgment of interest in environmental and ecological issues need look no further than Al Gore's 2007 Nobel Peace Prize for helping to raise awareness about man-made climate changes. In addition to titles that describe the fossil record and endangered animals, books are now being published for teen readers about plate tectonics and the damage that humans are causing on Earth, such as Shelley Tanaka's *Climate Change.* Readers interested in how the environment is being studied and what is being done to protect it will undoubtedly enjoy Molly Bang's combination picture book/graphic nonfiction book about marine ecology, which tells the story of one woman's quest to protect her local waters: *Nobody Particular: One Woman's Fight to Save the Bays.* This section is divided into two categories, "Ecology and Conservation" and "Animals." Books about the scientists who study endangered animals may be found in the "Adventures in Science" section.

## Ecology and Conservation

### Bang, Molly.

*Nobody Particular: One Woman's Fight to Save the Bays.* New York: Henry Holt, 2000. ISBN 9780805053968. **M** **J**

> Finding out that she lived in one of the most polluted counties in the entire country changed Diane Wilson's entire life. Her family had been shrimpers for four generations, giving her a love for the local bay and its waters. They would be in significant danger if the Formosa Plastics Corporation were to go ahead and build several new plants, especially since the company did not yet have the permits to do so, and no ecological studies had been undertaken. In this remarkable, graphic picture book, Wilson shows how her fight eventually led her to take on not just the corporation, but also the community and the EPA, for the sake of the local ecology.
>
> **Keywords:** Environmental protection • Environmentalism • Graphic nonfiction • Picture book nonfiction • Pollution • Waste disposal from chemical plants

### Burns, Loree Griffin.

🏵 *Tracking Trash: Flotsam, Jetsam, and the Science of Ocean Motion.* Scientists in the Field. Boston: Houghton Mifflin, 2007. ISBN 0618581316. **M** **J**

> Who would have guessed that a Nike sneaker washing up on a Seattle beach would lead an oceanographer to study ocean currents? Five containers of sneakers dumped in a larger cargo spill in 1990 did just that for scientist Curt Ebbesmeyer, also leading him to study other spills; develop a computer program for tracking drifts; and find explanations of latitude and longitude, waves, and gyres. In this readable and fact-filled book, which is a great resource for reports, readers will find copious information about what humans have put into the seas and its effects on the oceans and marine life that live in them. Especially welcome is a chapter on "what you can do." **BG-HB Honor**
>
> **Keywords:** Currents • Earth sciences • Environment • Garbage • Ocean

### Gore, Al.

🏵 *An Inconvenient Truth.* New York: Viking, 2007. ISBN 9780670062720. **M** **J**

> Global warming is not a new concept. The photographs in this book are powerful evidence of the changes that have occurred in the last century, showing where lakes and glaciers have melted. These, supplemented by graphs demonstrating population growth, rising temperatures, and greenhouse gas emissions, clearly explain the danger our planet is in.

This is an adaptation of the adult book intended to speak directly to the generation that must make the changes necessary to protect the planet. **ALA Notable**

**Keywords:** Environment • Global warming • Greenhouse gases

## Tanaka, Shelley.

*Climate Change.* <u>Groundwood Guides</u>. Toronto: Groundwood Books, 2006. ISBN 0888996799. **M J**

Although global warming is still a controversial topic, there is no doubt that there have been significant changes in the climate. Tanaka explains the science behind global warming, with a discussion of its possible causes, effects on plant and animal life, and what will happen in the future. This includes a discussion about what countries around the world are doing and suggestions for conserving energy.

**Keywords:** Climate • Energy • Global warming • Weather

**Now Try:** Readers interested in climate change may enjoy a graphic nonfiction title that explores environmental changes with an irreverent tone, Kate Evans's *Weird Weather: Everything You Didn't Want to Know About Climate Change But Probably Should Find Out.*

## Animals

The fascination that humans have with animals develops as very young children and remains a part of our lives. Human–animal relationships are the subject of Deborah Noyes's *One Kingdom: Our Lives with Animals: The Human–Animal Bond in Myth, History, Science, and Story.* The depth of attraction is reflected in the wide range of subjects, from Kelly Milner Halls's *Albino Animals* to Stephen Swinburne's *Saving Manatees.*

## Benchley, Peter, and Karen Wojtyla.

*Shark Life: True Stories About Sharks & the Sea.* New York: Delacorte Press, 2005. ISBN 0385731094. **M J**

Benchley's tales about diving with sharks and other sea creatures are a natural partner for information about these fascinating creatures of the deep. Readers are more likely to pay attention to the safety tips for safe surfing and swimming after reading some of Benchley's hair-raising encounters.

**Keywords:** Diving Shark attacks • Sharks

## Daigle, Evelyne, and Geneviève Wright. Illustrated by Daniel Grenier.

*The World of Penguins.* Toronto : Tundra Books, 2007. ISBN: 9780887767999. **M**

Evelyne Daigle gives readers more information about a popular group of birds than they are likely to have seen in one volume. Wildlife illustrator Daniel Grenier paints the seventeen species of penguins found in Antarctica in one comparative illustration as part of an introduction to the penguin world. Readers learn about their diet, reproduction, predators, habitat, threats to their ongoing survival, and the scientists who are studying them. Photographs from the author's travel journal add to the illustrations and are likely to tempt readers into using the bibliography or Web sites listed for further research.

**Keywords:** Antarctica • Ornithology • Penguins

## Greenberg, Nicki.

*It's True! An Octopus Has Deadly Spit.* It's True! Series. Toronto: Annick Press, 2007. ISBN 1554510775. **M** **J** **RR**

> Greenberg easily conveys her fascination with cephalopods for readers in this slim, fun volume. Chapters include information on the types of ocean dwellers in the cephalopod family, their incredible intelligence, their physical prowess, and the dangers inherent in getting close to them. Each chapter is supplemented with colorful pictures, and the book is likely to lead budding scientists to the recommended resources list.
>
> **Keywords:** Cephalopods • Octopus • Squid

## Halls, Kelly Milner.

🎃 *Albino Animals.* Plain City, OH: Darby Creek Publishing, 2004. ISBN 1581960123. **M** **RR**

> Halls pairs the basic science of this rare trait with straightforward text and pictures in an attractive format. The chapters are grouped by animal category, which makes for easy browsing, and the narrative is supplemented with interesting facts and anecdotes. **QP**
>
> **Keywords:** Albinism • Animals

## Harrington, Jane, and Bill Henderson.

*Extreme Pets!* New York: Tangerine Press/Scholastic, 2006. ISBN 9780439829489. **M** **J** **RR**

> This book considers the alternatives to having a labrador, siamese, or budgie as a pet. Chapters organize pets into four categories: cold-blooded, pocket pets, insects, and slimy. All choices are graded for coolness, aroma, neatness, ease of care, and cost, and the author explains exactly what one needs to know before bringing one of these interesting animals home. If readers are really interested and the great color photographs aren't enough of an enticement, suggestions are also provided on how to approach mom and dad.
>
> **Keywords:** Amphibians • Animals • Insects • Invertebrates • Pets • Reptiles

## Nouvian, Claire.

*The Deep: The Extraordinary Creatures of the Abyss.* Chicago: University of Chicago Press, 2007. ISBN 9780226595665. **H** **A**

> The single largest habitat on Earth is also the one about which the least is known. Unknown specimens are still being recovered from the depths of the oceans at an astounding rate. This beautiful coffee-table book offers breathtaking color photographs of the denizens of the deep, perfect for browsing, as well as fifteen essays from scientists that inform readers about all aspects of this environment. The source list includes both books and films.
>
> **Keywords:** Marine life • Nature • Science • Zoology
>
> **Now Try:** The seas are full of beings, ranging from beautiful to hideous. Erich Hoyt points out to readers that the use of the word "creature" is not always indica-

tive that an animal is a "monster," in *Creatures of the Deep: In Search of the Sea's "Monsters" and the World They Live In.*

### Noyes, Deborah.

*One Kingdom: Our Lives with Animals: The Human–Animal Bond in Myth, History, Science, and Story.* Boston: Houghton Mifflin, 2006. ISBN 9780618499144. M J H

Humans have shared the planet with animals as long as we have lived on it. The ways in which humans have interacted with animals have changed and evolved over time and in different cultures. Animals have been worshiped, domesticated, displayed, used as food sources, and endangered by our actions. An exploration of the evolving nature of these relations allows readers to think about this evolution in our relationships and what it means. Debates on conservation and using animals in entertainment are just a few of the discussions. **BBYA**

**Keywords:** Human–animal relationships • Psychology of animals

### Scott, Elaine.

*Poles Apart: Why Penguins and Polar Bears Will Never Be Neighbors.* New York: Viking, 2004. ISBN 0670059250; 9780670059256. M J

This volume presents an overview of the poles and their differences. A wide range of topics is covered, including seasons, magnetism, continental drift, the poles' contrasting climates, wildlife, explorers and settlers. Scientific discussions include research and potential changes caused by global warming.

**Keywords:** Antarctica • Continental drift • Penguins • Polar exploration • Polar regions

### Swinburne, Stephen.

*Saving Manatees.* Honesdale, PA: Boyds Mills Press, 2006. ISBN 9781590783191. M

Meet the unusual, likely unfamiliar, gentle giant that roams in wildlife refuges in Florida's "manatee county." Although these bewhiskered behemoths have been around long enough to be found in fossil records, those left are now facing unprecedented dangers from boaters and developers. Wildlife refuges offer information about these entrancing creatures, from their physiology to their behavior.

**Keywords:** Endangered animals • Manatees

## Consider Starting with . . .

These are some recommended titles for readers new to the genre.

Deem, James M. *Bodies from the Ash: Life and Death in Ancient Pompeii.*

Halls, Kelly Milner. *Albino Animals.*

Harrington, Jane, and Bill Henderson. *Extreme Pets!*

McClafferty, Carla Killough. *The Head Bone's Connected to the Neck Bone: The Weird, Wacky, and Wonderful X-Ray.*

Montgomery, Sy. *Quest for the Tree Kangaroo: An Expedition to the Cloud Forest of New Guinea.*

Rinard, Judith E. *Book of Flight: The Smithsonian National Air and Space Museum.*

Silverstein, Ken. *The Radioactive Boy Scout: The Frightening True Story of a Whiz Kid and His Homemade Nuclear Reactor.*

Szpirglas, Jeff, and Dave Whamond. *They Did What?: Your Guide to Weird & Wacky Things People Do.*

## Fiction Read-Alikes

- **Anderson, M. T.** In *Feed*, Titus lives in a world in which everything—information, marketing, media, conversation, and education—is available and regulated by corporate America through the feed linked straight into his brain. This isn't a problem, until his feed is hacked. This was chosen as one of YALSA's 2005 Best of the Best titles.

- **Crichton, Michael.** Readers who aren't scared of books that turn science and technology into gripping page-turners need look no further than Michael Crichton's books. Science offers both large and small nightmares in his work, from the horror of dinosaurs run amok in *Jurassic Park* to the nanotechnology in *Prey* and genetic engineering in *Next*.

- **Green, John.** When failed child prodigy Colin Singleton is dumped by his nineteenth girlfriend (all named Katherine), his best friend Hassan takes him on a road trip to cheer him up. Green's phenomenal humor is shown in the Printz Honor Book *An Abundance of Katherines*, in which Colin develops a mathematical theorem to predict the nature of all relationships. The math is explained in footnotes.

- **Hiaasen, Carl.** Carl Hiaasen provides readers with several feisty and determined protagonists determined to protect their local environment. In *Flush*, Noah is going to try to help save both his father and the local waters from waste; in *Hoot* the heroes want to save some burrowing owls.

- **McNaughton, Janet.** In *The Secret Under My Skin*, McNaughton presents a frightening, dystopian view of the future after a man-made, technological disaster. Blay Raytee is a valuable commodity in this world, one of its only "bio-indicators."

## References

Cords, Sarah Statz. 2006. *The Real Story: A Guide to Nonfiction Reading Interests*. <u>Genreflecting Advisory Series</u>. Westport, CT: Libraries Unlimited, 2006.

# Chapter 7

## Sports

## Definition

Sports by nature are competitive: People compete against themselves or others. To succeed in competition, a person must acquire the necessary skills to participate in the chosen activity and be able to maintain the activity for the amount of time it takes to finish.

Nonfiction titles in this area fulfill several purposes. Readers may find information about a sport that will help them improve their ability to prepare for, participate in, or be a more qualified spectator of an activity. On the other hand, they can also find stories about sports stars or role models. These books also feature heroes, high endurance, fighting against the odds, and lots of challenges.

## Appeal

Sports and games are more popular than ever. Teams have devoted fans who know their standings and the statistics of their favorite players on a day-to-day basis.

Many of the books in the "Rules and Tips" section use color photographs to show athletes breaking records, doing signature moves, and participating in "extreme sports." Several of these titles have been chosen as Quick Picks for Reluctant Readers. Yet readers do not need to be able to play a sport themselves to feel the pull of a well-written book; sports biographies offer stories with underdogs, heroes, races for a finish line, and breaking of records. These titles also appeal to readers who enjoy the "Sports Adventures" found in chapter 1.

## Chapter Organization

The "Sports Biographies" section includes fast-paced, engaging stories of heroes and people committed to becoming the best and attaining their goals. To participate in a sport or game, one must understand how it works, so the "Rules and Tips" section lists books that explain particular sports as well as how to participate in and excel at them. This is followed by "The Greatest Games" section, which covers sports histories, legends, and stories. The final section, "Sports in Action," contains collections of photographs and coffee table books.

## Sports Biographies

Athletes are heroic icons to many poeple. The qualities necessary to become a top competitor in any sport are admirable—strength, determination, self-discipline, and courage. A story behind the struggle to get to the finish line, a podium, or the end of a season has many appealing elements for readers, including exciting competitions, teamwork, drive, and overcoming difficulties. The sports-minded reader will often feel an empathy with the subject and seek validation of his or her own struggles.

### Burgan, Michael, and Brian Bascle.

*Muhammad Ali: American Champion.* Graphic Library. Mankato, MN: Capstone Press, 2008. ISBN 9781429601535. **M** **J** **RR**

The life of Muhammad Ali, born Cassius Clay, is presented in an enticing and readable graphic format as part of the Graphic Library. Readers will learn about the main events in his fascinating life and career, with actual quotations presented in a yellow box and an additional page of facts at the end. Interested readers may obtain more information from a list of suggested titles, or by entering the book's identification number at facthound.com.

**Keywords:** Ali, Muhammad • Boxers • Graphic nonfiction

### Cox, Lynne.

🏆 *Swimming to Antarctica: Tales of a Long-Distance Swimmer.* New York: A.A. Knopf, 2004. ISBN 9780375415074. **H**

What do a world-record, a goodwill visit from the United States to the Soviet Union, and the most dangerous three-mile stretch of water in the world have in common? They all relate to events in the remarkable thirty-year swimming career of the talented Lynne Cox, who discovered her propensity for open-water swimming at an early age and turned it into a lifetime of increasingly challenging tasks. There aren't many places in the world that her determination and devoted team haven't taken her, and readers will be able to experience both the dangers and her joy in making every attempt. **Alex**

**Keywords:** Cox, Lynne • Long-distance swimmers • Swimmers

### Doeden, Matt.

*Wayne Gretzky.* Sports Heroes and Legends. Minneapolis, MN: Twenty-First Century Books, 2008. ISBN 9780822571650. **M** **J**

Wayne Gretzky is synonymous with hockey. It's difficult to believe some people once thought that this hockey prodigy would be too small to play in the National Hockey League. Readers may follow the career of number 99 as he goes from the WHA to the Edmonton Oilers to the Hockey Hall of Fame.

**Keywords:** Gretzky, Wayne • Hockey players

### Finkel, Jon.

🏆 Greatest Stars of the NBA series. **RR** **BB**

Tokyopop introduced this sports series in their "cine-manga" format, in which they integrate full-sized digital images into cartoon spreads. With manga-style word balloons and captions that interpret the action, these books provide quick, fun reads loaded with information about some of today's most popular basketball stars. **QP**

*Jason Kidd.* Los Angeles: Tokyopop, 2004. ISBN 1595321829. **M** **RR**

Readers will see one of basketball's great point guards in action and get the inside scoop on his career path to his seventh all-star team in 2004.

**Keywords:** Basketball • Graphic nonfiction • Kidd, Jason • Point guard

*Tim Duncan.* Tokyopop, 2004. ISBN 1595321829. **M** **RR**

The pertinent moments of Tim Duncan's career are shown, including photographs that demonstrate his phenomenal bank shot. Readers will discover how he earned his two MVP awards.

**Keywords:** Basketball • Duncan, Tim • Graphic nonfiction

*Shaquille O'Neal.* Tokyopop, 2004. ISBN 1595321829. **M** **RR**

Finkel follows Shaq as he moves from the Lakers to the Miami Heat. The freeze-frame pictures highlight his famous blocks and dunks.

**Keywords:** Basketball • Graphic nonfiction • O'Neal, Shaquille

## Freedman, Russell.

🏃 *Babe Didrikson Zaharias: The Making of a Champion.* New York: Clarion, 1999. ISBN 0395633672; 9780395633670. **M** **J** **H**

Babe Didrikson Zaharias was a natural athlete at a time when women were neither encouraged nor accepted in sports. She competed with a basketball team before becoming an Olympic medalist, track star, and golfer, and arguably one of the greatest athletes of the twentieth century. **BBYA**

**Keywords:** Athletes • Sports • Zaharias, Babe Didrikson

## Hamilton, Bethany.

*Soul Surfer: A True Story of Faith, Family, and Fighting to Get Back on the Board.* New York: Pocket Books; MTV Books, 2004. ISBN 9780743499224; Trade pb., 2006; ISBN 9781416503460 **J**

The shark attack that took thirteen-year-old Bethany Hamilton's left arm made headlines around the world, not only because of the horrific nature of the attack, but also because of her determination to return to surfing. This is a fast-paced account of the attack and her dedication to her sport, as well as an acknowledgment of her family's support and faith as she journeyed back to the ocean that she loves.

**Keywords:** Amputations • Hamilton, Bethany • Recovery • Shark attacks • Surfing

## Hawk, Tony.

*Between Boardslides and Burnout: My Notes from the Road.* New York: ReganBooks, 2002. ISBN 9780060086312. **J** **H**

Tony Hawk is a superstar in the skateboarding world, the first person to successfully land a 900, two and a half rotations in the air. The reader will get a behind-the-scenes look at some of his tours, including the X-Games and the Teen Choice Awards, with a diary and color photographs provided by the man himself.

**Keywords:** Hawk, Tony • Skateboarder • Skateboarding

## Leonetti, Mike, and John Iaboni.

*Football Now!* Buffalo, NY; Richmond Hills, ON: Firefly Books, 2006. ISBN 1554071496. **J** **H**

This is not intended to be an instruction book for the sport; rather, it is a discussion of some of the NFL's best players. Eight chapters each take on a different position, with additional coverage for special teams and players to watch. Seventy players, including Drew Bledsoe and Ben Roethlisburger, are profiled. The commentary concentrates on their 2005 seasons, with added sidebars indicating their career highlights.

**Keywords:** Football • Football players • National Football League • Nonfiction collections • Quarterbacks

## McGrath, Jeremy, and Chris Palmer.

🏆 *Wide Open: A Life in Supercross.* New York: HarperEntertainment, 2004. ISBN 9780060537272. **H**

Supercross is a high-speed motorcycle sport held inside a stadium, with special motorcycles, steep jumps, and obstacles. The "King" of Supercross and one of the most successful racers in this relatively new sport explains what it took to make it to the top and stay there. Rivals, records, crashes, and comebacks are just a few of the things he deals with along the way in this high-octane story. **QP**

**Keywords:** McGrath, Jeremy • Motor sports • Supercross

## Miller, Timothy, and Steve Milton.

🏆 *NASCAR Now!.* Buffalo, NY; Richmond Hills, ON: Firefly, 2004. Reprinted 2006. ISBN 1554071488. **J** **H**

After an introduction and history of the popular sport for those new to it, Miller and Milton concentrate on the "business" of NASCAR, how it works, where it is run, and above all, whom to watch. Most of the book analyzes the top teams, drivers, and legends of the sport. Chosen as a Quick Pick for reluctant readers in 2005; there will be a new edition in 2008. **QP**

**Keywords:** NASCAR • Stock car racing

**Now Try:** Readers interested in a closer view of the sport will be interested in James Buckley Jr.'s *NASCAR* from the Eyewitness Books series. The books in the series provide the facts about one of the most popular spectator sports in the United States, complete with photographs and added information that make these volumes an appealing, eye-catching read. They identify the greatest drivers, their equipment, the procedures, and the tracks, with a glossary to help the reader understand what is going on. Janet Piehl's *Indy Race Cars* includes a history of Indy racing; information about Indy's racing cars and racing culture; and profiles of the greatest drivers, including Rick Mears, Helio "Spiderman" Castroneves, and Al Unser Sr.

## Morgan, David Lee.

🏵 *LeBron James: The Rise of a Star.* Cleveland, OH: Gray, 2003. ISBN 9781886228740. **J** **H**

LeBron James redefined high school sports in America. His amazing journey included national media appearances, consistently setting records in every year and gathering more attention than any other player before him. This six-foot-eight "gift to basketball" was no stranger to hardship and controversy, overcoming a difficult childhood and a scandal about promotions before becoming the number one pick in the 2003 NBA draft. **QP**

**Keywords:** Basketball • James, LeBron • NBA

**Now Try:** There is no doubt now that LeBron James was one of the best basketball players ever. When he played in high school, it was difficult to believe that a teenager could merit the attention being lavished upon him; but Ryan Jones, an editor at *SLAM*, a basketball magazine, was convinced. *King James: Believe the Hype: The LeBron James Story* shows readers the proof that James was always that good.

## Pitluk, Adam.

*Standing Eight: The Inspiring Story of Jesus "El Matador" Chavez, Who Became Lightweight Champion of the World.* Cambridge, MA: Da Capo Press, 2006. ISBN 9780306814549. **H** **A**

Most people probably have never heard of Gabriel Sandoval. His remarkable story includes his family entering the United States illegally, involvement in a gang, participation in a robbery that led to seven years in a maximum security facility, and deportation to Mexico. How can this history be reconciled with his becoming one of the world's greatest boxers? Gabriel's name change to Jesus "El Matador" Chavez was the first step on a journey that included becoming a youth counselor; acknowledging his background;and becoming a world champion in the featherweight, super-feather, and lightweight classes.

**Keywords:** Boxing • Chavez, Jesus • Gangs • Illegal immigration • World champion

## Platt, Larry.

🏵 *Only the Strong Survive: The Odyssey of Allen Iverson.* New York: ReganBooks, 2002. ISBN 9780060097738. **H**

Allen Iverson's story is a true rags-to-riches tale. The story of a teenage mother who knows her son is destined for great things may not seem exceptional, but add an incarcerated father, diminutive size, and sheer determination, and this is the truly remarkable story of Allen Iverson. Iverson's drive took him to five NBA championships and an MVP award. His tattoos, style, and strong sense of self make him a model for blazing his own trail without ever forgetting his own past. **QP**

**Keywords:** Basketball • Iverson, Allen • National Basketball Association

1

2

3

4

5

6

7

8

9

10

11

## Riner, Dax.

*Annika Sorenstam.* Sports Heroes and Legends. Minneapolis, MN: Twenty-First Century Books. 2007. ISBN 9780822571605. **M** **J**

Sorenstam has won eight ESPY awards, including two for best female athlete, and she is the only female golfer to have ever shot a 59 in competition. She wasn't a prodigy in the same vein as Tiger Woods, but he considers her a great friend. They have even played together in a Skins game. She has used her ups and downs to become a better golfer, enough to improve annually and make sure that her name was remembered long before she was eligible for the LPGA Tour Hall of Fame.

**Keywords:** Female golfers • Golf • Golfers • Ladies Professional Golf Association • Sorenstam, Annika

## Robinson, Sharon.

🎗 *Promises to Keep: How Jackie Robinson Changed America.* New York: Scholastic Press, 2004. ISBN 9780439425926. **M** **J**

The story of the first African American to play in the major leagues is one of an amazing athlete who also made waves in politics, business, and civil rights. Sharon Robinson, Jackie Robinson's daughter and the director of educational programming for major league baseball, writes with an immediacy and respect that captures the reader's attention. The photobiography she has produced, which also conveys the threats and dangers to Jackie Robinson's life when he entered the majors, gives the reader a front row seat to the life and times of one of America's greatest ball players. This is a fitting tribute to Jackie Robinson and his accomplishments. **BBYA**

**Keywords:** Baseball • Civil rights • Robinson, Jackie

**Now Try:** Sharon Robinson's book gives readers a sense not only of Jackie Robinson, but also of the time in which he lived. The integration of major league baseball was a major historical event. Readers interested in finding out more about the behind-the-scenes events, people, and culture of America's favorite pastime will enjoy Robert Lipsyte's *Heroes of Baseball: The Men Who Made It America's Favorite Game.* They will learn about some of the celebrities, rivalries, and scandals of this great game, along with enough statistics for any fan.

# Rules and Tips

Readers interested in becoming competent participants in or observers of a sport need look no further than these titles. They feature histories, equipment, rules, and setup and are generally written by people with a close association with and love of that particular activity. Many of these books are colorful and highly illustrated, which often appeals to boys and reluctant readers. Features generally include important competitors, which may lead interested readers to the "Sports Biographies" above. Rule books for board games, gaming information, and technology are covered in chapter 9.

## Extreme Sports Collection.

Written by various authors, these books include the history of a specific sport, appealing and age-appropriate photographs, and introductions to the sports and their assorted equipment and styles. Also discussed are techniques, biographies of notable people in the sport, and safety considerations.

**Keywords:** Extreme sports

**Burke, L. M.**

*Skateboarding! Surf the Pavement.* New York: Rosen Central, 1999. ISBN 0823930149. **M** **J**

> The history and evolution of the sport known as "sidewalk surfing" are covered in this volume, along with illustrations of moves, equipment, and styles of skating.
>
> **Keywords:** Skateboarding

**Hayhurst, Chris.**

*Mountain Biking: Get on the Trail.* New York: Rosen Central, 2000. ISBN 0823930130. **M** **J**

> Included are an introduction to mountain biking and its history, an explanation of how it differs from other kinds of cycling, and discussions of techniques for this kind of biking and safety. **QP**
>
> **Keywords:** All-terrain cycling • Mountain biking

*Bicycle Stunt Riding!: Catch Air.* New York: Rosen Central, 2000. ISBN 0823930114. **M** **J**

> Readers will turn their attention to stunt riding, along with its history, moves, and styles. Safety concerns aren't overlooked, either, and several suggestions are made about where to get additional information. **QP**
>
> **Keywords:** Motocross • Stunt riding

*Skydiving! Take the Leap.* New York: Rosen Central, 1999. ISBN 0823930157. **M** **J**

> Along with the history of this exciting sport, Hayhurst introduces the stars of the sport and gives an idea of what it takes to become involved in it, in terms of training, costs, types of jumps, and necessary equipment.
>
> **Keywords:** Skydiving

*Snowboarding!: Shred the Powder.* New York: Rosen Central, 1999. ISBN 0823930106. **M** **J**

> Biographies of snowboarding champions are included in this introduction to the sport, in addition to the regular features: history, venues, styles, and techniques.
>
> **Keywords:** Snowboarding • Winter sports

*Wakeboarding!: Throw a Tantrum.* New York: Rosen Central, 2000. ISBN 0823930084. **M** **J**

> Wakeboarding, a combination of waterskiing and snowboarding, is explored in this volume of the <u>Extreme Sports</u> series. Different styles and techniques are described and illustrated by photographs.
>
> **Keywords:** Wakeboarding • Water sports

**Kaminker, Laura.**

*In-Line skating!: Get Aggressive.* New York: Rosen Central, 1999. ISBN 0823930122. **M** **J**

> Here are the history, basic moves, techniques, necessary gear, and safety considerations for this popular sport.

> **Keywords:** In-line skating

**Roberts, Jeremy.**

🎗 *Rock & Ice Climbing: Top the Tower.* New York: Rosen Central, 2000. ISBN 0823930092. **M** **J**

> Along with a short history of climbing, readers will find discussion of climbing styles, venues, equipment, and techniques. A number of profiles of climbers are included. **QP**

> **Keywords:** Ice climbing • Rock climbing

## Fortin, François.

*Sports: The Complete Visual Reference.* Willowdale, ON; Buffalo, NY: Firefly Books, 2000. ISBN 9781552095409. **J** **H**

> Anyone who has ever watched a sporting event or competition and wondered what the judges were using as their criteria, or been confused about the differences among Australian, Canadian, and American football, will enjoy this book. This handy resource divides sports into twenty categories, such as track and field, nautical sports, gymnastics, ball sports (large ball), racquet sports, combat sports, motor sports and snow sports. Each entry contains material about the sport's history, equipment, organization, famous competitors, and signature moves. For example, the piece on figure skating includes illustrations and explanations of the death-drop spin, as well as five of the six different jumps: the Lutz, Salchow, flip, toe loop, and Axel.

> **Keywords:** Sports

## Kleh, Cindy.

🎿 *Snowboarding Skills: The Back-to-Basics Essentials for All Levels.* Toronto; Buffalo, NY: Firefly Books, 2002. Reprinted 2007. ISBN 1552976262. **J** **H** **RR**

> Thorough explanations from a championship snowboarder prepare every level, from novices getting ready for their first day to people looking for help in handling rough conditions and buying their own equipment. Kleh doesn't overlook proper gear, nutrition, equipment maintenance, safety, and etiquette on the slopes, either, making this a book to get any snowboarder into the best possible condition. **QP**

> **Keywords:** Instructions • Snowboarding • Winter sports

> **Now Try:** Readers interested in finding out more about winter sports can check out the photos and instruction in Pamela Pollack's *Ski! Your Guide to Jumping, Racing, Skiboarding, Nordic, Backcountry, Aerobatics, and More.* This guide from National Geographic's <u>Extreme Sports</u> series brings together information about skiing styles, equipment, training tips, and profiles of top competitors in one volume.

## Masoff, Joy, and Jack Dickason.

🎋 *Snowboard!: Your Guide to Freeriding, Pipe & Park, Jibbing, Backcountry, Alpine, Boardercross, and More.* Washington, DC: National Geographic Society, 2002. ISBN 9780792267409. **M** **J** **RR**

This slim volume packs a whole lot of information between its covers. The sections cover the different kinds of snowboarding, snowboarding moves, competitions, and notable competitors of the sport. Sidebars add glossaries and more in-depth information to each section. The book also includes tips about equipment and safety and a list of further sources. **QP**

**Keywords:** Extreme sports • Snowboarding • Winter sports

## Thomas, Keltie.

*Blades, Boards & Scooters.* <u>Popular Mechanics for Kids</u>. Toronto: Maple Tree Press, 2003. ISBN 1894379454. **M**

Thomas takes a look at scooters, in-line skates, skateboards, and snowboards, devoting a quarter of the book to each. Every section contains advice for beginners, explanations of moves seen in the extreme versions of the sport, and a user-friendly section on maintenance of the equipment in question. Legends in the sports are highlighted, including two women professionals. Beginning each section is an explanation of safety equipment and why it is not to be overlooked at any level of experience.

**Keywords:** In-line skating • Scooters • Skateboarding • Snowboarding

## Thomas, Keltie.

<u>How Sports Work.</u> **RR** **BB**

This series presents an in-depth look at some of today's most popular sports: the rules of play, the most important pieces of equipment, strategy, players, and how the sport developed through time and around the world. A highly illustrated, fast-paced tour through the history of each sport.

**Keywords:** Baseball • Basketball • Hockey • Soccer

*How Baseball Works.* Toronto: Maple Tree Press, 2004. ISBN 9781894379601. **M** **J**

The rules, the positions, legends of the sport, history, gear, play, and strategy are all covered in this book. Female legends and a discussion of the catcher's mask are included, along with the evolution of the baseball. Thomas introduces readers to kinetic energy, explains how hitters use it to their advantage, and even suggests some experiments for readers to try.

**Keywords:** Baseball • Baseball history • Sports

*How Basketball Works.* Toronto: Maple Tree Press, 2005. ISBN 9781897066188. **M** **J**

The third volume in the <u>How Sports Work</u> series covers basketball in seven chapters, from its invention in 1891 to its development into a fast-moving sport enjoyed worldwide. Thomas includes information on the sport's history, rules, and positions, along with a glossary and an explanation of reported statistics. Each chapter concludes with information on a legendary player and the development of the game, with reader-friendly material on the importance of improving equipment, such as the basketball, running shoes, and the basketball court.

**Keywords:** Basketball • Sports history • Sports instruction

*How Hockey Works.* Toronto: Maple Tree Press, 2006. ISBN 9781897066645. **M J**

In an interesting and fun introduction to hockey, Thomas covers everything from a history of the sport to its rules and regulations, and completes the book with a glossary to help translate what commentators say. Additional information is divided into of two categories: information about the game and how to better play it, and its development into the sport we know today, with details on ice surfaces, equipment, and the zamboni.

**Keywords:** Hockey • Sports history

*How Soccer Works.* Toronto: Maple Tree Press, 2007. ISBN 9781897349007. **M J RR**

How a "clunky" soccer boot evolved to become a player's most important piece of equipment is only one of the facts that helps enliven this history of one of the most popular sports. Readers will also find out about legends, from Pele to Mia Hamm and Ronaldinho, and get tips about using their heads and feet while finding out all about the game.

**Keywords:** Soccer • Sports history

## Tomlinson, Joe, and Ed Leigh.

*Extreme Sports: In Search of the Ultimate Thrill.* Richmond Hill, ON: Firefly Books, 2004. ISBN 9781552979921. **H**

Occasionally athletes test the limits of their endurance, competing individually against the elements in "extreme" sports. These very risky individual ventures are presented alphabetically in three categories: air, land and water. The entry for each sport is accompanied by several color photographs, a short history, and explanations of the equipment used.

**Keywords:** Extreme sports

# The Greatest Games

This subgenre shows how sports have changed, from the ten sports that debuted at the first Olympics, to the twenty that are expected to be at the 2010 Winter Olympic Games, to alerting the reader not only that girls have the right to compete, but they are also worth watching. The reader will find compelling sports histories, legends, and stories. There are also stories about sports and their effect on people's lives, such as Sue Macy's collection, *Girls Got Game: Sports Stories and Poems.*

## Bissinger, H. G.

*Friday Night Lights: A Town, a Team, and a Dream.* Cambridge, MA: Da Capo Press, 1990. Reprinted 2003. ISBN 9780306812828. **H A**

What makes football such an all-American sport? Every fall the small town of Odessa, Texas, circles around its high school football team. The reader will follow the captivating 1988 season of wins and losses with the Permian Panthers in a town where the team's play rules the lives of 20,000 rabid fans. This is the book that spawned the movie and television show of the same name.

**Keywords:** Football • Odessa (TX) • Permian Panthers • Texas

**Now Try:** Another story about how football not only brings a town together but also gives it a purpose is Carlton Stowers's *Where Dreams Die Hard: A Small American Town and Its Six-Man Football Team.* The high school in Penelope, Texas, has neither the numbers nor the wealth to field a regulation team, but that hasn't stopped them: the Penelope Wolverines play six-man football with the entire town behind them.

## Blumenthal, Karen.

🎗 *Let Me Play: The Story of Title IX: The Law That Changed the Future of Girls in America.* New York: Atheneum, 2005. ISBN 0689859570. **M J H**

Few girls today realize the changes in their rights and status that the last thirty years have wrought. This portrait of the battle to eliminate sex discrimination in U.S. schools and the changes effected by Title IX is eye-opening. It is highlighted by portraits of female athletes and politicians, and annual tables show ever-increasing numbers of females participating in sports as well as university enrollment. Readers have a front-row seat as politicians fight the prevailing views of the day, demonstrated by political cartoons that conveyed the message that girls did not need to and could not possibly compete with boys in school or on playing fields. **BBYA**

**Keywords:** Legal status of women athletes • Sex discrimination in sports • Title IX

## Macy, Sue, ed.

*Girls Got Game: Sports Stories and Poems.* New York: Henry Holt, 2001. ISBN 0805065687. **M J**

Sue Macy's anthology celebrates girls playing sports, and it is unusual if only because there are not many books with the same subject matter. Here she has gathered together original material from nine authors and four poets, setting it in the world of sports. Each selection is followed by the author's biography, including an explanation of what sports have meant to him or her. The writing is by experienced authors and features stories with girls involved in sports from football to tetherball, dealing with issues from school to family.

**Keywords:** Poetry • Sports • Women athletes

*Swifter, Higher, Stronger: A Photographic History of the Summer Olympics.* Washington, DC: National Geographic, 2004. ISBN 0792266676. **M J H**

In this thorough introduction to the Summer Olympics, Macy starts with the reintroduction of the modern Olympics by Pierre de Coubertin in 1896, alerting readers to the addition of new events and the changing of the rules to allow women to compete. Chapters on breakthrough athletes and unlikely heroes, followed by a capsule synopsis of the Olympiads through 2000, gives readers a portrait of the changing culture in sports and politics, as well as of the myriad of amazing athletes who have competed in the games. Triumphs of athletic prowess and sportsmanship, as well as tragedies, including scandals and the political low point of the 1972 terrorist act, are included. More than 150 captioned photographs showing the highs and lows of each of the games enhance the text.

**Keywords:** Olympics • Sports • Summer Olympics

**Now Try:** Macy's love of sports did not end with the Summer Olympics. In 2006 she turned her attention to ice and snow in *Freeze-Frame: A Photographic History of the Winter Olympics.* In addition to a history leading up to the creation of the winter games and a synopsis of each olympiad are chapters dealing with the difficulties and inevitable problems with weather, "heroes and superstars," and adding extreme sports such as snowboarding.

# Sports in Action

Given the number of photographers assigned to sporting events, the number of beautifully illustrated books is not surprising. Here are books devoted to a particular sport, as well as some titles that cover several sports. Reluctant readers will likely find many of these titles appealing, such as Mark Huebner's *Sports Bloopers.*

## Eichler, Christian.

*Soccer: 365 Days.* New York: Abrams, 2006. ISBN 9780810959194. **J H**

What makes soccer the most popular sport in the world? More than 600 photographs of the greatest moments and players from the FIFA World Cups played between 1954 and 2002 help explain the excitement surrounding the 2006 event.

**Keywords:** Photographs • Soccer

## Gottesman, Jane, and Geoffrey Biddle.

🏆 *Game Face: What Does a Female Athlete Look Like?* New York: St. Martin's Press, 2001. Reprinted 2006. ISBN 0375506020; 9780375506024. **M J H**

When Jane Gottesman worked in a store's sports department in the early 1990s, the prevailing attitude was that women's sports were "second-rate." Here she has gathered photographs of women involved in every aspect of sports to disprove that idea, from Olympic medalists and world cup soccer players to participants in more obscure sports such as discus throwing. The collection is organized by stages, from "getting ready" to "finish" to "aftermath," with each photograph captioned to indicate the subject and, occasionally, the drive and historical importance behind the athlete portrayed. Narratives also demonstrate the power that goes along with competitive women's athletics. A time line of women in sports demonstrates how far women's athletics has come. **QP**

**Keywords:** Photographs • Pictorial works • Women athletes

**Now Try:** Sue Macy and Jane Gottesman have been working for some time to prove that having someone say "you play like a girl" is a compliment rather than a putdown. For another great book about women's athletics, readers may enjoy *Play Like a Girl: A Celebration of Women in Sports,* in which Macy and Gottesman pair photographs of great athletes with quotes from people in the athletic world and add excerpts from books, articles, and short stories to illustrate the clout behind a female athlete.

**Huebner, Mark.**

🏵 *Sports Bloopers: All-Star Flubs and Fumbles.* Toronto; Buffalo, NY: Firefly Books, 2003. ISBN 1552976270: 9781552976272. **M** **J** **RR**
Professional photographers have the opportunity to see athletes, not to mention spectators, at their best—and their worst. . This collection of photographs demonstrates the potential for errors and awkwardness in almost every sport. **QP**

**Keyword**: Errors • Humor • Photographs • Sports

## Consider Starting with . . .

These are suggested titles for readers new to the genre.

Blumenthal, Karen. *Let Me Play: The Story of Title IX: The Law That Changed the Future of Girls in America.*

Cox, Lynne. *Swimming to Antarctica: Tales of a Long-distance Swimmer.*

Freedman, Russell. *Babe Didrikson Zaharias: The Making of a Champion.*

Gottesman, Jane, and Geoffrey Biddle. *Game Face: What Does a Female Athlete Look Like?*

Kleh, Cindy. *Snowboarding Skills: The Back-to Basics Essentials for All Levels.*

Macy, Sue. *Swifter, Higher, Stronger: A Photographic History of the Summer Olympics.*

Macy, Sue, ed. *Girls Got Game: Sports Stories and Poems.*

Robinson, Sharon. *Promises to Keep: How Jackie Robinson Changed America.*

Thomas, Keltie. *How Basketball Works.*

Tomlinson, Joe, and Ed Leigh. *Extreme Sports: In Search of the Ultimate Thrill.*

## Fiction Read-Alikes

- **Crutcher, Chris**. Many of the protagonists in Crutcher's complex novels are involved in sports. Swimming is the most common sport in his funny, tragic, beautifully written books (e.g., *Staying Fat for Sarah Byrnes, Stotan!*). *Whale Talk* was chosen for the 2005 YALSA Best of the Best list.

- **Lupica, Mike**. Among sportswriter Mike Lupica's books are several about a scrappy and determined basketball player named Danny. In *Travel Team* and *Summer Ball,* Danny is a fighter and a dogged little guy, proving that his small size will not keep him from playing.

- **Lynch, Chris.** Readers t interested in sports and humor or who empathize with characters who are not able to fit in with the sports crowd in school will find a soul mate in *Slot Machine*, in which Elvin must try out for each sport at a "retreat" before starting high school to find a niche with a particular team. Try as he might, sports are not Elvin's thing.

- **Murdock, Catherine Gilbert.** Girls play sports, too, as is ably and humorously shown in Murdock's novels. In the BBYA title *Dairy Queen: A Novel*, D.J. more than pulls her weight on her family's Wisconsin farm, so after she spends a summer training the rival high school's new quarterback, she decides to go out for the football team herself. Readers fond of D.J. can keep up with her in *Off Season*.

- **Ripslinger, Jon.** In *How I Fell in Love and Learned to Shoot Free Throws*, basketball is a starting point for a story about two teens getting to know one another and finding out that there is much more below the surface in their lives.

- **Zusak, Marcus.** In *Fighting Reuben Wolfe*, two brothers agree to join an underground boxing ring to get some badly needed money. In this traditional underdog story, Cameron and Reuben are drawn into the world of the boxing ring and eventually have to fight each other.

# Chapter 8

## All About You

## Definition

*Encyclopaedia Britannica* (2007) defines *adolescence* as "the transitional phase of growth and development between childhood and adulthood," which roughly encompasses the time between the ages of twelve and twenty. It is during this time that youngsters entering the "teenage" years undergo change in two primary areas. The first is the onset of puberty and questions that arise with it as the body matures physically and sexually; the second deals with psychological, social, and moral issues. This genre contains books that contend with physical changes and well-being, as well as the issues that teens deal with in their daily lives.

## Appeal

The transition to adulthood is a time when teenagers becoming increasingly independent. Books that give teens the opportunity to learn what is happening in their lives and how to take control of their own situations are frequently in demand. When they have questions too personal or embarrassing to ask someone else, about new and different things happening to their bodies and lives, it can be comforting to be able to consult a book and learn that these changes are not only normal, but happen to other people as well.

In our age of consumerism, supermodels, burgeoning anorexia, and unrealistic body images, there are solid examples available of what is normal, healthy, and realistic. Self-esteem, health, and nutrition are popular topics, and the books in this chapter provide realistic views about weight and body shapes. Books on relationships examine friendships and families. This is a complex time, and teens deal with serious concerns such as drugs and depression. Books on all of these topics often offer other resources for teens with further questions.

## Chapter Organization

The first section, "Self-Esteem," contains books that help readers develop a healthy self-image and find their inner beauty. The "Health and Nutrition" section lists informational books about what is healthy and how to stay healthy; interested readers will find some crossover with the "Cooking" section of chapter 9. This is followed by a section on "Sexuality." Here readers will find titles dealing with both puberty and sexuality. "Relationships" covers romantic relationships as well as relationships with friends and family. Some of today's most difficult issues, including drugs, violence, and depression, are covered in the books listed in the "Tough Stuff" section. "Career Directions" offers teens materials on finding jobs, adding to their resumes, networking, occupational outlook, and just having fun. The chapter concludes with "Fun Stuff," including personality tests and astrology.

# Self-Esteem

Self-esteem is a person's feelings of worth. For adults, this involves one's feelings about one's abilities, behaviors, and characteristics, but there is an overwhelming tendency among teens, especially girls, to measure self-worth solely by how they think they look. A 2007 study by Seidah and Bouffard identified teens by grade and gender and examined whether their self-esteem was determined by their physical appearance or their sense of self had priority. The group most concerned with their physical appearance had a lower overall sense of self-esteem. The books in this category provide a realistic view of the teenage years and help provide teens with coping strategies and a way to find their own intrinsic beauty, rather than the unrealistic and unhealthy images shown in the media. Books about beauty and self-esteem are very popular and usually directed at a female audience. Books that emphasize self-esteem also concentrate on inner beauty and creating a realistic self-image.

## Brashich, Audrey D.

*All Made Up: A Girl's Guide to Seeing Through Celebrity Hype and Celebrating Real Beauty.* New York: Walker, 2006. ISBN 0802780741. **M** **J**

A short turn as a model gave Brasich an insight into the so-called glamour of the celebrity world, which she uses here to explore the relationship between pop culture and self-esteem. Along with explanations of the reality behind marketing and challenges for teens to see beauty in different shapes and sizes, she also offers a chapter on real role models. Teens may post their thoughts on her blog.

**Keywords:** Beauty • Body image • Marketing • Self-esteem • Self-perception

## Cattrall, Kim

*Being a Girl: [Navigating the Ups and Downs of Teen Life].* New York: Little, Brown, 2006. ISBN 9780316011020. **M** **J**

It's difficult to imagine that a famous Hollywood actress would have the same problems with body image as a typical teenager, yet that is only one of the things that Kim Cattrall struggled with as a teen actress. Here she offers advice on many topics of interest, including style, nutrition, coping strategies, and the importance of developing a strong sense of self-esteem. The stories of this award-winning actor demonstrate the rewards of sticking up for oneself and making one's own choices.

**Keywords:** Adolescence • Body image • Cattrall, Kim • Self-esteem • Teenage girls

## Graydon, Shari.

🎗 *In Your Face: The Culture of Beauty and You.* Toronto: Annick Press, 2004. ISBN 1550378562. **M** **J** **H**

> Graydon presents a book about beauty, including how it is perceived and how such perceptions have changed over the years. She also considers the ways media affect people's views of what is beautiful, the different things people do to make themselves beautiful, and the possible dangers inherent in those actions. This book was awarded the 2005 Norma Fleck Award for Canadian Children's Nonfiction. **Norma Fleck**

> **Keywords:** Beauty • Body image • Health • Marketing • Self-esteem

# Health and Nutrition

According to the APA's *Developing Adolescents* (2002), 14 to 20 percent of adolescents aged twelve to nineteen years are overweight. Aside from the associated health risks, overweight or obese teens are likely to be discriminated against, teased, or victimized. The books in this section offer advice about lifestyle changes, exercise, and fitness for those who are overweight as well as for those who are not.

## Boutaudou, Sylvie, and Laetitia Aynie.

*Weighing In: How to Understand Your Body, Lose Weight, and Live a Healthier Lifestyle.* Sunscreen. New York: Amulet, 2006. ISBN 9780810992283. **M** **J**

> Being even a little bit overweight is enough to bring on a whole new level of abuse as a teenager. If losing weight is the right thing for a teenager, he or she shouldn't just go on a diet. This book discusses ways for teens to determine just what is healthy, how to talk to friends and family, and where to get help so that they can get started on a new lifestyle.

> **Keywords:** Diet • Health • Nutrition • Self-esteem • Weight

## Caldwell, Michaela.

*The Girls' Yoga Book: Stretch Your Body, Open Your Mind & Have Fun!* Illustrated by **Claudia Dávila**. Girl Zone. Toronto: Maple Tree Press, 2005. ISBN 1897066244. **M**

> The people behind the Girl Zone series propose yoga as one way for girls to cope with the multitude of stressors common in their everyday lives. It is a great way to relax, as well as to have fun. The four sections of the book cover yoga's history, breathing techniques, posture and meditation; the different poses; how yoga can help in day-to-day life; and integrating yoga into the "world around you." A number of sidebars are included throughout from girls describing their own experiences with yoga.

> **Keywords:** Health • Hygiene • Yoga

## Chryssicas, Mary Kaye. Illustrated by Angela Coppola.

*Breathe: Yoga for Teens.* New York: DK Publishing, 2007. ISBN 9787566266167. **M J H**

In this book Chryssicas, a long-time practitioner and teacher of yoga, introduces yoga to teens. She starts by discussing why teens might be interested in yoga and then covers various topics: breathing, the basic postures, and more advanced poses. Also included are chapters on "what's right for your body"; "your yoga journal"; and "practices" that include stress relief, yoga booty, and bedtime yoga. Each pose features instructions printed on one of Angela Coppola's photographs of a dozen female models. Readers are likely to find Chryssicas's enthusiasm for yoga infectious.

**Keywords:** Exercise • Stress relief • Yoga

**Now Try:** Girls looking for another friendly, fun book about yoga that concentrates on incorporating yoga into their lives might enjoy Evan Cooper's *Um, Like . . . OM: A Girl Goddess's Guide to Yoga.* In this book Cooper uses a casual, friendly tone and line drawings to describe poses, with an overall goal of using yoga to empower girls.

## Cosmogirl Editors.

*Ask CosmoGirl! About Nutrition and Fitness.* Ask Cosmo Girl! Series. New York: Hearst Books, 2007. ISBN 9781588166456; 1588166457. **J H**

The Cosmogirl editors answer girls' questions about health-related issues. Girls are given advice on primarily fitness and nutrition. Questions are answered with a regard for maintaining self-esteem.

**Keywords:** Advice • Health • Fitness • Nutrition • Teenage girls

## Douglas, Ann, and Julie Douglas.

*Body Talk: The Straight Facts on Fitness, Nutrition, and Feeling Great about Yourself!* Girl Zone. Toronto: Maple Tree Press, 2006. ISBN 1897066619. **M J**

*Body Talk* challenges girls to rethink their self-images by giving them the straight facts about fat, fad diets, eating disorders, and beauty. Information and tips on serious subjects are presented in a humorous, congenial style. This updated edition, part of the Girl Zone series, provides practical instructions for taking care of oneself inside and out.

**Keywords:** Diet • Health • Nutrition • Personal hygiene • Self-esteem

## Jukes, Mavis, and Lilian Cheung.

*Be Healthy! It's a Girl Thing: Food, Fitness, and Feeling Great.* **Illustrated by Debra Ziss.** New York: Crown, 2004. ISBN 0679990291. **M J**

Mavis Jukes provides a guide to smart lifestyle choices. With the assistance of a doctor and registered dietician, she explains nutrition, from the building blocks of food up. The authors propose what they call a "cactus plan," which, in the form of a food pyramid, is a way to achieve and maintain a balanced diet. Suggestions are also provided for how to read food labels, food shopping, and eating out. Because a diet plan needs balance, various chapters are devoted to exercise, watching out for false advertising, and maintaining healthy self-esteem.

**Keywords:** Diet • Exercise • Health • Lifestyle • Nutrition • Self-esteem

## Platkin, Charles Stuart.

*Lighten Up: Stay Sane, Eat Great, Lose Weight.* New York: Razorbill, 2005. ISBN 1595140654. **M** **J** **H**

Short-term weight loss is generally offset by a depressing reversal within a few months. In this book the author of the column "The Diet Detective" takes on miracle diets and more. His plan is a simple one, backed up with practical examples and discussions on how to change one's thinking about food and weight, teaching about diet modification that can fit into anyone's life.

**Keywords:** Health • Nutrition

---

# Sexuality

During the teenage years children develop secondary sexual characteristics (such as a deeper voice in boys, and development of breasts in girls) as their hormonal balance shifts strongly toward the adult state. During this time hormonal fluctuations also affect emotions and relationships and cause expected physical changes. A number of books that address these changes for each gender, for example, *The Boys' Body Book* talks about the changes that happen in all areas of a guy's life, and two doctors provide answers to the questions that their teenage patients have asked them in their Girlology books.

## Cosmogirl Editors.

🌸 *Ask Cosmogirl! About Your Body: All the Answers to Your Most Intimate Questions.* Ask CosmoGirl! Series. New York: Hearst Books, 2006. ISBN 1588164861. **J** **H** **RR**

Cosmogirl turns to girls' questions about themselves. Questions cover the gamut from what is normal in puberty, to everyday life, to physical and mental problems. This is a place for teen girls to find answers and to discover that other girls have the same questions, which indeed makes them all normal. **QP**

**Keywords:** Advice • Teenage girls

## Daldry, Jeremy

*The Teenage Guy's Survival Guide.* New York: Little, Brown, 1999. ISBN 9780316178242. **M** **J** **H**

The title says it all; who needs survival advice more than male teens? Here are practical, nonjudgmental tips that poke fun at urban myths and tackle situations from dating to sex, drugs, physical changes that go along with adolescence, and emotional highs and lows and tell teenage boys how to deal with some of the difficulties inherent in teen social life.

**Keywords:** Adolescence • Puberty • Sex instruction • Social situations • Teenage boys

## Dunham, Kelli S., and Steve Bjorkman.

*The Boy's Body Book.* Kennebunkport, ME: Cider Mill Press, 2007. ISBN 9781933662749. **M**

> A boy's life is just as affected by puberty as a girl's. There are changes in their bodies, homes, school, and relationships. These can be pretty tough to deal with and can cause stress over emotions, choices, and dealing with almost anything. Here are some answers to questions about those areas, as well as some extra places to go for more information.
>
> **Keywords:** Adolescence • Boys • Fitness • Growth • Health • Hygiene • Puberty

## Gravelle, Karen, and Jennifer Gravelle. Illustrated by Debbie Palen.

*The Period Book: Everything You Don't Want to Ask (But Need to Know).* New York: Walker, 1996. ISBN 0802780725. **M**

> Gravelle and her teenage coauthor's book is useful above all else for its matter-of-fact style and practical information. After presenting the facts about puberty and menstruation, they answer questions about what to wear, potentially embarrassing situations, body changes, and the difference between being "normal" and being "like everyone else."
>
> **Keywords:** Adolescence • Development • Menstruation

## Holmes, Melissa, and Patricia Hutchinson.

*Girlology: A Girl's Guide to Stuff That Matters: Relationships, Bodytalk & Girl Power!* Deerfield Beach, FL: Health Communications, 2005. ISBN 0757302955. **J H**

> There aren't many parts of a girl's life that don't go through changes during the teen years. Relationships change during this time, not only with friends but also with parents. Hormones rage, guys act weird, and girls' bodies are changing. All of that is normal. So is getting the right information about sex to make informed decisions about their bodies and life changes. This is a source for teen girls to use to increase their knowledge and confidence and develop their "girl power."
>
> **Keywords:** Adolescence • Fitness • Health • Menstruation • Puberty • Sexuality

*Girlology: Hang-Ups, Hook-Ups, and Holding Out: Stuff You Need to Know About Your Body, Sex, and Dating.* Deerfield Beach, FL: Health Communications, 2007. ISBN 9780757305863. **J H**

> Doctors are asked a lot of questions about sex and what is going on with teens' bodies. To improve family communications about "healthy sexuality" and make sure everyone has the right information to make the best possible decisions, two doctors started a program called girlology. This book explores what real girls wanted to know and the truth about sex, physical examinations, pregnancy, alcohol, and much more.
>
> **Keywords:** Hygiene • Sex instruction for girls • Sexuality

## Jukes, Mavis.

🎗 *The Guy Book: An Owner's Manual for Teens: Safety, Maintenance, and Operating Instructions for Teens.* New York: Crown Publishers, 2002. ISBN 0679990283. **J** **H**

A straightforward and frank guide for adolescent males about sex, STDs, birth control, and dating doesn't sound like something the average guy would want to read. However, by offering this information in the format of a 1950s car manual, along with the appropriate labeling and design, and a sense of humor, this book makes acquiring that information fun. **QP**

Keywords: Adolescence • Puberty • Sex instruction • Teenage boys

## Pardes, Bronwen.

🎗 *Doing It Right: Making Smart, Safe and Satisfying Decisions About Sex.* New York: Simon Pulse, 2007. ISBN 141691823X. **H**

An HIV and sex education counselor has written a direct, open, and honest book for teens about sex. She covers a multitude of topics, including puberty, sexual orientation, questions to ask before sex, safe-sex practices, masturbation, rape and sexual abuse, STDs, and HIV. She clears up myths, answers actual questions from teens, and suggests further resources and alternative choices. Pardes advocates responsibility, firmly stating to readers that ultimately, "what you choose to do, or not to do, is up to you." **PP, QP**

Keywords: Dating • Gender • Sex • Sexuality • Sexually transmitted diseases

## St. Stephen's Community House.

*The Little Black Book for Girlz: A Book on Healthy Sexuality.* Toronto: Annick Press, 2006. 9781550379549. **H**

To get real answers to questions about sex, the teens at St. Stephen's Community House in Toronto decided to produce their own guide to the subject. Chapters cover a long and varied list of topics, including relationships, periods, sex, birth control, pregnancy/miscarriage, abortion, STDs, AIDS, and sexual assault. Medical professionals vetted the personal responses penned by the authors, which will have a great appeal to and veracity for other teenagers.

Keywords: Adolescence • AIDS • Pregnancy • Sex instruction for girls • Sexual assault

# Relationships

The teenage years are a time for self-discovery, shifting boundaries, exploring one's identity, and establishing independence. It is only natural that the relationships teens have with friends and family will change a great deal during these years, not to mention the new relationships they form when they start to date. The books in this section contain more general advice about friends and family; information about sex can be found in the "Sexuality" section. Books on difficult relationship issues, such as abuse and violence, can be found in the "Tough Stuff" section.

## Cadier, Florence, and Claire Gandini.

*My Parents Are Getting Divorced: How to Keep It Together When Your Mom and Dad Are Splitting Up.* Sunscreen. New York: Amulet, 2004. ISBN 9780810991637. **M J H**

Every family that goes through a divorce goes through a lot of changes. This is a place for teens to find some answers about the process and the emotions that will arise along the way. The book covers three main phases of divorce, with accompanying advice for readers on how to keep their place amid the tumult of changing and difficult times.

**Keywords:** Divorce • Family

## Chicken Soup for the Teenage Soul: The Real Deal Series.

This series in the "Chicken Soup" group of books is intended for and written by teenage readers. The subjects are geared toward teens and the letters are written by teens. All are supplemented with additional materials.

### Canfield, Jack, Mark Victor Hansen, and Deborah Reber.

*Chicken Soup for the Teenage Soul's the Real Deal: Friends: Best, Worst, Old, New, Lost, False, True, and More.* Deerfield Beach, FL: Health Communications, 2005. ISBN 075730317X. **J H**

The first book in the Real Deal series focuses on friends and friendship. Teen letters are organized in chapters on friends who inspire, when friendships change, unusual friendships, and tough stuff. Added materials include quizzes and "For Real?" and "Consider This" sidebars that further discuss material in the letters.

**Keywords:** Friendship • Letters • Self-esteem • Self-help • Teenagers

**Now Try:** Kimberley Kirberger writes about being a friend, supplementing her thoughts with poems and stories from teens, in the first book in the new Teen Love series from the "Chicken Soup" publishers, entitled *On Friendship: Book for Teenagers.* Kirberger and coauthor Colin Mortensen, formerly of MTV's *The Real World,* have gathered a collection of stories that will not disappoint "Chicken Soup" fans, ranging from touching to sweet, and covering all bases in adolescent friendship.

*Chicken Soup for the Teenage Soul's the Real Deal: School, Cliques, Classes, Clubs, and More .* Deerfield Beach, FL: Health Communications, 2005. ISBN 0757302556. **M J**

Teenagers discuss school and all of its difficulties, including popularity, school violence, sports, everyday activities, and being an outsider. In addition to the essays, quizzes, and suggestions found in all of the series, questionnaires, teen poems, and references to music and films have been added.

**Keywords:** Cliques • Friendship • Letters • School • Self-esteem • Self-help

### Canfield, Jack, Mark Victor Hansen, Lisa Nichols, and Eve Hogan.

*Chicken Soup for the Teenage Soul's the Real Deal: On Girl Stuff.* Deerfield Beach, FL: Health Communications, 2007. ISBN 0757305873. **M J**

Girls today are dealing with completely unrealistic portrayals of beauty in magazines, movies, and television, not to mention the everyday pressures they face in academics and socially. This volume of the Real Deal features letters from girls on facing their problems, along with quizzes and advice to help teens discover and appreciate who they are and just how much they have to give. Acknowledgment of social problems and the possibility of working through them is given extra credence because these letters are written by peers.

**Keywords:** Advice • Letters • Self-esteem

## Cosmogirl Editors.

🔖 *Ask CosmoGirl! About Guys: All the Answers to Your Most Asked Questions About Love and Relationships.* Ask CosmoGirl! Series. New York: Hearst Books, 2006. ISBN 1588164853. **H RR**

Readers will find answers to their questions about dating, love, relationships and sex in this volume of the Ask CosmoGirl! Series. Readers are reminded not to change for or ever think themselves unworthy of a relationship, and the editors offer phone numbers for outside help with troubles beyond the scope of the book. **QP**

**Keywords:** Advice • Family • Interpersonal relationships • Letters • Relationships • Romance • Teenage girls

## Lanchon, Anne.

*All About Adoption: How to Deal with the Questions of Your Past.* **Illustrated by Monike Czarnecki.** Sunscreen. New York: Amulet, 2006. ISBN 9780810992276. **M J H**

Being a teenager comes with challenges. Being adopted adds more questions. With over 150,000 kids adopted each year in the United States, there are a lot of situations to cover, from establishing their own identity to overprotective parents. Some common questions and issues teens have about adoption are discussed in a casual style, and Web sites for further research are offered.

**Keywords:** Adoption • Family • Identity

# Tough Stuff

The books in this category address some of the difficult issues that teens deal with during adolescence, including drugs, violence, and depression. Minor emotional upheavals that happen between friends and families are common themes in young adult nonfiction, just as they are in fiction, and are covered in the "Relationships" section.

## Fearnley, Fran.

*I Wrote on All Four Walls: Teens Speak Out on Violence.* Toronto: Annick Press, 2004. ISBN 1550377574. **H**

Nine teens whose lives were affected by violence present their stories in a volume that shows how much damage it can inflict on both the abuser and the victim. The tales cross genders, and the mitigating factors vary from a reaction to a teen's coming out to familial histories of drugs, violence, and other disorders. All are presented in a matter of fact tone using strong language. An afterword offers suggestions for how to avoid violence.

**Keywords:** Bullying • Family violence • Nonfiction collections • Violence

## Gaskins, Pearl Fuyo.

🌺 *What Are You?: Voices of Mixed-race Young People.* New York: Henry Holt, 1999. ISBN 0805059687. **J H**

Eighty young people of mixed-raced backgrounds write about their experiences growing up. Each of their essays, interviews, or poems includes a sidebar indicating the author's name, age, and parents' ancestries. Although they are arranged by theme, all speak to the difficulties of growing up as an outsider, especially when one does not fit easily into an acknowledged category. The possibility of being rejected by more than one racial group is likely to be eye-opening to many readers; and the writers give a sense of pride and unwillingness to give up any part of their heritage. Also included are several lists of organizations, recommended reading, and Web sites for obtaining further information. **BBYA, IRA**

**Keywords:** Ethnicity • Identity • Nonfiction collections • Race relations • Racially mixed people • Teen writing

## Mezinski, Pierre.

*Drugs Explained: The Real Deal on Alcohol, Pot, Ecstasy and More.* Sunscreen. New York: Amulet, 2004. ISBN 9780810949317. **J H**

Drugs and alcohol are becoming more and more prevalent in society. What should teens know about them? This entry in the Sunscreen series is divided into three parts. The first presents a diary in which a teen describes what happened when he or she got involved with drugs; the second gives information about drugs, including what they do to the body and what to do to help oneself or any friend who tries them; and the final section looks at the debate about the legalization of drugs and statistics on teen use.

**Keywords:** Addiction • Alcohol • Drugs • Substance abuse

## Perrier, Pascale.

*Flying Solo: How to Soar Above Your Lonely Feelings, Make Friends, and Find the Happiest You.* **Illustrated by Klaas Verplancke.** Sunscreen. New York: Harry N. Abrams, 2007. ISBN 9781428740440. **M J**

There is a difference between being alone and feeling lonely. Readers may find out what they can do when they are overwhelmed by loneliness, from looking at possible reasons why they feel that way to potential steps to take to get out of that situation.

**Keywords:** Friendship • Identity • Loneliness • Solitude

**Piquemal, Michel, and Melissa Daly.**

*When Life Stinks: How to Deal with Your Bad Moods, Blues, and Depression.* **Illustrated by Olivier Tossan.** <u>Sunscreen</u>. New York: Amulet, 2004. ISBN 9780810949324. **M** **J**

> Feeling down every once in a while is normal, even expected. People find ways to cope as their bodies grow and change and they face challenging situations. But mental illness is something that cannot be dealt with without professional help. Knowing when and where to seek help is important. This book starts off with some practical suggestions for navigating the everyday ups and downs, then discusses places to go when help is needed.
>
> **Keywords:** Adolescent psychology • Depression • Emotions • Social situations

**Scowen, Kate.**

*My Kind of Sad: What It's Like to Be Young and Depressed.* Toronto: Annick Press, 2006. ISBN 1550379402. **J** **H**

> A youth counselor has written this informational book about how to differentiate between the normal moods and stresses that affect teens and other things that may require help. Chapters cover different types of depression as well as other problems that may require professional help, including cutting, eating disorders, and suicidal feelings. Gender differences and treatment options are discussed. Several types of resources are listed, including hotlines for anyone who has experienced depression's warning signs and Web sites for teens looking for more information.
>
> **Keywords:** Depression • Mental health

## Career Directions

What they will be "doing" with themselves after they finish school is a question that kids are asked from childhood. Nowadays teens start looking at jobs and schooling earlier than ever before. This section lists books about different kinds of jobs and the education they require, as well as guides for jobs teens might take while still in school, such as babysitting. Readers will also find suggested titles on rounding out a resume, networking, and volunteering.

Directories for colleges and test preparatory materials can best be found through specific, annually updated resources. Career materials need not be boring: *Odd Jobs* lists some unusual occupations, and the *Young Person's Occupational Outlook Handbook* offers a realistic picture of what sort of education is needed for all kinds of careers. Readers may follow along with a college admissions officer in Jacques Steinberg's memoir *The Gatekeepers: Inside the Admissions Process of a Premier College*, or find out about ways to get involved in their communities in Mikki Halpin's *It's Your World—If You Don't Like It, Change It: Activism for Teenagers*.

**Inside Special Operations.** New York: Rosen Central, 2003. Various authors. **M**

This six-volume series is intended to introduce readers to various Special Operations forces in the United States and Great Britain. The slim books are fast reads, with information about the history, duties, equipment, and training involved in being part of one of these units. Readers will also find resources for further reading and more information.

**Keywords:** Military • Military history • Military training • Special operations

Burnett, Betty. *Delta Force: Counterterrorism Unit of the U.S. Army.* ISBN 0823938077.

Ferguson, Amanda. *SAS: British Special Air Service.* ISBN 0823938107.

Goldberg, Jan. *Green Berets: The U.S. Army Special Forces.* ISBN 0823938085.

Payment, Simone. *Navy Seals: Special Operations for the U.S. Navy.* Reprinted 2005. ISBN 1404208747. **QP**

Poolos, J. *Army Rangers: Surveillance and Reconnaissance for the U. S. Army.* ISBN 0823938050.

Scheppler, Bill. *British Royal Marines: Amphibious Division of the United Kingdom's Royal Navy.* ISBN 0823938069.

## Murkoff, Heidi Eisenberg, and Sharon Mazel.

*The What to Expect Baby-sitter's Handbook.* New York: Workman, 2003. ISBN 9780761128458. **M J H A**

Babysitting is one of the most common first jobs in North America. This book can help anyone who looks after children or wants to start. Practical information covers feeding and diet, health and safety, and other subjects, providing information for different age groups because sitters won't do the same thing for a newborn that they would for an older child. Even an experienced sitter might be grateful for a first aid reference and answers to some of babysitting's common questions. Readers may use the forms at the back as a guide for their first visit to a new house to make sure they have everything they need and to impress prospective clients.

**Keywords:** Babysitting • Babysitting manuals

**Now Try:** If readers have questions about specific aspects of babysitting, they may find answers in one of the Snap Babysitting series. These guides are directed at specific aspects of the job. For advice on deciding if one wants to babysit, finding employers, and being a good employee, readers may consult Barbara Mehlman's *Babysitting Jobs: The Business of Babysitting.*

## Reber, Deborah.

*In Their Shoes: Extraordinary Women Describe Their Amazing Careers.* New York: Simon & Schuster/ Pulse, 2007. ISBN 9781416925781. **J H**

What is it like to be a professional woman today? This innovative guide lets readers find out directly from the women themselves. They describe what they do and how they do it and give a practical and realistic view of their careers, including potential salaries, educational requirements, stress levels, what it takes to work in the field, and tips to get started. The fifty women who are interviewed cover different cultures and an incredibly diverse range of interests, including law enforcement, the military, education, the media, medicine, and the arts.

**Keywords:** Careers • Occupations • Professional women

## Schiff, Nancy Rica

🏆 *Odd Jobs: Portraits of Unusual Occupations.* Berkeley, CA: Ten Speed Press, 2002. ISBN 1580084575. **J** **H** **RR**

Photographer Schiff has met a lot of people with unusual careers. Here she presents portraits of sixty-five of these people. Each person explains his or her job, and each entry contains a photograph demonstrating the person doing the job, whether Barbie's dress designer or a golf ball diver. Readers will probably learn about careers that they have never heard of and find out what is required to do them. **QP**

**Keywords:** Careers • Occupations • Portraits

*Odder Jobs: More Portraits of Unusual Occupations.* Berkeley, CA: Ten Speed Press, 2006. ISBN 1580087493. **J** **H**

More curious occupations are introduced in Schiff's second volume of job portraits. As in the first book, for each job there is an explanation, background information on the person being introduced, and a full-page portrait of that person in action. This is a good book for browsing, with jobs as varied as a Las Vegas dice inspector and a paleoscatologist.

**Keywords:** Careers • Occupations • Portraits

*Young Person's Occupational Outlook Handbook.* Indianapolis, IN: JIST Works. 2005. ISBN 9781593571252. **M** **J**

This book contains listings for more than 270 jobs in eleven different categories, from management to forestry. Readers will find out how much education or training is required and what subjects they should take in high school to prepare as well as an idea of what the job is really like: where one would work, how much one would make, and what the chances are for employment. There are also suggestions about similar jobs.

**Keywords:** Careers • Job descriptions • Occupations • Vocational guidance

## Zielin, Lara.

*Make Things Happen: The Key to Networking for Teens.* Montrèal: Lobster Press, 2003. ISBN 9781894222433. **M** **J**

The idea behind "networking" is to form a circle of people who can help each other reach their goals. Readers will find out how and why this can be helpful from people who have used networking strategies successfully. There are several suggestions for ways to build relationships and ideas for places to find out about prospective careers, such as job shadowing, internships, and volunteering. These are supplemented with sample resumes, brainstorming ideas, and practice scripts. The included lists of Web sites and organizations cover both the United States and Canada.

**Keywords:** Interpersonal relations • Networking • Social networks • Teenage employment • Teenage employment strategies

## Fun Stuff

When dealing with rapidly changing bodies, hormones, and emotions, teens have a multitude of questions. These titles, which present a lighter side to reading as well as insights into the human condition, are often popular with reluctant readers. Readers can find many lighthearted options in this category. The <u>CosmoGirl</u> series offers straightforward answers, as well as quotations and quizzes to give readers a new way of looking at something. In Tucker Shaw's *"What's That Smell?" (Oh, It's Me): 50 Mortifying Situations and How to Deal,* reading about other people's mortification may ease a reader's own embarrassment.

Readers interested in these titles will find more humorous titles in the "Popular Media and Consumer Culture" section of chapter 11.

### Cosmogirl Editors.

🌹 *Cosmogirl Quiz Book: All About You.* <u>Cosmo girl! Series</u>. New York: Hearst Books, 2004. ISBN 1588163814. 🇯 🇭

This selection of Cosmogirl quizzes is divided into three categories: fun, inner girl, and hear me roar. A lighthearted offering for girls to look at questions dealing with social situations, relationships, and themselves, without any serious repercussions, this is a good book for reading alone as well as in a group. **QP**

**Keywords:** Games and activities • Interpersonal relations • Questions • Quizzes • Social situations

🌹 *CosmoGIRL! Quiz Book: Discover Your Personality.* New York: Hearst Books, 2005. 9781588164896. 🇲 🇯

The latest book of Cosmogirl quizzes provides two dozen ways to help teens figure out who they are. The tests address different facets of personality, from color preference to leadership style to handwriting characteristics. Fun to do alone or with a group of friends; the last quiz is meant to be done with one's best friend. **QP**

**Keywords:** Personality tests • Psychology • Teenage girls

🌹 *Cosmogirl!: Words to Live By.* <u>Cosmo girl! Series</u>. New York: Hearst Books, 2006. ISBN 1588165280. 🇯 🇭

The thoughts and sayings collected in this book touch on subjects pertinent to every girl. They come from celebrities in all fields, movies, authors, sports figures, and Cosmogirl readers. A short, neatly designed book of quotes designed to provide inspiration and support. **QP**

**Keywords:** Advice • Conduct of life • Maxims • Quotations • Sayings

### Edut, Tali, and Ophira Edut.

*Astrostyle: Star-studded Advice for Love, Life, and Looking Good.* New York: Simon & Schuster, 2003. ISBN 9780743249850. 🇯 🇭

In this book readers can get the lowdown on what the alignment of the stars at the time of their birth says about them. Two astrologers offer profiles and style advice for each sign as well as thoughts on the results of possible pairings. Readers may learn what to watch for if they're mixing negative elements.

**Keywords:** Advice • Astrology

## Northcutt, Wendy.

*The Darwin Awards 4: Intelligent Design.* New York: Plume, 2006. ISBN 0525949607. **H** **A**

> This is the fourth annual publication of true tales about people lacking sound judgment. The awards are named after Charles Darwin; to be awarded one a person must have done something so foolish that the end result has actually left him or her unable to add to the gene pool. References are listed. This may not be suitable for the squeamish or those without a good sense of humor.
>
> **Keywords:** Black humor • Humor • Stupidity

## Shaw, Tucker.  Illustrated by Mike Reddy.

🏅 *"What's That Smell?" (Oh, It's Me): 50 Mortifying Situations and How to Deal.* New York: Alloy Books, 2003. ISBN 0142500119. **J** **H**

> Based on the premise that bad things happen and it's best to know how to deal with them and move on, Tucker Shaw presents survival techniques for situations likely not to be found in other manuals, such as advice for dealing with parents when a teen wrecks their car.. The book has several sections, including: "Family Nightmares," "Love Sucks," "Social Crises," "Online Problems," and "Hygiene Humiliation." The tone is similar to what one would expect from an older sibling—part comfort and part sarcasm—which is appropriate for some of these situations. The book provides practical, often amusing plans of action. **QP**
>
> **Keywords:** Advice • Dating • Errors • Humor • Survival

🏅 *Who Do You Think You Are?: 12 Methods for Analyzing the True You.* New York: Alloy Books, 2001. ISBN 014131091X. **J** **H**

> Tucker Shaw offers twelve different methods to use in analyzing personality types, from chakras to palm reading to personality typing to numerology. Each of the twelve comes with a short explanation, instructions, and a description for readers to see what aspects might apply to them or people they know. **QP**
>
> **Keywords:** Astrology • Numerology • Personality typing • Typology

🏅 *YM's the Best of Say Anything.* New York: Bantam, 2004. ISBN 0553376012. **J** **H** **RR**

> The editors of *YM* dug through their vault to present the most face-reddening moments from thirty years of letters sent to the "Say Anything" column. Presented in eight chapters, these are tales that show that we all have moments ranging from funny to gross to outright unbelievable. **QP**
>
> **Keywords:** Humor • Letters • Teenage girls

## Consider Starting with . . .

Daldry, Jeremy *The Teenage Guy's Survival Guide.*

Gravelle, Karen; Jennifer Gravelle. *The Period Book: Everything You Don't Want to Ask (But Need to Know).*

Holmes, Melisa; Patricia Hutchinson. *Girlology: Hang-Ups, Hook-Ups, and Holding Out: Stuff You Need to Know About Your Body, Sex, and Dating.*

Perrier, Pascale; Klaas Verplancke. *Flying Solo: How to Soar Above Your Lonely Feelings, Make Friends, and Find the Happiest You.*

## Fiction Read-Alikes

- **Friedman, Aimee, and Christine Norris.** In the graphic novel *Breaking Up,* four BFFs attending "Fashion High" deal with choices about friendship, popularity, and living up to the expectations of the fashion elite.

- **Vizzini, Ned.** Using his own experiences for background, Vizzini crafted a funny and hopeful novel about a young man whose call to a suicide hotline prompts him to get help for his depression in a nearby hospital. *It's Kind of a Funny Story* is just that, with a sense of humor amid the angst and troubles that the protagonist and other characters endure.

- **Vrettos, Adrienne Marie.** In *Skin,* the devastation and tragedy that arise in one dysfunctional family dealing with anorexia are seen through the eyes of the younger brother. Vrettos pulls no punches in her descriptions and language in this memorable and haunting book.

## References

"Adolescence." 2007. *Encyclopædia Britannica.* Available at http://search.eb.com. elibrary.calgarypubliclibrary.com/eb/article-9003766 (accessed September 8, 2007).

American Psychological Association (APA). 2002. *Developing Adolescents: A Reference for Professionals.* Available at http://www.apa.org/pi/pii/develop.pdf (accessed September 8, 2007).

Seidah, Amélie, and Thérèse Bouffard. 2007. "Being Proud of Oneself as a Person or Being Pround of One's Physical Appearance: What Matters for Feeling Well in Adolescence?" *Social Behavior & Personality: An International Journal* 35 (2): 255–68. *Psychology and Behavioral Sciences Collection*, EBSCOhost (accessed September 8, 2007).

# Chapter 9

## How To

## Definition

"Do it yourself" (DIY) is defined in Wikipedia as those areas in which people are "creating things for themselves without the aid of paid professionals" (2006). The phrase, which came into popular usage in the 1950s in reference to household work, applies equally well to any number of activities—from crafts and beauty to technology, games, and even survival skills. The subject matter's popularity is reflected in the numbers of reality television programs that show houses being remodeled and cars being remade, as well as competitions for chefs, hairdressers, dancers, fashion designers, and models. Rachael Ray and Emeril Lagasse remain mainstays, with their own television shows.

When Betty Carter surveyed junior high school libraries in 1987, books on drawing circulated frequently. This is still a popular subject, but it has since been joined by specialized craft books for teens, as well as books for making clothes or jewelry, adapting one's wardrobe, and creating one's own beauty products. This category includes titles that add to life skills, in terms of cooking and using technology, as well as a number of practical, artistic, and recreational subgenres.

## Appeal

These books provide more than just a chance to learn something new. There is great satisfaction in finishing a project that results in something tangible. Handcrafted items make great gifts and develop skills that last a lifetime. Some craft books provide historical details and are of interest to history buffs, while others will give teens ideas that are just seriously cool. As they test their abilities and interests and stretch their limits, teens are particularly drawn to how-to books.

DIY books also have a great appeal to reluctant readers; each year several titles are named to the Quick Picks for Reluctant Readers list. These books are colorful and clearly written and usually contain projects that are worth spending considerable time and attention on. Cookbooks provide mouthwatering recipes with helpful directions from chefs and teens.

Most crafts can be done in groups, with friends or family. Knitting, which has a long history as a social activity, has become a popular pastime and library program. Game books provide the same opportunity for competition as sports books, except that they generally allow people to interact with each other in a venue that often does not require a significant amount of physical activity. There are also abundant opportunities for escapist reading; several titles in the "Survival Skills" and "Beauty and Style" categories have been chosen for the American Library Association's Quick Picks for Reluctant Readers list.

## Chapter Organization

This chapter is organized into activity-based sections. Readers not sure what kind of project they would like to try will find a wide variety in "General Crafts." The following sections include books that tackle specific topics. Readers can give themselves a makeover with the books in the "Beauty and Style" section. They can add to their closets with the titles in the "Clothing and Accessories" section. The next sections list books on artistic pursuits, including "Acting," "Drawing," and "Comics and Graphic Novels." Hands-on sections include "Cooking," "Technology," "Games," and "Transportation." The final group of books cover "Survival Skills."

## General Crafts

Although many of the books and series in this category cover more than one kind of project, there is generally a theme to the book. A recent trend in this type of book is to take the approach of using crafts to study history, such as in Anderson's *Amazing Leonardo da Vinci Inventions You Can Build Yourself* or the <u>Crafts of the Ancient World</u> series. Environmental concerns have also become a more common theme in the media, popular culture, and mainstream publishing. This in turn means that repurposing, recycling, and using every last bit of material has been recognized as being important. These concerns have also been integrated into DIY books; instead of throwing something out, readers will find a new use for it in *ReadyMade*.

### Anderson, Maxine.

*Amazing Leonardo da Vinci Inventions You Can Build Yourself.* Norwich, VT: Nomad Press, 2006. ISBN 9780974934426. **M** **J**

The Mona Lisa is one of the best known examples of both Renaissance art and Leonardo da Vinci's genius. What isn't nearly as well known is the breadth of ideas and experiments da Vinci created. A short introduction to Renaissance history and a biography of the man himself are given before a discussion of da Vinci's creations in the fields of art, useful machines, water, flight, and war, which are reflected in the chosen activities. These include making a mask, a parachute, and a trebuchet. Sidebars explain the science. The well-illustrated instructions include pictures from da Vinci's own notebooks, offering an intriguing view of one of history's most forward-thinking technicians in art and science.

**Keywords:** da Vinci, Leonardo • Engineering • Handicrafts • Inventions • Models

## Berger, Shoshana, and Grace Hawthorne.

*ReadyMade: How to Make [Almost] Everything: A Do-It-Yourself Primer.* New York: Random House; Clarkson Potter, 2005. ISBN 1400081076; 9781400081073. **H**

> Authors Berger and Hawthorne, of *ReadyMade* magazine, take a direct approach to reusing materials usually discarded, offering instructions for projects to transform materials and fabrics into household items that may (or may not) be desirable, as well as offering a history of "raw" materials, such as paper, plastic, glass, and wood. The book offers humorous stories of failures as well as encouragement for creativity in terms of thinking of ways to reuse, instead of simply disposing of, items.
>
> **Keywords:** Crafts • Environment • Manufacturing • Recycling • Repurposing

## Bonnell, Jennifer.

🌲 *CosmoGIRL! Make It Yourself: 50 Fun and Funky Projects.* New York: Hearst Books, 2007. ISBN 781588166241. **M J**

> Whether looking for clothing projects, accessories, or beauty products, readers can find instructions on how to make them here. The ideas allow readers to adapt creations to show off their own style. They should begin with an "easy" project to get some practice, get some help, or make sure they have enough time to finish the "medium" and "hard" ones. The jeweled necklace T-shirt dress or honey-and-almond body scrub will take a lot less time than the ruched tube dress or customized tote bag. **QP**
>
> **Keywords:** Beauty • Clothing and dress • Crafts • Sewing

## Jovinelly, Joann.

### Crafts of the Ancient World.

> Jovinelly's series features a volume for each of four different civilizations in the ancient world. Each allows readers to learn about different aspects of the culture, government, and daily life of the citizenry. The introductions are followed by crafts related to the history. Warfare in the Greek volume is paired with a model of the Trojan horse; architecture is paired in the Roman volume with making a mosaic tile; the Egyptian volume has a plan for a sand pyramid; and beaded jewelry is made in the Aztec volume. Time lines and glossaries are included.
>
> **Keywords:** Ancient history • Crafts • Handicrafts

> *The Crafts and Culture of the Aztecs.* New York: Rosen Publishing Group, 2002. ISBN 0823935124. **M J**
>
> > **Keywords:** Aztecs • Crafts

> *The Crafts and Culture of the Egyptians.* New York: Rosen Publishing Group, 2002. ISBN 0823935094. **M J**
>
> > **Keywords:** Crafts • Egyptians

> *The Crafts and Culture of the Greeks.* New York: Rosen Publishing Group, 2002. ISBN 0823935108. **M J**
>
> > **Keywords:** Crafts • Greeks

*The Crafts and Culture of the Romans.* New York: Rosen Publishing Group, 2002. ISBN 0823935132. **M J**

Keywords: Crafts • Romans

## Jovinelly, Joann, and Jason Netelkos.

### Crafts of the Middle Ages.

This series focuses on the historical and cultural details of the time, which are then supplemented by craft projects appropriate for the place and people being described. The guilds, which gained greater power in medieval Europe, make jewelry; the town crafts include baking a bread trencher; a unicorn tapestry is a suitable decoration for a medieval castle; and a plague mask was a necessity for a monastery, which cared for the sick.

Keywords: Castles • Crafts • Handicrafts • Medieval history

Now Try: Readers who learn best by doing or who like combining interests will find another opportunity to do so in Rachel Dickinson's *Tools of the Ancient Romans: A Kid's Guide to the History & Science of Life in Ancient Rome.* This book considers several aspects of the Roman Republic, integrating related crafts. Among the projects are instructions for a ruin, an abacus, a laurel wreath, and a fresco.

*The Crafts and Culture of a Medieval Castle.* New York: Rosen Publishing Group, 2007. ISBN 1404207600. **M J**

Keywords: Castles • Medieval crafts

*The Crafts and Culture of a Medieval Cathedral.* New York: Rosen Publishing Group, 2006. ISBN 1404207589. **M J**

Keywords: Cathedrals • Churches • Medieval crafts

*The Crafts and Culture of a Medieval Guild.* New York: Rosen Publishing Group, 2006. ISBN 1404207570. **M J**

Keywords: Guilds • Jewelry • Medieval crafts

*The Crafts and Culture of a Medieval Manor.* New York: Rosen Publishing Group, 2006. ISBN 1404207562. **M J**

Keywords: Manor • Medieval crafts

*The Crafts and Culture of a Medieval Monastery.* New York: Rosen Publishing Group, 2006. ISBN1404207597. **M J**

Keywords: Medieval crafts • Monasteries

*The Crafts and Culture of a Medieval Town.* New York: Rosen Publishing Group, 2006 ISBN 1404207619. **M J**

Keywords: Medieval crafts • Towns

## Rogge, Hannah.

🌶 *Hardwear: Jewelry from a Toolbox.* Photographs by Marianne Rafter. New York: Stewart, Tabori & Chang, 2006. ISBN 9781584794806. **J H A**

Marrying the luxurious, decorative, and unnecessary with the practical, basic, and masculine results in unusual and groundbreaking jewelry made from materials found at a hardware store, as well as at a more traditional bead store or online. The projects here are divided into chapters according to their main materials: washers;

rope; metal connectors; nuts; or vinyl, plastic, and rubber. The projects produce gifts fit for anyone. All instructions are illustrated. A glossary is also provided. **QP**

**Keywords:** Crafts • Jewelry

## Schiedermayer, Ellie.

*Got Tape?: Roll Out the Fun with Duct Tape!* Iola, WI: Krause Publications, 2002. ISBN 9780873494267. **J H**

Duct tape is inexpensive, practically indestructible, and now available in at least a dozen colors, including red, purple, and gold. An inventive high school student has provided a book with full-sized patterns, photographs, and step-by-step instructions for projects that don't require much time or experience, and require only tape and scissors to complete. Crafters are encouraged to embellish or personalize the thirty projects, which include such things as wallets, frames, bracelets, and clothes.

**Keywords:** Crafts • Duct tape • Handicrafts

**Now Try:** Joe Wilson's updated *Ductigami: The Art of the Tape* includes a history of duct tape along with photographs of his finished projects, inserted into artworks using Photoshop. Instructions are given for practicing before starting any of the projects. The eighteen crafts make use of duct tape's strength for useful end products that include a cell phone cover, pet raingear, a phone book cover, and a cooler/lunchbox.

## Traig, Jennifer.

### The Crafty Girl Series.

This series includes ideal projects to interest anyone in crafts, style, fashion, and makeup. Intended to offer alternatives to hanging around at home, the books offer lists of supplies and complete instructions for useful, practical, and tempting projects. Options include possibilities for theme parties and useful tools for babysitting.

**Keywords:** Accessories • Crafts • Handicrafts • Makeup

🎀 *Accessories: Things to Make and Do.* San Francisco: Chronicle Books, c2002. ISBN 0811831515. **M J H**

Fashion projects to glam up nights, days, and every possible occasion, whether beachside, at school, or just "on the go." A belt, collar, cuff, barrette, and messenger bag to keep them in are just a few of the projects, all with a list of supplies and instructions. Stencils are also included for creating further adornment.

**Keywords:** Accessories • Clothing • Handicrafts

*Beauty: Things to Make and Do.* San Francisco: Chronicle Books, 2001. ISBN 0811829995. **J H**

Traig and coauthor Julianne Balmain offer new ways for teens to look at beauty aisles in stores. This entry in the <u>Crafty Girl</u> series explains the basic ingredients in many of the most popular beauty products and then offers clear, easy-to-follow recipes for teens to make their own alternative products at home. In this fun little volume readers may learn to make such things as their own massage oils or soaps while reading about aromatherapy.

**Keywords:** Beauty • Crafts • Health • Hygiene

*Cool Stuff: Things to Make and Do.* San Francisco: Chronicle Books, 2001. ISBN 0811829456. **M** **J** **H**

Traig and coauthor Julianne Balmain present projects that convert everyday objects into things that are a lot more fun—such as picture frames, desk and dresser accessories, decorations for windows and walls, and bedroom items. The clear instructions include a notice indicating whether help or supervision may be needed for novices.

**Keywords:** Crafts • Handicrafts

*Fun and Games: Things to Make and Do.* San Francisco: Chronicle Books, 2001. ISBN 0811831256. **M** **J**

This volume includes rules, recipes, games, activities, and board games as alternatives to boredom. Guidelines, rules, necessary equipment, and anything else required for completing tasks are included. Some of these experiments and outdoor games could be very handy when babysitting.

**Keywords:** Crafts • Games • Handicrafts

🌂 *Hair: Things to Make and Do.* San Francisco: Chronicle Books, c2004. ISBN 0811840336. **M** **J**

Readers will learn how to maintain a healthy head of hair, find the right hairstyle for the shape of their faces, and make some great accessories for their crowning glory. Instructions are given for achieving particular looks and handcrafted hair accessories. Recipes for hair products include tips on how and when to use them. **QP**

**Keywords:** Hair accessories • Hair care • Hairstyles

*Makeup: Things to Make and Do.* San Francisco: Chronicle Books, c2003. ISBN 0811836797. **M** **J**

Every aspect of makeup in which a crafty girl would be interested is considered, broken down by cosmetic types and their uses. Readers will then find different kinds of looks and what is needed to achieve each one. An additional section includes recipes for homemade cosmetics, including several lip glosses.

**Keywords:** Cosmetics • Handicrafts • Makeup • Skin care

🌂 *Slumber Parties: Things to Make and Do.* San Francisco: Chronicle Books, 2002. ISBN 0811835715. **M** **J**

This book contains plans for fourteen themed slumber parties, from an all-night Sweet Dreams candy fest to a more relaxed Bliss-Out Spa party. Each party plan comes with suggestions for music, recipes, and other crafts or games. **QP**

**Keywords:** Crafts • Parties • Recipes

**Vitkus, Jessica. Illustrated by Elizabeth Lee.**

🎖 *Alternacrafts: [20+ Hi-style, Lo-budget Projects to Make].* **Photographs by Brian Kennedy.** New York: Stewart, Tabori & Chang, 2005. ISBN 9781584794561. **H**

Crafts make great gifts because they show care and creativity on the part of the giver, no matter how much time and effort is required. This unique guide offers crafters an opportunity to make use of materials that they already have, presenting "ten commandments of crafting" that will set them on the way to producing useful, fun projects by recycling things that they would otherwise be throwing out. Instructions for making snack-wrapper wallets, remaking T-shirts, and turning a bottle cap into a pendant are just a few of the ideas to be found in this book dedicated to repurposing and improvising. **PP**

**Keywords:** Crafts • Recycling

# Beauty and Style

Why wouldn't people want to learn how to take the sting out of their wallets, when, as Shari Graydon's *In Your Face: The Culture of Beauty and You* tells us, they spend over $6 billion on makeup alone? These DIY guides are intended to help people avoid paying professionals for services in two important areas: beauty and style. Both are very popular with female readers.

## Beauty

Books in this section are devoted to the process of beautification: helping to improve one's outward appearance. Readers will find recipes for making products, as well as information about finding and using the right colors, makeup, tools, and discussions on what to do to look one's best.

### Brown, Bobbi, and Annemarie Iverson.

🎖 *Bobbi Brown Teenage Beauty: Everything You Need to Look Pretty, Natural, Sexy & Awesome.* New York: Cliff Street, 2000. ISBN 006019636X. **M J H RR**

Brown and Iverson concentrate on using very little makeup to make teens stand out, with great results, featuring "Makeunders" that emphasize the small amount of makeup that is actually needed. Advice is given about specific facial features, and there are chapters for African Americans, Latin Americans, Asian Americans, and "Global Beauties." The authors also offer their thoughts on diet and exercise, dermatologists, and where to buy beauty products. **QP**

**Keywords:** Beauty • Makeup • Skin care

## McCann, Lauren.

🌸 *Teen People Celebrity Beauty Guide: Star Secrets for Gorgeous Hair, Makeup, Skin and More!* Plattsburgh, NY: Time Inc., 2005. ISBN 1932273395. **M** **J**

The editors of *Teen People* use photos of stars to illustrate the best and worst in hair, makeup, and fashion. Included are explanations and examples of makeup, tools, hair types, styles, and problems, all clearly illustrated. Readers may find out how to get the look they love, the products they need, and how to use them, in this great and fun guide for anyone who loves makeup. **QP**

**Keywords:** Beauty • Hair • Fashion • Makeup • Style

## Milano, Selene.

🌸 *Unforgettable Color: Makeup with Confidence.* Toronto: Carlton Books; distributed by Firefly Books, 2003. ISBN 155297670X; 9781552976708. **J** **H** **RR**

Milano takes the science of color typing one step further in this book about makeup. Chapters about seven colors are preceded by a discussion of what color preference says about a person. Readers will then see which shades of that color family are the most flattering for different skin tones and hair colors. Guides for makeup application include the basics, as well as tips for special occasions. **QP**

**Keywords:** Beauty • Colors • Cosmetics • Makeup

## Naylor, Caroline.

🌸 *Beauty Trix for Cool Chix: Easy-to-Make Lotions, Potions, and Spells to Bring Out a Beautiful You.* New York: Watson-Guptill, 2003. ISBN 0823069575. **M** **J**

Caroline Naylor presents a book of fun and easy recipes for homemade beauty "boosts." Readers will learn how to make lotions, shampoos, conditioners, cream, and bath oil and how to scent these with any of several suggested combinations of essential oils for aromatherapy benefits. Tips and tricks are also offered for makeup, manicures, and pedicures as well as gift wrappings, should any readers like to share these crafts with friends. **QP**

**Keywords:** Aromatherapy • Beauty • Crafts • Makeup

## Schlip, Joanna.

*Glamour Gurlz: The Ultimate Step-by-Step Guide to Great Makeup and Gurl Smarts.* New York: Clarkson Potter, 2006. ISBN 9780307339355. **H** **RR**

A world-renowned celebrity makeup artist presents seventy looks and how to find the look that will work for the reader. The photos of and step-by step instructions about favorite looks may be adapted if the reader wishes. The models and "gurls" have been chosen for their great attributes that need to be defined and celebrated.

**Keywords:** Beauty • Personal hygiene

## Worthington, Charles.

🌸 *The Complete Book of Hairstyling.* Willowdale, ON; Buffalo, NY: Firefly Books, 2002. ISBN: 1552975762; 9781552975763. **J** **H**

Hairstylist Worthington answers every question about hair care and styling, from cuts and products to salon practices and procedures. Cuts from the simple to the stylish are provided, with instructions and advice on choosing a look is suitable for the shape of one's face. **QP**

**Keywords:** Beauty • Grooming • Hairstyles

## Style

Books in this section concentrate on wardrobe and accessories—how to put clothes and accessories together for a great look. These books are very popular with female readers.

### Beker, Jeanne

*The Big Night Out.* Toronto: Tundra Books, 2005. ISBN 0887767192. **M J**

A host from fashion television presents a guide for finding one's own style and getting ready for any big night. Chapters include shopping, styles, accessories, makeup, and getting ready. In each chapter Beker answers questions appropriate to the subject, from budgets to the right kind of bra, always in a straightforward manner and with a reminder that true style comes from within.

**Keywords:** Fashion • Self-esteem • Style

### Koopersmith, Chase.

*How to Be a Teen Fashionista: Put Together the Hottest Outfits and Accessories—on Any Budget.* Gloucester, MA: Fair Winds, 2005. ISBN 1592331629. **H**

Koopersmith decided to go through ninth grade without wearing the same outfit twice. She managed to do it, too—with good shopping, embellishments, repurposing, and accessories. This book shows readers how they can do this too, starting off with suggestions for becoming style conscious, buying the right clothes, accessorizing, and putting things together properly and offering rules for maintaining one's wardrobe. Several craft projects are included. Chase, who is now a correspondent for *Teen Newsweek*, illustrates her wardrobe styles on real girls and adds a list of her favorite stores for readers who are interested in the brands she uses in the book.

**Keywords:** Accessories • Fashion • Repurposing • Style

### Leive, Cindi, and Rebecca Sample Gerstung.

*Glamour's Big Book of Dos & Don'ts: Fashion Help for Every Woman.* New York: Gotham Books, 2006. ISBN 9781592402335. **H**

The editors of *Glamour* magazine present the fruits of one of the style magazine's most popular columns: "Dos and Don'ts." Asserting that everyone can have an off-day in fashion, including the magazine's editor-in-chief, the book illustrates how to choose the best styles for one's shape, then offers more than 750 examples of ways to get fashion right and wrong. Twelve different style makeovers for particular effects are included. All other pictures were taken by photographers on the street, of people as they actually appeared. Real people and celebrities are seen, for once, as not necessarily being perfect.

**Keywords:** Beauty • Clothing and dress • Fashion • Style

## Teen People Magazine.

*Celebrity Style Guide.* New York: Time Home Entertainment, 2006. ISBN 9781933405353. **M** **J**

Do readers check out what the stars wear on the red carpet? Do they wish they had the style sense of their favorite celebs? Readers may not have the stars' money, a stylist, and access to their closets, but thanks to the editors of a magazine that is everywhere the stars are, readers can learn what fashions accentuate or hide different features and find a primer on colors, fabrics, and accessories. All of these are shown on some of today's hottest stars.

**Keywords:** Celebrities • Clothing • Fabrics • Fashion • Style

**Now Try:** Janice Weaver looks at fashion through the ages and across cultures in *From Head to Toe: Bound Feet, Bathing Suits, and Other Bizarre and Beautiful Things.* This fun and light book examines how men and women have dressed, painted themselves, and added to their looks. The author also alerts the reader to the concept of fashion being a reflection of its society and times, which led to the rise of fads. For a broader look at clothes and their importance in Western society, the reader may look at L. Rowland-Warne's and Liz McAulay's *Costume.* This entry in the Eyewitness Books series starts by asking, "Why bother with clothes?" and answers the question for successive historical periods and with the copious photographs common to the series.

# Clothing and Accessories

Knitting has enjoyed a resurgence in recent years, among teens as well as adults. The ability to produce something wearable, durable, and beautiful is a life skill that may be taken up at any age. Guides are also produced for teen sewing and crocheting. A recent trend has seen the publication of books on repurposing clothing and sweaters. *Second-Time Cool* turns old sweaters into felt that may be reused, and the Popular Paperback title *Generation T* finds innovative ways to make fashion out of discarded T-shirts.

## Blakeney, Faith, Justina Blakeney, and Ellen Schultz.

🏃 *99 Ways to Cut, Sew & Deck Out Your Denim.* New York: Potter Craft, 2007. 9780307351708. **H** **A**

Almost everyone has an old pair of jeans in their closet that they don't wear anymore. How about transforming them into a skirt, bag, shirt, vest, hat, or even an iPod case? If readers don't know how to sew or use a sewing machine, they'll need to go through the glossary and practice making a pattern. Fortunately there are instructions, and the ninety-nine patterns included in this volume are graded for difficulty so that readers can start with something simple and work their way up. **QP**

**Keywords:** Fashion • Jeans • Repurposing • Sewing

## Haab, Sherri.

🏆 *The Hip Handbag Book: 25 Easy-to-Make Totes, Purses and Bags.* New York: Watson-Guptill Publications, 2004. ISBN 9780823022632. **M** **J** **RR**

Haab's guide to handbags starts with a guide to the tools and techniques used in her projects, illustrating each to make it understandable for the novice hobbyist. The projects themselves are divided by level of experience, providing choices for those with more time and experience. Each project is accompanied by a plan, a list of supplies, and step-by-step instructions. **QP**

Keywords: Hobbies • Plans • Purses • Sewing

## Lindén Ivarsson, Anna-Stina, Katarina Brieditis and Katarina Evans.

*Second-time Cool: The Art of Chopping Up a Sweater.* Translated by Maria Lundin. Toronto: Annick Press, c2005. ISBN 9781550379112. **J** **H**

This book shows how to use a washing machine to turn wool sweaters into felt that can be used for something new: bags, hats, and trims. Additional chapters suggest ways to use knitting, crocheting, and embroidery to personalize and embellish projects. Resources for learning basic stitches are included. Readers can take repurposing to the next level with this innovative DIY guide. The creative crafter can find many new possibilities here.

Keywords: Crafts • Crocheting • Knitting • Remaking clothes • Repurposing • Style

## Nicolay, Megan.

🏆 *Generation T: 108 ways to Transform a T-shirt.* New York: Workman Publishing, 2006. ISBN 9780761137856. **J** **H**

T-shirts are one of the most common garments in almost every teen's closet, the fabric equivalent of the rabbit, multiplying exponentially and providing a legacy of fashion history in colors and logos. What could be better than finding an easy way to change these unused articles into something fun and useful? Starting with a guide to the terms, tools, and stitches required, crafters will find projects divided by clothing styles, before moving to "accents for the home and body" and suggestions for the leftovers. The possibilities are limitless—funky T-shirts, tanks and skirts, pillow cases, handbags, hair bands, and more. Each project is graded for difficulty, and at least a third of them don't require any sewing at all, making this a fun guide for teens at any skill level. **PP**

Keywords: Crafts • DIY • Fashion • Refashioning • Remaking clothing • Remaking T-shirts

## Okey, Shannon.

*Knitgrrl: Learn to Knit with 15 Fun and Funky Patterns.* New York: Watson-Guptill, 2005 ISBN 9780823026180. **M** **J** **H**

A knitting guide for beginners, with patterns intended to specifically appeal to teens. The chapters start at a basic level and add on a new skill with each pattern, supplementing directions with color photos and online resources.

**Keywords:** Crafts • Hobbies • Knitting

## Rannels, Melissa.

🔖 *Sew Subversive: Down and Dirty DIY for the Fabulous Fashionista.* Newtown, CT: The Taunton Press, 2006. ISBN 9781561588091. **H**

This fun book gives novice sewers all of the basics. An introductory chapter covers "hand-sewing basics," including enough stitches to get started and explanations for basic tasks. This is followed by an introduction to the sewing machine and other equipment and a buying guide. The projects that follow vary from making new things to refashioning, altering, and embellishing tired clothing to spice up a tired wardrobe and make something just for oneself. The projects have a lot of options and don't require much time to complete, from ten minutes for a hip belt to an hour for a pillow tank dress. **QP**

**Keywords:** Crafts • Fashion • Sewing

## Sadler, Judy Ann, and Esperança Melo.

*Quick Knits.* Kids Can Do It. Toronto: Kids Can Press, 2006. ISBN 1563891654. **M J**

This knitting book, suitable for beginners, starts out with knitting basics, including casting on and the basic stitches required for all of the projects in the second half of the book. There are illustrations for every step, and Sadler includes tips on how to fix mistakes. The patterns are fun and concentrate on projects that do not require advanced techniques and will produce something that is useable, such as a fuzzy scarf, a drawstring backpack, trim for clothing, and a fuzzy foot mat. The final garment is a "Quick-knit" sweater, with finishing instructions included.

**Keywords:** Crafts • Knitting • Patterns

## Zent, Sheila.

*Sew Teen: Make Your Own Cool Clothes.* New York: Sixth & Spring Books, 2006. ISBN 1931543909. **J H**

This guide opens with basic techniques, terminology, and directions on how to take measurements. Each project has further instructions for calculating how much fabric to buy and tips on sewing different fabrics, as well as drawings to help with construction. The twenty-one projects vary from simple "no-sew" projects to ones that require more advanced techniques.

**Keywords:** Clothing • Crafts • Hobbies • Instructions • Sewing

**Now Try:** A beginner may also find an introduction to hand and machine sewing in Judy Ann Sadler's *Simply Sewing*, from the Kids Can Do It series. Similar in layout to her knitting book, it provides a demonstration of sewing techniques and then directions for twelve patterns, each of which includes a picture of the finished product, a list of items required, and complete directions.

# Acting

Acting must be done very well indeed if it is to be done successfully. This subgenre contain books about the craft of acting and what it is like to make a living as an actor.

## Belli, Mary Lou, and Dinah Lenney.

*Acting for Young Actors: The Ultimate Teen Guide.* New York: Back Stage Books/Watson-Guptil, 2006. ISBN 9780823049479. **J** **H**

This is a book for teens who are seriously interested in the craft of acting: Actors offer practical information and differentiate reality programming from real acting, covering both film and television acting. In addition to monologues and improvisation, readers will find "Dos and Don'ts" for auditions, information about rehearsals, and what it is like to work as an actor. Anyone serious about acting can find out how to do it for fun, in school, camps, and with other training opportunities. Supplementary information is offered about the practicalities of unions, classes, and making use of what one has.

**Keywords:** Acting • Auditions

## Friedman, Lise

*Break a Leg!: The Kids' Book of Acting and Stagecraft.* **Photographs by Mary Dowdle.** New York: Workman Publishing, 2002. ISBN 9780761122081. **M** **J**

This book explains all about acting techniques, from warm ups, to acting exercises, to overcoming stage fright, as well as performance highs and lows and making a living as an actor. Readers will also be given practical advice about getting started in the business. Information about head shots, audition advice, and pictures of working child actors are provided throughout the book. Different kinds of acting and jobs done behind the scenes in stage, film, and television are covered also.

**Keywords:** Acting • Theater direction • Theater production

## Nevraumont, Edward J., and Nicholas P. Hanson.

*The Ultimate Improv Book: A Complete Guide to Comedy Improvisation.* Colorado Springs, CO: Meriwether Publishing, 2001. ISBN 9781566080750. **H**

Improvisation provides an alternative to traditional theater as well as a way to help readers practice in front of an audience and learn to think on their feet. It can also be done with groups of almost any size: The exercises and games here may be adapted to be used with pairs and large teams and use a wide range of skills appropriate for budding thespians to help sharpen their wits.

**Keywords:** Acting • Improvisation • Stand-up comedy

1

2

3

4

5

6

7

8

9

10

11

# Drawing

Drawing was a popular subject with young adult readers when Betty Carter did her circulation study in the early 1970s, and it still is. What has changed since then is the subject matter. The overwhelming popularity of graphic novels is evident in the number of books that give teens instructions and advice about cartooning, manga, and anime. This section is divided into two categories, "Techniques" and "Anime and Manga," in which readers will be able to find books specifically on those subjects. Teens interested in writing and creating graphic novels will find material in the "Comics and Graphic Novels" section.

## Techniques

In this section are some guides to help readers refine their drawing. Most of these have step-by-step illustrations to help the work take off. Supplemental information often includes interviews, suggestions for supplies, and tips.

### Caldwell, Ben

🏆 *Fantasy! Cartooning.* New York, Sterling Publishing, 2005. ISBN 9781402716126. **M** **J** **H** **RR**

Artists interested in fantasy create their own worlds, complete with heroes, villains, lords and ladies, and the sidhe. In each sketch, tips show why and how each part of the figure matters, from nails to stance to the length of faces. **QP**

Keywords: Cartooning • Cartoons • Drawing • Fantasy

### Hart, Christopher.

*Drawing Cutting Edge Anatomy: The Ultimate Reference Guide for Comic Book Artists.* Cutting Edge. New York: Watson-Guptill Publications, 2004. ISBN 9780823023981. **H** **A**

Readers will not only find an incredibly detailed look at virtually every muscle group, shown posed and in motion, but they will also find three sections with additional information: elements to practice, starting out strategies in "the biz," and interviews with comic book artists.

Keywords: Anatomy • Drawing

### Lee, John.

🏆 *Street Scene: How to Draw Graffiti-Style.* Cincinnati, OH: IMPACT Books, 2007. ISBN 9781581808476. **J** **H**

A dash of cartooning with some manga thrown in results in Lee's "ultracool" and fun "graffiti-style" of drawing. It is meant to be fun, playful, and done at any and all times. Readers are shown how to build up characters, interiors, and exteriors, piece by piece. Drawings may be done in ink, pencil, or both. Lots of extra tips accompany the sketches to provide help and inspiration. **QP**

Keywords: Drawing, Graffiti, Popular culture, Street scenes

## Miller, Steve.

*Hi-Yah: How to Draw Fantastic Martial Arts Comics.* New York: Watson-Guptill Publications, 2007. ISBN 9780823022465. **H**

Included here are step-by-step instructions for drawing favorite martial arts moves as well as a cornucopia of additional information, including background for each drawing, suggestions for supplies, and lessons on techniques such as foreshortening, and drawing parts of the body. There are chapters that provide some great ideas for creating one's own comic, such as the "Fight Club" chapter, which has sections on "adding oomph" and "cyber chicks."

**Keywords:** Cartooning • Drawing • Martial arts cartoons

## Miller, Steve, and Bryan Baugh.

🎗 *Scared!: How to Draw Fantastic Horror Comic Characters.* New York: Watson-Guptill Publications, 2004. ISBN 9780823016648. **J** **H**

This is much more than just a how-to of ghoulish, creepy characters, although it has an abundance of those, in categories including "The Dead & the Undead," "It Came from Outer Space," and "Creature Features." Readers will also find interviews with illustrators, including Vincent Locke and Bernie Wrightson, and a fascinating history of horror comics. **QP**

**Keywords:** Cartooning • Comics • Drawing techniques

## Anime and Manga

*Manga* is a Japanese genre of cartoons and animation, usually recognizable by the style of illustration. *Anime* refers to Japanese animation. The books in this category help readers copy these distinctive illustration styles.

## DesignEXchange.

🎗 *Japanese Comickers: Draw Anime and Manga Like Japan's Hottest Artists.* Tokyo: DesignEXchange; New York: Harper Design International, 2003. ISBN 0060513551. **H**

More a lesson in art appreciation and anime than a how-to about drawing, this book covers twelve of Japan's feature illustrators and their work. A gallery of representative works is presented for each artist, who then explains his or her technique using a single work shown in several stages. The artists use different methods, including computers, drawings, pencils, or combinations of these to produce works of art that are shown in full-page spreads. The end result is both instructive and beautiful. **QP**

**Keywords:** Anime • Art • Japanese art • Manga

## Hart, Christopher.

🎗 *Anime Mania: How to Draw Characters for Japanese Animation.* New York: Watson-Guptill Publications, 2002. ISBN 082300158X. **M** **J**

In this introduction to the Japanese form of animation, Hart entices all levels of cartoonists. It starts with "basic character construction" and works its way through characters and creatures and how to use them, from the basics of storyboarding to how an animation studio works. Interviews with anime directors are included. **QP**

**Keywords:** Animation • Anime • Drawing instruction

## Hart, Christopher.

### The Manga Mania Series.
One of today's most popular comic formats, *manga* means "comics" in Japanese. The elements of the format are introduced in this series of books intended for those interested in drawing or manga.

🔥 *Manga Mania: How to Draw Japanese Comics.* New York: Watson Guptill Publications, 2001. ISBN 0823030350. **M J**

Hart starts with a short introduction to manga before breaking down the basic elements of the drawing style. He progresses through poses, genres, scenes, and characters, with a step-by-step visual guide to aid instruction. **QP**

**Keywords:** Cartooning • Drawing • Instruction • Manga

🔥 *Manga Mania Chibi and Furry Characters: How to Draw the Adorable Mini-People and Cool Cat-Girls of Japanese Comics.* New York: Watson-Guptill Publications, 2006. ISBN 0823029778. **M J RR**

The "adorable, naughty, mischievous" creatures that populate the Japanese comics are given Hart's full attention in this volume. From the beginnings of facial shapes to costumes and fantasy animals, readers are given a thorough background in these popular characters. **QP**

**Keywords:** Cartooning • Chibi • Drawing • Instruction • Manga

🔥 *Manga Mania Fantasy Worlds: How to Draw the Amazing Worlds of Japanese Comics.* New York: Watson-Guptill Publications, 2003. ISBN 0823029727. **M J**

What fantasy would be complete without the strange characters found in the fantasy realm? Hart teaches young cartoonists how to add everything and everyone necessary to place their manga in the world of science fiction and fantasy. **QP**

**Keywords:** Cartooning • Drawing techniques • Fantasy • Instructions Manga • Science fiction

*Manga Mania Magical Girls and Friends: How to Draw the Super-Popular Action-Fantasy Characters of Manga.* New York: Watson-Guptill Publications, c2006. ISBN 0823029689. **M J**

Christopher Hart concentrates on the female characters found in manga, starting with faces and moving on through bodies, poses, and costumes. As in his other books, he then takes a step-by-step approach to using those characters to best effect in comics.

**Keywords:** Instruction • Manga • Technique

*Manga Mania Shoujo: How to Draw the Charming and Romantic Characters of Japanese Comics.* New York: Watson Guptill Publications, 2004. ISBN 0823029735. **M J RR**

Shoujo manga is one of the most popular genres of manga. Its stories focus on peer pressure, romance, and friendship. Hart explores the facial expressions, body types, body language, characters, and clothing needed to draw in this format.

**Keywords:** Cartooning • Drawing techniques • Instruction • Manga • Shoujo

🏵 *Manga Mania Villains: How to Draw the Dastardly Characters of Japanese Comics.* New York: Watson-Guptill, 2003. ISBN 0823029719. **M** **J**

Christopher Hart's book on manga villains goes further than giving instructions on how to draw them. He also includes sections on their costumes, powers, and weapons and how to best use them in comic panels and pages. As in his other books, all of his instructions are illustrated. **QP**

**Keywords:** Cartooning • Drawing techniques • Instructions • Manga • Manga villains

*Mecha Mania: How to Draw the Battling Robots, Cool Spaceships, and Military Vehicles of Japanese Comics.* New York: Watson-Guptill, 2002. ISBN 0823030563. **M** **J**

Focusing on the "mechanically-based humanoids" found in anime and manga, Hart starts with the basics and shows how to build 'bots that can fly, swim, use weapons, and be integrated into comics. Includes some 300 illustrations.

**Keywords:** Cartooning • Drawing techniques • Instructions • Manga • Robots

**Now Try:** Readers interested in drawing might be looking for something more specific about robots, or something a little bit easier. Aaron Sautter and Jason Knudson have created a simple guide with a handful of projects for novice artists, *How to Draw Terrifying Robots*. Other books in the <u>Drawing Cool Stuff</u> series, which also include step-by-step instructions, show readers *How to Draw Manga Warriors* or *How to Draw Comic Heroes*.

## Hart, Christopher.

🏵 *Manhwa Mania: How to Draw Korean Comics.* New York: Watson Guptill Publications, 2004. ISBN 082302976X. **M** **J** **RR**

Christopher Hart differentiates between manga and manhwa (Korean comic books), offering a comparison between the two formats before introducing the elements of manhwa. He finishes this book with suggestions for "designing the comic book page" and "extreme manhwa" that will help more experienced cartoonists improve their drawing. **QP**

**Keywords:** Cartooning • Drawing • Instruction • Manhwa

# Comics and Graphic Novels

Graphic novels are one of the fastest growing and most popular formats available today. They are receiving more critical praise and recognition, as well as room on library bookshelves. The books in this section provide information about how to create comics and graphic novels. Books about cartooning, including drawing manga and anime, may be found in the previous section.

## Eisner, Will.

*Graphic Storytelling.* Tamarac, FL: Poorhouse Press, 1996. 0961472832.
**J H A**

The acknowledged master of graphic novels shows how to "write with pictures."
Readers will learn about the different kinds of stories and how to get them across
to an audience in a graphic medium. Eisner discusses ideas, storytelling, and writing and then looks at how to apply them to a visual format, with a multitude of
examples.

**Keywords:** Comics • Storytelling • Writing for comics

## Macloud, Scott.

*Making Comics: Storytelling Secrets of Comics, Manga and Graphic Novels.* New
York: Harper, 2006. ISBN 9780060780944. **H**

How and why are cartoon panels laid out the way they are? How can artists
achieve different effects? Macleod breaks comics down into the most basic parts
here, illustrating everything as he shows exactly how to get started. There is also a
supplementary bibliography. Budding artists will find all of the building blocks to
start their own comic.

**Keywords:** Art • Comics • Drawing • Graphic nonfiction

**Now Try:** Readers interested in comics or who would like to understand the burgeoning
popularity of comics and graphic novels might consider Scott Macleod's Eisner
award–winning *Understanding Comics: The Invisible Art*. This classic look at the medium examines in comic format the elements that make up comics..

## Rollins, Prentis.

🎖 *The Making of a Graphic Novel: The Resonator.* New York: Watson-Guptill,
2006. ISBN 9780823030538. **J H**

One side of this flip book presents a world in which humans have lost the capacity
to sleep, until Bronsen comes into contact with a Resonator and learns what it is to
dream, never thinking that this could affect humanity. The other side tells how the
story was conceived, with a step-by-step guide on the process of creating, writing,
drawing, and inking the graphic novel. Many of the drafts and information on
needed supplies are included. This title was included on the 2007 Great Graphic
Novels for Teens list.

**Keywords:** Cartoons • Graphic nonfiction • Writing

## Todd, Mark, and Esther Pearl Watson.

🎖 *Whatcha Mean, What's a Zine?: The Art of Making Zines and Mini-comics.*
Boston: Graphia, 2006. ISBN 1415677506. **M J H**

An introduction and guide to zines from longtime zinesters Todd and Watson. Includes useful information and guides from more than twenty other zine and
mini-comic creators on widely varying topics from zine subjects to copying, bind-
ing, and printing tips. Creative teens are offered new outlets in these discussions.
**ALA**

**Keywords:** Graphic novels • Self-publishing,

**Now Try:** All published authors need to start somewhere. Elizabeth and Timothy Harper's *Your Name in Print: A Teen's Guide to Publishing for Fun, Profit, and Academic Success* offers a number of suggestions about where to begin, including blogs, Web sites, and school newspapers. Readers will also find a realistic explanation of the writing and publication process.

## Cooking

Cooking is an activity that many teens become interested in as they prepare for independence. Teen cookbooks are usually illustrated and often feature glossaries and supplementary information that is not found in adult cookbooks. Their authors are often subject specialists. Male chefs, like Sam Stern, author of *Cooking up a Storm: The Teen Survival Cookbook*, can offer male readers a viable role model as a presence in the kitchen. For crossover reading opportunities, readers may check the "Working Life" section of chapter 3

### Carle, Megan, Jill Carle, and Judy Carle.

🏆 *Teens Cook: How to Cook What You Want to Eat.* **Illustrated by Jessica Boone.** Berkeley, CA: Ten Speed Press, 2004. ISBN 1580085849. **J H**

Two teens, Megan and Jill Carle, wrote this cookbook to explain how to become self-sufficient in the kitchen. Incorporating basic cooking instructions into the recipes, they offer shortcuts from traditional cooking to make easier versions, with plenty of vegetarian options, albeit far from low-fat. Their own "Kitchen Disasters" lend a sincere, friendly tone to the book. **PP**

Keywords: Cooking • Vegetarian cooking

*Teens Cook Dessert.* Berkeley, CA: Ten Speed Press, 2006. ISBN 1580087523. **J H**

Teen cooks Megan and Jill Carle add to their repertoire with a volume dedicated to their favorite part of any meal: dessert. Each recipe includes a personal opinion or anecdote that speaks directly to the reader, with historical facts, shortcuts, and vocabulary help added in sidebars. The recipes start with the basics and get more difficult, moving from chocolate chip cookies to peppermint ice cream sandwiches and banana spring rolls with cinnamon-caramel sauce, among dozens of others.

Keywords: Cooking • Desserts

### Krizmanic, Judy.

🏆 *The Teen's Vegetarian Cookbook.* **Illustrated by Matthew Wawiorka.** New York: Puffin, 1999. ISBN 0140385061. **M J H**

In addition to the usual cookbook sections of breakfasts, soups, main courses, and desserts, this valuable book contains many extras for teens considering a vegetarian lifestyle, such as a glossary to explain ingredients and terms for new vegetarian cooks, a chart to make sure that meals have complete nutritional values, hints, and menus. Recipes that are especially fast or "insanely easy" to prepare are also marked. **BBYA**

Keywords: Cooking • Vegetarian cooking

## Raab, Evelyn.

*Clueless in the Kitchen: A Cookbook for Teens.* Buffalo, NY: Firefly Books, 1998. ISBN 1552092240. Reprinted 2006. ISBN 1552092240. **M J H RR**

> This is a cookbook intended for those people who need help from beginning to end of a recipe. Using both humor and good sense, the author provides instructions that run the gamut from loading the fridge, to preparing complete meals, to what to do with leftovers, including when and how to defrost the refrigerator. A conversion chart, glossary, and other instructions will be especially helpful to novices in the kitchen.
>
> **Keywords:** Cooking • Nutrition

## Stern, Sam.

*Cooking up a Storm: The Teen Survival Cookbook.* Cambridge, MA: Candlewick Press, 2006. ISBN 076362988X. **M J H BB**

> An English teen offers a fresh entry in the cookbook field. Although this is generally directed toward guys, it will work for either gender. Readers are offered reasons for cooking's appeal and suggestions for snacks and parties, in addition to the recipes. They will find out what to do to ensure pre-exam brainpower. The enthusiastic, clear text, supplemented by color photos, may convince readers try out their inner Emeril.
>
> **Keywords:** Cooking • Teen authors

# Technology

Technology offers today's young adults ample opportunities for creative outlets. The books in this section go beyond providing basic introductions to equipment and software. The authors provide suggestions on how to use the knowledge. For example, in *The Big Book of Pop Culture: A How-to Guide for Young Artists,* John Gosney offers possibilities for how teens might use a blog, and readers are shown examples from several different forms of media.

## Gaines, Thom.

🏆 *Digital Photo Madness!: 50 Weird & Wacky Things to Do with Your Digital Camera.* New York: Lark Books, 2006. ISBN: 9781579906245. **J H**

> After a basic introduction to digital cameras and how they work, Gaines covers programming features, using camera features, color and light, subjects, and composition. He then adds fun with chapters on how to take advantage of digital technology and software advances, giving readers examples with close-ups, patterns, filters, tools, and backgrounds. The basic information and technical advice on photography will help readers make sure they are making full use of the camera's potential. **PP**
>
> **Keywords:** Digital cameras • Digital photography • Photography
>
> **Now Try:** Readers eager to improve their picture-taking have another option with Alan Buckingham's *Digital Photo Magic.* Included with an introduction to the technology are tips on how to improve common mistakes, illustrated by comparing good and bad photographs. A chapter also discusses software effects.

## Gosney, John.

*Blogging for Teens.* Boston: Thomson Course Technology, 2004. ISBN 9781592004768. **M** **J**

> Keeping a journal is a great way to express one's thoughts, and having a blog lets readers share and discuss their thoughts with others in a space that they create and maintain. This guide discusses how a blog differs from e-mail, provides examples of what readers can do with one, and then shows exactly how to set one up. Chapters also include pros and cons of different hosting services, managing the blog, a FrontPage overview, keeping the blog interesting, designing and publishing, and care and feeding of the blog.

> **Keywords:** Blogs • Computers • Programming

## Niedzviecki, Hal.

*The Big Book of Pop Culture: A How-to Guide for Young Artists.* **Illustrated by Marc Ngui.** Toronto: Annick Press, 2007. ISBN 1554510554. **H**

> Author and editor Hal Niedzviecki introduces readers to the concept of popular culture and its two forms: corporate and independent. Niedzviecki, cofounder of the magazine *Broken Pencil*, offers readers a DIY guide for different media, including zines, movies, music, radio, and the Internet. Each section includes possibilities for creative inspiration, from further reading and project suggestions to Internet keywords and interviews with people involved in alternative formats, such as filmmaker Paula Tiberius and zinester Iza Bourret.

> **Keywords:** Media • Popular culture • Self-publishing • Zines

## Pardew, Les.

*Game Art for Teens.* Boston: Thomson Course Technology/Premier Press, 2004. ISBN 978-1592003075. **H**

> Readers can learn about how game art works right from the beginning. The chapters examine both two- and three-dimensional (2D and 3D) art, as well as light and reflections, objects, interiors, characters, and special effects. Each chapter provides exercises for practice.

> **Keywords:** Videogame art • Videogames

## Sethi, Maneesh.

*Game Programming for Teens.* Premier Press Game Development Series. Boston: Thomson Course Technology, 2005. ISBN 9781592000685. **H**

> Readers can start to create their own games using BASIC. They do not need any experience and will start right from the beginning before adding animation, sound, and graphics. They will even get information on artificial intelligence.

> **Keywords:** Computer programming • Videogame programming

**Now Try:** Videogames have changed into an art form since the days of single joy sticks. Shanna Compton's *Gamers: Writers, Artists & Programmers on the Pleasures of Pixels* provides a chance not only to reflect on those changes but for the contributors to discuss different games and ponder games' influence in other areas, including fashion, music, and film. In Heather Chaplin and Aaron Ruby's *Smartbomb: The Quest for Art, Entertainment, and Big Bucks in the Videogame Revolution,* readers may follow the development of video games from the days of the first table tennis game to today's complex and multiperson worlds, with introductions to the people and the companies behind the most popular games, including the creator of Donkey Kong and Zelda, Shigeru Miyamoto.

## Shaner, Pete, and Gerald E. Jones.

*Digital Filmmaking for Teens.* Boston: Thomson, 2005. ISBN 9781592006038. **J** **H**

This guide covers filmmaking from the planning stages and storyboarding, through filming and editing, to adding music and releasing the film. Because the largest part of a filmmaking project is the editing, the supplementary CD offers examples and advice to help improve one's work.

**Keywords:** Digital cinematography • Digital filmmaking • Film editing • Film production • Videorecording

## Shulman, Mark, Martha Newbigging, and Hazlitt Krog.

*Attack of the Killer Video Book: Tips and Tricks for Young Directors.* Toronto: Annick Press, 2004. **M** **J**

If the words "lights, camera, action" are appealing to readers but leave them puzzled where to start, this is the guide for them. From the story ideas to storyboarding, lights and sound, technical aspects, and post-production, aspiring directors will find ideas as well as instructions for using their video cameras to produce movies. The cartoon illustrations complement the lighthearted, humorous tone of the writing.

**Keywords:** Video production • Videorecording

# Games

The books in this subgenre provide information about how to play a particular game. They are intended to help readers learn about, participate in, and get ready to play a game or to compete with others. Readers will also find information about great players and where to play, such as Daniel King's *Chess: From First Moves to Checkmate.* Information about creating games may be found in the "Technology" section.

## King, Daniel.

🏆 *Chess: From First Moves to Checkmate.* New York: Kingfisher, 2000. (reprinted 2004) ISBN 0753452790; 9780753452790. **M** **J** **H**

After discussing the history of chess, International Grandmaster King moves on to explain the game from the beginning move. More experienced players can improve their game with these exercises and strategies. Added information includes chess organizations, Web sites, and features on the great players. **BBYA**

**Keywords:** Chess • Games

## Morehead, Albert H., Geoffrey Mott-Smith, and Philip D. Morehead.

*Hoyle's Rules of Games: Descriptions of Indoor Games of Skill and Chance, with Advice on Skillful Play: Based on the Foundations Laid Down by Edmond Hoyle, 1672–1769.* New York: Signet. 2001. ISBN 9780451204844. **H** **A**

This book offers more than the rules about a new game of chance; readers will also find strategy tips for more than 250 card, board, dice, and computer games in this revised third edition. The cards section includes multiple variations for bridge, poker, rummy, cribbage, hearts, and solitaire.

**Keywords:** Board games • Card games • Computer games

## Spadaccini, Stephanie

*The Big Book of Rules: Board Games, Kids' Games, Card Games, from Backgammon and Bocce to Tiddlywinks and Stickball.* New York: Plume, 2005. ISBN 9780452286443. **M** **J** **H**

This is ultimate source for something fun to do and how to do it. A former editor of *Games* magazine gathers all of the information needed to play over 300 games, including the equipment, object, number of players, setup, play, and variations. Categories of games include childhood, outdoor, travel, sporty, parlor, board, card, and party games for kids.

**Keywords:** Games • Rules

# Transportation

The books in this category help readers prepare to own, operate, and maintain their favorite modes of transport, be they two- or four-wheeled. Readers looking for information about the history and development of their favorite car, bike, train, or motorcycle will find them in the "Transportation" subsection in chapter 6.

## Christensen, Lisa.

*Clueless about Cars: An Easy Guide to Car Maintenance and Repair.* Buffalo, NY: Firefly Books, 2004. ISBN 9781552979754. **H** **A**

Knowing what exactly is under the hood of one's car will not only keep it running longer and save money, it can ensure that one gets the best possible deal when buying and selling a car and when taking it into a garage. Readers might even be able to help themselves if they get into trouble on the road. They will learn how a car runs, what the proper upkeep of a vehicle entails, and what to do in an emergency; they will also find lists for car trips.

**Keywords:** Car maintenance • Car repair • Cars

**Now Try:** In Phil Edmonston's and Maureen Sawa's *Car Smarts: Hot Tips for the Car Crazy,* the reader will find a short history of the car, learn what makes a good car, and find a great guide to buying a used car, from the writer of the <u>Lemon-Aid</u> car guides and a children's librarian.

## Gravelle, Karen. Illustrated by Helen Flook.

*The Driving Book: Everything New Drivers Need to Know But Don't Know to Ask.* New York: Walker & Co, 2005. ISBN 0802789331. **H**

> In this handbook, written in Gravelle's trademark, readable style, advice is presented in short chapters outlining things practiced drivers wish they had known about. Topics include car maintenance, things one should have in the car, driving safely in different kinds of conditions, road rage, peer pressure, passenger etiquette, drinking, medications, and other possible distractions. The author's advice is supplemented by teen stories and Karen Flook's humorous illustrations.
>
> **Keywords:** Car maintenance • Driving • Transportation

## Sidwells, Chris.

*The Complete Bike Book.* New York: DK Publishing, 2005. ISBN 0756614279. **H**

> Here is a book that covers every aspect of bicycles, including a gallery with the various types of bikes that labels and defines each part to help cyclists differentiate among them. Chapters also cover getting started, the history of the bicycle, guides for riding on different sorts of terrain, equipment maintenance and repair, health and fitness, and competitive cycling. A glossary and index help readers understand the abundant information.
>
> **Keywords:** Bicycle maintenance • Bicycle repair • Bicycles
>
> **Now Try:** Readers will find lots of photographs, trivia, and concrete instructions in Richard Ballantine and Richard Grant's *Ultimate Bicycle Book.* It explains how to adjust the seat to the perfect position and provides information about roadside maintenance in a form that is suitable for browsing and shows new riders information about becoming roadworthy.

# Survival Skills

We live in a dangerous world—but books can help. The titles in this subgenre are intended to help readers cope with possible problems or hazards that are a part of everyday life (*The Worst-Case Scenario Survival Handbook: College*) or those that are beyond our control (*Terrorists, Tornadoes, and Tsunamis: How to Prepare for Life's Danger Zones*). Some of the authors rely on professionals to impart knowledge that demonstrates their expertise and provides a welcome source of humor, offering comic relief from reading about the dangers being discussed. One such example is *Don't Try This at Home: How to Win a Sumo Match, Catch a Great White Shark, and Start an Independent Nation and Other Extraordinary Feats (for Ordinary People).* Although the experts and skills used as sources in these books are legitimate, the skills are generally outside the realm of possibility for the average reader and offer instead a humorous reading experience.

## Fulghum, Hunter S.

🎗 *Don't Try This at Home: How to Win a Sumo Match, Catch a Great White Shark, and Start an Independent Nation and Other Extraordinary Feats (for Ordinary People).* New York: Broadway Books, 2002. ISBN 0767911598. **J** **H** **A**

This is a perfect book for anyone who has ever wondered what one would need to accomplish a mission from a *James Bond, Mission Impossible,* or a *Galaxy Quest*-type movie. Fulghum presents instructions, complete with the necessary materials from personality types and required bail, for objectives from short-sheeting Prince Charles's bed to robbing Fort Knox. Since the disclaimers do include the likelihood of jail time and serious injury, this is a book for armchair adventurers to enjoy, perhaps while playing the soundtrack from their favorite Bond movie. **QP**

Keywords: Adventurers • Humor • Rescues • Survival skills

## Orndorff, John Christian, and Suzanne Harper.

*Terrorists, Tornadoes, and Tsunamis: How to Prepare for Life's Danger Zones.* New York: Abrams Books for Young Readers. 2007. ISBN 9780810957671. **M** **J**

There is no denying that there are many dangers in today's world, both natural and man-made. Given that they are both generally random and outside of one's control, one's best defense is an understanding of the possibilities and knowledge of how to handle them. The authors examine terrorism, crime, and a multitude of weather scenarios to explain how to stay safe and be prepared. A number of Web sites and sources for further information are also included.

Keywords: Emergency management • Safety education • Survival skills

## Piven, Joshua, and David Borgenicht.

🎗 *The Worst-Case Scenario Survival Handbook.* San Francisco, Calif.: Chronicle Books, c1999. ISBN 0811825558. **H** **A**

This is the ideal guide for anyone seeking to learn how to deal with unusual situations. Sections about entrances and exits, the best defense, leaps of faith, emergencies, and adventure survival, provide instructions and necessary warnings for situations as varied as wrestling an alligator, treating frostbite, escaping from killer bees, and surviving an avalanche. The authors list the experts consulted for each scenario and issue a warning not to try any of these on purpose. This is a fun, light read that gives one an understanding of where the Darwin Award winners could have started out. **QP**

Keywords: Humor • Survival skills

🎗 *The Worst-Case Scenario Survival Handbook: Travel.* San Francisco: Chronicle Books, c2001. ISBN 0811831310. **H** **A**

Anyone who has traveled knows that accidents and mishaps occur. The authors of the worst-case scenario guides offer the opinions of professionals to help readers be prepared for almost anything. Some scenarios may be more useful than others, given that not all travelers may need to know how to foil a UFO abduction, but the travel strategies are useful. **QP**

**Keywords:** Humor • Survival skills • Travel

## Piven, Joshua, David Borgenicht, and Brenda Brown.

*The Worst-Case Scenario Survival Handbook: LIFE.* San Francisco: Chronicle Books, 2006. ISBN 0811853136. **H A**

In short, easily readable explanations and clear illustrations, the authors of the worst-case guides turn their attention to the everyday world, with an eye to making sure that readers have a way to combat problems from the mundane to the outrageous. The seven parts of the book are divided into sections that make for easy browsing, including home, family, travel, sports and hobbies, pets, school, beauty and fitness, stages of life, food and cooking, and relationships and family.

**Keywords:** Crisis survival • Everyday life • Family relationships • Survival

## Piven, Joshua, David Borgenicht, and Jennifer Worick.

*The Worst-Case Scenario Survival Handbook: College.* San Francisco: Chronicle Books, 2004. ISBN 0811842304. **H**

The authors behind the worst-case scenario survival guides lend their own collegiate experience to help prospective students learn the proper skills to find the right college and thrive there. Included are instructions for dealing with common problems from roommate troubles, poor cafeteria food, and the "freshman fifteen" to sports injuries and classroom or party problems.

**Keywords:** College • Humor • Survival

# Consider Starting with . . .

Brown, Bobbi, and Annemarie Iverson. *Bobbi Brown Teenage Beauty: Everything You Need to Look Pretty, Natural, Sexy & Awesome.*

Leive, Cindi, and Rebecca Sample Gerstung. *Glamour's Big Book of Dos & Don'ts: Fashion Help for Every Woman.*

Milano, Selene. *Unforgettable Color: Makeup with Confidence.*

Okey, Shannon. *Knitgrrl: Learn to Knit with 15 Fun And Funky Patterns.*

Raab, Evelyn. *Clueless in the Kitchen: A Cookbook for Teens.*

Rogge, Hannah. *Hardwear: Jewelry from a Toolbox.*

Vitkus, Jessica, Brian Kennedy, and Elizabeth Lee. *Alternacrafts: [20+ Hi-style, Lo-Budget Projects to Make].*

Worthington, Charles. *The Complete Book of Hairstyling.*

## Fiction Read-Alikes

- **Elliot, Jessie**. Four girls contend with their lives and problems over meals in *The Dinner Club*. Romance, heartaches, and cooking are the glue that holds the friendships of these four together.

- **Giles, Gail**. Gail Giles's books are known for their engaging characters and often feature suspenseful story lines, with twists and turns along the way. Their characters can be depended on to be very resourceful: Skye makes a skirt out of duct tape in *Playing in Traffic*.

- **Lenhard, Elizabeth**. Lenhard converted her interests in writing and knitting into the recent trilogy about four friends with a knitting club, *Chicks with Sticks: It's a Purl Thing*, *Chicks with Sticks: Knit Two Together*, and *Chicks with Sticks*.

- **Shaw, Tucker**. Tucker is a relationship columnist at alloy.com. He is equally well known for his teen self-help titles, and a group of fiction titles for teens with strong protagonists who know their own minds. One of those is Cyril, a cooking prodigy in *Flavor of the Week*, who helps a friend woo the beauty next door through food before falling for her himself.

- **Wittlinger, Ellen**. The world of underground publishing is at the forefront of Wittlinger's 2000 BBYA and Michael L. Printz Honor Book *Hard Love*. Readers will get to know John and Marisol through their zines *Bananafish* and *Escape Velocity*.

## References

Carter, Betty. 1987. "A Content Analysis of the Most Frequently Circulated Information Books in Three Junior High Libraries." Ed.D. thesis, University of Houston.

"DIY." 2006. *Wikipedia*. Available at http://en.wikipedia.org/wiki/DIY (accessed August 30, 2007.)

# Chapter 10

## The Arts

## Definition

This chapter includes books about art history and appreciation, books about music and film history, reviews, and literature, as well as books about some of the artists and musicians who produced the works we remember. Readers will also find books about popular culture, folklore, and myths and legends.

## Appeal

The arts provide one of the best means of self-expression. Although art is a product of the mind and imagination of the artist, the product itself is tangible. Reading books about art and creative people from around the world is one way to find inspiration. Titles *about* creative people are listed in chapter 4. Readers may get ideas for drawing, crafts, and filmmaking in chapter 9.

Art conveys emotions, thoughts, and ideas. It is up to the audience to interpret what they see, and their perceptions may change as they mature. As our knowledge of culture, the world, and its denizens increases we are able to better appreciate literature and popular culture.

The wide variety of styles in these books provide something for every reader. Reluctant readers may be attracted to Dave Barry's humor, John Grandit's concrete poetry, or the speculative *Tales of the Cryptids*.

## Chapter Organization

The first section, "Visual Arts," contains the subheadings "Art" and "Artists." This is followed by "All about Music," which is divided into "Music" and "Musicians." The next section covers film. A general section on literature is next, listing books about genres, writing, authors, and the times in which they lived. "Poetry" is next, divided into three subcategories: "About Poetry and Poets," Poetry Collections and Anthologies," and "Verse Biographies." The last section is "Folklore, Myths, and Legends," subdivided into "General" and "Urban Legends."

# Visual Arts

## Art

These books cover both art history and art appreciation. Readers may find not only depictions of the arts, but also discussions about their history and merits (e.g., in *Art Attack: A Short Cultural History of the Avant-Garde*) as well as examples of how they have been used in everyday life (e.g., in *My So-Called Digital Life*).

### Aronson, Marc.

*Art Attack: A Short Cultural History of the Avant-Garde.* New York: Clarion Books, 1998. ISBN 9780395797297. **H**

Avant-garde art embraces many different styles, including bohemianism, impressionism, and cubism, and has affected lifestyles, fashions, dance, and music. The common thread among all of these styles and facets is an ability to outrage sensibilities. Aronson covers the history, formats, artists, and movements of the avant-garde from the nineteenth century through contemporary times. With each movement set within its cultural and political context, it becomes clear why it was so shocking at the time. Discographies are given in each chapter, along with numerous reproductions of the discussed artwork.

**Keywords:** Art • Art appreciation • Art history • Avant-garde • Modern art

### Clarke, Michael.

*Watercolor.* <u>Eyewitness Books</u>. New York: Dorling Kindersley, 2000. ISBN 9780789468178. **J**

The use of watercolor in art dates back to ancient civilizations. Today it is the most popular f painting medium. Readers may follow its history from illuminated manuscripts to twentieth-century cubism and expressionist paintings.

**Keywords:** Art • <u>Eyewitness Books</u> (series) • Painting • Watercolor painting

### Desnoëttes, Caroline.

*Look Closer: Art Masterpieces Through the Ages.* New York: Walker, 2006. ISBN 9780802796141. **M** **J**

Eighteen paintings from five centuries create a gallery used to introduce readers to the styles and techniques behind history's great artists. Each double-page spread presents the artist's work, with two flaps showing selected details from the work. Behind one flap is a history of the era and a description of the artist's technique, with questions about the work, while the other flap indicates the artist's palette. This allows readers to appreciate the optical effect in Georges Seurat's use of pointillism in *The Circus* and learn about backgrounds, with artists from Da Vinci to Matisse. Backgrounds are given for all of the artists.

**Keywords:** Art • Art appreciation • Art history • Art techniques • Flap books

## Grody, Steve.

🏺 *Graffiti L.A.: Street Styles and Art.* New York: Abrams, 2007. ISBN 9780810992986. **H** **A**

The evolution of graffiti, from crude markings used strictly by hoodlums and gangs to highly stylized art forms, has been slow to be recognized. Through photographic portrayals of four different styles found on L.A. streets, Grody recognizes and celebrates these paintings. His relationship with the crews allows for an examination of the other issues that go along with graffiti: equipment, relationships with police, and the evolution and meaning of the art itself. **QP**

**Keywords:** Art • Graffiti • Popular culture • Street art

## Paniccioli, Ernie.

🏺 *Who Shot Ya?: Three Decades of Hip Hop Photography.* New York: Amistad, 2002. ISBN 0066211689. **H**

According to former *Vibe Magazine* editor Kevin Powell's introduction, hip-hop has developed into a "cultural phenomenon." Ernie Paniccioli follows the development of hip-hop, including some of the major names behind what has become a billion dollar industry, in a pictorial history made up of 150 photographs taken over a span of thirty years. In this fun-to-browse book, the photographs have no other captions than the identification of the subjects, so readers can dive in at any page, or follow the evolution of styles and appearance of now-familiar faces. **QP**

**Keywords:** Culture • Hip-hop • Photographs • Style

**Now Try:** Readers more interested in reading about the evolution of the hip-hop sound will enjoy *Yes Yes Y'all: The Experience Music Project Oral History of Hip-hop's First Decade,* by Jim Fricke and Charlie Aherne. The thoughts of more than fifty people, including musicians and DJs, are interwoven into a readable text that covers people, events, and trends that combined to make hip-hop what it is today.

## Pletka, Bob.

🏺 *My So-Called Digital Life: 2,000 Teenagers, 300 Cameras, and 30 Days to Document Their World.* Santa Monica, CA: Santa Monica Press, c2005. ISBN 1595800050. **J** **H**

Hundreds of California teens documented their lives with digital cameras in an effort to answer the common question of what a teenager does all day. The teens then chose, sorted, and captioned the photographs by topic, from classrooms to extracurricular activities to their neighborhoods. The result shows the fast pace and pressures that teens experiences in daily life. **QP**

**Keywords:** Adolescence • High school • Photography • Teenage life

## Rochelle, Belinda.

🏺 *Words with Wings: A Treasury of African-American Poetry and Art.* New York: HarperCollins/Amistad, 2001. ISBN 9780688164157. **J** **H**

Belinda Rochelle joins twenty works of art with twenty poems, all meant to show a range of experiences and emotions portrayed in the works of African American artists and poets. The pairings are subtle, allowing the reader/viewer to discover underlying themes and connections. In this well-designed and accessible book, readers will discover two generations of African American artists and poets, from nineteenth- century Braithewaite and Dunbar to contemporaries Alice Walker and Maya Angelou. A short biographical note is provided for each poet and artist. **BBYA, IRA**

**Keywords:** African American art • Art • Poetry

### Sousa, Jean.

*Faces, Places, and Inner Spaces: A Guide to Looking at Art.* New York: Published in Association with The Art Institute of Chicago by Harry N. Abrams, 2006. ISBN 9780810959668. **M J**

Artists can render the same objects and ideas in so many different ways that it can be confusing. Using examples from the wonderful and varied collection of The Art Institute of Chicago, Sousa explains art techniques and their meanings in three sections: faces, spaces, and inner spaces. The influences on and backgrounds of the artists are considered with each artwork. Sidebars demonstrate the concepts covered. For example, a close-up from Georges Seurat's *A Sunday on La Grande Jatte* illustrates pointillism, and perspective is shown in a seventeenth-century Dutch work entitled *The Terrace*. Paintings are not the only form discussed; readers will also find sculpture, pottery, furniture, and photographs. A glossary of terms is included.

**Keywords:** Art appreciation • Art Institute of Chicago

### Welton, Jude.

*Impressionism.* Eyewitness Books. London; New York: Dorling Kindersley in Association with The Art Institute of Chicago, 2000. ISBN 9780789468123. **M J**

Readers will find out about impressionism and the impressionist painters, including Monet, Renoir, Degas, Caillebotte, Pisarro, a Berthe Morisot, and Mary Cassatt. Also explored and illustrated are the themes and influences in their works.

**Keywords:** Art history • Eyewitness Books (series) • Impressionism • Painting

## Artists

Artists are some of the most influential and visionary people in society. Their stories are full of creativity, drive, and difficulties. More titles on artists can be found in the "The Creative Life" section of chapter 4.

### Greenberg, Jan, and Sandra Jordan.

🎋 *Andy Warhol: Prince of Pop.* New York; Delacorte Press, 2004. ISBN 9780385900799. **J H**

The story of Andy Warhol's art is the story of pop art. Greenberg and Jordan start with Warhol's Pittsburgh beginnings, follow him through art school, and then through his experimentation with art, into various other media. Warhol's personal life is also explored, as it is only by showing who Andy Warhol was that his art and world can be understood. **BBYA**

**Keywords:** Art history • Pop art • Warhol, Andy

*Frank O. Gehry: Outside In.* New York: DK Ink, 2000. ISBN 9780789426772. **M** **J**

Architect Gehry's work may best be described by the banner with his photograph used to advertise Apple computers, "THINK DIFFERENT." What looks like a thin, quick book is actually a neatly presented entry into the postmodern world of world-famous architect Frank O. Gehry. The authors start with Gehry's move from Canada to Los Angeles, where he was introduced to new art and architectural forms. A look at Gehry's work provides a new understanding of what architecture can be, accompanied by many pictures of his works, representative of the client and always alive with possibilities. This is the reader's chance to explore his work and read explanations of it by the "genius" himself.

**Keywords:** Architect • Architecture • Gehry, Frank O. • Postmodern architecture

🏵 *Runaway Girl: The Artist Louise Bourgeois.* New York: Harry N. Abrams, 2003. ISBN 0810942372. **J** **H**

The French artist Louise Bourgeois was definitely a woman ahead of her time. Recognized for her postmodern arachnid sculptures, hemp and naturalistic material pieces, as well has her rebellious attitude, she is also known for coining the phrase, "Art is the promise the artist makes to the community that they [sic] will not commit murder." This is a great art history book, especially for girls who really want to learn about women who have succeeded in establishing independence. Bourgeois's accomplishment in becoming the first female sculptor to have a retrospective of her work at the Museum of Modern Art is inspiring, to say the least. **BBYA**

**Keywords:** Art • Biography • Bourgeois, Louise

🏵 *Vincent Van Gogh: Portrait of an Artist.* New York: Delacorte Press, 2001. ISBN 9780385328067. Reprinted New York: Dell Yearling, 2003. ISBN 9780440419174pb. **M** **J** **H**

If all readers knows about Van Gogh is that he was the "crazy" one—this is the book for them. Readers will find out about his life, what led him into art, and his relationship with the brother who supported him. This is a well-rounded presentation of the artist, including his personal difficulties and incorporating his letters to his brother. Even the paperback version contains color reproductions of his artwork that will help readers appreciate the discussion of his techniques and motivations. In addition to being named an honor book for the 2002 Robert F. Sibert Informational Book Award, this title was chosen for the 2007 Popular Paperbacks list and was named a Best Book for Young Adults. **BBYA, PP, Sibert Honor**

**Keywords:** Artist • Painter • Van Gogh, Vincent

## Sis, Peter.

🏵 *The Wall: Growing up Behind the Iron Curtain.* New York: Farrar, Straus and Giroux, 2007. ISBN 9780374347017. **M** **J**

The multiple design formats in this picture book autobiography add a compelling element to Peter Sis's story of growing up in Soviet-controlled Czechoslovakia. His rebellion, artistic growth, and desire for freedom are certain to appeal to teenage readers. This title was awarded the Robert F. Sibert Informational Book Medal. **Sibert**

**Keywords:** Autobiography • Czechoslovakia • Picture book nonfiction • Sis, Peter

## Sullivan, George.

*Berenice Abbott, Photographer: An Independent Vision.* New York: Clarion, 2006. ISBN 0618440267. **M** **J**

Anyone interested in either strong women or photography will find an intriguing subject in Berenice Abbott, one of America's first established female photographers. She is known primarily for her photographs of "Changing New York," taken during the 1930s as part of a Federal Art Project. This work was followed by innovations in science photography and a career in teaching. Abbott was a practicing photographer for sixty years; her work is reproduced throughout the book. An extensive bibliography will help readers find further information.

**Keywords:** Abbott, Berenice • Photographer • Photography

# All about Music

There are an overwhelming number of music genres and styles. The books listed in this section cover styles of music, either contemporary or of past eras, followed by books about some of the great musicians who helped define those eras.

## Music

These books present music histories as well commentaries and reviews about different music styles. Readers interested in current music will also find photographs and background of hip-hop artists in the "Visual Arts" section.

## Barry, Dave.

*Dave Barry's Book of Bad Songs.* Kansas City, MO: Andrews McMeel, 2000. ISBN 9780740706004. **H** **A**

This book is the perfect tool to point out to anyone who doesn't like a reader's favorite song that there have been many, many horrible songs put out over the last thirty years. When humorist Dave Barry asked his readers which song would get their vote as the worst song, he never expected to receive more than 10,000 responses. Warning: Either reading or listening to this book is guaranteed to leave really, really bad lyrics running through one's head, although the commentary is surely worth it.

**Keywords:** Humor • Music

**Now Try:** Readers who like their music with a dash of humor may want to try Gavin Edwards's *'Scuse Me While I Kiss This Guy, and Other Misheard Music Lyrics.* Edwards pairs the "mondegreens," otherwise known as misheard and incorrect (albeit) humorous song lyrics, with Chris Kalb's illustrations to provide an amusing picture of what people were sure they heard on the radio.

## Bertholf, Bret.

*Long Gone Lonesome History of Country Music.* New York: Little, Brown, 2006. ISBN 9780316523936. **M**

> Country music tells stories about people. This is a fun and meandering history of country music that covers the who, what, where, when, and why. Irreverent and instructive sections include notes on country instruments, "vee-hickles," and the development of new sounds. Bertholf, a country singer, musters an enthusiasm that is hard to match for evocative, cartoonlike drawings, and a story that takes readers from the days of Whitey Ford and Lulu Belle to Garth Brooks and Faith Hill.
>
> **Keywords:** Country music • Country music history

## Bogdanov, Vladimir, Chris Woodstra, and Stephen Thomas Erlewine.

*All Music Guide to Rock: The Definitive Guide to Rock, Pop, and Soul.* AMG All Media Guide. San Francisco: Backbeat Books, 2002. ISBN 9780879306533. **H**

> Readers will discover the opinions of music critics about rock, pop, soul, R&B, rap, and easy listening, all under one cover. The third edition of this easy-to-use guide makes for fun browsing, allowing readers to look up a specific artist or group and find information about them before reading the rated reviews on their recordings. A series of essays at the end introduces readers to the evolution of different genres.
>
> **Keywords:** Discography • Music reviews • Popular music • Reviews of sound recordings

## Harcourt, Nic.

*Music Lust: Recommended Listening for Every Mood, Moment, and Reason.* Seattle: Sasquatch Books, 2005. ISBN 9781570614378. **H**

> In the age of MP3s and iPods, what better way do we have to find out about music than to start with themed lists, custom made for moods and chosen from the best of recorded music? DJ Nic Harcourt accompanies each list with notes that let readers know where to start, and identifies the momentous albums and songs in an astounding variety of genres. In more than eighty lists Harcourt presents an incredibly diverse range of music from around the globe. For example, one list covers "One Hundred Essential Albums from the Last Half of the Twentieth Century" and includes jazz, rock, punk rock, and hip-hop.
>
> **Keywords:** Music • Music reviews • Recommended music lists

## Musicians

What makes a great singer? These books explore the most influential singers and their musical legacies. Readers will find more choices in the section "The Creative Life" in chapter 4, which lists detailed examinations of individual performers

## Bolden, Tonya.

*Take-Off: American All-Girl Bands during WWII.* New York: Alfred A. Knopf, 2007. ISBN 0375927972. **M J**

This is a fresh, bouncy look at an almost unknown slice of music history: the all-girl bands that filled in the gap left when male musicians went overseas during World War II. Primarily swing and jazz musicians, these ladies had their moment in the spotlight, often performing in USO tours under wartime conditions, before fading away after the war. Bolden highlights three groups: Ada Leonard's All-American Girl Orchestra, the Prairie View State College Co-eds, and the International Sweethearts of Rhythm. Interested readers are given further sources from books to videos to CDs, including an attached CD with songs by the performers discussed.

**Keywords:** Big bands • Music history • Women jazz musicians

## Marsalis, Wynton, and Phil Schaap. Illustrated by Paul Rogers.

🎙 *Jazz Abz: An A to Z Collection of Jazz Portraits.* Cambridge, MA: Candlewick Press, 2005. Reprinted 2007. ISBN 9780763634346. **M J**

Readers will encounter an alphabet of jazz greats, including Louis Armstrong, Miles Davis, and Dizzy Gillespie. Jazz great Wynton Marsalis uses a different form of verse for each musician, depicted in illustrations by Paul Rogers. In this clever book the alliteration, rhyme, and rhythm of the poetry celebrate and underscore the musical style of each musician. Musical historian Phil Schaap contributes biographies for each performer. The biographical notes and discography at the end will be of interest to musically inclined students. This title was awarded the 2006 Bologna Ragazzi Special Award for words and music. **IRA**

**Keywords:** Jazz • Music • Poetry

**Now Try:** Fans of jazz or poetry may find an accessible, enticing read in *Jazz*, a melding of words and pictures that expresses the development of jazz as well as its rhythms. Walter Dean Myers's poetry and Christopher Myers's illustrations pair perfectly and will entice a wide range of readers. This title was named an honor book for the 2007 Coretta Scott King Award as well as being awarded the 2007 Lee Bennett Hopkins Poetry Award.

## Orgill, Roxane.

🎙 *Shout, Sister, Shout: Ten Girl Singers Who Shaped a Century.* New York: Margaret K. McElderry Books, 2001. ISBN 0689819919. **J H**

Music critic Roxanne Orgille chooses one singer to represent each decade of the twentieth century. Criteria for selection include an interesting story and strong music. Orgille also presents in sidebars different musical genres and formats that arose at different times in the century and helped to define their times. She admits that many strong singers, including some of her favorites, may have been missed, but presents a lively biography that may direct readers to some new voices, among them Sophie Tucker, Ma Rainey, Bessie Smith, Ethel Merman, Judy Garland, Anita O'Day, Joan Baez, Bette Midler, Madonna, and Lucinda Williams. **BBYA**

**Keywords:** Music • Musicians • Performing arts • Singers

**Now Try:** Readers interested in reading about female singers overcoming odds and making their mark might like to try Heather Ball's *Magnificent Women in Music*, which presents ten performers with different musical backgrounds and styles, from Clara Schumann and Marian Anderson to Ella Fitzgerald and Chantal Kreviazuk. Leslie Gourse took on the task of profiling the greatest female jazz singers in *Sophisticated Ladies: The Great women of Jazz*. These ladies' voices influenced the music of a century, from Bessie Smith in the 1920s to Diana Krall's music today.

## Tanner, Mike.

*Flat-out Rock: Ten Great Bands of the '60s.* Toronto: Annick Press, 2006. ISBN 9781554510368. **M** **J** **H**

Tanner chooses ten rock bands from the sixties that were undeniably in the spotlight and influenced the music that followed them. Arranged chronologically, the chapters offer summaries of the groups, their careers, and their lives since the sixties. Tanner's choices include Bob Dylan; the Beatles; the Who; the Doors; Janis Joplin; Jimi Hendrix; Creedence Clearwater Revival; the Rolling Stones; Neil Young; Crosby, Stills, and Nash; and Led Zeppelin. Sidebars explain what inspired the music, from other musicians to social and political situations. Readers will find new possibilities for their iPods in the lists of musicians who were influenced by these bands, as well as a list of other great songs.

**Keywords:** Rock groups • Rock music of the 1960s • Rock musicians

# Film

Movies are one of the most popular forms of entertainment in North America today. Books in this section help readers find movies, give them information about films and the cinema, and provide film buffs with light reading that allows them to expand their cinematic knowledge. Readers interested in making their own films can find titles on that topic in the "Technology" section of chapter 9.

## Grahame-Smith, Seth.

*How to Survive a Horror Movie: All the Skills to Dodge the Kills.* Philadelphia: Quirk Books, 2007. ISBN 978159474179. **H** **A**

Readers may use this guide to all things horror to acquaint themselves with the genre or use their knowledge of the various types of scary movies to make sure they will be ready if they did something last summer or find children in their corn or snakes on their plane. Sidebars include preparations to help readers understand stereotypical characters, escape methods, and potential house haunting. **QP**

**Keywords:** Films • Horror movies • Humor

## Heimberg, Jason, and Justin Heimberg.

*The Official Movie Plot Generator: 27,000 Hilarious Movie Plot Combinations.* Los Angeles: Bros. Heimberg Publishing, 2003. Reprinted 2004. ISBN 0974043915. **J** **H**

> This is a book for movie fans or would-be screenwriters with writer's block or time on their hands. The brothers provide an almost endless array of possible new movie plots in an interactive, spiral-bound flip book, with selections for stars, action, and setting that range from humorous to outrageous. **QP**

> **Keywords:** Film and movies • Humor

## Miller, Ron.

*Special Effects: An Introduction to Movie Magic.* Minneapolis, MN: Twenty-first Century Books, 2006. ISBN 9780761329183. **J** **H**

> Readers will enjoy finding out how very far special effects have come, from the novelty of moviemaking itself to the wonders of today's CGI effects. This comprehensive book includes chapters on miniatures, stop-motion effects, makeup, mechanical effects, and digital effects. The supplementary material includes a glossary and a list of Academy Award winners.

> **Keywords:** Movies • Special effects • Trick cinematography

> **Now Try:** Readers will discover the wonders behind all kinds of visual effects in Al Seckel's *Optical Illusions: The Science of Visual Perception.* They may have fun with 275 optical illusions that make use of different techniques, from illustrations and photographs to computer technology. The science behind each illusion is explained, making this a great book for flipping back and forth or perusing at length. This title was chosen as a Quick Pick for Reluctant Readers.

## Roeper, Richard.

*Ten Sure Signs a Movie Character Is Doomed and Other Surprising Movie Lists.* New York: Hyperion, 2003. ISBN 078688830X. **J** **H** **RR**

> Film critic Richard Roeper presents a fun and unusual book of lists guaranteed to arouse laughter and debate, from "highly stupid habits of movie people" to his picks for the all-time greatest and worst movies. These are enjoyable lists, written by Roger Ebert's partner, with enough humor to make them appealing to movie buffs and those looking for new genres alike. **QP**

> **Keywords:** Film and video • Movie guide • Movie reviews • Performing arts

> **Now Try:** Richard Roeper acknowledges the fascination the public has with both gossip and famous people in his *Hollywood Urban Legends: The Truth Behind All Those Delightfully Persistent Myths of Film, Television and Music.* This is a fun book for both browsing and reading, as Roeper has written a tongue-in-cheek debunking of rumor and innuendo about people in all three arenas.

## Sarvady, Andrea.

*The Ultimate Girls' Movie Survival Guide: What to Rent, Who to Watch, How to Deal.* **Illustrated by Jamie Bennett.** New York: Simon Spotlight Entertainment, 2004. ISBN 9780689873737. **M** **J** **H**

> Readers who have a hard time picking out a movie will enjoy this guide. They can use the "Mood Control," the "Girl Rating," or some of the other fun features to help pick out a perfect movie from over 100 possibilities. Each review includes notes on the girl and guy to watch, soundtrack and plot notes, the "scene worth the rewind," and "how this movie helps."
>
> **Keywords:** Movie reviews • Movies

## Sklar, Robert.

*A World History of Film.* New York: Harry N. Abrams, 2002. ISBN 9780810906068. **H** **A**

> Readers will find an introduction to film from around the world, from the very beginnings of movies to *Titanic* and the Farrelly brothers. They will also be introduced to European and Soviet cinema in this comprehensive, well-illustrated volume.
>
> **Keywords:** Film history • Films

# Literature

In books about literature, readers may explore their favorite poets and authors, their lives, and their work, and find new favorites. They can also learn about the history and development of their favorite format or genre in this wide assortment of titles.

## Janeczko, Paul B.

*Seeing the Blue Between: Advice and Inspiration for Young Poets.* Cambridge, MA: Candlewick Press, 2002. ISBN 0763608815. **M** **J**

> Thirty-two poets—from Joseph Bruchac, who initially was discouraged from writing poetry because he was a wrestler, to the humorous poet Jack Prelutsky, who demonstrates the comic techniques he uses—suggest ways for young poets to continue, improve upon, experiment with, and enjoy poetry. Advice is accompanied by poems from each of the poets. The book is rounded out by photos and biographical information on the poets.
>
> **Keywords:** Authorship • Creative writing • Nonfiction collections • Poetry • Poets

## Krensky, Stephen.

*Comic Book Century: The History of American Comic Books.* People's History. Minneapolis, MN: Twenty-First Century Books. 2008. ISBN 9780822566540. **M** **J**

> Long before graphic novels became popular, cartoons reflected the politics of the day. Comic strips were gathered together in anthologies and

became the first comic books, which faced an uphill battle to be recognized as being worthy of reading. Restrictions on story lines and characters led to the development of underground publishers and a number of the most popular formats available today, including comic strips, cartoons, and graphic novels. Additional resources include a time line, bibliography, and list of Web sites.

**Keywords:** Comics • History of comics

**Now Try:** Books both beloved and totally unfamiliar provide fodder for satirical and amazingly detailed, punny illustrations in Chris Riddell's *The Da Vinci Cod and Other Illustrations for Unwritten Books.* "Oliver Bust" finds the hero contemplating an empty bowl and a losing card hand; "The Da Vinci Cod" finds a large fish taking the place of the *Mona Lisa*. Readers, artists, and art lovers alike will find many sources of inspiration in these clever "unwritten books."

## Marcus, Leonard S., ed.

🏆 *The Wand in the Word: Conversations with Writers of Fantasy.* Cambridge, MA: Candlewick Press, 2006. ISBN 0763626252. **M J**

Thirteen interviews with fantasy authors, among them Brian Jacques, Tamora Pierce, Philip Pullman, Garth Nix, and Ursula K Le Guin, give readers insights into and a chance to better understand their work habits, literary influences, reasons for writing fantasy, and advice for young authors. Each chapter includes a sample page from a manuscript, a photograph, and a selected list of the author's works. **BBYA**

**Keywords:** American authors • Authorship • English authors • Fantasy • Literary influences • Nonfiction collections • Writers • Writing

## Rosen, Michael, and Robert Ingpen.

*Shakespeare: His Work and His World.* Cambridge, MA: Candlewick Press, 2001. Reprinted 2006. ISBN 9780763632014. **M J**

Every year since our great-great-grandmother's time, in classes all over the English-speaking world, students have studied Shakespeare. Why? That is just the first question pondered here. Readers will find out what we know about Shakespeare, the Globe Theatre, the dangerous times in which he lived, and how they are reflected in four of his plays. The detailed illustrations and explanations may just inspire readers to attend or read the plays with a new understanding.

**Keywords:** Globe Theatre • Literary criticism • Shakespeare

**Now Try:** Rosen and Ingpen follow the same format to introduce another literary giant, in *Dickens: His Work and His World.* An introduction to Dickens is followed by biographical material that introduces the man and the tumultuous times in which he lived, followed by an examination of four of his works. Illustrations include portraits of book characters and may lead readers to try a new title. Gary Blackwood transports readers to the Globe Theatre in *Shakespeare's Stealer, Shakespeare's Scribe,* and *Shakespeare's Spy.* These historical novels center around young apprentices in Shakespeare's company and are infused with period details.

# Poetry

Poetry is defined by its sound, meaning, and rhythm, with various types of poetry dependent on the use of line. Poetry covers a broad span of topics and forms. Readers are introduced to twenty-nine different types of poems in Paul Janeczko's *A Kick in the*

*Head: An Everyday Guide to Poetic Forms.* Poetry—writing and reading—is very popular with teens.

This section is organized in three subcategories. "About Poetry and Poets" lists works that help provide background and understanding of poetry, poetic forms, and the writing process. This is followed by "Poetry Collections and Anthologies" and "Verse Biographies." The number of collections and anthologies is evidence of the popularity of poetry writing in classrooms and with teens in general, which is underscored by the number of titles that celebrate teen writing. The last section examines the recent trend of composing biographical tributes in verse, four of which were penned by Marilyn Nelson, Connecticut's Poet Laureate.

## About Poetry and Poets

This section lists works that help readers understand poetry and poetic forms.

### Andronik, Catherine M.

*Wildly Romantic: The English Romantic Poets: The Mad, the Bad, and the Dangerous.* New York: Henry Holt, 2007. ISBN 0805077839. **H**

> The Romantics were the rock stars of their times, with lives of excess, tragedy, and scandal that make for fun reading and provide readers with background not only on the poets but also on their views about poetry. This unique introduction to the world of nineteenth-century English Romantic poetry starts with biographies of the poets, integrating their poetry into their life stories. Included are Wordsworth, Coleridge, Shelley, Byron, and Keats, incorporating others in their circle such as Mary Shelley.
>
> **Keywords:** Poets • Romantic poetry • Romantic poets

### Janeczko, Paul B.

*A Kick in the Head: An Everyday Guide to Poetic Forms.* **Illustrated by Chris Raschka.** Cambridge, MA: Candlewick Press, 2005. ISBN 0763606626. **M J**

> Using a fun, alluring approach, Janeczko and Raschka demonstrate twenty-nine different poetic forms. Works from poets ranging from Ogden Nash (the couplet) to Gary Soto (the ode) are illustrated with Chris Raschka's lively, colorful paper collages and accompanied by a few words giving the basic outline of the format. Longer explanations are given at the back of the book. Students interested in poetry may be challenged or amused by new, unfamiliar formats such as double dactyl or clerihew. Janeczko points out that knowing the "rules makes the writing of a poem more challenging." Readers given an example of this with the sonnet, a poem written in the style of Shakespeare, may go on to use the rules given here to write their own poems.
>
> **Keywords:** Poetic forms • Poetry • Poetry anthology

## Wolf, Alan.

*Immersed in Verse: An Informative, Slightly Irreverent and Totally Tremendous Guide to Living the Poet's Life.* **Illustrated by Tuesday Mourning.** New York: Lark Books, 2006. ISBN 1579906281. **M** **J** **H**

In his guide to writing and appreciating poetry, Wolf, a poet and poetry lover, includes practical information that makes writing and reading poetry accessible and fun. All kinds of poetry, poetic forms, and poets are examined, with humor and an appealing appreciation of language. This is a useful tool for the novice poetry reader as well as the creative writer.

**Keywords:** Journaling • Poetry • Poetry appreciation • Writing

## Poetry Collections and Anthologies

This section covers both collections by one poet and anthologies of works by more than one poet.

## Carlson, Lori Marie, ed.

🌶 *Red Hot Salsa: Bilingual Poems on Being Young and Latino in the United States.* New York: Henry Holt, c2005. ISBN 9780805076165. **M** **J** **H**

Lori Carlson offers a collection of poems in English and Spanish, with the occasional poem written in both languages, and biographical notes on each of the poets. She includes not only the better-known writers, such as Gary Soto, but also several teenage poets. Translation was done by the poets, and a glossary is included. Universal themes cover language, identity, *amor*, and neighborhoods. This book will give all readers a better understanding of the Latino experience in the United States and may spur young writers in their work. **QP**

**Keywords:** American poetry • Bilingual (Spanish-English) • Hispanic American poetry • Poetry • Poetry anthologies

**Now Try:** It has been ten years since Lori Carlson published her *Cool Salsa: Bilingual Poems on Growing up Latino in the United States.* Still a delightful read, it speaks to teens in a musical cadence with varying subject matters and styles. Carlson celebrates twenty-nine different Latino authors in a collection that lets the authors share their heritage and culture.

## Clinton, Catherine.

*A Poem of Her Own: Voices of American Women Yesterday and Today.* **Illustrated by Stephen Alcorn.** New York: Harry N. Abrams, 2003. ISBN 9780810942400. **M** **J** **H**

This introduction to women's poetry discusses twenty-five poets, whose poems are them presented chronologically. Each is accompanied by a full-page illustration and a biography of the poet. This is an eclectic and interesting collection, in which poetry readers are likely to find "sounds, sweet airs/that give delight," not only in Julia Alvarez's poem, but also in the story behind "The Battle Hymn of the Republic" by Julia Ward Howe.

**Keywords:** Poetry • Poetry anthology • Poets • Women authors

## Crisler, Curtis L

�(flower) *Tough Boy Sonatas.* **Illustrated by Floyd Cooper.** Honesdale, PA: Wordsong, 2007. ISBN 9781428732209. **J** **H**

Gary, Indiana, is a tough town, filled with tough young men who know it and aren't afraid to say so. "Our lives are symphonies, and pain's our aria." The sharp lines, rhythms, and forms inform readers about their lives, while the softer illustrations complement their words. This collection provides a complete picture of a life that is not often seen and may offer inspiration to teens who wouldn't otherwise approach poetry. **BBYA**

**Keywords:** Indiana • Poetry • Poetry collections

## Franco, Betsy, ed.

�(flower) *Things I Have to Tell You: Poems and Writing by Teenage Girls.* Cambridge, MA: Candlewick Press, 2001. ISBN 0763609056. **J** **H**

Poets and authors from fourteen to eighteen years old share thoughts and concerns pertinent to their peers. This collection displays different poetic forms and a smart use of language, whether speaking of a bad hair day or sexual orientation. Budding authors and poets may find inspiration here, and teen girls may find solace in the words of their peers. **BBYA, QP**

**Keywords:** Poetry • Poetry anthologies • Short stories • Teen writing

*You Hear Me?: Poems and Writing by Teenage Boys.* Cambridge, MA: Candlewick Press, 2000. ISBN 0763611581. **J** **H** **RR**

Teen boys speak out in this collection of verse and short prose. Subjects range from families and friends to drugs and sex, all of which are appealing to the twelve- to eighteen-year-old authors and audience. The book also has motivational potential for teen poets. **BBYA, QP**

**Keywords:** Poetry • Poetry anthologies • Teen writing

## Grandits, John

�(flower) *Blue Lipstick.* New York: Clarion Books, 2007. ISBN 978061856804. **M** **J** **H**

The cover of this book, taking its title from a poem about blue lipstick, lets the reader know that ninth-grade Jessie sees things differently than her family does. The thirty-three poems in this collection take full advantage of fonts and the space afforded for exploring Jessie's thoughts and world, giving readers a chance to learn about life along with this smart, fun girl. Frequent musings include her annoying younger brother, high school, and the ups and downs of her days, which are rendered effectively on the page. **QP**

**Keywords:** Concrete poetry • Poetry • Poetry collections

🌐(flower) *Technically, It's Not My Fault: Concrete Poems.* New York: Clarion Books, c2004. ISBN 061842833X. **M** **J** **RR** **BB**

Grandits uses his background as a print designer to perfectly present his funny poems. The concrete poetry here illustrates the everyday thoughts of eleven-year-old Robert, from a clever toilet use to evil thoughts about his sister. All demonstrate a love of language. The different typefaces used in the poems are identified for readers who would like to experiment with their own poetry . **QP**

**Keywords:** Concrete poetry • Poetry • Poetry collections

## Greenberg, Jan.

🕏 *Heart to Heart: New Poems Inspired by Twentieth-century American Art.* New York: Harry N. Abrams, 2001. ISBN 0810943867. **M J**

Contemporary American authors have written poems about some of the finest American art. Here readers have a chance to experience the artwork along with the authors. The poems are divided into four sections. In the first, "stories," poets tell an anecdote or share a memory in response to the art. In "voices," the poems speak from the point of view of the subject of the artwork. The third section offers the artists' "impressions" from the art, followed by the "expressions" the poet believes the artist to be making through the art in the last section. This is a novel way for readers to experience both art and poetry. Biographical information is given for both the poets and the artists. **BBYA, Printz Honor**

**Keywords:** American art • Art • Modern art • Poetry • Poetry anthologies

## Janeczko, Paul B.

*A Poke in the I: A Collection of Concrete Poems.* **Illustrated by Chris Raschka.** Cambridge, MA: Candlewick, 2001. Reprinted 2005. ISBN 0763623768. **M J RR**

Paul Janeczko's creative collection of concrete poetry demonstrates the perfect marriage of text and illustration, giving readers a visual feast. No page has been ignored: The notes from the editor are the lines from a bullhorn, even the copyright information forms the symbol "©". Readers will discover that a concrete poem may indeed take on all shapes and sizes, sometimes depending on the artwork. On the other hand, they are very easy to enjoy. Robert Carola's poem "STOWAWAY" is illustrated with a ship but demonstrates the concept of simplicity.

**Keywords:** Concrete poetry • Poetry anthologies

## Myers, Walter Dean.

🕏 *Here in Harlem: Poems in Many Voices.* New York: Holiday House, 2004. ISBN 0823418537. **M J H**

Readers gain a sense of the Harlem that Walter Dean Myers grew up in through the fifty-three voices that speak in this volume. The varied characters present their hopes, dreams, and disappointments in verse, with vintage photographs, combining to present a clear and memorable picture. **BBYA**

**Keywords:** Harlem • Poetry • Poetry collections

**Now Try:** Readers who enjoy experiencing poetry through someone else's eyes can voyage back in time with Lewis and Clark as fourteen different voices—including the president, crew members, Sacagawea, and the crew's Newfoundland dog—share their thoughts, hopes, and fears, in Allan Wolf's novel and fast-moving *New Found Land: Lewis and Clark's Voyage of Discovery*, a 2005 BBYA title re-released in 2007.

## Nye, Naomi Shihab.

🎗 *19 Varieties of Gazelle: Poems of the Middle East.* New York: HarperCollins/Greenwillow,2002. Reprinted New York: HarperTempest, 2005. ISBN 9781415583449. **J** **H**

Nye had a uniquely cross-cultural childhood, relocating with her Palestinian father and German American mother to places such as St. Louis, Missouri; San Antonio, Texas; and Jerusalem. Stories of the Middle East are presented through the eyes of an American child, and stories of America are shown through the eyes of Middle Easterners. **BBYA**

**Keywords:** Middle East • Poetry • Poetry collections

## WritersCorps.

🎗 *Paint Me Like I Am: Teen Poems.* New York: HarperTempest, 2003. ISBN 9780064472647. **M** **J** **H** **RR**

Readers will find out what other teens can say in poems when they have the chance. These are poems from teens who participated in workshops with WritersCorp. This gives readers a chance to see what they have to say about real, everyday things like family, friends, drugs, and relationships. They may then try expressing themselves using the sample exercises included at the beginning of each section.

**Keywords:** Poetry • Poetry anthologies • Teen writing

## Verse Biographies

In the past few years a number of books of poetry have been written about people. Readers who enjoy these will be able to find a number of alternate choices in chapters 3 and 4, including books about some of the same people.

## Alexander, Elizabeth, and Marilyn Nelson.

🎗 *Miss Crandall's School for Young Ladies and Little Misses of Color: Poems.* **Illustrated by Floyd Cooper.** Honesdale, PA: Wordsong, 2007. ISBN 9781428764767. **M** **J** **H**

Blind hatred and prejudice are nothing new; in the nineteenth century, they often went hand in hand. When Prudence Crandall dared to open a girls' school in Connecticut in 1833, she knew it would be unpopular, yet she did not know the lengths to which her neighbors, the town leaders, and even the government would go to ensure that African American girls would not be allowed to attend her classes. Twenty-four sonnets explore the events at Miss Crandall's school, expressing the voices of the students, protestors, lawyers, and Miss Crandall. The illustrations underscore the feelings in the poems. Readers will find supplementary historical information in the foreword, as well as an inspiring letter from the poets that explains how they worked together. **ALA**

**Keywords:** Crandall, Prudence • Poetry • Segregation in education • Sonnets • Women educators

**Now Try:** Readers interested in this story will find more information on it in Suzanne Jurmaine's *The Forbidden Schoolhouse: The True and Dramatic Story of Prudence Crandall and Her Students.*

## Engle, Margarita.

🎗 *The Poet Slave of Cuba: A Biography of Juan Francisco Manzano.* **Illustrated by Sean Qualls.** New York: Henry Holt, 2006. ISBN 0805077065. **M** **J** **H**

Margarita Engle describes the difficult boyhood and suffering of a Cuban poet, Juan Francisco Manzano, who was born a slave. The book covers the period between the death of his first owner and his escape at the age of sixteen. He learned to read in secret and developed a love of poetry and words, which he used to preserve beauty and faith in a horrible and cruel world. This title was chosen for the 2007 Teachers' Choices list of the International Reading Association. **BBYA, IRA, Pura Belpre**

Keywords: Manzano, Juan Francisco • Poetry • Poets • Slavery

## Hemphill, Stephanie.

🎗 *Your Own, Sylvia: A Verse Portrait of Sylvia Plath.* New York: Alfred A. Knopf, 2007. ISBN 9780375937996. **J** **H** **BG**

Sylvia Plath was undeniably a talented poet and writer. Here another talented poet melds biography and poetry to present Plath's life through her own medium. The poems, presented in the voices of the people around Plath, are supplemented with biographical footnotes. Readers see her life through her family, friends, doctors, and colleagues, and occasionally "in the style" of specific poems, which not only gives a picture of the artist and her works, but will also likely inspire many to read the originals. **Printz Honor**

Keywords: Confessional poetry • Plath, Sylvia • Poetry

## Nelson, Marilyn

🎗 *Carver: A Life in Poems.* Asheville, NC: Front Street, 2001. ISBN 1886910537. **M** **J** **H**

A portrait of George Washington Carver is presented in fifty-nine poems. Connecticut's poet laureate presents a journey that begins with Carver's rescue from slave-stealers as an infant, covers his academic accomplishments, and finishes with the Tuskegee airmen flying in the sky above the campus where he worked for more than thirty years. Readers are shown a scientist and chemist with an artistic side. Among this title's honors are the Boston Globe-Horn Book Award, a Newbery Honor Award, and a Coretta Scott King Honor Award. **BBYA, CSK Honor, Newbery Honor**

Keywords: Carver, George Washington • Poetry • Slaves • Tuskegee, Alabama

🎗 *Fortune's Bones: The Manumission Requiem.* Asheville, NC: Front Street, 2004. ISBN 1932425128. **J**

A slave who died in 1789, Fortune is remembered in a traditional requiem. His owner, Dr Preserved Porter, preserved Fortune's bones for anatomical studies. The bones were lost for years and then recovered, before ending up at a museum in Connecticut. Poems told in multiple voices, including those of Dr. Porter, Fortune, his wife, their descendants, and museum visitors, illuminate not only his life but also his afterlife and final journey to freedom. *Fortune's Bones* was named a Coretta Scott King Honor book. **BBYA, CSK Honor**

Keywords: Poetry • Requiem • Slavery

🎗 *A Wreath for Emmett Till.* Boston: Houghton Mifflin, 2005. ISBN 780618397525. **J** **H**

> A heroic crown—a cycle of fifteen sonnets that uses the last line of one poem as the first line of the next—is used to reflect upon the lynching of Emmett Till. This remarkable literary achievement contemplates a horrific act and, in speaking of mourning and remembrance, uses that act to look forward. The book was named an honor book for both the Michael L. Printz and the Coretta Scott King Awards in 2006, as well as being named to the BBYA list. Readers interested in more information about the original story may be referred to Chris Crowe's *Getting Away with Murder: The True Story of the Emmett Till Case.* **BBYA, CSK Honor, Printz Honor**
>
> **Keywords:** Hate crimes • Murder victims • Poetry • Sonnets • Till, Emmett
>
> **Now Try:** In *Mississippi Trial, 1955,* Chris Crowe presents a fictional take on the Emmett Till case from the point of view of Hiram, a sixteen-year-old white outsider attending the trial while he stays with his grandfather. Hiram learns some hard lessons about injustice and prejudice and his own family's feelings about them.

## Folklore, Myths, and Legends

The books in this section contain traditional tales, divided into a "General" section of fairy tales and mythology and a section for popular but unverifiable urban legends. These titles are not what one normally thinks of as nonfiction, but technically they are nonfiction.

### General

### Andersen, Hans Christian, Tiina Nunnally, and Jackie Wullschlager.

*Fairy Tales.* London; New York: Penguin Books, 2004. ISBN 978-0670033775. **H** **A**

> There is no doubt that a good translation can make a work much more accessible. Andersen's bicentennial is celebrated by an award-winning translator and Andersen's biographer to make his stories vibrant, enticing, and attractive to an older audience.
>
> **Keywords:** Fairy tales
>
> **Now Try:** The denizens of the high court are given their own fashion week in the beautiful *Fairie-Ality: The Fashion Collection,* which marries fashion and fantasy. What will the fairies choose to wear this season? Eugenie Bird, David Downton, and David Ellwand present an imaginative catalog, with illustrations, photographs, and text, of a dream wardrobe using stunning things from nature. The high court would love to be seen in lilies, roses, and snakeskin. Would-be designers will get some wonderful ideas

### Halls, Kelly Milner, Rick Spears, and Roxyanne Young.

🎗 *Tales of the Cryptids: Mysterious Creatures That May or May Not Exist.* Plain City, OH: Darby Creek, 2006. ISBN 1581960492. **M** **J** **RR**

> Cryptozoology is the study of and search for legendary animals. Readers shouldn't dismiss cryptozoology outright; for every definite hoax like the

Cardiff Giant, scientists have found creatures such as the coelacanth. The book is divided into four sections: bigfoot, sea serpents, prehistoric cryptids, and mammals. The "cryptidictionary" that follows summarizes the information on each creature and rates the "reality factor" of each. **QP**

**Keywords:** Bigfoot • Cryptids • Legendary animals

## Philip, Neil.

*Mythology.* <u>Eyewitness Books</u>. New York: Dorling Kindserley, 2000. ISBN 9780789462886. **M J**

This basic introduction to myths from around the world starts by defining "myths" as "a collection of truth" and then looks at various mythical elements from around the world, noting common elements that recur around the globe. Some of the double-page spreads include creation myths, supreme beings, the elements, fertility and birth, superheroes, tricksters, and universal creatures.

**Keywords:** Gods • Mythology

## Philip, Neil, and Nicki Palin.

*Mythology of the World.* London: Kingfisher, 2004. ISBN 9780753409640. **J H**

This in-depth examination starts by defining myths, then provides examples of where they are found in culture, society, and geography. The myths themselves are then presented geographically, introducing readers to tales from Europe, Asia, America, Australasia and Oceania, and Africa.

**Keywords:** Mythology

## Wilkinson, Philip.

*Illustrated Dictionary of Mythology: Heroes, Heroines, Gods, and Goddesses from Around the World.* New York: Dorling Kindersley, 2006. ISBN 078943413X. **M J**

After an introductory chapter that looks at recurring themes in world mythologies, the material is then broken down geographically. For each region creation myths, gods and goddesses, heroes and tricksters, mythical monsters, animals and plants, and endings are presented. Since this is a dictionary and not an encyclopedia, the material is meant for browsing rather than detailed research. The entire book is lavishly illustrated, with boldfaced cross-references that help readers find further explanations. An index is included as a starting point.

**Keywords:** Dictionary of mythology • Mythology

# Urban Legends

The books in this section are collections of popularized, sensationalized tales whose main characteristic is that they are purported to be true. The books here are collections of these stories as well as a collection testing the veracity of such stories.

## Brunvand, Jan Harold.

*Be Afraid, Be Very Afraid: The Book of Scary Urban Legends.* New York: Norton, 2004. ISBN 978-0393326130. **H**

In his new collection urban folklore scholar Jan Harold Brunvand has chosen the most chilling tales, from the familiar tale of the hook in the car door to chilling stories of dismembered arms and deaths from fright. The stories are organized thematically and are often offered with more than one variation, to show how spreading a tale can change a story. Brunvand also demonstrates his research skills by explaining where some of the stories started, which makes the other stories more interesting.

**Keywords:** Folklore • Myths • Urban legends

**Now Try:** Jan Harold Brunvand adapted roughly 200 FOAF (Friend of a Friend) tales from his books about urban legends into the *Big Book of Urban Legends* in 1994. The tales are particularly suited to comic format, and DC Comics included a wide variety of artists, who make this a fun book to curl up to read short stories that are all "true."

## Holt, David.

*The Exploding Toilet: Modern Urban Legends.* **Illustrated by Kevin Pope.** Little Rock, AR: August House, 2004. ISBN 9781415545560. **J H**

Whether readers like implausible stories scary, funny, or downright unbelievable, they will find a selection from which to choose here. The traditional Friend of a Friend (FOAF) tales, which include sections on workplace, school, and scary stories, are told without adornment and make for enjoyable reading. There is also a chapter that passes on information taken from the Internet, including virus warnings and an e-mail "warning."

**Keywords:** Humor • Scary stories • Urban legends

## Zimmerman, Keith, and Kent Zimmerman.

*Mythbusters: The Explosive Truth Behind the Thirty Most Perplexing Urban Legends of All Time.* New York: Simon Spotlight Entertainment, 2005. ISBN 9781416909293. **J H**

Adam Savage and Jamie Hyneman combined science and myths with reality television on their show *Mythbusters*, on which they used scientific methods to find out the truth behind popular urban legends. Can one save oneself in a falling elevator by jumping at the last moment? Is there really such a thing as an exploding toilet? Readers will find out which legends are true, which have been busted, and how.

**Keywords:** Science experiments • Urban legends

# Consider Starting with . . .

These titles cover a wide age range and are recommended as an introduction to the genre.

Franco, Betsy, ed. *Things I Have to Tell You: Poems and Writing by Teenage Girls.*

Grandits, John *Technically, It's Not My Fault: Concrete Poems.*

Harcourt, Nic. *Music Lust: Recommended Listening for Every Mood, Moment, and Reason.*

Hemphill, Stephanie. *Your own, Sylvia: A Verse Portrait of Sylvia Plath.*

Sousa, Jean. *Faces, Places, and Inner Spaces: A Guide to Looking at Art.*

# Fiction Read-Alikes

- **Bingham, Kelly**. Jane Arrowood lost more than just her right arm when she was attacked by a shark; she had defined herself as an artist and now she not only can't draw, she is known by everyone as *Shark Girl*. Follow Jane's story in verse as she struggles with herself and everyone around her.

- **Castellucci, Cecil**. Several of the books by this author feature art and music. She helped launch DC Comics' <u>Minx</u> line of graphic novels with *Plain Janes*. Four misfit Janes band together to launch "art attacks" that aren't appreciated by the town's adults. Katy, sent to stay with her father, lead singer of the Punk band Suck, is derided as being *Beige* by the girl her dad has asked to keep an eye on her.

- **Chevalier, Tracy**. The popular works by this adult author combine coming-of-age tales with artists and authors bringing forth their most famous works. *The Girl with a Pearl Earring*, about Johannes Vermeer and his sixteen-year-old muse and maid, was recognized with an Alex award.

- **Geras, Adele**. Geras offers novelizations of famous classical stories, retelling the Trojan War in *Troy: A Novel* and offering the story of *Ithaka*, whose people await Odysseus.

- **Grimes, Nikki**. In *Bronx Masquerade*, eighteen inner-city teens in Mr. Ward's English class tell about their lives through text and poetry as they participate in weekly Open Mike Fridays. This exercise brings them together, opens them up to one another, and gives them the chance to learn about themselves and the people around them. This BBYA and 2003 Coretta Scott King Award winner is a verse novel that could also be used for readers' theatre.

- **Koja, Kathe**. The story of an outsider who is easily bullied is nothing new, although Jinsen, the hero in Koja's *Buddha Boy*, is strange enough to make himself a target at school. Only when Justin is paired with this begging, Buddhist-dressing outcast does he find out that there is more to this artistically gifted boy.

- **Korman, Gordon**. In *Born to Rock*, Leo Caraway is a gifted high school senior, a Young Republican on the fast track to Harvard. Everything is going his way, until he finds out that his biological father is King Maggot, lead singer of the punk rock band Purge. Readers familiar with Korman's humorous writing will enjoy Leo's quandary over meeting his father. More humor can be found in Korman's *No More Dead Dogs*, in which Wallace Wallace sticks to his guns and turns the school's play upside down when he is on detention for a book report denouncing his teacher's favorite childhood book, which is also the play being performed.

- **Woodson, Jacqueline**. Known for writing that appeals to a wide age range, one of Woodson's many enticing books is *Locomotion*. The unusual feature of this verse novel is that it introduces the readers and the main character, an eleven-year-old boy named Lonnie, to poetry in order for him to recover from the trauma of losing his parents. Use of a male protagonist and the wide variety of poetry, including sonnets, haiku, epistle, and free verse, translate into a lyrical, beautiful, and often funny verse novel that was awarded the Boston Globe-Horn Book award.

# Chapter 11

## Understanding and Changing the World

## Definition

This chapter includes books about popular culture, folklore, myths and legends, media and consumer culture, social concerns, and religions. What all of these books have in common is that they help teens better understand the world in which they live.

## Appeal

It is not surprising that with the rise of the modern media and the Internet there has been an increase in the number of books published about advertising and consumerism. These books also provide background about both sides of relevant issues in our society and how people are affected by them, fostering debate and offering the chance to see how other people live.

## Chapter Organization

The sections in this chapter look at the world in which we live. "Popular Media and Consumer Culture" is followed by "Social Concerns and Issues" and "Religion."

## Popular Media and Consumer Culture

This category includes books that explore the idioms, allusions, and advertising that help to make up the foundation of our informal popular culture. The books explore advertising, news, humor, and different forms of media.

**Geissman, Grant.**

🏆 *MAD About the '90s: The Best of the Decade.* New York: MAD Books, 2005. ISBN 1401206603; 9781401206604. 🇯 🇭

A collection of the best *MAD* parodies of film, television, commercials, politics, and assorted pop culture from the 1990s, gathered into one volume. The book is arranged chronologically, with a brief introduction that reminds readers what the number one hits and events were, along with the backstory for several of the included spoofs. The tone of the cartoons reflects the views of the day, which is particularly noticeable in the jokes about political correctness. **QP**

Keywords: 1990s—Humor • Comic strip • Pop culture

### Graydon, Shari, and Warren Clarke.

*Made You Look: How Advertising Works and Why You Should Know.* Toronto: Annick Press, 2003. ISBN 1550378155. **M** **J**

This is a book about advertising written directly for the audience at whom more and more advertising is being directed. It includes a history of marketing, with concrete examples to help readers understand how advertising works. Also included are further resources for consumers, including a sample complaint letter.

Keywords: Advertising • Business • Economics • Marketing

### Koon, Jeff, and Andy Powell.

🎗 *Wearing of This Garment Will Not Enable You to Fly: 101 Real Dumb Warning Labels.* New York: Free Press, 2003. ISBN 9780743244756. **J** **H**

The litigiousness of modern society has resulted in some ridiculous warnings being placed on products. The author presents this collection of labels that inform consumers about what would seem to be obvious. These submissions from the Web sites www.dumblaws.com and www.dumbwarnings.com, maintained by the authors, are a mixture of unlikely contingencies that various companies feel they need legal protection from, for example, that upholstery cleaner is an "eye irritant." **QP**

Keywords: Humor • Warning labels

### Perel, David, and Editors of the *Weekly World News*.

🎗 *Bat Boy Lives!: The* Weekly World News *Guide to Politics, Culture, Celebrities, Alien Abductions, and the Mutant Freaks That Shape Our World.* New York: Sterling, 2005. ISBN 1402728239. **H**

A collection of stories from the *Weekly World News*, which prides itself on finding the news that other journalists miss attracts more than a million subscribers. Where else could we find out about the aliens among us? These are the correspondents who "discovered" that Elvis was still alive, that astronauts found beer cans on the moon, and that the center of the earth is actually candy, not magma. **PP, QP**

Keywords: American humor • Humor

### Shayne, David.

*MADvertising: A MAD Look at 50 Years of MADison Avenue.* New York: Watson-Guptill Publications, 2005. ISBN 0823030814. **H**

A look at one aspect of *MAD Magazine's* very pointed satire: advertising. Featuring the best and most popular advertising satires, it not only points out how pop culture and marketing have changed, but also serves as an important and readable education in marketing strategies.

Keywords: Advertising • Humor • Marketing • Satire

# Social Concerns

The books in this category examine some of the social and political issues in the world we live in today, the lives of others, hard economic times, and the possibility of bringing about change in the world.

## Atkin, S. Beth.

*Gunstories: Life-Changing Experiences with Guns.* New York: HarperTempest, 2006 ISBN 9780060526597. **J** **H**

The teenagers in these stories agree that guns are a fact of modern society. For some, they have been a good thing, associated with sports, protection, or hunting, while others remember only accidents, drive-bys, and death. All are true stories, told by the teens involved, with an eye to opening discussion and debate.

**Keywords:** Firearm history • Firearms • Guns • Nonfiction collections

**Now Try:** It is important to see both sides of an issue. Rudy Adler, Victoria Criado, and Brett Huneycutt handed out disposable cameras to groups on both sides of the U.S.–Mexico border to document illegal immigration. Some of the 2,000 photographs they collected are documented in *Border Film Project: Photos by Migrants & Minutemen on the U.S.–Mexico Border.*

## Ehrenreich, Barbara.

🐦 *Nickel and Dimed: On (Not) Getting by in America.* New York: Henry Holt, 2001. ISBN 9780805063882. **H** **A**

During a time of great economic prosperity, is it really possible to "get by" without welfare or government assistance? This sharp social critic decided to find out. Relying only on the low-paying jobs she could get without any reference to her educational background and living in the least expensive places she could find, she worked her way from Florida to Maine and Wisconsin. Her experiences, living on just over $300 per week while working long hours at two jobs with no healthcare, were made tolerable by her coworkers, who suffered along with her without the same possible end to their plight. What emerges is a sobering view of the lives of low-skilled workers, even in times of economic prosperity. **Alex**

**Keywords:** Business • Economics • Labor • Political science • Poverty

## Ellis, Deborah.

🐦 *Our Stories, Our Songs: African Children Talk about AIDS.* Markham, ON: Fitzhenry & Whiteside, 2005. ISBN 9781550419139. **M** **J**

The number of AIDS cases in Sub-Saharan Africa is overwhelming and continues to rise. Deborah Ellis traveled to Malawi and Zambia in 2003 to meet some of the 11.5 million children orphaned by AIDS at that time. These are the personal stories of children she met. Whether living on the street, in jail, at clinics, or in crowded homes, the children offer their opinions about AIDS, tuberculosis, and their futures in a place where there is little education or medical help, but a remarkable amount of hope and

**11**

courage. Sidebars offer statistics and information about AIDS. Additional resources are also listed. **Norma Fleck Honor**

**Keywords:** Africa • African children • AIDS

## Halpin, Mikki.

*It's Your World—If You Don't Like It, Change It: Activism for Teenagers.* New York: Simon Pulse, 2004. ISBN 0689874480. **J** **H**

Is there an issue readers care about, but have thought that they couldn't make a difference? This book defines the basics of activism and examines the issues one by one, helping readers decide which one might be their best fit, providing real-life examples from other teens about what they are doing, and offering suggestions and resources to get readers started making the world a better place. Readers can start practicing in any of several different areas, including helping animals; fighting racism; saving the environment; ending war; fighting the spread of HIV/AIDS; defending women's rights; protecting civil rights; and promoting tolerance toward lesbian, gay, bisexual, transgendered, and questioning youth.

**Keywords:** Activism • Adolescent psychology • Values • Volunteering

## Warren, Frank.

*PostSecret: Extraordinary Confessions from Ordinary Lives.* New York: ReganBooks, 2005. ISBN 9780060899196. **J** **H** **A**

When Frank Warren started handing out postcards for a community art project, he didn't know that it would spawn a Web site and several books. This project was meant as a way for people to express themselves and share any kind of secret, as long as it was honest and had never been told to anyone before. Cards were sent in from all over the world and were shown in art galleries as a method of art therapy to demonstrate common humanity. Some of the best cards from www.postsecret.com are featured in this first collection. This was one of the top ten 2007 Quick Picks for Reluctant Readers. **QP**

**Keywords:** Art therapy • Postcards • Secrets

**Now Try:** Davy Rothbart, the founder and editor of *Found* magazine, showed a collection of items he and his readers had collected over the years in *Found: The Best Lost, Tossed, and Forgotten Items from Around the World*. The writing ranges from the outright strange or funny to the erudite, maudlin, or haunting. Readers will get a small taste of the lives of the people who deposited these notes, postcards, and scraps of paper.

# Religion

In this section are books that explore the different religions practiced around the world, as well as a moving look at what their faith means to teens.

## Barnes, Trevor.

### World Faiths.

Readers may explore some of the world's religions in these highly researched and illustrated volumes. Each volume explores the history, people, traditions, and events of the religion, in straightforward and readable text.

*Hinduism and Other Eastern Religions.* Boston: Kingfisher, 2005. ISBN 9780753458815. **J** **H**

> **Keywords:** Buddhism • Hinduism • Jainism • Sikhism

*Islam.* **World Faiths.** Boston: Kingfisher, 2005. ISBN 9780753458822. **J** **H**

> **Keywords:** Islam • Koran • Muhammad

*Judaism.* **World Faiths.** Boston: Kingfisher, 2005. ISBN 9780753458839. **J** **H**

> **Keywords:** Judaism

## Gaskins, Pearl Fuyo.

*I Believe in. . . : Christian, Jewish, and Muslim Young People Speak About Their Faith.* Chicago: Cricket Books, 2004. ISBN 9780812627138. **J** **H**

> After interviewing almost 1,000 teens, Gaskins presents their answers to questions about faith and religion in their lives. Jewish, Christian, and Muslim teens' answers are divided into sections that include religious symbols, following religious laws, women's issues, and living in a world with many different faiths. The teens are giving their own opinions about how they integrate faith into their world, whether by wearing a kippah or a crucifix in public or deciding which religious laws to follow.
>
> **Keywords:** Faith • Religions • Religious lives

## Siddiqui, Haroon.

*Being Muslim.* <u>Groundwork Guides</u>. Toronto: Groundwood Books, 2006. ISBN 9780888997852. **H** **A**

> This is not merely a discussion of the beliefs and practices of Islam but an informed, balanced, and thought-provoking look at being Muslim in the post 9/11 world. With chapters taking a penetrating look at politics, European Muslims, faith, jihad and terrorism, women, and the future, this book is guaranteed to provide many opportunities for debate and discussion. The notes list is supplemented by a list of essential reading.
>
> **Keywords:** Islam • Muslims

## World Religions.

> This series describes the practice of six major religions in the world today: Judaism, Christianity, Hinduism, Buddhism, Sikhism, and Islam. Each book starts by looking at the experiences of a person of that faith before providing a discussion of the religion's origins, beliefs, and practices. Sidebars address some of the potential challenges and issues. For example, homosexuality is not recognized in Hinduism, and a discussion about modern medicine touches on several issues, including birth control, in the Islam volume.
>
> **Keywords:** Buddhism • Christianity • Hinduism • Islam • Judaism • Religion • Sikhism

11

**Barrow, Joy.**

*Sikhism.* North Vancouver, BC: Whitecap Books, 2004. ISBN 9781552856529. **M** **J**
    **Keywords:** Religion • Sikhism

**Brown, Alan.**

*Christianity.* North Vancouver, BC: Whitecap Books, 2005. ISBN 9781552856512. **M** **J**
    **Keywords:** Catholicism • Christianity • Protestantism • Religion

**Graham, Ian.**

*Judaism.* North Vancouver, BC: Whitecap Books, 2005. ISBN 9781552856567. **M** **J**
    **Keywords:** Judaism • Religion

**Prime, Ranchor.**

*Hinduism.* North Vancouver, BC: Whitecap Books, 2005. ISBN 9781552856550. **M** **J**
    **Keywords:** Hinduism • Religion

**Thompson, Jan**

*Islam.* North Vancouver, BC: Whitecap Books, 2005. ISBN 9781552856543. **M** **J**
    **Keywords:** Islam • Religion,

**Thompson, Mel.**

*Buddhism.* North Vancouver, BC: Whitecap Books, 2005. ISBN 9781552856536. **M** **J**
    **Keywords:** Buddhism • Religion

## Consider Starting with . . .

These titles cover a wide age range and are recommended as an introduction to the genre.

Ehrenreich, Barbara. *Nickel and Dimed: On (Not) Getting by in America.*

Gaskins, Pearl Fuyo. *I Believe in . . . : Christian, Jewish, and Muslim Young People Speak About Their Faith.*

Geissman, Grant *MAD About the '90s: The Best of the Decade.*

Graydon, Shari, and Warren Clarke. *Made You Look: How Advertising Works and Why You Should Know.*

Halpin, Mikki. *It's Your World—If You Don't Like It, Change It: Activism for Teenagers.*

Koon, Jeff, and Andy Powell. *Wearing of This Garment Will Not Enable You to Fly: 101 Real Dumb Warning Labels.*

Warren, Frank. *PostSecret: Extraordinary Confessions from Ordinary Lives.*

# Fiction Read-Alikes

- **Abdel-Fattah, Randa**. In *Does My Head Look Big in This?*, Amal deals with integrating her culture and her faith into her everyday life when she decides to wear the hijab, a Muslim headcovering, full time.

- **Bauer, Joan**. The protagonists in Joan Bauer's novels have a talent for making a difference, as well as finding something that they are good at and sticking to it. The reader will learn about politics and how to stand up for oneself in the Newbery Medal Honor Book *Hope Was Here*, meet the world's best shoe salesman and personal assistant in *Best Foot Forward*, and laugh while a great photographer fights off cupid in *Thwonk*.

- **Stratton, Allan**. In *Chanda's Secrets*, Allan Stratton gives readers a view of the ugly realities of life in an unnamed African country. The reader is introduced to Chanda as she makes funeral arrangements for her sister, Sara. When no neighbors will attend the funeral because her mother is bad luck, a string of secrets, all connected to AIDS, starts tearing apart her world. This is a 2005 Michael L. Printz Award Honor book as well as a BBYA title.

1

2

3

4

5

6

7

8

9

10

**11**

# Appendix A

## Nonfiction Readers' Advisor Resources for YA Librarians

Although there are no readers' advisory or reviewing resources devoted solely to young adult nonfiction, there are sources that will help with both readers' advisory and collection development.

## Reference and Readers' Advisory Sources

### Gillespie, John Thomas, and Catherine Barr.

*Best Books for High School Readers Grades 9–12.* Westport, CT: Libraries Unlimited, 2004.

*Best Books for Middle School and Junior High Readers Grades 6–9.* Westport, CT: Libraries Unlimited, 2004.

> These two guides list titles for virtually every subject, with multiple access points. Supplements were added in 2006.

### Jones, Patrick, Patricia Taylor, and Kirsten Edwards.

*A Core Collection for Young Adults.* Teens @ the Library Series. New York: Neal-Schuman, 2003.

> This terrific guide for creating a well-rounded collection includes a well-annotated starter nonfiction collection.

### Pawuk, Michael.

*Graphic Novels: A Genre Guide to Comic Books, Manga, and More.* Genreflecting Advisory Series. Westport, CT: Libraries Unlimited, 2007.

> Teen titles are marked in this cornucopia of graphic novels.

**Silvey, Anita.**

*500 Best Books for Children.* Boston: Houghton Mifflin, 2006.
> Chapter headings, such as "Information" and "Adventure and Survival," give readers the opportunity to find nonfiction titles mixed in with the standard "Fantasy" and "Mystery" chapters.

## Review Journals

*Booklist.* P.O. Box 607, Mt. Morris, IL 61054-7564. Phone: 888-350-0949.
> Contains critical reviews of books. Published twenty-two times annually.

*Horn Book.* 56 Roland Street, Suite 200, Boston, MA 02129. Phone: 617-628-0225; 800-325-1170. E-mail: info@hbook.com www.hbook.com.
> A bimonthly magazine for children's and young adult literature. The companion *Horn Book Guide* contains reviews of most books from each publishing season.

*School Library Journal.* 360 Park Ave. South. New York, NY 10010. Phone: 646-746-6759. Web site: www.schoollibraryjournal.com.
> Contains reviews of nonfiction, with online blogs, including Marc Aronson's "Nonfiction Matters." Published monthly.

*VOYA: Voice of Youth Advocates.* Scarecrow Press, 4501 Forbes Blvd., Suite 200, Lanham, MD 20706. Web site: www.voya.com/. E-mail: journals@rowman.com. Phone: (800) 233-1687.
> *VOYA* reviews nonfiction in every issue, with the Nonfiction Honor List published annually in August. Young adult reviewers are included in the editorial process. Published bimonthly.

## Online Sources

- **ATN Reading Lists** (http://atn-reading-lists.wikispaces.com/). The ATN (All Together Now) reading lists date back to 1996. The lists, which were administered by Nancy Keane, have been converted to a wiki format and number more than 1,400, many of which are nonfiction.

- **Cybils (Children's and YA Bloggers' Literary Awards)** (http://dadtalk. typepad.com/cybils/). A literary award administered and chosen by bloggers, with nominations open to the public. The Cybils are awarded in eight categories, including middle grade and YA nonfiction and picture book nonfiction.

- **Kathleen Baxter Nonfiction Booktalker** (http://www.kathleenbaxter.com). Kathleen Baxter has written several guides on booktalking children's nonfiction, including *Gotcha, Gotcha Again, Gotcha Covered,* and *Gotcha for Guys.* Her Web site includes handouts from her presentations, with suggested titles for nonfiction booktalks as well as booktalking tips.

- **Reads 4 Teens** (http://reads4teens.org). This teen review site from the Carmel Clay Public Library in Carmel, Indiana, contains a good number of nonfiction book reviews.

- **Reading Rants** (http://www.readingrants.org). Jennifer Hubert's review site, converted into a blog format. The reviews, which include some wonderful biographies and memoirs, have also been turned into *Reading Rants: A Guide to Books That ROCK* (Neil-Schuman, 2007).
- **Scholastic Booktalks (Dr. Joni Richards Bodart)** (http://teacher.scholastic. com/products/tradebooks/booktalks.htm). Contains ready-made booktalks and ideas for books with hooks from librarian and expert booktalker Dr. Joni Richard Bodart.

## Discussion Lists

Although there are no listservs specifically for young adult nonfiction, there are a few open listservs that discuss young adult books. Nonfiction books are discussed on both lists.

- **Adbooks** (http://www.adbooks.org/). An e-mail list created to discuss books written for adolescent readers. Its members include children, teens, and adults who love to read and to talk about good books.
- **YALSA-bk** (http://lists.ala.org/wws/info/yalsa-bk). Subscribers are invited to discuss specific titles, as well as other issues concerning young adult reading and young adult literature. The listserv also provides opportunities for subscribers to learn what has been nominated for Best Books for Young Adults, Popular Paperbacks for Young Adults, and Quick Picks for Reluctant Young Adult Readers and to discuss those books. Cumulative lists of nominations for the lists are posted by each of the committees. Queries may be posted if one is looking for help with a readers' advisory question.

## Book Awards

The increasing amount of quality nonfiction for young adults is well reflected in the recognition these books receive. Following is an explanation of the awards cited in this book and the organizations that award them.

- **The Young Adult Library Services Association (YALSA)** has several committees that work to find the best books for teens aged twelve to eighteen. These annual lists have the specific purpose of identifying (1) the Best Books for Young Adults, which are those that balance literary quality and popularity; (2) Quick Picks for Reluctant Young Adult Readers, pleasurable books for teens who do not like to read; and (3) Popular Paperbacks, pleasurable reading in a variety of accessible themes and genres.
- The **Michael L. Printz Award** is given annually by YALSA to the book that exemplifies literary excellence in young adult literature. As many as four "Printz" honor books may be chosen annually.
- **The Alex Awards,** chosen by YALSA, are given annually to the best adult books for young adults.
- **The Coretta Scott King Task Force** commemorates the life and works of Dr. Martin Luther King Jr. and honors Mrs. Coretta Scott King with the Coretta Scott King Award. These titles promote understanding of the cultures of all people

and their realization of the American dream. The CSK and the John Steptoe New Talent Award, which celebrates the beginning of a career, are given to African American authors and illustrators for outstanding inspirational and educational contributions.

- **The Bologna Book Fair** is held annually for children's publishers in Bologna, Italy. At the fair an international panel chooses the Bologna Ragazzi award winners in fiction and nonfiction in four age categories, including young adult.

- **The International Reading Association** (IRA) is a professional organization for people involved in teaching reading to any age. Their children's book awards include fiction and nonfiction books in primary, intermediate, and young adult categories up to age seventeen.

- **The Robert F. Sibert Informational Book Award** is awarded annually by the ALA's Association for Library Services to Children (ALSC) at its Midwinter meeting in January. The "Sibert" is given to the author, author/illustrator, coauthor or author, and illustrator of the most distinguished informational book published in the United States during the preceding year. Honor books may also be awarded.

- **The Norma Fleck Award for Canadian Children's Nonfiction** (http://www. bookcentre.ca/awards/norma_fleck/index.shtml) is overseen by the Canadian Children's Book Centre. It was established in 1999 to recognize the high quality of informational literature available to children and young adults.

- **The Boston Globe-Horn Book Award** (http://www.hbook.com/bghb/default. asp) is cosponsored by the *Boston Globe* and *Horn Book* magazine. Nonfiction is one of the three categories of the award, which is judged by three children's literature professionals.

- **The National Book Award for Young People's Literature** (http://www. nationalbook.org/nba.html) has been celebrating "the best in American literature" since 1950.

- **The Orbis Pictus Award** (http://www.ncte.org/elem/awards/orbispictus) for Outstanding K–8 nonfiction is chosen by the National Council of Teachers of English.

- **ALSC Recommended Titles** (http://www.ala.org/ala/alsc/awardsscholarships/). The Association for Library Service to Children makes available the Notable Book Lists as well as information about the Newbery Award and the Pura Belpre Award.

# Appendix B

## Bibliography

Abrahamson, Richard F., and Betty Carter. "Nonfiction: The Missing Piece in the Middle." *English Journal* 80, no. 1 (1991): 52–58.

American Psychological Association. *Developing Adolescents: A Reference for Professionals.* 2002. Available at http://www.apa.org/pi/cyf/develop.pdf.

Aronson, Marc. "Battle of the Bulge." *School Library Journal: SLJ* 52, no. 10(2006): 34.

———. *Beyond the Pale: New Essays for a New Era.* Scarecrow Studies in Young Adult Literature, 9. Lanham, MD: Scarecrow Press, 2003, 69–72.

———. "Consider the Source—A Glaring Omission." *School Library Journal: SLJ* 52, no. 11 (2006): 32.

———. *Exploding the Myths: The Truth About Teens and Reading.* Lanham, MD: Scarecrow Press, 2001.

———. "Originality in Nonfiction." *School Library Journal: SLJ* 52, no. 1 (2006): 42–43.

———. "The Shape of Things to Come." *School Library Journal* 52, no. 9 (September 2006): 33.

Bamford, Rosemary A., and Janice V. Kristo. *Making Facts Come Alive: Choosing & Uusing Quality NonfictionLiterature K–8.* Norwood, MA: Christopher-Gordon Publishers, 2003.

Booth, David W. *Even Hockey Players Read: Boys, Literacy, and Learning.* Markham, ON: Pembroke Publishers, 2002.

Burns, M. M., et al. "Whatever Happened to—? A List of Recovered Favorites and What Makes a Book Memorable after All." *The Horn Book* 75, no. 5 (September/October 1999): 574–86.

Carter, Betty. "Alex: The Why and the How." *The Booklist* 99, no. 15 (2003): 1389.

———. "A Content Analysis of the Most Frequently Circulated Information Books in Three Junior High Libraries." Ed.D. thesis, University of Houston, 1987.

———. "Features—Formula for Failure—Reading Levels and Readability Formulas Do Not Create Lifelong Readers." *School Library Journal: SLJ* 46, no. 7 (2000): 34.

———. "Reviewing Nonfiction Books for Children and Young Adults: Stance, Scholarship, and Structure." In *Evaluating Children's Books*, 59–71. Urbana-Champaign: University of Illinois Graduate School of Library and Information Science, 1993.

Carter, Betty, and Richard F. Abrahamson. *Nonfiction for Young Adults: From Delight to Wisdom*. Phoenix, AZ: Oryx Press, 1990.

Carter, Betty, Sally Estes, and Linda L. Waddle. *Best Books for Young Adults*. Chicago: American Library Association, 2000.

Jones, Patrick. "Nonfiction: The Real Stuff—A YA Librarian Makes the Argument for Noncurriculum-related Nonfiction." *School Library Journal: SLJ* 47, no. 4 (2001): 44.

Jones, Patrick, Michele Gorman, and Tricia Suellentrop. *Connecting Young Adults and Libraries: A How-to-Do-It Manual for Librarians*. New York: Neal-Schumans, 2004.

Jones, Patrick, Maureen L. Hartman, and Patricia Taylor. *Connecting with Reluctant Teen Readers: Tips, Titles, and Tools*. New York: Neal-Schuman, 2006.

Lodge, S. A. "Fresh Takes on the Tried and True." *Publishers Weekly* 248, no. 48 (November 26, 2001): 20–22.

Parsons, Les. "Challenging the Gender Divide: Improving Literacy for All." *Teacher Librarian* 32, no. 2 (2004): 8–11.

Pierce, Jennifer Burek. "Picking the Flowers in the 'Fair Garden': The Circulation, Non-Circulation and Disappearance of Young Adult Materials." *School Libraries Worldwide* 9, no. 2 (2003): 62–72.

Smith, Karen M. "The Power of Information: Creating a YA Nonfiction Collection." *School Library Journal: SLJ* 5, no. 1 (2006): 28–30.

Sullivan, E. "Race Matters." *School Library Journal* 48, no. 6 (June 2002): 40–41.

Sullivan, Ed. "Some Teens Prefer the Real Thing: The Case for Young Adult Nonfiction." *English Journal* 90, no. 3 (2001): 43.

Sullivan, Michael. *Connecting Boys with Books: What Libraries Can Do*. Chicago: American Library Association, 2003.

———. "Why Johnny Won't Read." *School Library Journal: SLJ* 50, no. 8 (2004): 36–39.

Watson, Jamie, and Jennifer Stencel. "Reaching Reluctant Readers with Nonfiction." *Young Adult Library Services* 4, no. 1 (2005): 8–11.

# Author/Title Index

Abdel-Fattah, Randa, 203
*Absolutely True Diary of a Part-Time Indian, The*, 43
Abu-Jaber, Diana, 36
*Abundance of Katherines, An*, 115
*Accessories: Things to Make and Do*, 151
*Acting for Young Actors: The Ultimate Teen Guide*, 159
Adler, David, 49
Adler, Rudy, 199
Adventure Travel Books, 11–12
*Adventures of Marco Polo, The*, 12
Aherne, Charlie, 177
Ahmedi, Farah, 36
*Airborne: A Photobiography of Wilbur and Orville Wright*, 51
Ajak, Benjamin, 32
Akbar, Said Hyder, 36
*Alamo, The: Surrounded and Outnumbered, They Chose to Make a Defiant Last Stand*, 74
*Albino Animals*, 112, 114
Alcorn, Stephen, 64, 188
*Alexander the Great Rocks the World*, 47, 65
Alexander, Caroline, 4
Alexander, Elizabeth, 191
Alexie, Sherman, 43
*All Aboard!: Passenger Trains Around the World*, 106
*All About Adoption: How to Deal with the Questions of Your Past*, 139
*All Made Up: A Girl's Guide to Seeing Through Celebrity Hype and Celebrating Real Beauty*, 132
*All Music Guide to Rock: The Definitive Guide to Rock, Pop, and Soul*, 181
Almond, David, 28
Almond, Steve, 42
*Alternacrafts: [20+ Hi-style, Lo-budget Projects to Make]*, 153, 172
Alvarez, Julia, 91
*Amazing Leonardo da Vinci Inventions You Can Build Yourself*, 148
*American Plague, An: The True and Terrifying Story of the Yellow Fever Epidemic of 1793*, 81

AMG All Media Guide, 181
Andersen, Bethanne, 64
Andersen, Hans Christian, 193
Anderson, Laurie Halse, 91
Anderson, M. T., 115
Anderson, Maxine, 148
Andronik, Catherine M., 187
*Andy Warhol: Prince of Pop*, 178
*Angel of Death*, 24
Angelou, Maya, 31–32
*Anime Mania: How to Draw Characters for Japanese Animation*, 161
*Anne Frank*, 86
*Anne Frank: The Diary of a Young Girl*, 28
*Annika Sorenstam*, 122
Ansary, Mir Tamim, 36
*Apprentice, The: My Life in the Kitchen*, 40
*Archers, Alchemists, and 98 Other Medieval Jobs You Might Have Loved or Loathed*, 71
Armstrong, Jennifer, 4, 13, 77
Armstrong, Lance, 27, 32
*Army Rangers: Surveillance and Reconnaissance for the U. S. Army*, 142
Aronson, Marc, 10, 52, 176
*Art Attack: A Short Cultural History of the Avant-Garde*, 176
Ask Cosmo Girl! Series, 134–135, 139
*Ask CosmoGirl! About Guys: All the Answers to Your Most Asked Questions About Love and Relationships*, 139
*Ask CosmoGirl! About Nutrition and Fitness*, 134
*Ask Cosmogirl! About Your Body: All the Answers to Your Most Intimate Questions*, 135
*Asteroids, Comets, and Meteors*, 109
*Astrostyle: Star–studded Advice for Love, Life, and Looking Good*, 144
*At the End of Words: A Daughter's Memoirs*, 35
Atkin, S. Beth, 199
*Attack of the Killer Video Book: Tips and Tricks for Young Directors*, 168
Aynie, Laetitia, 133

*B. Franklin, Printer,* 49
*Babe Didrikson Zaharias: The Making of a Champion,* 119, 129
Babysitting, 142
*Babysitting Jobs: The Business of Babysitting,* 142
*Bad Boy: A Memoir,* 29, 43
Bahn, Paul G., 98
Ball, Heather, 183
Ballantine, Richard, 170
Bang, Molly, 110–111
Banyard, Antonia, 4–5
Barakat, Ibtisam, 37, 43
Barnard, Bryn, 78
Barnes, Trevor, 200
Barnett, Charles, 80
Barrett, Angela, 86
Barrow, Joy, 201
Barry, Dave, 175, 180
Bartoletti, Susan Campbell, 79, 86–87, 90
Bascle, Brian, 118
*Bat Boy Lives!: The* Weekly World News *Guide to Politics, Culture, Celebrities, Alien Abductions, and the Mutant Freaks That Shape Our World,* 198
Batten, Jack, 78
*Battle Dress,* 29
Bauer, Joan, 202–203
Baugh, Bryan, 161
Bausum, Ann, 52, 58, 62
*Be Afraid, Be Very Afraid: The Book of Scary Urban Legends,* 194
*Be Healthy! It's a Girl Thing: Food, Fitness, and Feeling Great,* 134
*Beast of Chicago, The,* 17, 23
*Beauty: Things to Make and Do,* 151
*Beauty Trix for Cool Chix: Easy–to–Make Lotions, Potions, and Spells to Bring Out a Beautiful You,* 154
Beck, Gregor Gilpin, 107
*Beet Fields, The,* 44
*Before We Were Free,* 91
Behnke, Alison, 47
*Beige,* 196
*Being a Girl: [Navigating the Ups and Downs of Teen Life],* 132
*Being Muslim,* 201
Beker, Jeanne, 155
Belli, Mary Lou, 159
*Ben Franklin's Almanac: Being a True Account of the Good Gentleman's Life,* 49

Benanav, Michael, 11
Benchley, Peter, 112
Bennett, Jamie, 185
*Berenice Abbott, Photographer: An Independent Vision,* 180
Beres, D. B., 20
Berger, Shoshana, 149
Bernstein, Judy, 32
Bertholf, Bret, 181
Bertozzi, Nick, 59
*Best Foot Forward,* 203
*Between Boardslides and Burnout: My Notes from the Road,* 119
*Bicycle Stunt Riding!: Catch Air,* 123
Biddle, Geoffrey, 128–129
*Big Book of Pop Culture, The: A How–to Guide for Young Artists,* 166–167
*Big Book of Rules, The: Board Games, Kids' Games, Card Games, from Backgammon and Bocce to Tiddlywinks and Stickball,* 169
*Big Book of Urban Legends,* 195
*Big Night Out, The* 155
Bingham, Kelly, 196
Bird, Eugenie, 193
Bishop, Nic, 94–95
Bissinger, H. G., 126
Bjorkman, Steve, 136
*Black Potatoes: The Story of the Great Irish Famine, 1845–1850,* 79
*Black, White and Jewish: Autobiography of a Shifting Self,* 31
Blackwood, Gary, 91, 186
*Blades, Boards & Scooters,* 125
Blakeney, Faith, 156
Blakeney, Justina, 156
*Blizzard!: The Storm That Changed America,* 84
*Blogging for Teens,* 167
*Blue Jean Book, The: The Story Behind the Seams,* 83
*Blue Lipstick,* 189
Blumberg, Rhoda, 11
Blumenthal, Karen, 81, 127, 129
*Bobbi Brown Teenage Beauty: Everything You Need to Look Pretty, Natural, Sexy & Awesome,* 153, 172
Bober, Natalie, 46
*Bodies from the Ash: Life and Death in Ancient Pompeii,* 98, 114
*Bodies in the Bog,* 99

*Body Art Book, The: A Complete, Illustrated Guide to Tattoos, Piercings, and Other Body Modification,* 108
*Body Brokers: Inside America's Underground Trade in Human Remains,* 103
*Body Marks: Tattooing, Piercing, and Scarification,* 108
*Body Talk: The Straight Facts on Fitness, Nutrition, and Feeling Great about Yourself!,* 134
Boese, Alex, 16, 23
Bogdanov, Vladimir, 181
Bolden, Tonya, 53, 56, 89–90, 182
*Bone Detectives, The,* 101
Bonnell, Jennifer, 149
*Book of Flight: The Smithsonian National Air and Space Museum,* 105, 114
*Book of Rock Stars, The: 24 Musical Icons That Shine Through History,* 45, 64
Boone, Jessica, 165
*Borden Tragedy, The,* 17
*Border Film Project: Photos by Migrants & Minutemen on the U.S.–Mexico Border,* 199
Borgenicht, David, 171–172
Boring, Mel, 63, 65
*Born to Rock,* 196
*Bound for the North Star: True Stories of Fugitive Slaves,* 76
Boutaudou, Sylvie, 133
Bowers, Vivien, 22
*Boy's Body Book, The,* 135–136
Branzei, Sylvia, 110
Brashich, Audrey D., 132
*Break a Leg!: The Kids' Book of Acting and Stagecraft,* 159.
*Breaking Up,* 146
Breashears, David, 7, 13
*Breathe: Yoga for Teens,* 134
Brewster, Todd, 72, 91
Bridman, Rodger, 105
Brieditis, Katarina, 157
*British Royal Marines: Amphibious Division of the United Kingdom's Royal Navy,* 142
*Bronx Masquerade,* 196
Brown, Alan, 202
Brown, Bobbi, 153, 172
Brown, Brenda, 172
Brown, Chester, 56
Brown, Martin, 90

*Bruce Lee: The Celebrated Life of the Golden Dragon,* 61
Brunvand, Jan Harold, 194–195
Bryson, Bill, 93, 97
Buckingham, Alan, 107, 166
Buckley, James, Jr., 120
*Buddha Boy,* 196
*Buddhism,* 202
Buller, Laura, 107
*Bullet Proof!: The Evidence That Guns Leave Behind,* 20
Burgan, Michael, 118
Burke, L. M., 123
*Burn: The Life Story of Fire,* 83
*Burn Journals, The,* 34
Burnett, Betty, 142
Burns, Loree Griffin, 111
Bursztynski, Sue, 22
Burton, Susan, 36
*Bury the Dead: Tombs, Corpses, Mummies, Skeletons & Rituals,* 100
Butts, Ed, 5
*By Truck to the North: My Arctic Adventure,* 12

Cadier, Florence, 138
*Caged Eagles,* 92
Calabro, Marian, 4
Caldwell, Ben, 160
Caldwell, Michaela, 133
*Candyfreak: A Journey Through the Chocolate Underbelly of America,* 42
Canfield, Jack, 138
Cannell, Jon, 96
Caputo, Philip, 70
Capuzzo, Michael, 79
*Car,* 106
*Car Smarts: Hot Tips for the Car Crazy,* 169
Carle, Jill, 165
Carle, Judy, 165
Carle, Megan, 165
Carlson, Lori Marie, 188
*Carver: A Life in Poems,* 192
*Case of Madeleine Smith, The,* 17
Castellucci, Cecil, 196
Cattrall, Kim, 132
*Caught by the Sea: My Life on Boats,* 42
*Celebrity Style Guide,* 156
*Century for Young People, The,* 72, 91
Chambers, Aidan, 45
*Chanda's Secrets,* 203

Chaplin, Heather, 168
Cheney, Annie, 103
*Chess: From First Moves to Checkmate*, 168
Cheung, Lilian, 134
Chevalier, Tracy, 196
*Chew on This: Everything You Don't Want to Know About Fast Food*, 108
Chiappe, Luis M., 101
Chicken Soup for the Teenage Soul: The Real Deal Series, 138
*Chicken Soup for the Teenage Soul's the Real Deal: Friends: Best, Worst, Old, New, Lost, False, True, and More*, 138
*Chicken Soup for the Teenage Soul's the Real Deal: On Girl Stuff*, 138
*Chicken Soup for the Teenage Soul's the Real Deal: School, Cliques, Classes, Clubs, and More*, 138
*Chicks with Sticks*, 173
*Chicks with Sticks: It's a Purl Thing*, 173
*Chicks with Sticks: Knit Two Together*, 173
Child, Julia, 38
*Children of the Great Depression*, 87
*Children's Blizzard, The*, 80
Childress, Diana, 12
*Chinese Cinderella: The True Story of an Unwanted Daughter*, 33, 43
Christensen, Lisa, 169
*Christianity*, 201
*Christopher Killer, The*, 24
Chryssicas, Mary Kaye, 134
*Circle of Blood, The*, 24
*Clara Schumann: Piano Virtuoso*, 62
Clark, Warren, 104
Clarke, Michael, 176
Clarke, Warren, 198, 202
Clement, Frederic, 56
*Climate Change*, 110, 112
Clinton, Catherine, 188
*Close to Shore: The Terrifying Shark Attacks of 1916*, 79
*Clueless about Cars: An Easy Guide to Car Maintenance and Repair*, 169
*Clueless in the Kitchen: A Cookbook for Teens*, 166, 172
*Coal: A Human History*, 82
Codell, Esmé Raji, 28, 38, 43
Coffey, Maria, 10–11
Coker, Cheo Hodari, 60
Coleman, Janet Wyman, 23
Collins, Mary, 51

Colman, Penny, 72, 100
Colton, Larry, 8
*Come Back to Afghanistan: A California Teenager's Story*, 36
*Comic Book Century: The History of American Comic Books*, 185
*Complete Bike Book, The*, 170
*Complete Book of Hairstyling, The*, 154, 172
*Complete Collected Poems of Maya Angelou, The*, 32
*Complete Maus, The*, 78
Compton, Shanna, 168
*Confucius: The Golden Rule*, 56
Conniff, Richard, 81
*Conquering the Beast Within: How I Fought Depression and Won . . . and You Can, Too*, 33
*Conquests of Alexander the Great, The*, 47
Conroy, Pat, 28
*Cooking up a Storm: The Teen Survival Cookbook*, 165–166
*Cool Salsa: Bilingual Poems on Growing up Latino in the United States*, 188
*Cool Stuff: Things to Make and Do*, 152
Cooper, Evan, 134
Cooper, Floyd, 189, 191
Cooper, Ilene, 59
Cooper, Michael L., 56, 75
Coppola, Angela, 134
Coria, Rodolfo A., 101
*Corpses, Coffins, and Crypts: A History of Burial*, 100
Corrigan, Eireann, 32
Cosmo Girl! Series, 144
Cosmogirl Editors, 134–135, 139, 144
*CosmoGIRL! Make It Yourself: 50 Fun and Funky Projects*, 149
*CosmoGIRL! Quiz Book: Discover Your Personality*, 144
*Cosmogirl!: Words to Live By*, 144
*Cosmogirl Quiz Book: All About You*, 144
*Costume*, 156
Coulter, Laurie, 71
*Counting Coup: A True Story of Basketball and Honor on the Little Big Horn*, 8
*Cowboys and Coffin Makers: One Hundred 19th-Century Jobs You Might Have Feared or Fancied*, 71
Cox, Lynne, 118, 129
*Crafts and Culture of a Medieval Castle, The*, 150

*Crafts and Culture of a Medieval Cathedral, The,* 150
*Crafts and Culture of a Medieval Guild, The,* 150
*Crafts and Culture of a Medieval Manor, The,* 150
*Crafts and Culture of a Medieval Monastery, The,* 150
*Crafts and Culture of a Medieval Town, The,* 150
*Crafts and Culture of the Aztecs, The,* 149
*Crafts and Culture of the Egyptians, The,* 149
*Crafts and Culture of the Greeks, The,* 149
*Crafts and Culture of the Romans, The,* 150
Crafts of the Ancient World, 148
Crafts of the Middle Ages, 150
Crafty Girl Series, The, 151–152
Craig, David, 7, 13
Crawford, Elizabeth, 66
*Creatures of the Deep: In Search of the Sea's "Monsters" and the World They Live In,* 114
Criado, Victoria, 199
Crichton, Michael, 115
*Crime Scene: How Investigators Use Science to Track Down the Bad Guys,* 22
*Crime Scene: The Ultimate Guide to Forensic Science,* 22
Crisler, Curtis L., 189
Crowe, Chris, 75, 90, 193
Crutcher, Chris, 42, 129
*Crystal & Gem,* 110
*Curse of the Pharaohs, The: My Adventures with Mummies,* 100
Cutting Edge, 160
Czarnecki, Monike, 139

*Da Vinci Cod and Other Illustrations for Unwritten Books, The,* 186
Daigle, Evelyn, 41, 112
*Dairy Queen: A Novel,* 130
Daldry, Jeremy, 135, 146
D'Aluisio, Faith, 108
Daly, Melissa, 141
*Dangerous Crossings!,* 4–5
*Darkness over Denmark: The Danish Resistance and the Rescue of the Jews,* 10
*Darwin Awards 4, The: Intelligent Design,* 145
*Dave Barry's Book of Bad Songs,* 180
Davidson, Sue, 55

Davila, Claudia, 84, 133
Day That Changed America, A, 7, 74
*D–Day: The Greatest Invasion—A People's History,* 74
*Dear Miss Breed: True Stories of the Japanese American Incarceration During World War II and a Librarian Who Made a Difference,* 88
Deary, Terry, 69, 90
Deem, James M., 98–99, 114
*Deep, The: The Extraordinary Creatures of the Abyss,* 113
Delano, Marfé Ferguson, 47
Delisle, Guy, 28, 38–39
*Delta Force: Counterterrorism Unit of the U.S. Army,* 142
Dendy, Leslie, 63, 65
Denega, Danielle, 20
Deng, Alephonsion, 32
Deng, Benson, 32
DeSaix, Deborah Durland, 9
DesignEXchange, 161
Desnoëttes, Caroline, 176
*Devil in the Details: Scenes from an Obsessive Girlhood,* 35
*Devil in the White City, The: Murder, Magic, and Madness at the Fair That Changed America,* 17
Dickason, Jack, 124
*Dickens: His Work and His World,* 186
Dickinson, Rachel, 150
Diclaudio, Dennis, 108
*Digital Filmmaking for Teens,* 168
*Digital Photo Madness!: 50 Weird & Wacky Things to Do with Your Digital Camera,* 166
*Digital Photo Magic,* 166
Dingus, Lowell, 101
*Dinner Club, The,* 173
*Dinosaur Eggs Discovered!: Unscrambling the Clues,* 101
*Dinosaur Mummies: Beyond Bare-Bone Fossils,* 101
Discovery!, 99, 109
*Disguised: A Wartime Memoir,* 35
Dixon, Dougal, 101–102
*Do You Read Me?: Famous Cases Solved by Handwriting Analysis!,* 21
Dobson, Clive, 107
Doeden, Matt, 118
*Does My Head Look Big in This?,* 203

*Doing It Right: Making Smart, Safe and Satisfying Decisions About Sex*, 137

Dominguez, Richard, 80

*Don't Try This at Home: How to Win a Sumo Match, Catch a Great White Shark, and Start an Independent Nation and Other Extraordinary Feats (for Ordinary People)*, 170–171

D'Orso, Michael, 8

*Dougal Dixon's Dinosaurs*, 101

Douglas, Ann, 134

Douglas, Julie, 134

Dowd, Olympia, 28, 59

Dowdle, Mary, 159

*Down the Yukon*, 91

Downton, David, 193

*Dr. Jenner and the Speckled Monster: The Search for the Smallpox Vaccine*, 50

Drake, Jane, 84

Drawing Cool Stuff, 163

*Drawing Cutting Edge Anatomy: The Ultimate Reference Guide for Comic Book Artists*, 160

*Dream of Freedom, A: The Civil Rights Movement from 1954 to 1968*, 73, 91

*Dress Your Family in Corduroy and Denim*, 43

*Driving Book, The: Everything New Drivers Need to Know But Don't Know to Ask*, 170

*Drugs Explained: The Real Deal on Alcohol, Pot, Ecstasy and More*, 140

*Ductigami: The Art of the Tape*, 151

Duncan, Tim, 119

Dunham, Kelli S., 136

*Dusted and Busted!: The Science of Fingerprinting*, 20

*Eagle Blue: A Team, a Tribe, and a High School Basketball Team in Arctic Alaska*, 8

*Eagle Strike*, 24

*Earthquake!: On a Peaceful Spring Morning Disaster Strikes San Francisco*, 7, 13

Ebadi, Shirin, 37

Editors of the *Weekly World News*, 198

Edmonston, Phil, 169

*Educating Esmé: Diary of a Teacher's First Year*, 38, 43

Edut, Ophira, 144

Edut, Tali, 144

Edwards, Gavin, 180

Efaw, Amy, 29

Ehrenreich, Barbara, 199, 202

Eichler, Christian, 128

Eisenhower, John S. D., 74

Eisner, Will, 164

*Elephant Rescue: Changing the Future for Endangered Wildlife*, 95

Elliot, Jessie, 173

Ellis, Deborah, 199

Ellwand, David, 193

*Elvis Presley, a Twentieth Century Life*, 60

Encyclopedia Prehistorica, 102

*Endurance, The: Shackleton's Legendary Antarctic Expedition*, 4

Engle, Margarita, 192

Erlewine, Stephen Thomas, 181

*Escape!: The Story of the Great Houdini*, 59

*Escapes!*, 6

Evans, Katarina, 157

Evans, Kate, 112

*Exploding Toilet, The: Modern Urban Legends*, 195

*Extreme Pets!*, 113–114

Extreme Sports, 124

Extreme Sports Collection, 122–124

*Extreme Sports: In Search of the Ultimate Thrill*, 126, 129

Eyewitness Books, 69–70, 104–107, 110, 120, 156, 176, 178, 194

*Faces, Places, and Inner Spaces: A Guide to Looking at Art*, 178, 195

*Failure Is Impossible: The History of American Women's Rights*, 83

*Fairie-Ality: The Fashion Collection*, 193

*Fairy Tales*, 193

Fama, Elizabeth, 13

*Fantasy! Cartooning*, 160

*Far North*, 91

*Farewell to Manzanar: A True Story of Japanese American Experience During and after the World War II Internment*, 75

Farrell, Jeanette, 78

*Father Water, Mother Woods: Essays on Fishing and Hunting in the North Woods*, 43

*Fear This Book: Your Guide to Fright, Horror, & Things That Go Bump in the Night*, 110

Fearnley, Fran, 139

*Feed*, 115

*Feed the Children First: Irish Memories of the Great Hunger*, 79

Feldman, Jane, 46, 58

Ferguson, Alane, 24

Ferguson, Amanda, 142

Ferris, Timothy, 103

*Fever, 1793*, 91

*Fields of Fury: The American Civil War*, 73

*Fight for Peace, The: A History of Antiwar Movements in America*, 89

*Fight On! Mary Church Terrell's Battle for Integration*, 53

*Fighting Reuben Wolfe*, 130

Finkel, Jon, 118–119

Firefly Animal Rescue, 95

*Fires!: Ten Stories That Chronicle Some of the Most Destructive Fires in Human History*, 5

Fisher, David Hackett, 70–71

*5,000 Miles to Freedom: Ellen and William Craft's Flight from Slavery*, 76, 91

*Flat-out Rock: Ten Great Bands of the '60s*, 183

*Flavor of the Week*, 173

Fleischman, John, 47, 65

Fleischman, Sid, 59

Fleming, Candace, 48, 53, 65

Flook, Helen, 170

*Flush*, 115

*Flying Solo: How to Soar Above Your Lonely Feelings, Make Friends, and Find the Happiest You*, 140, 146

*Food*, 107

*Football Now!*, 120

*Forbidden Schoolhouse, The: The True and Dramatic Story of Prudence Crandall and Her Students*, 76, 191

Forrester, Tina, 10

Fortin, François, 124

*Fortune's Bones: The Manumission Requiem*, 192

*Fossil Fish Found Alive: Discovering the Coelacanth*, 95

*Found: The Best Lost, Tossed, and Forgotten Items from Around the World*, 200

Fradin, Dennis Brindell, 53–54, 75–76, 91, 96

Fradin, Judith Bloom, 53–54, 76, 91

Franco, Betsy, 189, 195

Frank, Anne, 28

Frank, Otto, 28

*Frank O. Gehry: Outside In*, 179

*Free Fall*, 14

Freedman, Russell, 12, 45, 54, 56, 60, 65, 82, 87, 90–91, 119, 129

*Freedom Riders: John Lewis and Jim Zwerg on the Front lines of the Civil Rights Movement*, 52

*Freedom Walkers: The Story of the Montgomery Bus Boycott*, 87, 91

*Freedom Writers Diary, The: How a Teacher and 150 Teens Used Writing to Change Themselves and the World around Them*, 38

Freese, Barbara, 81–82

*Freeze-Frame: A Photographic History of the Winter Olympics*, 128

Fricke, Jim, 177

*Friday Night Lights: A Town, a Team, and a Dream*, 126

Friedman, Aimee, 146

Friedman, Lise, 159

*From Boneshakers to Choppers: The Rip-roaring History of Motorcycles*, 105

*From Head to Toe: Bound Feet, Bathing Suits, and Other Bizarre and Beautiful Things*, 156

Fulghum, Hunter S., 171

*Fun and Games: Things to Make and Do*, 152

*Future*, 104

*Future Is Wild, The*, 101–102

Gaines, Thom, 166

Galloway, Priscilla, 71, 88

Galvin, Jack, 8, 13

*Game Art for Teens*, 167

*Game Face: What Does a Female Athlete Look Like?*, 128–129

*Game Programming for Teens*, 167

*Gamers: Writers, Artists & Programmers on the Pleasures of Pixels*, 168

Gandini, Claire, 138

Gantos, Jack, 33, 43

Gaskins, Pearl Fuyo, 36, 140, 201–202

*Gatekeepers, The: Inside the Admissions Process of a Premier College*, 41, 141

Gay, Kathlyn, 108

Geary, Rick, 16–18, 23

Geissman, Grant, 197, 202

*Generation T: 108 ways to Transform a T-shirt*, 156–157

*Genius: A Photobiography of Albert Einstein*, 47

*Genocide*, 84
Geoffrey Mott-Smith, 169
*George Washington & the Founding of a Nation*, 47
*Gerald R. Ford*, 47
Geras, Adele, 196
Gerstung, Rebecca Sample, 155, 172
*Getting Away with Murder: The True Story of the Emmett Till Case*, 75, 90, 193
Giants of Science, 49
Giblin, James Cross, 57, 78, 88, 91
Giles, Gail, 173
*Girl with a Pearl Earring, The*, 196
Girl Zone, 133–134
Girlology, 135
*Girlology: A Girl's Guide to Stuff That Matters: Relationships, Bodytalk & Girl Power!*, 136
*Girlology: Hang–Ups, Hook–Ups, and Holding Out: Stuff You Need to Know About Your Body, Sex, and Dating*, 136, 146
*Girls Got Game: Sports Stories and Poems*, 126–127, 129
*Girls Think of Everything: Stories of Ingenious Inventions by Women*, 98
*Girls' Yoga Book, The: Stretch Your Body, Open Your Mind & Have Fun!*, 133
*Give Me Liberty: The Story of the Declaration of Independence*, 82
*Glamour Gurlz: The Ultimate Step-by-Step Guide to Great Makeup and Gurl Smarts*, 154
*Glamour's Big Book of Dos & Don'ts: Fashion Help for Every Woman*, 155, 172
Goering, Dag, 11
Goldberg, Jan, 142
Goldenberg, Linda, 99
Goldman-Rubin, Susan, 52
Goldsmith, Barbara, 50
Golus, Carrie, 60
*Good Brother, Bad Brother: The Story of Edwin Booth & John Wilkes Booth*, 88, 91
*Good Girl Work: Factories, Sweatshops, and How Women Changed Their Role in the American Workforce*, 80
Gore, Al, 111
*Gorilla Doctors: Saving Endangered Great Apes*, 94
Gosney, John, 166–167

*Got Tape?: Roll Out the Fun with Duct Tape!*, 151
Gottesman, Jane, 128–129
Gottfried, Ted, 89
Gottlieb, Lori, 27, 33
Gourley, Catherine, 71, 80
Gourse, Leslie, 183
*Graffiti L.A.: Street Styles and Art*, 177
Graham, Ian, 202
Grahame-Smith, Seth, 183
Grandits, John, 175, 189, 195
Grant, Richard, 170
Graphic Library, 12, 80, 118
*Graphic Storytelling*, 164
Gravelle, Jennifer, 136, 146
Gravelle, Karen, 136, 146, 170
Gray, Dianne E., 91
Graydon, Shari, 133, 153, 198, 202
Greatest Stars of the NBA, 118–119
Green, John, 115
*Green Berets: The U.S. Army Special Forces*, 142
Greenberg, Jan, 178–179, 190
Greenberg, Nicki, 113
Greene, Meg, 72
Greenlaw, Linda, 39
Grenier, Daniel, 112
*Grief Girl: My True Story*, 35
Grimes, Nikki.
Grody, Steve, 177
*Gross Universe: Your Guide to All Disgusting Things under the Sun*, 110
*Grossology: The Science of Really Gross Things*, 110
Groundwood Guides, 84, 112, 201
*Growing Up in a New Century, 1890 to 1914*, 73
*Growing Up in Coal Country*, 87
*Growing Up in Pioneer America, 1800 to 1890*, 73
*Growing Up in Slavery: Stories of Young Slaves as Told by Themselves*, 65
*Growing Up in World War II, 1941–1945*, 73
Gruwell, Erin, 38
*Guilty by a Hair!: Real-Life DNA Matches!*, 21
*Guinea Pig Scientists: Bold Self-experimenters in Science and Medicine*, 62–63, 65
Gunderson, Jessica, 12
*Gunstories: Life-Changing Experiences with Guns*, 199

*Gut-Eating Bugs: Maggots Reveal the Time of Death!*, 20
*Guts: The True Stories Behind Hatchet and the Brian Books*, 42
*Guy Book, The: An Owner's Manual for Teens: Safety, Maintenance, and Operating Instructions for Teens*, 137

Haab, Sherri, 157
*Hail to the Chiefs: Presidential Mischief, Morals, & Malarky from George W. to George W.*, 63
*Hair: Things to Make and Do*, 152
Hakim, Joy, 97
Halls, Kelly Milner, 101, 112–114, 193
Halpin, Mikki, 141, 200, 202
Hamilton, Bethany, 119
Hampton, Wilborn, 60, 69, 70, 72, 76, 79–80
*Hana's Suitcase*, 77
Haney, Eric L., 29, 39, 43
Hansen, Mark Victor, 138
Hanson, Nicholas P., 159
Harcourt, Nic, 181, 195
*Hard Love*, 173
Harding, R. R., 110
*Hardwear: Jewelry from a Toolbox*, 150, 172
Harper, Elizabeth, 165
Harper, Suzanne, 171
Harper, Timothy, 165
Harrington, Jane, 113–114
Hart, Christopher, 160–163
Haskins, James, 29
*Have You Seen This Face?: The Work of Forensic Artists*, 20
Hawass, Zahi, 100
Hawk, Tony, 119
Hawthorne, Grace, 149
Hayhurst, Chris, 123
*Head Bone's Connected to the Neck Bone, The: The Weird, Wacky, and Wonderful X–ray*, 109, 114
*Hear My Cry*, 66
*Heart in Politics: Jeannette Rankin and Patsy T. Mink, A*, 55
*Heart to Heart: New Poems Inspired by Twentieth–century American Art*, 190
Heimberg, Jason, 184
Heimberg, Justin, 184
*Helen Keller: Rebellious Spirit*, 54
Hemphill, Stephanie, 192, 195
Henderson, Bill, 113–114

*Here in Harlem: Poems in Many Voices*, 190
*Hero of the High Seas: John Paul Jones and the American Revolution*, 56
*Heroes of Baseball: The Men Who Made It America's Favorite Game*, 122
Hewitt, Kathryn, 64
Hiaasen, Carl, 115
*Hidden Evidence: Forty True Crimes and How Forensic Science Helped Solve Them*, 22, 24
*Hidden on the Mountain: Stories of Children Sheltered from the Nazis in Le Chambon*, 9
*Hidden Secrets: A Complete History of Espionage and the Technology Used to Support It*, 23
*High Exposure: An Enduring Passion for Everest and Unforgiving Places*, 7, 13
Hillenbrand, Laura, 8, 13
Hillman, Laura, 86
*Hinduism*, 202
*Hinduism and Other Eastern Religions*, 201
*Hip Handbag Book, The: 25 Easy-to-Make Totes, Purses and Bags*, 157
*Hippo Eats Dwarf: A Field Guide to Hoaxes and Other B.S.*, 16, 23
*Hitler Youth: Growing Up in Hitler's Shadow*, 86, 90
*Hitler's Canary*, 92
*Hi-Yah: How to Draw Fantastic Martial Arts Comics*, 161
Hobbs, Will, 13, 91
Hogan, Eve, 138
*Hole in My Life*, 33, 43
Holland, Barbara, 63
*Hollywood Urban Legends: The Truth Behind All Those Delightfully Persistent Myths of Film, Television and Music*, 184
Holmes, Melissa, 136, 146
Holt, David, 195
*Hoodwinked: Deception and Resistance*, 10
Hoose, Philip, 63, 83
Hoover, Dave, 80
*Hope Was Here*, 203
Horowitz, Anthony, 24
*Houdini: The Handcuff King*, 59
Houston, Jeanne Wakatsuki, 75
*How Angel Peterson Got His Name: And Other Outrageous Tales about Extreme Sports*, 43
*How Baseball Works*, 125

*How Basketball Works,* 125, 129

*How Hockey Works,* 126

*How I Fell in Love and Learned to Shoot Free Throws,* 130

*How Soccer Works,* 126

How Sports Work, 125–126

*How to Be a Teen Fashionista: Put Together the Hottest Outfits and Accessories—on Any Budget,* 155

*How to Draw Comic Heroes,* 163

*How to Draw Manga Warriors,* 163

*How to Draw Terrifying Robots,* 163

*How to Survive a Horror Movie: All the Skills to Dodge the Kills,* 183

*How to Survive a Robot Uprising: Tips on Defending Yourself Against the Coming Rebellion,* 105

*Hoyle's Rules of Games: Descriptions of Indoor Games of Skill and Chance, with Advice on Skillful Play: Based on the Foundations Laid Down by Edmond Hoyle, 1672–1769,* 169

Hoyt, Erich, 95, 113

Huebner, Mark, 128–129

Huneycutt, Brett, 199

*Hunger, The,* 92

*Hungry Ocean, The: A Swordboat Captain's Journey,*

*Hungry Planet: What the World Eats,* 108

*Hunt for Justice, A: The True Story of a Woman Undercover Wildlife Agent,* 19

*Hurricanes, Tsunamis, and Other Natural Disasters,* 109

Hutchinson, Patricia, 136, 146

*Hypochondriac's Pocket Guide to Horrible Diseases You Probably Already Have, The,* 108


*I, Dred Scott: A Fictional Slave Narrative Based on the Life and Legal Precedent of Dred Scott,* 66

*I Believe in . . . : Christian, Jewish, and Muslim Young People Speak About Their Faith,* 201–202

*I Know Why the Caged Bird Sings,* 31

*I Will Plant You a Lilac Tree: A Memoir of a Schindler's List Survivor,* 86

*I Wrote on All Four Walls: Teens Speak Out on Violence,* 139

Iaboni, John, 120

Ibatoulline, Bagram, 12

*Ice Maiden, The: Inca Mummies, Mountain Gods, and Sacred Sites in the Andes,* 101

*Illustrated Dictionary of Mythology: Heroes, Heroines, Gods, and Goddesses from Around the World,* 194

*Immersed in Verse: An Informative, Slightly Irreverent and Totally Tremendous Guide to Living the Poet's Life,* 188

*Impressionism,* 178

In American History, 80

*In Defense of Liberty: The Story of America's Bill of Rights,* 82

*In My Enemy's House,* 91

*In My Hands: Memories of a Holocaust Rescuer,* 77

*In Real Life: Six Women Photographers,* 65

*In the Company of Men: A Woman at the Citadel,* 29

*In the Line of Fire: Presidents' Lives at Stake,* 47, 89

*In Their Shoes: Extraordinary Women Describe Their Amazing Careers,* 142

*In Your Face: The Culture of Beauty and You,* 133, 153

*Inconvenient Truth, An,* 111

Incredible Deep-Sea Adventure, 96

*Incredible Hunt for the Giant Squid, The,* 96

*Indy Race Cars,* 120

Ingpen, Robert, 186

*In-Line skating!: Get Aggressive,* 124

*Inside Delta Force: The Story of America's Elite Counterterrorist Unit,* 29, 39, 43

*Inside Out: Portrait of an Eating Disorder,* 34

Inside Special Forces, 29

Inside Special Operations, 142

*Inside the Alamo,* 74

*Into the Land of Freedom: African Americans in Reconstruction,* 72

*Into the West: From Reconstruction to the Final Days of the American Frontier,* 73

*Inventing the Future: A Photobiography of Thomas Alva Edison,* 47

*Invisible Allies: Microbes That Shape Our Lives,* 78

*Invisible Enemies: Stories of Infectious Disease,* 78

*Iran Awakening: A Memoir of Revolution and Hope,* 37

Irwin, Cait, 33

*Isaac Newton,* 49

*Islam* (no author), 201
*Islam* (Thompson), 202
*It's Kind of a Funny Story*, 146
*It's Not About the Bike: My Journey Back to
    Life*, 32
*It's True! An Octopus Has Deadly Spit*, 113
It's True! Series, 22, 113
*It's Your World—If You Don't Like It,
    Change It: Activism for Teenagers*,
    141, 200, 202
*Ithaka*, 196
Iverson, Annemarie, 153, 172

*Jackie's Wild Seattle*, 13
Jackson, Donna M, 101
Jacobs, Thomas A., 18, 24
Jacobson, Sid, 76
*Jane Addams: Champion of Democracy*, 54
Janeczko, Paul B., 23, 185–187, 190
Jansen, Hanna, 66
*Japan 1945: A U.S. Marine's Photographs
    from Ground Zero*, 69, 77
*Japanese Comickers: Draw Anime and Manga
    Like Japan's Hottest Artists*, 161
*Jason's Gold*, 91
*Jazz*, 182
*Jazz Abz: An A to Z Collection of Jazz
    Portraits*, 182
*Jeannette Rankin: A Political Pioneer*, 55
*Jefferson's Children: The Story of One
    American Family*, 46, 58
Jennings, Peter, 72, 91
*John Adams*, 102
*John Lennon: All I Want Is the Truth: A
    Biography*, 61, 65
*Johnny Cash: A Twentieth-century Life*, 61
Johnson, Dolores, 51
Jones, David, 105
Jones, Gerald E., 168
Jones, Ryan 121
Jordan, Sandra, 178–179
Josephson, Judith Pinkerton, 73
Jovinelly, Joann, 149–150
Joyce, Jaime, 20
*Judaism*, 201, 202
Jukes, Mavis, 134, 137
*Jungle Islands: My South Sea Adventure*, 11
*Jurassic Park*, 115
Jurmain, Suzanne, 76, 191
Just the Facts Biographies, 60

Kalb, Chris, 180
Kaminker, Laura, 124
Karwoski, Gail, 5
Kendall, Martha E., 83
Kennedy, Brian, 153, 172
*Kennedy Assassinated!: The World Mourns:
    A Reporter's Story*, 80
*Kick in the Head, A: An Everyday Guide to
    Poetic Forms*, 186–187
*Kid Who Named Pluto, The: And the Stories
    of Other Extraordinary Young People
    in Science*, 96
Kidd, Jason 119
Kids Can Do It, 158
*Kids on Strike!*, 87
*Killer at Large: Criminal Profilers and the
    Cases They Solve!*, 20
*Killer Rocks from Outer Space: Asteroids,
    Comets, and Meteorites*, 109
*Killer Wallpaper: True Cases of Deadly
    Poisonings*, 21
Kimmel, Elizabeth Cody, 55, 62–63
King, Daniel, 168
*King James: Believe the Hype: The LeBron
    James Story*, 121
*King of the Mild Frontier: An Ill-Advised
    Autobiography*, 42
Kirberger, Kimberley, 138
Kirkpatrick, Katherine, 51
Kleh, Cindy, 124, 129
*Knitgrrl: Learn to Knit with 15 Fun and
    Funky Patterns*, 157, 172
Knudson, Jason, 163
Koja, Kathe, 196
Koon, Jeff, 198, 202
Koopersmith, Chase, 155
Koppes, Steven N., 109
Korman, Gordon, 196
Krensky, Stephen, 185
Krizmanic, Judy, 165
Krog, Hazlitt, 168
Krüger, Kobie., 40
Krull, Kathleen, 49, 62, 64
Kulikov. Boris, 49
Kurson, Robert, 12–13
Kyi, Tanya Lloyd, 5–6, 83

*Ladies First: 40 Daring American Women
    Who Were Second to None*, 55, 63
Lanchon, Anne, 139
*Land, The*, 66

Langley, Andrew, 109
*Language of Baklava, The: A Memoir*, 36
Lanier, Shannon, 46, 58
LaReau, Jenna, 23
Larson, Erik, 17–18
Laskin, David, 80
Lauber, Patricia, 99
Lawlor, Laurie, 54
*LeBron James: The Rise of a Star*, 121
Lee, Bruce, 61
Lee, Elizabeth, 153, 172
Lee, John, 160
*Left for Dead: A Young Man's Search for Justice for the USS* Indianapolis, 90–91
Leigh, Ed, 126, 129
Leive, Cindi, 155, 172
Lemke, Donald B., 80
Lenhard, Elizabeth, 173
Lenney, Dinah, 159
Leonetti, Mike, 120
*Let Me Play: The Story of Title IX: The Law That Changed the Future of Girls in America*, 127, 129
Levine, Ellen, 10, 49
Levine, Karen, 77
*Lewis and Clark Expedition, The*, 12
*Library of Alexandria, The*, 70, 85
Lieurance, Suzanne, 80
*Life and Death of Adolf Hitler, The*, 57
*Lighten Up: Stay Sane, Eat Great, Lose Weight*, 135
*Lincoln: A Photobiography*, 45
Lindén Ivarsson, Anna-Stina, 157
Lindop, Laurie, 96
*Lipstick Jihad: A Memoir of Growing up Iranian in America and American in Iran*, 37
Lipsyte, Robert, 122
*Listen to Us!: The World's Working Children*, 87
Little, John R., 61
*Little Black Book for Girlz, The: A Book on Healthy Sexuality*, 137
*Little Girls in Pretty Boxes: The Making and Breaking of Elite Gymnasts and Figure Skaters*, 34
*Little People and a Lost World: An Anthropological Mystery*, 99
*Lives of Extraordinary Women: Rulers, Rebels (and What the Neighbors Thought)*, 64
*Locomotion*, 196

*Long Gone Lonesome History of Country Music*, 181
*Look Closer: Art Masterpieces Through the Ages*, 176
*Louis Riel: A Comic-Strip Biography*, 56
Love, Ann, 84
*Lucky*, 34
Lundin, Maria, 157
Lupica, Mike, 129
Lutes, Jason, 59
Lynch, Chris, 129
Lyons, Mary E, 79

Macaulay, David, 103
MacDonald, John, 5
Mace, Nancy, 29
MacEachern, Stephen, 6
Macloud, Scott, 164
Macy, Sue, 126–127
*MAD About the '90s: The Best of the Decade*, 197, 202
*Made You Look: How Advertising Works and Why You Should Know*, 198, 202
*MADvertising: A MAD Look at 50 Years of MADison Avenue*, 198
*Magnificent Women in Music*, 183
Mah, Adeline Yen, 33, 43
*Make Things Happen: The Key to Networking for Teens*, 143
*Makeup: Things to Make and Do*, 152
*Making Comics: Storytelling Secrets of Comics, Manga and Graphic Novels*, 164
*Making of a Graphic Novel, The: The Resonator*, 164
Manga Mania, 162–163
*Manga Mania: How to Draw Japanese Comics*, 162
*Manga Mania Chibi and Furry Characters: How to Draw the Adorable Mini-People and Cool Cat-Girls of Japanese Comics*, 162
*Manga Mania Fantasy Worlds: How to Draw the Amazing Worlds of Japanese Comics*, 162
*Manga Mania Magical Girls and Friends: How to Draw the Super-Popular Action-Fantasy Characters of Manga*, 162
*Manga Mania Shoujo: How to Draw the Charming and Romantic Characters of Japanese Comics*, 162

*Manga Mania Villains: How to Draw the Dastardly Characters of Japanese Comics,* 163
*Manhwa Mania: How to Draw Korean Comics,* 163
*Marco Polo's Journey to China,* 12
Marcus, Leonard S., 186
*Margaret Bourke-White: Her Pictures Were Her Life,* 52
*Maritcha: A Nineteenth-century American Girl,* 56
Markle, Sandra, 6
Marrin, Albert, 47, 50, 82
Marsalis, Wynton, 182
Marshall, Robina MacIntyre, 85
*Martha Graham: A Dancer's Life,* 60
Masoff, Joy, 124
Massotty, Susan, 28
Matas, Carol, 91
Matsen, Bradford, 96
Maurer, Richard, 86
*Maus I: A Survivor's Tale: My Father Bleeds History,* 78
*Maus II: A Survivor's Tale: And Here My Troubles Began,* 78
Mazel, Sharon, 142
McAulay, Liz, 156
McCann, Lauren, 154
McClafferty, Carla Killough, 50, 109, 114
McCutcheon, Marc, 96
McGrath, Jeremy, 120
McKernan, Victoria, 13
McNaughton, Janet, 115
McPherson, James M., 73
McWhorter, Diane, 73, 91
*Mecha Mania: How to Draw the Battling Robots, Cool Spaceships, and Military Vehicles of Japanese Comics,* 163
*Mega-beasts,* 102
Mehlman, Barbara, 142
Melo, Esperança, 158
*Meltdown: A Race Against Nuclear Disaster at Three Mile Island: A Reporter's Story,* 79
Meltzer, Milton, 64
*Men of Salt: Crossing the Sahara on the Caravan of White Gold,* 11
Menzel, Peter, 108
Mezinski, Pierre, 140
*Mighty Robots: Mechanical Marvels That Fascinate and Frighten,* 105

Mikaelson, Ben, 13
Milano, Selene, 154, 172
Miles, Victoria, 94
Miller, Jean-Chris, 108
Miller, Ron, 109, 184
Miller, Sarah, 66
Miller, Steve, 161
Miller, Timothy, 120
Milton, Steve, 120
*Miss Crandall's School for Young Ladies and Little Misses of Color: Poems,* 191
*Miss Spitfire,* 66
*Mississippi Trial,* 1955, 193
*M.L.K.: Journey of a King,* 53
Moaveni, Azadeh, 37
Montgomery, Sy, 94–95, 114
Mordan, C. B., 63
Morehead, Albert H., 169
Morehead, Philip D., 169
Morgan, David Lee, 121
Morgan, Jody, 95
Moses, Sheila P., 66
*Mountain Biking: Get on the Trail,* 123
Mourning, Tuesday, 188
*Muckrakers: How Ida Tarbell, Upton Sinclair, and Lincoln Steffens Helped Expose Scandal Inspire Reform, and Invent Investigative Journalism,* 58
*Muhammad Ali: American Champion,* 118
*Mummies: The Newest, Coolest & Creepiest from Around the World,* 100
*Mummies, Bones & Body Parts,* 100
*Murder of Abraham Lincoln: A Chronicle of 62 Days in the Life of the American Republic, March 4–May 4, 1865, The,* 17
Murdock, Catherine Gilbert, 130
Murkoff, Heidi Eisenberg, 142
Murphy, Jim, 57, 65, 69, 74, 81, 84
Murray, Stuart, 70
*Museum of Hoaxes, The: A Collection of Pranks, Stunts, Deceptions, and Other Wonderful Stories Contrived for the Public from the Middle Ages to the New Millennium,* 16
Musgrave, Susan, 34
*Music Lust: Recommended Listening for Every Mood, Moment, and Reason,* 181, 195
*My Fundamentalist Education: A Memoir of a Divine Girlhood,* 30

My Kind of Sad: What It's Like to Be Young and Depressed, 141

My Life in France, 38

My Losing Season, 28

My Parents Are Getting Divorced: How to Keep It Together When Your Mom and Dad Are Splitting Up, 138

My Sahara Adventure: 52 Days by Camel, 12

My Season with Penguins: An Antarctic Journal, 4, 41

My So-Called Digital Life: 2,000 Teenagers, 300 Cameras, and 30 Days to Document Their World, 176–177

Myers, Christopher, 182

Myers, Walter Dean, 29, 43, 190

Mystery of Mary Rogers, The, 16

Mythbusters: The Explosive Truth Behind the Thirty Most Perplexing Urban Legends of All Time, 195

Mythology, 194

Mythology of the World, 194


Naidoo, Beverly, 92

NASCAR, 120

NASCAR Now!, 120

Naughton, Terry, 47, 65

Navy Seals: Special Operations for the U.S. Navy, 142

Naylor, Caroline, 154

Neimark, Anne E., 61

Nelson, Marilyn, 191–192

Nelson, Peter, 90–91

Nerves Out Loud: Critical Moments in the Lives of Seven Teen Girls, 34

Netelkos, Jason, 150

Nevraumont, Edward J., 159

New Found Land: Lewis and Clark's Voyage of Discovery, 190

New Way Things Work, The, 103

Newbigging, Martha, 22, 71, 168

Next, 115

Ngui, Marc, 167

Nibbling on Einstein's Brain: The Good, the Bad and the Bogus in Science, 104

Nichols, Lisa, 138

Nickel and Dimed: On (Not) Getting by in America, 199

Nicolay, Megan, 157

Niedzviecki, Hal, 167

9/11 Report, The: A Graphic Adaptation, 76

19 Varieties of Gazelle: Poems of the Middle East, 191

99 Ways to Cut, Sew & Deck Out Your Denim, 156

No End in Sight: My Life as a Blind Iditarod Racer, 9

No More Dead Dogs, 196

Nobody Particular: One Woman's Fight to Save the Bays, 111

Nobody's Child, 92

Norris, Christine, 146

Northcutt, Wendy, 145

Nouvian, Claire.

Noyes, Deborah, 112, 114

Nunnally, Tiina, 193

Nye, Naomi Shihab, 191


Obsessive Genius: The Inner World of Marie Curie, 50

Odd Jobs: Portraits of Unusual Occupations, 143

Odder Jobs: More Portraits of Unusual Occupations, 143

O'Donnell, Jim, 69

O'Donnell, Joe, 77

Off Season, 130

Official Movie Plot Generator, The: 27,000 Hilarious Movie Plot Combinations, 184

Oh Rats! The Story of Rats and People, 82

Okey, Shannon, 157, 172

One Kingdom: Our Lives with Animals: The Human–Animal Bond in Myth, History, Science, and Story, 112, 114

Only the Strong Survive: The Odyssey of Allen Iverson, 121

Onward: A Photobiography of African-American Polar Explorer Matthew Henson, 51

Opdyke, Irene Gut, 77

Oppenheim, Joanne, 88

Oprah Winfrey: Media Queen, 59

Optical Illusions: The Science of Visual Perception, 184

Orgill, Roxane, 182

Orndorff, John Christian, 171

Our America, 73

Our Country's First Ladies, 62

Our Country's Presidents, 62

Our Eleanor: A Scrapbook Look at Eleanor Roosevelt's Remarkable Life, 53, 65

Our Stories, Our Songs: African Children Talk about AIDS, 199

*Out of Bounds: Seven Stories of Conflict and Hope,* 92
*Out of the Shadows: An Artist's Journey,* 30
*Outbreak: Plagues That Changed History,* 78
Outwitting the Enemy: Stories from the Second World War, 10
*Over a Thousand Hills I Walk with You,* 66
*Overboard,* 13
Owen, David, 22–24

*Paint Me Like I Am: Teen Poems,* 191
Palen, Debbie, 136
Palin, Nicki, 194
Palmer, Chris, 120
Paniccioli, Ernie, 177
Pardes, Bronwen, 137
Pardew, Les, 167
Parks, Rosa, 29
Partridge, Elizabeth, 51, 61, 65
*Paul Revere's Ride,* 71
Paulsen, Gary, 28, 42–44
Payment, Simone, 142
*Peak,* 13
Pearson, Debora, 11–12
*Pedro and Me: Friendship, Loss, and What I Learned,* 55, 66
People's History, 72, 89, 185
Pepin, Jacques, 40
Perel, David, 198
Perez, Ramon, 110
*Perilous Journey of the Donner Party, The,* 4
*Period Book, The: Everything You Don't Want to Ask (But Need to Know),* 136, 146
Perrier, Pascale, 140, 146
*Persepolis: The Story of a Childhood,* 37, 43
*Persepolis 2: The Story of a Return,* 38
Pfetzer, Mark, 8, 13
Philbrick, Nathaniel, 6
Philip, Neil, 194
*Phineas Gage: A Gruesome But True Story about Brain Science,* 45, 48, 65
*Photography,* 107
Piehl, Janet, 120
Piquemal, Michel, 141
Pitluk, Adam, 121
Piven, Joshua, 171–172
Pivotal Moments in American History, 71
Pivotal Moments in History, 12, 47
*Plain Janes,* 196
Platkin, Charles Stuart, 135
Platt, Larry, 121

Platt, Richard, 22
*Play Like a Girl: A Celebration of Women in Sports,* 128
*Playing in Traffic,* 173
Pletka, Bob, 177
*Poem of Her Own, A: Voices of American Women Yesterday and Today,* 188
*Poet Slave of Cuba, The: A Biography of Juan Francisco Manzano,* 192
*Point Blank,* 24
*Poke in the I, A: A Collection of Concrete Poems,* 190
*Poles Apart: Why Penguins and Polar Bears Will Never Be Neighbors,* 41, 114
Pollack, Pamela, 124
Poole, Josephine, 86
Poolos, J., 142
Pope, Kevin, 195
Popular Mechanics for Kids, 125
*PostSecret: Extraordinary Confessions from Ordinary Lives,* 200, 202
Powell, Andy, 198, 202
*Power of One, The: Daisy Bates and the Little Rock Nine,* 54
Premier Press Game Development Series, 167
Pressler, Mirjam, 28
*Prey,* 115
Prime, Ranchor, 202
Prokos, Anna, 21
*Promises to Keep: How Jackie Robinson Changed America,* 122, 129
Prud'homme, Paul, 38
*Pyongyang: A Journey in North Korea,* 39

Qualls, Sean, 192
*Quest for the Tree Kangaroo: An Expedition to the Cloud Forest of New Guinea,* 94, 114
*Quick Knits,* 158

Raab, Evelyn, 166, 172
*Race to Save the Lord God Bird, The,* 83
*Rachel Carson: Environmentalist,* 49
*Radioactive Boy Scout, The: The Frightening True Story of a Whiz Kid and His Homemade Nuclear Reactor,* 66, 96–97, 115
Rafter, Marianne, 150
Rall, Ted, 40
Rannels, Melissa, 158
Raschka, Chris, 187, 190

Raskin, Laurie, 12
*Rats Saw God*, 44
*Rats!: The Good, the Bad, and the Ugly*, 81
*Rats: Observations on the History and Habitat of the City's Most Unwanted Inhabitants*, 82
*ReadyMade: How to Make [Almost] Everything: A Do-It-Yourself Primer*, 148–149
*Real Benedict Arnold, The*, 57, 65, 69
Reber, Deborah, 138, 142
*Red Hot Salsa: Bilingual Poems on Being Young and Latino in the United States*, 188
*Red Land, Yellow River: A Story from the Cultural Revolution*, 57
*Red Midnight*, 13
*Red Sea*, 14
Reddy, Mike, 145
Reich, Susanna, 62
Reinhard, Johan, 101
*Remembering Manzanar: Life in a Japanese Relocation Camp*, 75
*Rescues!*, 6
*Rescues!: Ten Dramatic Stories of Life–saving Heroics*, 6
*Restless Spirit: The Life and Work of Dorothea Lange*, 51
*Revenge of the Whale: The True Story of the Whaleship* Essex, 6
Riddell, Chris, 185
*Right Bite, The: Dentists as Detectives*, 21
Rinard, Judith E., 105, 114
Riner, Dax, 122
Ripslinger, Jon, 130
Roach, Mary, 103
*Road to There, The: Mapmakers and Their Stories*, 84
*Robert E. Lee: Virginian Soldier, American Citizen*, 57
*Robert F. Kennedy: Crusader*, 52
*Robert F. Kennedy and His Times*, 52
Roberts, Jeremy, 124
Robertson, James I., 57
Robinson, Sharon, 122, 129
*Robot*, 105
Rochelle, Belinda, 177
*Rock & Ice Climbing: Top the Tower*, 124
Roeper, Richard, 184
Rogers, Paul, 182
Rogge, Hannah, 150, 172

*Roll of Thunder*, 66
Rollins, Prentis, 164
*Rosa Parks: My Story*, 29
Rosen, Christine, 30
Rosen, Michael, 186
Ross, Val, 84
Rothbart, Davy, 200
Rowland-Warne, L., 156
Ruby, Aaron, 168
Ruelle, Karen Gray, 9
*Run*, 66
*Runaway Girl: The Artist Louise Bourgeois*, 179
Runyon, Brent, 34
Ryan, Joan, 34

Sabuda, Robert, 102
Sadler, Judy Ann, 158
Salzman, Mark, 41
Sarvady, Andrea, 185
*SAS: British Special Air Service*, 142
Satrapi, Marjane, 37–38, 43
Sautter, Aaron, 163
*Saving Manatees*, 112, 114
Sawa, Maureen, 169
*Scams!: Ten Stories That Explore Some of the Most Outrageous Swindlers and Tricksters of All Time*, 18
Scandiffio, Laura, 6
*Scared!: How to Draw Fantastic Horror Comic Characters*, 161
Scdoris, Rachael, 9
Schaap, Phil, 182
Scheppler, Bill, 142
Schiedermayer, Ellie, 151
Schiff, Nancy Rica, 143
Schlesinger, Arthur Jr., 52
Schlip, Joanna,154
Schlosser, Eric, 108
*Schoolchildren's Blizzard, The*, 80
Schroeder, Andreas, 18–19, 24
Schroeder, Lucinda Delaney, 19
Schulke, Flip, 52
Schultz, Ellen, 156
<u>Scientists in the Field</u>, 94–95, 111
Scott, Elaine, 41, 114
Scowen, Kate, 141
*'Scuse Me While I Kiss This Guy, and Other Misheard Music Lyrics*, 180
*Seabiscuit: An American Legend*, 8, 13
Sebold, Alice, 34

Seckel, Al, 184

*Second-time Cool: The Art of Chopping Up a Sweater,* 156–157

*Secret Under My Skin, The,* 115

*Secrets of a Civil War Submarine: Solving the Mysteries of the* H.L. *Hunley,* 85, 91

*Secrets, Lies, Gizmos, and Spies: A History of Spies and Espionage,* 23

Sedaris, David, 43

*Seeing in the Dark: How Backyard Stargazers Are Probing Deep Space and Guarding Earth from Interplanetary Peril,* 103

*Seeing the Blue Between: Advice and Inspiration for Young Poets,* 185

*September 11, 2001: Attack on New York City,* 76

Sethi, Maneesh, 167

*Sew Subversive: Down and Dirty DIY for the Fabulous Fashionista,* 158

*Sew Teen: Make Your Own Cool Clothes,* 158

*Shackleton's Stowaway,* 13

*Shadow Divers: The True Adventure of Two Americans Who Risked Everything to Solve One of the Last Mysteries of World War II,* 3, 12–13

*Shakespeare: His Work and His World,* 186

*Shakespeare's Scribe,* 186

*Shakespeare's Spy,* 186

*Shakespeare's Stealer,* 186

Shakur, Afeni, 60

Shaner, Pete, 168

Shapiro, Stephen, 10

*Shaquille O'Neal,* 119

*Shark Girl,* 196

*Shark Life: True Stories About Sharks & the Sea,* 112

Shaw, Tucker, 144–145, 173

Shayne, David, 198

Shecter, Vicky Alvear, 47, 65

*Shenzhen: A Travelogue from China,* 39

*Shipwreck at the Bottom of the World: The Extraordinary True Story of Shackleton and the* Endurance, 4, 13

*Shipwrecked!: The True Adventures of a Japanese Boy,* 11

Shivack, Nadia, 34

*Short History of Nearly Everything, A,* 93, 97

*Shot and Framed: Photographers at the Crime Scene,* 21

*Shout, Sister, Shout: Ten Girl Singers Who Shaped a Century,* 182

Shulman, Mark, 168

Siddiqui, Haroon, 201

Sidwells, Chris, 170

Siegel, Siena, 30, 59

*Sikhism,* 201

*Silent in an Evil Time: The Brave War of Edith Cavell,* 78

Sills, Leslie, 65

Silverstein, Ken, 97, 115

*Simply Sewing,* 158

*Sir Walter Ralegh and the Quest for El Dorado,* 10

Sis, Peter, 50, 179

*Six Days in October: The Stock Market Crash of 1929,* 70, 81

*Skateboarding! Surf the Pavement,* 123

*Skeleton Key,* 24

*Ski! Your Guide to Jumping, Racing, Skiboarding, Nordic, Backcountry, Aerobatics, and More,* 124

*Skin,* 146

Sklar, Robert, 185

Skrypuch, Martha Forchuk, 92

*Skydiving! Take the Leap,* 123

Slavin, Bill, 104

Sloan, Christopher, 100

*Slot Machine,* 129

*Slumber Parties: Things to Make and Do,* 152

*Smartbomb: The Quest for Art, Entertainment, and Big Bucks in the Videogame Revolution,* 168

Smedman, Lisa, 105

Smith, Roland, 13

*Snow Baby, The: The Arctic Childhood of Admiral Robert E. Peary's Daring Daughter,* 51

*Snowboard!: Your Guide to Freeriding, Pipe & Park, Jibbing, Backcountry, Alpine, Boardercross, and More,* 124

*Snowboarding!: Shred the Powder,* 123

*Snowboarding Skills: The Back-to-Basics Essentials for All Levels,* 124, 129

*Soccer: 365 Days,* 128

*Something Out of Nothing: Marie Curie and Radium,* 50

*Sophisticated Ladies: The Great Women of Jazz,* 183

*SOS: Stories of Survival: True Tales of Disaster, Tragedy, and Courage,* 5

*Soul Surfer: A True Story of Faith, Family, and Fighting to Get Back on the Board,* 119

Sousa, Jean, 178, 195

Spadaccini, Stephanie, 169

Spears, Rick, 101, 193
*Special Effects: An Introduction to Movie Magic*, 184
Spiegelman, Art, 78
*Spook: Science Tackles the Afterlife*, 103
*Sports Bloopers*, 128–129
*Sports: The Complete Visual Reference*, 124
Sports Heroes and Legends, 118, 122
Springer, Jane, 84, 87
St. George, Judith, 47, 89
St. Stephen's Community House, 137
*Standing Eight: The Inspiring Story of Jesus "El Matador" Chavez, Who Became Lightweight Champion of the World*, 121
*Stars and Galaxies*, 109
*Staying Fat for Sarah Byrnes*, 129
*Steamboats: The Story of Lakers, Ferries, and Majestic Paddle-Wheelers*, 107
Steber, Rick, 9
Steinberg, Jacques, 41, 141
Stern, Sam, 165–166
*Stick Figure: A Diary of My Former Self*, 33
*Stiff: The Curious Lives of Human Cadavers*, 103
Stone, Miriam, 35
*Stormbreaker*, 24
*Story of My Life, The: An Afghan Girl on The Other Side of the Sky*, 36
*Story of Science, The: Aristotle Leads the Way*, 97
*Stotan!*, 129
Stowers, Carlton, 127
Stratton, Allan, 203
*Street Scene: How to Draw Graffiti–Style*, 160
Sullivan, George, 180
Sullivan, Robert, 82
*Summer Ball*, 129
Sunscreen, 133, 138–141
Sutton, Richard, 106
Swanson, Diane, 6, 104
Sweeney, Joyce, 14
Sweet, Melissa, 98
*Sweet!: The Delicious Story of Candy*, 84
*Swifter, Higher, Stronger: A Photographic History of the Summer Olympics*, 127, 129
*Swimming to Antarctica: Tales of a Long-distance Swimmer*, 118, 129
Swinburne, Stephen, 94, 112, 114
Symes, R. F., 110
Szpirglas, Jeff, 104, 110, 115

*Take-Off: American All-Girl Bands during WWII*, 182
*Tales of the Cryptids: Mysterious Creatures That May or May Not Exist*, 175, 193
Tambini, Michael, 104
Tanaka, Shelley, 7, 13, 74, 100, 110, 112, 183
*Tarantula Scientist, The*, 95
*Tasting the Sky: A Palestinian Childhood*, 37, 43
*Tattoo Nation: Portraits of Celebrity Body Art*, 108
Taylor, Mildred D., 66
Taylor, Yuval, 65
*Team Moon: How 400,000 People Landed Apollo 11 on the Moon*, 45, 58, 66
*Technically, It's Not My Fault: Concrete Poems*, 189, 195
Teen Love, 138
*Teen People Celebrity Beauty Guide: Star Secrets for Gorgeous Hair, Makeup, Skin and More!*, 154
Teen People Magazine (author), 156
*Teenage Guy's Survival Guide, The*, 135, 146
*Teens Cook Dessert*, 165
*Teens Cook: How to Cook What You Want to Eat*, 165
*Teens Take It to Court: Young People Who Challenged the Law—and Changed Your Life*, 18
*Teen's Vegetarian Cookbook, The*, 165
*Ten Kings: And the Worlds They Ruled*, 64
*Ten Queens: Portraits of Women in Power*, 64
*Ten Sure Signs a Movie Character Is Doomed and Other Surprising Movie Lists*, 184
10,000 Days of Thunder: A History of the Vietnam War, 70
*Terrorists, Tornadoes, and Tsunamis: How to Prepare for Life's Danger Zones*, 170–171
*They Broke the Law—You Be The Judge: True Cases of Teen Crime*, 18, 24
*They Did What?!: Your Guide to Weird & Wacky Things People Do*, 104, 115
*They Poured Fire on Us from the Sky: The True Story of Three Lost Boys from Sudan*, 32
*Thieves!*, 19, 24
Thimmesh, Catherine, 45, 58, 66, 98
*Things I Have to Tell You: Poems and Writing by Teenage Girls*, 189, 195

*33 Things Every Girl Should Know: Stories,
    Songs, Poems, and Smart Talk by 33
    Extraordinary Women,* 89
*33 Things Every Girl Should Know About
    Women's History: From Suffragettes to
    Skirt Lengths to the ERA,* 89–90
*This Book Is Being Bugged,* 22
*This Is All: The Pillow Book of Cordelia Kenn,*
    44
*This Land Was Made for You and Me: The
    Life & Songs of Woody Guthrie,* 61
*Thomas Jefferson: Draftsman of a Nation,* 46
Thomas, Keltie, 125–126
Thomas, Rob, 44
Thompson, Jan, 202
Thompson, Mel, 202
*Thunderstruck,* 18
*Thwonk,* 203
*To Afghanistan and Back: A Graphic
    Travelogue,* 40
*To Dance: A Ballerina's Graphic Novel,* 30
*To the Top: The Story of Everest,* 9
Todd, Mark, 164
*Together Apart,* 91
Toksvig, Sandi, 92
Tomlinson, Joe, 126, 129
*Tomorrow the River,* 91
*Too Young to Fight: Memories from Our
    Youth During World War II,* 88
*Tools of the Ancient Romans: A Kid's Guide
    to the History & Science of Life in
    Ancient Rome,* 150
*Top Secret: A Handbook of Codes, Ciphers,
    and Secret Writing,* 23
Tossan, Olivier, 141
*Tough Boy Sonatas,* 189
*Tracking Trash: Flotsam, Jetsam, and the
    Science of Ocean Motion,* 111
Traig, Jennifer, 35, 151
*Transformed: How Everyday Things Are
    Made,* 104
*Travel Team,* 129
Treasury of Victorian Murder, A, 16–18
*Treasury of Victorian Murder, A,* Volume 1,
    16
*Tree of Life: A Book Depicting the Life of
    Charles Darwin, Naturalist, Geologist
    & Thinker, The,* 50
*Triangle Shirtwaist Fire and Sweatshop
    Reform in American History, The,* 80
*Troy: A Novel,* 196

*True Notebooks: A Writer's Year at Juvenile
    Hall,* 41
True Stories from the Edge, 4–6, 16, 18–19
Trumble, Kelly, 85
*Tsunami: The True Story of an April Fools'
    Day Disaster,* 5
Tullson, Diane, 14
*Tunnels!,* 6
*Tupac: Resurrection, 1971–1996,* 60
*Tupac Shakur,* 45, 60
Turnbull, Andy, 12
Turner, Pamela, 94
24/7: Science Behind the Scenes: Forensic
    Files, 19–21

*Ultimate Bicycle Book,* 170
*Ultimate Classic Car Book, The,* 106
*Ultimate Girls' Movie Survival Guide, The:
    What to Rent, Who to Watch, How to
    Deal,* 185
*Ultimate Harley-Davidson,* 106
*Ultimate Improv Book, The: A Complete
    Guide to Comedy Improvisation,* 59
*Ultra Hush-Hush: Espionage and Special
    Missions,* 10
*Um, Like . . . OM: A Girl Goddess's Guide to
    Yoga,* 134
*Unbelievable: The Life, Death, and Afterlife of
    the Notorious B.I.G.,* 60
*Understanding Comics: The Invisible Art,*
    164
*Unforgettable Color: Makeup with
    Confidence,* 154, 172
Up Close, 49, 52, 59–61

Van der Vat, Dan, 74
Venables, Stephen, 9
*Venturing the Deep Sea,* 96
Verplancke, Klaas, 140, 146
*Vietnam War,* 70
*Vincent Van Gogh: Portrait of an Artist,* 179
Vincent, Erin, 35
Vitkus, Jessica, 153, 172
Vizzini, Ned, 146
*Voice That Challenged a Nation, The: Marian
    Anderson and the Struggle for Equal
    Rights,* 54, 65
Vrettos, Adrienne Marie, 146

*Wakeboarding!: Throw a Tantrum,* 123
Waldman, Neil, 30

Walker, Rebecca, 31

Walker, Sally M., 85, 91, 95

*Wall, The: Growing up Behind the Iron Curtain*, 179

Walters, Eric, 66, 92

*Wand in the Word, The: Conversations with Writers of Fantasy*, 186

*War, Women, and the News: How Female Journalists Won the Battle to Cover World War II*, 71

*War in the Middle East: A Reporter's Story: Black September and the Yom Kippur War*, 70, 72

*War of the Eagles*, 92

*War Within, The: A Novel of the Civil War*, 91

Warren, Frank, 200, 202

*Washington's Crossing*, 70–71

*Watercolor*, 176

*Watersheds: A Practical Handbook for Healthy Water*, 107

Watson, Esther Pearl, 164

Wawiorka, Matthew, 165

*Wayne Gretzky*, 118

*We Were There Too!: Young People in U.S. History*, 63

*Wearing of This Garment Will Not Enable You to Fly: 101 Real Dumb Warning Labels*, 198, 202

Weaver, Janice, 156

Webb, Sophie, 4, 41

Webber, Diane, 21

*Weighing In: How to Understand Your Body, Lose Weight, and Live a Healthier Lifestyle*, 133

*Weird Weather: Everything You Didn't Want to Know About Climate Change But Probably Should Find Out*, 112

Welton, Jude, 178

*Whale Rescue: Changing the Future for Endangered Wildlife*, 95

*Whale Talk*, 129

Whamond, Dave, 104, 115

*What Are My Rights?: 95 Questions and Answers about Teens and the Law*, 18

*What Are You?: Voices of Mixed-race Young People*, 36, 140

*What to Expect Baby-sitter's Handbook, The*, 142

*Whatcha Mean, What's a Zine?: The Art of Making Zines and Mini–comics*, 164

*"What's That Smell?" (Oh, It's Me): 50 Mortifying Situations and How to Deal*, 144–145

*When I Was a Soldier: A Memoir*, 31, 43

*When Life Stinks: How to Deal with Your Bad Moods, Blues, and Depression*, 141

*When Plague Strikes: The Black Death, Smallpox, AIDS*, 78

*Where Dreams Die Hard: A Small American Town and Its Six–Man Football Team*, 127

*Where the Action Was: Women War Correspondents in World War II*, 72

Whittington, Christine, 108

*Who Came First: New Clues to Prehistoric Americans*, 99

*Who Do You Think You Are?: 12 Methods for Analyzing the True You*, 145

*Who Shot Ya?: Three Decades of Hip Hop Photography*, 177

*Who Was First?: Discovering the Americas*, 90

*Wicked History of the World, The: History with the Nasty Bits Left In*, 69, 90

*Wide Open: A Life in Supercross*, 120

Wilcox, Charlotte, 100

*Wild Man Island*, 13

*Wild Science: Amazing Encounters Between Animals and the People Who Study Them*, 94

*Wilderness Family, The: At Home with Africa's Wildlife*, 40

*Wildly Romantic: The English Romantic Poets: The Mad, the Bad, and the Dangerous*, 187

Wilkinson, Philip, 194

Willson, Quentin, 106

Wilson, Charles, 108

Wilson, Daniel H., 105

Wilson, Hugo, 106

Wilson, Joe, 151

Winchester, Elizabeth Siris. 21

Winget, Mary, 47

Winick, Judd, 55, 66

*With a Little Luck: Surprising Stories of Amazing Discoveries*, 96

*Within Reach: My Everest Story*, 3, 8, 13

*Witness to Our Times: My Life as a Photojournalist*, 52

Wittlinger, Ellen, 173

Woelfle, Gretchen, 55

Wojtyla, Karen, 112
Wolf, Allan, 188, 190
*Woods Scientist, The,* 94
Woodson, Jacqueline, 196
Woodstra, Chris, 181
*Words with Wings: A Treasury of
    African-American Poetry and Art,* 177
Worick, Jennifer, 172
World Faiths, 200–201
*World History of Film, A,* 185
*World of Penguins, The,* 41, 112
World Religions, 201–202
Worlds Beyond, 109
*Worst-Case Scenario Survival Handbook, The,*
    171
*Worst-Case Scenario Survival Handbook, The:
    College,* 170, 172
*Worst-Case Scenario Survival Handbook, The:
    LIFE,* 172
*Worst-Case Scenario Survival Handbook, The:
    Travel,* 171
Worthington, Charles, 154, 172
*Wreath for Emmett Till, A,* 193
*Wright Sister, The: Katharine Wright and
    Her Famous Brothers,* 86
Wright, Geneviève, 112
WritersCorps, 191
*Written in Bones: How Human Remains
    Unlock the Secrets of the Dead,* 98
Wullschlager, Jackie, 193

*Year of the Hangman, The,* 91
*Yes Yes Y'all: The Experience Music Project
    Oral History of Hip-hop's First
    Decade,* 177
*YM's the Best of Say Anything,* 145
*You Hear Me?: Poems and Writing by
    Teenage Boys,* 189
*You Remind Me of You: A Poetry Memoir,*
    32
Young, Roxyanne, 193
*Young Dancer's Apprenticeship, A: On Tour
    with the Moscow City Ballet,* 28
*Young Person's Occupational Outlook
    Handbook,* 18, 141, 143
*Your Name in Print: A Teen's Guide to
    Publishing for Fun, Profit, and
    Academic Success,* 165
*Your Own, Sylvia: A Verse Portrait of Sylvia
    Plath,* 192, 195

Zenatti, Valerie, 31, 45
Zent, Sheila, 158
Zhang, Ange, 57
Zielin, Lara, 143
Zimmerman, Keith, 195
Zimmerman, Kent, 195
Zimmermann, Karl, 106–107
Ziss, Debra, 134
Zubli, Rita la Fontaine de Clercq, 35
Zusak, Marcus, 130

# Subject Index

Abbott, Berenice, 180
Abolitionists, 76
Abu-Jaber, Diana, 36
Abuse, 32, 34
Accessories, 151, 155
Accidents, 13
Acting, 159
Activism, 200
Activists, 52–55, 89
Actors and actresses, 59, 88
Addams, Jane, 54
Addiction, 140
Adolescence, 132, 134–137
Adolescent psychology, 141, 200
Adoption, 139
Adventure, 5–6, 9, 13
Adventurers, 4, 12, 104, 171
Advertising, 104, 198
Advice, 89, 134–135, 139, 144–145
Afghanistan, 36, 40, 51, 59, 105
Africa, 200
African American art, 178
African Americans, 31, 72, 77
African children, 200
Ahmedi, Farah, 36
AIDS, 55, 77–78, 137, 200, 202
Air pollution, 107
Ajak, Benjamin, 32
Akbar, Said Hyder, 36
Al-Qaeda, 76
ALA. *See* Association for Library Services
    to Children, Notable Books for
    Children
Alamo, the, 74
Albinism, 113
Alcohol, 140
Alex Award, xii, 4, 7–8, 13, 28, 31, 38–42,
    103, 118, 196, 199
Alexander the Great, 47
Alexandrian library, 85
Ali, Muhammad, 118
All-terrain cycling, 123
Alternative history, 92
American antiquities, 99
American art, 190
American authors, 32, 186

American explorers, 90
American history, 73
American humor, 198
American political leaders, 46–48
American Revolution, 56–57
American women, 63
Amphibians, 113
Amputations, 119
Anatomy, 160
Ancient Egypt, 100
Anderson, Marian, 54, 183
Andes, 101
Angelou, Maya, 32
Animals, 82, 112–114
    habitats of, 94
Animation, 162
Anime, 161–163
Anorexia, 32, 35, 92, 146
Antarctic, 4, 41
Antarctica, 41, 112, 114
Anthropology, 100–101
Antique cars, 106
Antiquities, American, 99
Antislavery movements, 76
Apartheid, 92
Arab–Israeli conflict, 37
Arachnologists, 95
Archaeology, 85, 98–101
    excavations, 13
Architects, 179
Architecture, 179
Arctic circle, 51
Armenian massacres, 91
Armstrong, Lance, 32
Arnold, Benedict, 57
Aromatherapy, 154
Art, 65, 161, 164, 176–180, 190
    American, 190
    appreciation, 176, 178
    history, 176, 178
    techniques, 176
    therapy, 200
Art Institute of Chicago, 178
Artists, 30, 178–180
Asia, 12
Assassination attempts, 47, 52, 80, 88

Assassinations, pictorial works about, 17
Association for Library Services to
    Children, Notable Books for
    Children, xii, 37, 58, 90, 112, 164,
    191
Asteroids, 109
Astrology, 144–145
Astronautics, 59, 105
Astronomers, 103
Astronomy, 103, 109
Athletes, 119
Atomic energy, 97
Attempted suicide, 32, 34
Auditions, 159
Audubon Society, 83
Auschwitz (Poland), 86
Austria, 38
Authors, American, 32, 186
Authorship, 185–186
Autobiography, 29, 30, 32, 180. *See also*
    Biography
Automobiles, 106
Avant-garde art, 176
Aviation, 86, 105
Aztecs, 149

Babysitting, 142
    manuals, 142
Bacteria, 110
Bahariya Oasis, 100
Ballerinas, 30
Ballet, 28, 30
Ballistics, 20
Barakat, Ibtisam, 37
Baseball, 122, 125
    history, 125
Basketball, 8, 28, 119, 121, 125–126, 130
    for women, 8
Beauty, 132, 149, 152–156
Bereavement, 35
Best Books for Young Adults, xii, 4, 6, 8, 10,
    22, 29, 31–33, 36, 38–44, 47–59, 61–63,
    72–85, 87–88, 90, 97, 99, 103, 114, 119,
    122, 127, 130, 140, 165, 168, 173,
    178–9, 182, 186, 189–193, 196, 202
Bicycles, 170
    maintenance of, 170
    repair of, 170
Big bands, 182
Bigfoot, 194
Bilingual (Spanish-English) poems, 188

Biography, 33, 38, 50, 53, 55, 61–62, 88, 97,
    179. *See also* Autobiography
    collections of, 62–65
    group/partner, 58, 63
    historical, 55–58, 85–88
    political, 49
    professional, 50–52
    religious, 30, 201
    of scientific figures, 48–50
    verse, 191–193
Biologists, 94
Biomes, 107
Biracial people, 31
Black Death, 78
Black humor, 145
Blindness, 9, 54–55
Blizzards, 80, 84
Blogs, 167
Blue jeans, 83
Board games, 169
Boats, 42
Body image, 132
Body marking, 108
Body piercing, 108
Bologna Ragazzi Award, 58, 88, 182
Booth, Edwin, 88
Booth, John Wilkes, 17, 88
Borden, Lizzie, 17
Boston Globe-Horn Book Award, xii, 11,
    81, 83, 192, 196
Boston Globe-Horn Book Honor, 88, 111
Boston Tea Party, 82
Bourgeois, Louise, 179
Bourke-White, Margaret, 52
Boxing, 118, 121, 130
Boys, 136
Brain damage, 48
Breast cancer, 35
Breed, Clara, 88
Buddhism, 201–202
Bulimia, 32, 34
Bullying, 140
Burial customs and rites, 98, 100
Burns, 34
Burrowing owls, 115
Bus integration, 53
Business, 198–199

Cadavers, 103
Cameras, 107
Cancer, 32, 35

Candy, 42, 84
    industry, 42
Cannibalism, 4
Car maintenance/repair, 169–170
Caravans, 11
Card games, 169
Careers, 41, 141–143
Carson, Rachel, 49
Cartographers, 84
Cartography, 84
Cartooning, 160–163
Cartoons, 160, 164
Carver, George Washington, 192
Cash, Johnny, 61
Castles, 150
Castroneves, Helio, 120
Cathedrals, 150
Catholicism, 202
Cattrall, Kim, 132
Cavell, Edith, 78
Celebrities, 156
Cephalopods, 113
Chatterton, John, 13
Chavez, Jesus, 121
Chefs, 40
Chernobyl, 79
Chess, 168
Chibi, 162
Child, Julia, 38
Child labor, 87
Children
    in history, 63
    and social conditions, 87
    as slaves, 65
    war, 88
    in World War II, 35
China, 33, 39, 58
Chinese Americans, 33
Chinese social life and customs, 33
Chocolate, 42
Choreographers, 60
Christian lives, 30
Christianity, 201–202
Churches, 150
Cinematography, 7
Ciphers, 23
Citadel, The (South Carolina), 28, 29
Civil rights, 30, 39, 53, 54, 74–75, 77, 82,
        122
    movement, 74, 88
    workers, 30, 53–54
Civil War, 57, 66, 73, 85, 88, 91

Clark, William, 12, 190
Classic cars, 106
Climate, 112
Cliques, 138
Clothing and accessories/dress, 149, 151,
        156–158
    remaking, 157
Coal, 82, 87
Code talkers, 10
Codell, Esmé Raji, 38
Codes, 23
Coelacanth, 96
Coffey, Maria, 11
Colleges, 41, 172
Colors, 154
Comets, 109
Comics, 161, 164, 186
    graphic novels, 163–165
    strips, 198
Coming-of-age, 28–31, 44
Composers, 61
Composite drawing, 20
Computers, 167
    games, 169
    programming, 167
Concrete poetry, 189–190
Confederate generals, 57
Confederate States of America, 57
Confessional poetry, 192
Confucianism, 56
Confucius, 56
Conroy, Pat, 28
Conservation, 95
Continental Congress, 82
Continental drift, 114
Cooking, 38, 40, 165–166
Coretta Scott King Award, xii, 66, 182, 196
Coretta Scott King Honor, xii, 56, 192–193
Cosmetics, 152, 154
Counterfeiters, 18
Country music, 61, 181
    history of, 181
Courtiers in Great Britain, 11
Covert operations, 10
Cowboys, 73
Cox, Lynne, 118
Crafts, 149–154, 157–158
Crandall, Prudence, 77, 191
Creative writing, 41, 185
Crime, 18
Crime scene photography, 21
Crime sciences, 22

Criminal investigations, 16, 19–22
Criminal profiling, 20
Criminals, 20
Criminology, 19
Crippen, Hawley Harvey, 18
Crisis survival, 172
Crocheting, 157
Crutcher, Chris, 42
Cryptids, 194
Cryptography, 23
Crystallography, 110
Crystals, 110
Cultural Revolution, 58
Culture, 177
Curie, Marie, 50
Currents, 111
Cycling, 32
Czechoslovakia, 180

da Vinci, Leonardo, 148
Dance, 28, 30
Dancers, 60
Danish history, 10
Dating, 137, 145
D–Day, 74
DDT, 49
Deafness, 54–55
Death and dying, 35, 103
Declaration of Independence, 82
Deep-water diving, 13
Delaware River, crossing of the, 71
Delta Force, 40
Deng, Alephonsion, 32
Deng, Benson, 32
Denmark, 91
Depression (economic), 8
Depression (mental), 33, 141
Desserts, 165
Development (human), 136
Dickens, Charles, 186
Dictatorship, 91
Diet, 133–134
Digestion, 108
Digital cameras, 166
Digital cinematography, 168
Digital filmmaking, 168
Digital photography, 166
Dinosaur eggs, 102
Dinosaurs, 101, 115
Disasters, 5, 7
    technological, 115
Discography, 181

Discovery and exploration of America, 90
Discrimination, 58
    in education, 77
Disease, 50, 55, 81, 108
    communicable, 78
    epidemics, 78–81
Diving, 112
Divorce, 138
DIY, 157
DNA profiling, 21
Doctors, 63
Dominican Republic, 91
Donner Party, 4
Drawing, 160–164
Drawing instruction, 162
Drawing techniques, 160–163
Driving, 170
Drugs, 140
Duct tape, 151
Duncan, Tim, 119

Earth sciences, 111
Earthquakes, 7
Eating disorders, 32, 34
Ebadi, Shirin, 37
Ecological succession, 102
Ecology and conservation, 107, 111–112
Economic depression, 8
Economics, 198–199
Edison, Thomas Alva, 48
Educators, 77
Egypt, 100
Egyptians, 149
Einstein, Albert, 48
Elephants, 95
Emancipation Proclamation, 72–73
Emergency management, 171
Emigrant, 36
Emotions, 110, 141
Endangered species, 94–96, 114
Energy, 82, 112
Engineering, 148
English authors, 186
Enigma machine, 10
Entertainers, 59–62
Environment, 111–112, 115, 149
Environmental protection, 19, 111
Environmental writing, 110–114
Environmentalism, 111
Environmentalists, 49, 94
Epidemics, 78, 92
Epistolary nonfiction, 88

Equal Rights Amendment (ERA), 83
Errors, 129, 145
Escape artists, 59
Escapes, 6
Espionage, 10, 22–23
Essays, 40, 43
Ethnic killings, 85
Ethnic relations, 10
Ethnicity, 140
Evacuation and relocation, 75
Everest. *See* Mount Everest
Everyday life, 172
Evolution, 102
Exercise, 134
Experimentation, 104
Exploitation, 87
Exploration and discovery, 12, 90, 96
Explorers, 12, 51
    American, 90
Extinct animals, 102
Extinction, 83
Extreme sports, 122, 124–126

Fabrics, 156
Facial reconstruction, 20
Fads, 104
Fairy tales, 193
Faith, 201
Family, 138–139
Family relationships, 34–35, 43, 172
Family violence, 140
Famine, 79
Fantasy, 160, 162, 186, 193
Fashion, 154–158, 193
    history of, 89
Fast food, 108
Fear, 110
Feelings, 110
Female golfers, 122
Female reporters, 72
Feminism, 55, 89
Feminists, 55
Field biology, 95
Figure skaters, 34
Film, 183–185
    editing, 168
    history of, 185
    and movies, 184
    production, 168
    and video, 184
Film stars, 61

Fingerprints, 20
    analysis of, 20
Fire, 83
Firearms, 199
    history of, 199
First ladies, 62
Fish, 96
Fishing, 39, 42
Fitness, 134, 136
Flap books, 176
Floods, 109
Florida childhoods, 30
Florida fundamentalists, 30
Folk music, 61
Folklore, myths, and legends, 193–195
Food, 108
Football, 120, 127, 130
Football players, 120
Ford, Gerald R., 48
Forecasting, 104
    technological, 104
Forensic anthropologists, 101
Forensic artists, 20
Forensic dentistry, 21
Forensic entomology, 20
Forensic sciences and scientists, 21, 22
Forensics, 19, 21–22, 85, 98, 103
Forged documents, 21
Fossil animals, 102
Fossil hominids, 99
Fossils, 101–102
Fox, Terry, 66
Frank, Anne, 29, 86
Franklin, Benjamin, 49
Fraud, 16, 18
Freedmen, 72
Freedom rides, 53
French cooking, 38
French Guiana, 95
Friendship, 138, 140
Frontier and pioneer life, 73, 80
Fugitive slaves, 76
Funeral rites, 100–101

Gambling, 8
Games and activities, 144, 152, 168
Gangs, 121
Gantos, Jack, 33
Garbage, 111
Gehry, Frank O., 179
Gender, 137

Genealogy, 58
Genetic engineering, 115
Genocide, 85
Geography, 84
Germany, 57, 87
    occupation of Denmark, 10
Ghosts, 110
Giant squid, 96
Gies, Miep, 39
Global warming, 82, 112
Globe Theatre, 186
Gods, 194
Goering, Dag, 11
Gold Rush, 91
Golf, 122
Golfers, 122
Gorillas, 94
Graffiti, 160, 177
Graham, Martha, 60
Grand Banks, 39
Graphic nonfiction, 12, 16–18, 30, 38–40,
    55–56, 76, 80, 111–112, 118–119, 164
Graphic novels, 163–165, 196
Great apes, 94
Great Britain, 16
Great Depression, 52, 81, 87
Greeks, 149
    generals, 47
Greenhouse gases, 112
Greenlaw, Linda, 39
Gretzky, Wayne, 118
Grief, 35
Grooming, 155
Group stories, 86–88
Growth, 136
Gruwell, Erin, 38
Guatemala, 13
Guiana, discovery of, 11
Guilds, 150
Guns, 199
Guthrie, Woody, 61
Gymnasts, 34

Habitat, 83
Hair, 154
Hair accessories, 152
Hair care, 152
Hairstyles, 152, 155
Hamilton, Bethany, 119
Handicrafts, 148–152
Handwriting analysis, 21
Hardin High School, 8

Harlem, 29, 190
Harley-Davidson, 106
Hate crimes, 193
Hawaii, 5
Hawass, Zahi, 100
Hawk, Tony, 120
Health and nutrition, 133–136, 152
Health education, 110
Hemings, Sally, 58
Henson, Matthew, 51
High school, 177
Hijab, 202
Hillary, Edmund, 9
Hillman, Laura, 86
Hinduism, 201–202
Hip-hop, 177
Hiroshima, 79
History, 23, 74–81, 88, 90. *See also*
        Biography
    American, 73
    ancient, 99, 149
    of burials, 98
    of candy, 84
    comics, 186
    of fires, 5
    ideas of, 89
    science, 97–98
    transportation, 106
Hitler, Adolf, 57
Hitler Jugend (Youth), 87
*H.L. Hunley* (submarine), 85
Hoaxes, 104
Hobbies, 157–158
Hockey, 125–126
Hockey players, 118
Holocaust, 10, 29, 38, 77–78, 86
Horror movies, 183
Horse racing, 8
Horses, 8
Houdini, Harry, 59
Human anatomy, 110
Human behavior, 110
Human biology, 110
Human remains (archaeology), 98–99, 101
Human rights advocates, 37
Human–animal relationships, 114
Humor, 16, 42–43, 105, 108, 129, 145,
        171–172, 180, 183–184, 195, 198
    American, 198
    memoirs, 42–43
Hunting, 42
Hurricanes, 109

Hygiene, 133, 136, 152
Hypothermia, 80

Ice age, 101
Ice climbing, 124
Identity, 139–140
Iditarod, 9
Illegal immigration, 121, 199
Illustrators, 30
Immersion journalism, 41
Immigrants, 80
Imperial Trans-Antarctic Expedition, 4
Imposters and imposture, 16
Impressionism, 178
Improvisation, 159
Incas, 101
In-line skating, 124–125
Indian athletes, 8
Indian origins, 99
Indiana, 189
Indians of North America, 73
Indonesia, 99
Insects, 113
Instructions, 158, 162–163
Integration, 53
Intelligence service, 23
International Reading Association, xii, 34,
     53–54, 64, 70, 77–78, 85, 88, 140, 178,
     182, 192
International security, 40
Interpersonal relations, 139, 143–144
Inventions, 83, 96, 98, 104, 109, 148
Inventors, 97–98
Invertebrates, 113
Investigation, 79
Investigative reporting, 58
Investigative sciences, 22
IRA. See International Reading
     Association
Iran, 37–38
Ireland, 79
Irwin, Cait, 33
Islam, 201–202
Israel, 31, 37
Israeli army, 31
Iverson, Allen, 121
Ivory-billed woodpecker, 83

Jail, 33
Jainism, 201
James, LeBron, 121
James Madison Book Award, xii, 56, 81

James Madison Book Honor, xii, 48, 77, 88
Japanese Americans, 75, 88
Japanese art, 161
Japanese history, 11
Japanese internment, 52, 92
Jazz, 182–183
Jeans, 156
Jefferson, Thomas, 46
Jenner, Edward, 50
Jewelry, 150–151
Jewish daughter, 31
Jewish children in World War II, 9, 77, 86
Job descriptions, 143
Jones, John Paul, 56
Jordan, 36
Journaling, 33, 188
Journalism and journalists, 37, 71
Judaism, 201–202
Juvenile delinquents, 41

Keller, Helen, 55, 63, 66
Kennedy, John F., 80
Kennedy, Robert F., 52
Kidd, Jason, 119
King, Martin Luther, Jr., 53, 88
King Tut, 100
Kings, 64
   of Greece, 47
Knitting, 157–158
Kohler, Rich, 13
Koran, 201
Kruger, Kobie, 40
Kruger National Park, 40

Labor, 199
   reform, 80
Ladies Professional Golf Association, 122
Lange, Dorothea, 52
Law, 16, 18, 22, 34, 82
Le Chambon (France), 9
Lee, Bruce, 61
Lee, Robert E., 57
Legal status of women athletes, 127
Legal system, 18
Legendary animals, 194
Lennon, John, 61
Letters, 138–139, 145
Lewis and Clark expedition, 12, 190
Lewis, John, 53
Lewis, Meriwether, 12, 190
Life-changing events, 34
Lifestyle, 134

Lincoln, Abraham, 17, 88
Lions, 40
Literary criticism, 186
Literary influences, 186
Literature, 185–185
Little Rock (AR), 54
Lockouts, 87
Loneliness, 140
Long-distance swimmers, 118
Lost boys, 32
Lyons, Maritcha Remond, 56

Mace, Nancy, 29
Machinery, 106
Magicians, 59
Mah, Adeline Yen, 33
Makeup, 151–154
Manatees, 114
Manga, 161–163
    villains, 163
Manhwa, 163
Manjiro, 11
Manor, medieval, 150
Manufacturing, 104, 149
Manzanar, 75
Manzano, Juan Francisco, 192
Mapmakers, 84
Maps, 84
Marconi, Guglielmo, 18
Marine life, 113
Marine research, 96
Marketing, 83, 132, 198
Martial arts, 61
    cartoons, 161
Mathematical theorems, 115
Matschie's tree kangaroo, 95
Maxims, 144
McGrath, Jeremy, 120
Media, 167
Medical ethics, 103
Medical research, 103
Medicine, 48, 63, 81
Medieval crafts, 150
Medieval history, 71, 150
Medieval life, 71
Medieval occupations, 71
Memoirs, 31, 34, 39
    humorous, 42–43
    working life, 38–41
Menstruation, 136
Mental health, 141
Meteorites, 109

Métis, 56
Michael L. Printz Honor Book, xii, 33, 61, 115,
    173, 190, 192, 173, 190, 192–193, 202
Micro-histories, 81–85
Micro-science, 107–110
Microbes, 78
Middle East, 37, 72, 191
    twentieth century, 72
Middle Eastern cookery, 36
Military, 31, 77, 142
    history, 142
    training, 142
Military cadets, 29
Mines and mine work, 87
Mink, Patsy T., 55
Moaveni, Azadeh, 37
Models, 148
Modern art, 176, 190
Modern dance, 60
Monasteries, 150
Monsters, 110
Montgomery (AL), 88
Montgomery bus boycott, 30, 88
Monticello (VA), 46
Mothers and daughters, 35
Motocross, 123
Motor sports, 120
Motorbikes, 106
Motorcycles, 106
Mount Everest, 7–9, 13
Mount Vesuvius, 99
Mountain biking, 123
Mountaineering, 7–9, 13
Mountaineers, 8
Movie guides, 184
Movie reviews, 184–185
Movie stars, 61
Movies, 184–185. See also Film
Mudgett, Herman, 17
Muhammad, 201
Mummies, 100–101
Mung, John, 11
Murder, 18, 75
    mysteries, 16
    in New York State, 17
    in the nineteenth century, 16
    in Scotland, 17–18
    victims, 21, 193
Murderers, 17
Music, 61, 180–182
    history of, 182
    popular, 181

Music reviews, 181
Musician, 54, 61, 64, 181–183
Muslims, 201
Mythology/myths, 194
   dictionary of, 194

Nagasaki, 77
Nanotechnology, 115
NASCAR, 120
National Basketball Association, 121
National Football League, 120
National Socialism, 57
Natural disasters, 78–81, 109
Natural history, 102
Natural selection, 50
Nature, 113
Naval history, 85
Nazis, 91
NBA, 121
Nebraska, 92
Networking, 143
Neurology, 48
New York city, history of, 56
New York State
   blizzards, 84
   history of, 84
New York Stock Exchange, 81
Newbery Award, 66
Newbery Honor, 81, 87, 192, 202
Newton, Isaac, 49
Nineteenth century, 71, 80, 91
Nineteenth-century murders, 16
Ninjas, 22
Nobel Peace Prize, 64
   winners, 37, 53–54
Nobel Prize, 48, 50
Nonfiction collections, 5–6, 18–19, 65, 94,
   96–98, 120, 140, 185–186, 199
Nonfiction picture books, 86, 111, 180
Norma Fleck Award, xii, 12, 34, 84, 104,
   133
Norma Fleck Honor, 200
Normandy, 74
North Korea, 39
North Pole, 51
Notorious B.I.G., 60
Nuclear energy/power, 79, 97
Numerology, 145
Nutrition, 108, 133–136

Obsessive-compulsive disorder (OCD), 35
Ocala National Forest, 13

Occupations, 71, 143
Ocean, 111
Octopus, 113
Odessa (TX), 127
Olympics, 128
O'Neal, Shaquille, 119
Opdyke, Irene Gut, 78
Operation Neptune, 74
Operation Overlord, 74
Oppression, 37
Optical illusions, 184
Orbis Pictis Honor, xii, 48, 50, 54, 59, 77,
   82–83, 87
Orbis Pictis Nonfiction Award, xii, 53, 81,
   87
Ornithology, 41, 112
Outdoors, 42
Overland journeys to the West, 73

Painter, 179
Painting, 176, 178
Paleontology, 99, 101–102
Palestine, 37
Papua New Guinea, 95
Parks, Rosa, 30, 88
Parties, 152
Partridge, Elizabeth, 51
Passenger trains, 106
Patagonia, 102
Patterns, 158
Paulsen, Gary, 43–43
Peace movements, 89
Peary, Marie Ahnighito, 51
Penguins, 112, 114
   Adélie, 41
Pennsylvania, 87
People with disabilities, 55
Pepin, Jacques, 40
Performing arts, 28, 182, 184
Permian Panthers, 127
Perseverance, 36
Personal hygiene, 134, 154
Personal narratives, 78
Personal rights, 18
Personality tests, 144
Personality typing, 145
Pesticides, 49
Pets, 113
Pfetzer, Mark, 8
Philadelphia, 921
Philanthropists, 59
Philosophers, 56

Photographers, 52, 72, 180
Photographs, 52, 65, 128–129, 107, 166,
    177, 180
Photojournalism/photojournalists, 52, 77
Physicists, 48–49
Pianists, 62
Pictorial record of World War II, 77
Pictorial works, 128
Pioneer children, 73
Pioneers, 4, 63, 80
Pirates, 13
Plagues, 78
Plans, 157
Plantation life, 46
Plath, Sylvia, 192
Poetic forms, 187
Poetry and poets, 32, 35, 127, 178, 182,
    185–193, 196
    American poetry, 188
    anthologies, 187–191
    appreciation, 188
    collections and anthologies, 188–191
    concrete poetry, 189–190
    confessional poetry, 192
    Hispanic American, 188
    romantic, 187
Point guard, 119
Poisonings, 18
Poland, 78
Polar exploration, 114
Polar regions, 41, 114
Political science, 36–37, 199
Politicians, 52
Politics, 40, 52, 89
Pollution, 111
Polo, Marco, 12
Pompeii, 99
Pop art, 178
Popular culture, 16, 43, 160, 167, 177, 198
Pop-up books, 102
Portraits, 143
Postcards, 200
Postmodern architecture, 179
Poverty, 199
Prairies, 80
Pre-Columbian discovery and
    exploration, 90
Precious stones, 110
Pregnancy, 137
Prejudice, 91

Presidents, 46–48, 62, 71
    assassination of, 17, 47
    spouses, 53, 62
Presley, Elvis, 60
Prisoners of war, 35
Professional women, 143
Programming, 167
Protestantism, 202
Psychology, 144
    of animals, 114
Puberty, 135–137
Pura Belpre Award, xii, 91, 192
Purses, 157
Pygmies, 99

Qin dynasty, 100
Quarterbacks, 120
Queens, 64
Questions, 144
Quizzes, 144
Quotations, 144

Race, 58
    relations, 140
Racially mixed people, 140
Racism, 32, 54
Radiation, 50
Radioactivity, 79
Radiography, 109
Radium, 50
Railroads, 106
Raleigh, Sir Walter, 11
Rankin, Jeannette, 55
Rap musicians, 60
Rape, 34
Rats, 82
Recipes, 36, 40, 152
Reconstruction, 72–73
Recovery, 119
Recycling, 149, 153
Refashioning, 157
Relationships, 115, 137–139
Religion, 56, 200–202
Reptiles, 113
Repurposing, 149, 155–157
Requiem, 192
Rescue work, 6
Rescues, 6, 171
Research, 74, 104
Resistance, 10, 91

Revere, Paul, 71
Revolutionary War, 71
Riel, Louis, 56
Robbery, 19
Robert F. Sibert Informational Book
    Award, xii, 11, 30, 33, 54, 57, 59, 79,
    81, 180
Robert F. Sibert Informational Honor
    Book, xii, 41, 53, 55, 81, 84, 87, 95,
    179
Robinson, Jackie, 122
Robots, 105, 163
Rock climbing, 124
Rock groups, 183
Rock music, 64
    of the 1960s, 183
Rock musicians/stars, 60, 64, 183
Rogers, Mary, 17
Romance, 139
Romans, 150
Roosevelt, Eleanor, 53
Rosen, Christine, 30
Rulers, 64
Rules and tips, 122–126, 169
Runyon, Brent, 34
Rwanda, 6, 66

Safety education, 171
Sahara, 11
Sailing, 13, 42
Salt industry/trade, 11
Salzman, Mark, 41
San Francisco earthquake and fire, 7
Satire, 198
Satrapi, Marjane, 38
Sayings, 144
Scarification, 108
Scary stories, 195
Schindler, Oscar, 86
School, 138
    integration, 54
Schroeder, Lucinda, 19
Schulke, Flip, 52
Schumann, Clara, 62, 183
Science, 49–50, 63, 79, 81, 97, 104, 109–110,
    113
    adventures, 94–96
    biography, 48–50
    experiments, 195
    history, 97
    and nature, 83
    and technology, 49, 97, 103–104

Science fiction, 162
Scientific discoveries, 98
Scientific method, 104
Scientific research, 94–96
Scientists, 49, 63
    science enthusiasts, 96–97
Scodoris, Rachael, 9
Scooters, 125
Scott, Dred, 66
Scrupulosity, 35
Scythians, 100
Sea kayaking, 11
Seabiscuit (race horse), 8
Sebold, Alice, 34
Secret Service, 47
Secrets, 200
Segregation, 88
    in education, 191
Self-esteem, 132–134, 138–139, 155
Self-help, 138
Self-perception, 132
Self-publishing, 164, 167
September 11, 2001, 76
Serial killers, 17. *See also* Murder
Sewing, 149, 156–158
Sex, 137
Sex discrimination in sports, 127
Sex instruction, 135, 137
    for girls, 136–137
Sexism, 32
Sexual assault, 137
Sexuality, 135–137
Sexually transmitted diseases, 137
Shackleton, Sir Ernest, 4
Shakespeare, William, 186
Shakur, Tupac, 60
Sharks, 79, 112
    attacks by, 112, 119, 196
Shipwrecks, 4
    New Jersey, 13
Shivack, Nadia, 34
Short stories, 189
Shoujo, 163
Siegel, Siena Cherson, 30
Sikhism, 201
Sinclair, Upton, 58
Singers, 54, 60, 182
Sis, Peter, 180
Six-Day War, 37
Skateboarding, 120, 123, 125
Skiing, 124
Skin care, 152–153

Skydiving, 123
Slavery, 46, 56, 65, 192
Slaves, 192
    writings by, 65
Sled dog racing, 9
Smallpox, 50, 78
    vaccine, 50
Smith, Madeleine Hamilton, 18
Snowboarding, 123–125
Soccer, 125–126, 128
Social networks, 143
Social science, 16, 85, 100
Social situations, 135, 141
Solar system, 109
Solitude, 140
Solomon Islands, 11
Sonnets, 191, 193
Sorenstam, Annika, 122
South Africa, 40, 91
Space flight, 59, 105
Space science, 59
Special effects, 184
Special operations, 142
Spelunking, 13
Sperm whales, 6
Spies, 22-23
Sports, 7, 32, 119, 124–125, 127–129
    biographies, 118–122
    history, 126
    in action, 128–129
    instruction, 126
Squid, 113
Stand-up comedy, 159
Steamboats, 107
Steffens, Lincoln, 58
Stock car racing, 120
Stock market, 81
Stone, Miriam, 35
Storms, 109
Stories
    group, 86–88
    short, 189
Storytelling, 164
Strauss, Levi, 83
Street art, 177
Street scenes, 160
Stress relief, 134
Strikes, 87
Stunt riding, 123
Stupidity, 145
Style, 154–157, 177
Submersibles, 96

Substance abuse, 140
Sudan, 32
Suffrage, 83, 89
Sullivan, Anne, 66
Sumatra, 13
Summer Olympics, 128
Supercross, 120
Surfing, 119
Survival, 4–7, 13, 145, 172
    skills, 13, 170–172
Swimmers, 118
Swindlers, 18

Tarantulas, 95
Tarbell, Ida, 58
Tattooing, 108
Teaching, 38, 41
Technique, 162
Technology, 103, 105, 115, 166–168
Teen authors, 166
Teen writing, 140, 189, 191
Teenage boys, 135, 137
Teenage crime, 18
Teenage employment, 143
    strategies, 143
Teenage girls, 34, 132, 134-135, 139,
    144-145
Teenage life, 177
Teenagers, 138
Tehran, 38
Television, 59
Terrell, Mary Church, 53
Terrorism, 76
    prevention of, 40, 76
Texas, 74, 127
Theater direction, 159
Theater production, 159
Theft, 19
Thieves, 19
Till, Emmett, 193
Title IX, 127
Tombs, 98, 100
Totalitarianism, 38
Towns, 150
Toxicology, 21
Tragedy, 90
Traig, Jennifer, 35
Trains, 106
Traitors, 23, 57
Transportation, 105–107, 169–170
Travel, 5, 36, 172
    in Africa, 11

Travelogue, 40
Trials, 34
Triangle Shirtwaist Company fire, 80
Trick cinematography, 184
Trojan War, 196
True crime, 16, 19, 22
Tsunamis, 5, 109
Tunnels, 7
Tuskegee (AL), 192
Twentieth century, 72
Typology, 145

U-869, 13
Underdogs, 8
Underground railroad, 76
Underwater archaeology, 13
Underwater exploration, 96
Underwater photography, 52
Unionization, 87
Unser, Al, Sr., 120
Urban legends, 184, 194–195
U.S. admirals, 56
U.S. Army, 40
U.S. Congress, 55
U.S. Constitution, 82
U.S. generals, 47
U.S. history, 63, 71, 72
U.S.–Mexico border, 199
U.S. Navy, 56
U.S. presidents. *See* Presidents

Values, 200
Van Gogh, Vincent, 179
Vegetarian cooking, 165
Venables, Stephen, 9
Verse novel, 32, 196
Vice presidents, 48
Video production, 168
Videogames
    art, 167
    programming, 167
Videorecording, 168
Vietnam War, 70
Vincent, Erin, 35
Violence, 140
    in society, 85
Visual arts, 176–180
Vocational guidance, 143
Volunteering, 200
Voyages, 5

Wakeboarding, 123
Waldman, Neil, 30
War, 32, 90
    correspondents, 71
    photography, 77
War Relocation Center, 75
Warhol, Andy, 178
Warning labels, 198
Washington, George, 47, 71
Waste, 115
Waste disposal from chemical plants, 111
Water pollution, 107
Water sports, 123
Watercolor painting, 176
Watersheds, 107
Weather, 5, 13, 42, 112
Weight, 133
West Point, 29
Whales, 95
Whaling, 6, 95
Winfrey, Oprah, 59
Winter sports, 123–125
Women, 63
    athletes, 127–128
    authors, 188
    educators, 191
    heads of state, 64
    inventors, 98
    jazz musicians, 182
    legislators, 55
    photographers, 65
    in politics, 64
Women's rights, 83, 89
Women's studies, 37
Working children, 87
World champion, 121
World history, 64, 72, 90
World War I, 78
World War II, 9–10, 29, 35, 57, 71–75, 78,
        87–88, 91–92
    campaigns, 74
    personal narratives, 35
World's Fair, 17
Wright, Katharine, 86
Wright, Orville, 51, 86
Wright, Wilbur, 51
Writers, 29, 59–62, 186
Writing, 28, 33, 42, 164, 186, 188
    for comics, 164

X-rays, 109

Yellow fever outbreak, 91
Yoga, 133–134
Yom Kippur War (1973), 72
Young Adult Library Services Association
    Popular Paperbacks, xii, 16, 18, 22,
    32, 34, 36, 41, 51, 55, 83, 105, 108,
    110, 137, 153, 157, 165–166, 179, 198
Young Adult Library Services Association
    Quick Picks for Reluctant Young
    Adult Readers, xii, 8, 18, 22, 33, 55,
    82, 101, 105, 108, 113, 119–121,
    123–124, 128–129, 135, 137, 139,
    143–145, 148–149, 151–158, 160–163,
    171, 177, 183–184, 188, 190–194, 198,
    200

Zaharias, Babe Didrikson, 119
Zenatti, Valerie, 31
Zhang, Ange, 58
Zines, 167
Zoologists, 94
Zoology, 40, 94, 113
Zubli, Rita la Fontaine de Clercq, 35
Zwerg, Jim, 53

# About the Author

ELIZABETH (BETSY) FRASER has been a librarian for more than ten years. She is active in ALA and CLA, having served on several committees, including Best Books for YAs, the Michael Printz Award, and the Young Adult Canadian Book Award Committees. She is currently serving on YALSA's "Award for Excellence in Nonfiction" committee. She has also been a reviewer for *VOYA*, *School Library Journal*, *Audiofile*, and *CM* (*Canadian Materials*).